DON'T
THROW
IT OUT

DON'T THROW IT OUT

LORI BAIRD and the Editors of

YANKEE MAGAZINE.

RODALE

YANKEE PUBLISHING STAFF

President: Jamie Trowbridge
Book Editors: Lori Baird, Myrsini Stephanides
Contributing Writers: Tom Cavalieri, Marjorie Galen, Rose Kennedy,
Dougald MacDonald, Deb Martin, Diana Reese, Donna Shryer, Delilah Smittle
Interior Design: Shamona Stokes, Brian MacMullen
Illustrator: Molly Borman-Babich
Fact-Checker and Copy Editor: Diana Reese
Proofreaders: Franchesca Ho Sang, John K. Finkbeiner
Indexer: Lina B. Burton
Layout Production Manager: Brian MacMullen

RODALE INC. EDITORIAL STAFF

Senior Editor: Karen Bolesta
Senior Project Editor: Marilyn Hauptly
Cover Design: Christina Gaugler

The information in this book has been carefully researched, and all efforts have been made to ensure accuracy. Rodale Inc. and Yankee Publishing Inc. assume no responsibility for any injuries suffered or damages or losses incurred during or as a result of following this information. All information should be carefully studied and clearly understood before taking any action based on the information or advice in the book.

When using any commercial product, always read and follow label directions. Mention of specific companies, organizations, or authorities in this book does not imply endorsement by the publisher, nor does mention of specific companies, organizations, or authorities imply that they endorse this book.

Internet addresses and telephone numbers given in this book were accurate at the time it went to press.

Direct and trade editions are both being published in 2007.

Rodale books may be purchased for business or promotional use or for special sales. For information, please write to: Special Markets Department, Rodale Inc., 733 Third Avenue, New York, NY 10017

Printed in the United States of America

Rodale Inc. makes every effort to use acid-free ∞, recycled paper ♻.

Library of Congress Cataloging-in-Publication Data is on file with the publisher.

ISBN-13: 978–0–89909–402–1   hardcover
ISBN-10: 0–89909–402–3   hardcover
ISBN-13: 978–1–59486–577–0   paperback
ISBN-10: 1–59486–577–9   paperback

Distributed to the book trade by Holtzbrinck Publishers

2   4   6   8   10   9   7   5   3   1   hardcover
4   6   8   10   9   7   5   3   paperback

We inspire and enable people to improve their lives and the world around them
For more of our products visit **rodalestore.com** or call 800-848-4735

CONTENTS

INTRODUCTION

Remember the good old days, when stuff was built to last? Most of us have at least one story about a family member or friend who owned the same refrigerator or car or washing machine for 10, 20, even 30 years. Craftsmanship and quality seemed to be more important back then. Of course, once in a while, a repair was necessary. But that was no problem, because most every town was home to at least one "fix-it" shop—you know, the local guy to whom you could take a mixer or a radio or a sewing machine that was on the fritz, and he'd fix it up in a jiff—and for just a few bucks.

But these days, it seems as though most of the consumer products in our lives are designed to last only a short while before they break and end up in the landfill. Today, most of us don't think twice throwing away an item because it seems to be easier to replace it than to repair it.

But that kind of thinking is no good for the environment or your wallet. Well here's some good news: You don't need to be a slave to this planned obsolescence (that's a fancy term for "disposable goods") There are lots of ways to get the most out almost every item in your life. All it takes is a little bit of creativity and the book you're holding right now—*Don't Throw It Out.*

On the following pages are hundreds of clever and practical ways to make your possessions live a long, hard-working life, saving you time, money, and frustration. We've left nothing out: Every room in the house gets the full treatment, from the kitchen to the bedroom, the rec room to the laundry room, the bedroom to the home office. We head outdoors, too, to offer tips about the lawn and garden, as well as useful *and* money-saving advice about cars and trucks.

But wait—as they say on TV (your still good-as-new set that's 12 years old, that is!)—there's more. In addition to all that great "make it last" advice, we help you keep your possessions out of the trash or landfill by describing simple and inexpensive repairs you can make at home when household items go on the fritz. And when the time does come to get rid of something, we tell you how you can pass it along easily—by recycling, donating, selling, or throwing them away—when it's time. It adds up to three kinds of tips in every chapter:

• *Make It Last* tips that describe how to care for an item so that it lives a longer life;

• *Fix It Fast* tips that explain how to make quick-and-easy repairs to the item when it breaks; and

• *Pass It Along* tips, which detail how you can get rid of the item when it's no longer wanted—by selling or donating it to another person or organization, recycling it, or throwing it away in the safest manner possible.

So how does it work? Easy: Let's say you want some information about cell phones. Just turn to page 158, where you'll find an entire section devoted to these handy electronic devices. First you'll find all of the Make It Last tips grouped together. There's clever advice about how to keep a cell phone dry in a downpour, how to prevent the LED screen from getting scratched, and the right way to charge the phone's battery for longest life.

Immediately following those are the cell phone Fix It Fast tips. Does your phone cut out unexpectedly? We have a clever solution, and all you'll need is a pencil eraser. Maybe the problem is that you often have a hard time connecting to whomever you're calling. We'll tell you how to solve that issue, too. And we promise, all of the Fix It Fast tips in *Don't Throw It Out* are simple. We've provided easy-to follow instructions and crystal-clear how-to illustrations where necessary so you never have to worry, even if you're all thumbs.

Finally, when your phone has given its all and is ready for retirement (or you're just finished with that particular model), take a look at the Pass It Along tips that come next in the text for ways to donate working phones to people who can use them, as well as environmentally friendly and convenient methods of recycling cell phones that no longer work.

Throughout *Don't Throw It Out*, you'll find sidebars that provide additional information or true-life stories that will make you smile. In the One Man's Trash sidebars, for instance, you'll read some truly out-of-this-world stories of recycling taken to the extreme. Take for instance, the tale of John Milkovisch. He used almost 50,000 recycled beer

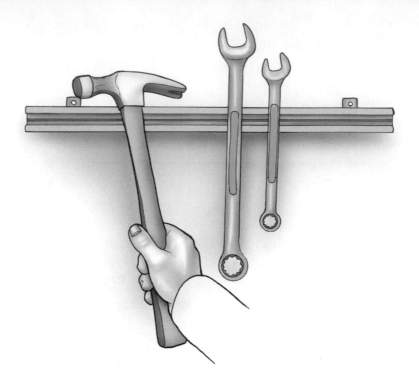

cans to side his Houston, Texas, home—today, it's a popular roadside attraction. And woodworker Denis Roy of Winnipeg, Manitoba, Canada, crafts beautiful wooden bowls out of . . . discarded hockey sticks.

Among the other information-packed sidebars we've included are those we call "Fix It or Forget It?" Each instructs you about whether a broken item is worth the time or money to repair or whether it makes more sense to toss it into the recycling bin. "Smart Buys" sidebars help you shop wisely for products that will last longer (always a clever strategy, especially in our throw-it-away world.) "The Fine Print" sidebars clue you into vital information that manufacturers don't always make clear. For instance, although electric lawn mowers sound like a smart, environmentally friendly purchase, they're most appropriate for small lawns. If your yard is large, gas-powered is the way to go.

After you've finished reading each chapter, why not put your new-found knowledge to the test with our "Domestic Challenge" quizzes. Not only will these mini-exams allow you to put what you've learned to use, but they'll also offer even more valuable information about how to take care of what you own, how to make quick and simple fixes, and how to pass along what's outlived its usefulness.

The back pages of *Don't Throw It Out* are just as useful and informative as the rest of the book. There you'll find a Resources section that includes a handy reading list, loads of Web sites where you can get even more information, and a guide to our Top 10 Pass It Along Projects.

Don't Throw It Out's goal is to help you reduce waste and clutter by showing you how to get the most out of the products you already own or will purchase. Sure, it's good for the wallet and the planet, but you get personal satisfaction out of it, too. Imagine yourself in 10 years, showing off the good ol' toaster oven (or tennis racket or washing machine or power drill. . .) that you purchased way back when. It's still working good as new, thanks to your own creativity and resourcefulness and a little help from *Don't Throw It Out*.

—THE EDITORS

PART

INSIDE THE HOUSE

1

THE KITCHEN

The kitchen is the heart of the home. It's the nutritional center, of course—the emporium where fresh, frozen, canned, dry, and bottled goods are chopped, sizzled, and whirled together into memorable recipes and treats. It's the social center, too—where even the busiest families gather around the table face-to-face and where party guests gravitate for munchies and conversation. The kitchen may also serve as the communication center, the sanitation center, and the family art gallery. Supporting all of that activity are a range of possessions, ranging from the vinyl floor to the walnut cabinets, from the dishwasher to the microwave oven, and from the ice maker to the cheese shredder. Each possession within these very busy four walls has special needs to keep it functioning and clean. When you consider the financial investment involved in operating even the simplest kitchen in the twenty-first century, a homeowner has no choice but to get optimum life and performance out of every item.

REFRIGERATORS

Chill out! The following tips will help you handle any problem your fridge might have. And once it's time to replace the components inside that faithful Frigidaire, just consult our clever Pass It Along tips for ingenious advice.

MAKE IT LAST

KEEP THAT COMPRESSOR THIRSTY. Because moist air takes longer to cool than dry air, excess moisture inside your refrigerator means that the compressor has to work extra hard, causing unnecessary wear. To prevent this, keep all liquids in tight-fitting jars and jugs with tight-fitting lids, and keep all food well-wrapped in plastic or plastic containers with the lids fully snapped on.

TAKE THE HEAT OFF YOUR FRIDGE. If your refrigerator is located next to a heat source, the compressor will have to work harder to keep up and will wear out faster. So if your icebox is near the stove or a heating duct, relocate it to a cooler spot.

UNCOVER THE COILS. Your refrigerator works by removing the heat from its interior and releasing it on the exterior through a network of little pipes called condenser coils. These coils get rid of heat more readily if they aren't insulated by a layer of dust. Cleaning them a couple of times a year will give your refrigerator a break, meaning it will last longer, and keep your energy bills down, as well.

Most condenser coils are on the bottom of the refrigerator. To clean them, you'll need to pull off that little grille that runs along the front bottom of the appliance. Put the crevice tool (or whatever attachment looks like it will do the best job) onto your vacuum cleaner and suck the dust off of the coils. You also can buy special brushes for this purpose at your home improvement store. Or just wrap a cleaning cloth around the end of a yardstick, secure it with rubber bands, and use that. Replace the grille, and check the coils again in 6 months.

RUN A RETIRED APPLIANCE. If you have a refrigerator or freezer that you're not using at the moment, "exercise" it once a month to keep it in good working order. Turn it on for an hour or so—just long enough to allow the internal fluids to circulate well and prevent corrosion. When you're ready to put it back into regular service, your appliance will still be in tip-top shape.

USE THE "THINK-FIRST" RULE. When you open the refrigerator door—even for just a moment—the appliance's compressor has to run for an extra 8 to 10 minutes to restore the interior's temperature. To save wear and tear on this machinery, establish a family rule: No standing at the open door of the fridge trying to figure out what you might want to eat. Think it over first, and then open the door only when you know what you want.

FEED FREEZERS WELL. A freezer with little food in it has to work harder to keep the compartment cold and will wear out faster. So keep your freezer fully packed with food that will "hold the cold" and put less stress on your appliance.

KEEP THE SEALS HAPPY. Those rubbery seals running around the perimeter of your refrigerator and freezer door are called gaskets. They're designed to last as long as your refrigerator does. It's fairly easy to make sure they do: Every time you clean your refrigerator, clean the gaskets, too. Wipe them down with a sponge dipped in a mixture of warm water and a squirt of dishwashing liquid. Rinse out the sponge, and then wipe again.

SET THE RIGHT TEMP. Your refrigerator will last longer if you set it at the right temperature. The optimum setting allows your appliance to keep your food cold by expending the minimum amount of work and energy. When your appliance doesn't work as hard, it lasts longer—and keeps your energy bills down, too. So check your manual or use this guideline: Refrigerator temperature should be between 36°F and 38°F; freezer temperature between 0° and 5°F.

WARM UP TO DEFROSTING. When ice builds up on the coils inside a freezer, it has to work harder to keep the interior cold; meaning it will wear out more quickly. If you own a frost-free unit, there's no worry. But if your freezer doesn't defrost itself automatically, do it when there's a quarter-inch buildup inside.

DRAIN THE PAN, ELIMINATE ODOR. You spent time scrubbing the interior of the fridge and even stowed a box of baking soda inside, but you can still detect an unpleasant odor. The problem may be under, not in, the refrigerator. Under the refrigerator is a receptacle called a drain pan. That's where the melting ice in an auto-defrosting freezer goes once it leaves the freezer. Normally, that water just evaporates, but sometimes, bits of food end up in the pan, too, and after a while, mold and odors can develop. To clean the pan, just remove the grate or panel at the front bottom of the fridge. Then reach under and grab the pan. Wash it well, and then replace it. If you're unsure about how to proceed, check the owner's manual or visit the manufacturer's Web site for guidance.

SIMPLE SOLUTIONS

Blast Those Drip Pans Clean

You're so disgusted with the burned-on stains in your stove-top drip pans that you're ready to buy a whole new set. Keep your wallet in your pocket. If you have a self-cleaning oven, remove the drip pans from the stove top, slip them into the oven compartment, and run the oven through the self-cleaning process. Your drip pans will come out sparkling.

"RAIN" IN THE FRIDGE IS A DRAIN. If water is dripping into your refrigerator compartment from the freezer above it, you have a drain that's dammed up, so the water has nowhere else to go. Here's the problem: Self-defrosting freezers have a tube of some kind at the bottom of the freezer compartment to drain off the water created by defrosting. The tube leads down to the drip pan beneath the refrigerator. But if the opening to the tube gets blocked, the water will back up and drip into the refrigerator compartment. Some of that excess water is probably freezing into a drippy glacier behind the walls of the freezer. Here's how to solve the problem.

Pack all of the food in your freezer into a cooler to keep items cold while you work. To be safe, unplug the refrigerator. Remove the screws that secure the interior back and floor panels of the freezer. Place the screws in a safe place. Next, check the bottom of the freezer for the opening to the drain tube and clear away any debris blocking it. Use a hairdryer to melt any ice that has built up. Keep a sponge handy to mop up any resulting water. For good measure, dribble some hot water into the drain hole to make sure it's clear. Then replace the plastic panels, return the food to the freezer, and plug the unit back into the outlet. The drain pan probably needs emptying and cleaning, too. Pull away that narrow grate from the front bottom of the refrigerator to reach it.

SPRAY THE TRAYS. Sometimes an automatic icemaker just doesn't want to let go. The cubes don't spill out of the tray, so the machine's productivity grinds to a halt. To fix the problem, remove the icemaker's tray, dry it well, and then spray it very lightly with cooking oil. Wipe it with a paper towel so there's only a thin film of oil left, then replace the tray. The new ice cubes will slide out with no hesitation, and no, you won't end up with an oily beverage.

PASS IT ALONG

REUSE THE RACKS. If you're replacing an old fridge, save the racks and give them a new life. They're perfect for draining foods such as fried chicken (set over plenty of paper towels or newspapers, of course) or cooling cookies or biscuits.

TRANSFER TRAYS. Once it's time to purchase new ice cube trays, move the old ones into a dresser drawer where you can use them to organize earrings and other small pieces of jewelry. Or take them to the office and set them in a drawer, where they can hold small sticky notes, pushpins, stamps, and the like.

RANGES

We're so much luckier than our distant ancestors, who really did slave over a hot stove all day to produce a filling and nutritious dinner. These days, life is easier. Our ranges are easy to maintain and operate—especially when you employ our expert tips.

MAKE IT LAST

WATCH OUT FOR "GOOD" IDEAS. Sometimes the best intentions will cause rapid wear on your stove. So here are two precautionary notes from the "It-Sounded-Like-a-Good-Idea" department.
- **It's not a heater.** Don't run your oven continuously to warm the house during cold weather. This can permanently damage the oven's heating element and thermostat.
- **Don't be foiled by foil.** You may be tempted to keep your oven clean by placing a sheet of aluminum foil across the bottom to catch drips. Don't! The reflected heat can damage the heating element.

FIX IT FAST

TEST DEAD BURNERS. Got a defunct burner on your electric stove top? If you have the kind of burner element that simply unplugs from its receptacle, there's an easy way to diagnose the problem. Swap the suspect burner element into another receptacle that's working fine.

If the suspect element doesn't work in its new position either, you know the element is broken—buy a new one. If the suspect element does work in its new position, the *receptacle* on the original burner needs to be replaced. If you're comfortable with small wiring jobs, consult your owner's manual. Otherwise, call an appliance repairman.

GIVE THE RANGE HOOD FILTER A BATH. If your range hood isn't drawing up air (and those steamy, oily cooking smells) well enough any more, the filter may be clogged. Look up under the hood and detach that aluminum mesh filter. Fill the sink with enough hot water to cover the filter, add two squirts of dishwashing liquid, and drop the filter in. After 20 minutes, slip on some rubber gloves and slosh the filter around in the sudsy water, then wipe it with a sponge. Let the sudsy water go down the drain and rinse the filter in fresh hot water, then towel it dry. If you have the kind of range hood that does not lead to an outside vent, look for the charcoal filter, which you ought to change a couple of times a year.

REINVIGORATE A GAS OVEN. Does your gas oven seem like it's, well, running out of gas? It could be that the minute holes for the burner flames are clogged by debris. Here's how to fix them.
1. Let the oven cool and then open it. If there's a burner cover at the roof of the oven compartment, unscrew it.
2. Pour warm water into a bowl and add a couple squirts of dishwashing liquid. Dip a synthetic scrubber into it, squeeze out the excess, and clean the grime off the burner.
3. Use a needle or stiff wire to clean any dirt out of the flame holes on the burner.
4. Pull the bottom pan out of the oven, and clean the burner you find underneath in the same way.
5. Sponge up any excess water, and leave the oven door open while the interior air-dries.
6. Put the burner covers back into place.

OVEN BROKEN? ELEMENTARY, MY DEAR. Since the element in your oven is the device that actually delivers the heat, replacing one seems like serious business. It's actually quite easy, however. There are two elements in your oven: The broiler (near the roof of the oven) and the regular oven element (at the bottom of the oven). If either of these fails to turn orangey-hot when the appropriate controls are switched on, you probably need to change it. The procedure will go more easily if you remove the oven door first. In most cases, all you need to do is open the door partway and lift it off the hinges. Remember, don't start working on your oven until everything has cooled down.

1. Switch off the circuit breaker that feeds electricity to your oven.
2. Find the bracket that holds the element to the back of the oven. Remove its screws and pull the element toward you enough to expose the wires.
3. Use tape or some other method for marking the wires so you'll remember what goes where later. Unhook the wires from the clips that connect them to the element.
4. Remove the element and buy one like it at your home improvement store or appliance shop.
5. Attach the wires to the new element and put it back into the bracket on the back of the oven, replacing any screws you removed earlier.
6. Turn on the power to check your repair.

DISHWASHERS

There's the old joke that says if a woman has a husband, then she has a dishwasher. The kind we're talking about below are mechanical—but they need just as much TLC. Here's how to give it to them.

WASH LABELED BOTTLES BY HAND. Resist the temptation to wash bottles and jars with adhesive labels in the dishwasher. In the intense heat and moisture of the dishwasher, the labels are likely to slide off and could jam up the inner workings of the machine, shortening the life of the mechanism.

MAKE IT LAST

RUST-PROOF THE DISH RACK. When one of the wire prongs of the dish rack breaks inside a dishwasher, unsightly rust will follow close behind. Most appliance stores sell a number of products that will halt the rust damage and rejuvenate the look of your dish rack as well. Your choices include super-tough paint-on sealants and little slide-on rubber caps.

POWER UP THOSE SPRAY ARMS. When debris or deposits build up on the spray arms inside your dishwasher, they'll be less effective at cleaning your dishes. Open the door of your dishwasher and examine the little spray holes along the top of the spray arms. If you see some kind

FIX IT FAST

of grime starting to narrow the spray holes, it's time to remove the arms (upper and lower) and clean those holes. Spray arms come in various designs, but they tend to be secured by screws and clips that are easy to work with. When you remove the lower spray arm, wipe off any debris from the screen or filter that you see underneath it at the base of the washer. Put the spray arms in the sink. Use a pipe cleaner or wire to poke at the deposits blocking the spray arm holes. Then run warm water into the spray arm, and slosh it around to wash out any loosened dirt. Put the spray arms back into place, reattaching all screws and clips. You have just rejuvenated your dishwasher—and saved yourself a service call.

UN-JAM THE VALVE. If your dishwasher doesn't fill with water when you turn it on, your overflow protection valve may be the culprit. This is usually simple to fix. Look for the valve on the floor of the dishwasher. It has a little float that rises as the water level inside increases. Find the valve, clear away any obstruction, and push the float back down. If the valve is actually defective, you'll need to have it replaced; but in most cases, a push with a finger is all that's required.

BOOST THE WATER TEMPERATURE. Are your dishes still a little dirty when the dishwasher has finished its cleaning cycle? The problem might be that the water being pulled into your washer isn't hot enough. There are two simple fixes for this problem.

Before you start a load in the dishwasher, run the kitchen faucet on hot to clear all of the tepid water out of the pipe. This ensures that fully heated water will move into your dishwasher at the beginning of the cycle.

If the dirty-dish problem persists, check the temperature of your hottest water. Put a candy or meat thermometer stem-down into a glass measuring cup. Run the kitchen tap on hot for a minute or so until the water is as hot as it's going to get, then fill the measuring cup. The ideal hot-water temperature is 120°F. If your water is cooler than that, adjust the water heater. Be sure to warn the rest of the family that they will now get water that's hotter than they're accustomed to.

RINSE AWAY ODORS. A bunch of dirty dishes left in a closed compartment—your dishwasher—are going to stink after a while. This is particularly true if you wait two or three days between loads. If the odor singes your eyebrows and causes the dog to yowl every time you open the dishwasher door, there's a simple cure. Run your washer through a rinse cycle once or twice a day until you build up a full load for a genuine washing. This will keep the odor to a minimum.

TAKE A VINEGAR BATH. If white hard-water spots have built up on your glassware, dishes, and inside your dishwasher, let the dishwasher fix the problem itself—with a vinegar bath.

1. First, run all of your dishes through a wash cycle, using the air-dry option.
2. Remove all of the metal implements from the dishwasher and leave the "clean" but spotty dishes in the racks.
3. Pour 2 cups of white vinegar into a dishwasher-safe measuring cup and place the cup on the lower rack of the dishwasher.
4. Without adding any detergent, run the washer through its cleaning cycle, using the air-dry setting again. The acid in the vinegar will eat away the white spots, leaving your dishes and the interior of your dishwasher sparkling.

MIXING MACHINES

Food processors, blenders, and mixers. When cared for properly, not only do they last a good long time, but they'll also keep you looking like a pro in the kitchen. Our tips show you how to maintain and fix the niggling little issues that can crop up with these appliances.

SHIELD THE LID FROM SCRATCHES. The clear plastic cover for the typical food processor takes on a foggy-white tinge after a year or two of service. This is caused by the minute scrapes and scratches that result from cleaning. There's a simple way to prevent this wear and tear—don't clean the lid if it doesn't need it. If the recipe you're working on doesn't require the use of the feed tube on top, cover the bowl part of your food processor with plastic wrap before you lock the top into place. This will keep the top clean, prevent the wear that comes with cleaning, and save you some effort to boot.

GO GENTLE ON THAT BLADE. The crucial "business end" of your food processor is the blade that whirls and chops your food at lightning speed. It would be a pity if your blade got dull prematurely—but many people accomplish just that. Many food processor parts do just fine in the dishwasher (except the base with the motor in it, of course), but that's too rough an environment for the blade. So treat it to some loving care when it needs cleaning: Immerse it in hot, sudsy water, sponge it off, rinse, and dry it with a cloth. When all parts of your processor are clean, reassemble it for storage. This way, the blade is protected, the cover keeps dust out of the interior, and it's ready for service the next time you need it.

DRY THE PARTS THOROUGHLY. Many food processors have a metal spring that engages when you fit the bowl onto the heavy base. If this spring is left wet for too long, it can rust. If this continues, the spring will eventually break. Here's how to avoid all the headache: When you have finished cleaning your food processor, wipe the parts

THE FINE PRINT

He Ain't Heavy, He's My Blender

As with many appliances, the huge menu of features available for blenders may distract you from the core issues. Here are the important points to consider.

- **Stability or weight?** What are the jar and base made of? If they're both plastic, your blender will be less expensive in some cases—but also less stable. But if the weight of the blender is an issue for you, remember that a glass jar and metal base will weigh more.

- **Is it easy to feed?** Is there a feeder mechanism that allows you to add ingredients while the machine is running?

- **Does it have extras?** Are there other special options you'll want—such as a pulse switch?

- **Is it too big?** Will the new blender fit where you are hoping to store it, such as under a counter? Measure the counter-to-cabinet gap before you go shopping.

with a dry towel as well as you can, and then leave them unassembled so air can get to the spring for air-drying. This will prevent the need for an annoying (and potentially expensive) repair.

EASY DOES IT. If you work too hard, you burn out, right? Same thing with ice cream makers, juicers, and mixers. Follow the manufacturer's instructions carefully. If you hear the motor slowing or straining, it probably is working too hard. Use a smaller amount of ingredients or, in the case of juicers, cut the ingredients into smaller, thinner pieces.

KEEP VENTS SPLATTER-FREE. If splattered food or dust is clogging the vents on the housing of your blender or food processor, the motor will have restricted access to cool air. Overheating will shorten the life of your appliance. Use an old toothbrush or a pipe cleaner to clear out the vents any time you see a blockage.

LIGHTEN UP. Your blender is loaded with food, you flick on the switch—and you get nothing but a hum. No whirling blades. First, turn off the motor—you don't want to burn it out. Remember that your blender is built for speed, not for power-grinding. If you have heavy, chunky food or frozen food or ice in the jar, the blades may not be able to get started. So lighten the machine's load. Remove half of the food, and try the blender again. Adding some liquid and selecting a higher speed also will move things along.

FIX IT FAST

TEST THE BLADES. Humans may slow down as they get older, but your blender shouldn't. If your blender doesn't seem as powerful as it once was, try this simple diagnostic test: Run the blender for a few seconds with the jar in place. Then remove the jar and run the blender with just the bare shaft spinning. Does it spin more freely without the jar? If so, there's probably nothing wrong with the motor—the blade mechanism of your blender is jammed. Pull out your owner's manual and see whether your blender's blade assembly is the type that can be dismantled and lubricated.

CLEAN WITH A TOOTHPICK. If you don't feel that the machine is operating at full speed when you depress a button, unplug the appliance and poke around the buttons with a toothpick to dislodge crumbs or grimy buildup. The button may not be able to fully engage if there's something in the way.

COFFEEMAKERS AND GRINDERS

If you don't feel human until you've had your morning cup, then you know why coffeemakers and coffee grinders are among the most important appliances in the home. These tips are all about the machine that grinds the beans and the one that brews them up.

MAKE IT LAST

CAREFUL WITH THAT CARAFE. Coffeemaker carafes need a little tender loving care if you want them to last for years. Tempting as it might be, don't try to warm up a carafe of coffee on a stove-top burner—it could crack. Also, don't wash a hot glass carafe until it has cooled completely.

BREW AWAY DEPOSITS. Few things can gum up an automatic coffeemaker more readily than mineral deposits. This is a particular hazard if you have hard water. Follow this cleaning procedure at least once a month to keep all of the internal channels flowing properly.

1. Fill the coffeemaker's tank halfway with white vinegar; add enough water to fill it to the top.
2. Turn on the coffeemaker, let it run halfway through its cycle, and then turn it off.
3. Let the machine sit with the carafe half full for at least a half hour.
4. Pour the vinegar and water from the carafe back into the tank.
5. Return the carafe to its station, flick the coffeemaker on again, and run it through a full cycle.
6. Pour the vinegar and water out, and then rinse: Refill the tank with fresh water, and run the coffeemaker through another full cycle.

GRIND IN BURSTS. A coffee grinder is happiest when its blades are knocking against coffee beans, slicing them into a grainy powder. It *doesn't* like spinning freely or working for several minutes at a time—either of which will burn the motor out quickly. So turn your grinder on only when there's something inside to grind. Preferably, grind in bursts of just a few seconds each. For every minute of use, give the grinder a few minutes' rest.

AVOID THE GRIND. If your coffee grinder doubles as a spice grinder, or if your blender has a plastic or polycarbonate pitcher, don't use it to grind spices like cloves and cinnamon sticks. Those spices contain volatile oils that can permanently discolor plastic and will leave behind odors that won't wash out.

ADJUST THE SPRINKLER. Your coffeemaker has mysteriously started serving up weak coffee. You're using the same amount of coffee, and you haven't changed coffee brands. So what could possibly be going wrong? The culprit is probably the spreader plate, a little device positioned above the coffee basket. It works something like a showerhead, sprinkling hot water through little holes onto the ground coffee. If deposits are clogging up some of those holes, then the water is sprinkling onto the coffee unevenly and weakening the coffee. Here's how to fix the problem on many coffeemakers.

FIX IT FAST

1. Remove the carafe and coffee basket, unplug the unit, and turn it upside down. You should have easy access to the spreader plate now. (On some models, all you have to do is flip up a hinging lid on top of the machine.)
2. Work a stiff wire or a toothpick around in the holes of the spreader plate to loosen any deposits. With that accomplished, your favorite brew should be back to full strength.

HELP THOSE HOLES. You say your percolator-type coffeemaker is serving up a light-brown brew with just a weak hint of coffee flavor? It could be that the basket that holds the coffee grounds is stopped up, meaning much of the water is flowing over the sides of the basket rather than through the

FIX IT OR FORGET IT?
DON'T BE A CRACKPOT

With a lot of kitchen items, you can forgive little flaws such as dents, nicks, and chips. But if there's even the slightest crack in your coffeemaker's carafe, throw it away and get a new one. You don't want to be anywhere near a carafe full of hot coffee when a minor crack in the glass decides to shatter.

grounds. Hold the percolator basket over the sink and push a straight pin or toothpick into the holes to loosen any residue or grounds. Rinse the basket under the faucet, and percolate another pot—a deep, rich, dark brown brew this time.

PASS IT ALONG

START A PARTS DEPOT. Unfortunately, coffeemakers come and go. Some last for years, and others unaccountably break down when they're 35 seconds out of warranty. To save yourself some trouble down the line, set aside a cardboard box in your basement for coffeemaker parts. When one dies on you, drop the still-working parts into the box (carafes and carafe lids, especially) and trash the rest. Some parts are interchangeable between models. In an emergency, you may be surprised at how you can cobble together a perfectly good coffeemaker.

BREW UP CLEVER USES FOR FILTERS. Great news: You just got a brand new coffeemaker. Not so great news: The old coffeemaker used basket filters, and your new one uses cone filters. So what are you supposed to do with that bulk pack of 1,000 basket filters you bought last week? Here are just a few ideas.

- **Polish 'em off.** Polish your eyeglasses and camera lenses with filters. They make terrific polishing cloths because they're lint-free.
- **Fry away.** Flatten the filters, lay them on a plate in a couple of layers, and drain fried foods including falafel, bacon, and fish.
- **Use petite plates.** Make perfect improvised plates for snacks like cake, peanuts, candies, and even sandwiches.
- **For small spills.** Use a coffee filter as a substitute paper towel. They are very absorbent.

One Man's Trash
Keep the Carafe

My mother grew up during the Depression, and so she hated to throw anything away. If she thought she could get a second life out of something, she did, using plastic shopping bags to line small trash bins, recycling her coffee grounds into compost, and storing leftovers in margarine tubs.

Her best idea may not have been the cleverest, but it was certainly the longest lasting. We got our first electric coffeemaker some-time in the early 1970s, when I was a kid. What that one went kaput, she held onto the carafe and used it to water the houseplants. That carafe lasted a good 20 years before it finally gave up the ghost. Although I'm definitely not as thrifty as Mom was, I did inherit the old-coffee-carafe-as-plant-pitcher gene. Thanks, Mom.

—Jenn Lewis
Astoria, New York

- **Gas up your fuel**. Strain the fuel for a gas camp stove through a coffee filter. If that camping gas has been hanging around for awhile, it may have sediments in it that will make your stove sputter.
- **Lose the cork.** Strain wine if pieces of cork fall into the bottle.
- **Groom the gloss.** Keep a few filters in your purse—they'll come in handy when traveling and you need something to blot your lipstick.
- **Let flowers bloom.** Line a flowerpot with a filter before adding soil. The filter will prevent soil from escaping through the drainage hole, but will allow excess water to seep through.
- **They're real shiners.** Put some filters in your shoe-shine kit and use them to apply polish and buff.
- **Make cheese.** Put your filters to work making yogurt cheese (yummy as a base for dip or salad dressing), if you like to experiment with fresh ingredients. Place a filter in a mesh colander, then pour the yogurt into the filter. Let the yogurt drain for a few hours or overnight. You'll have rich and creamy yogurt cheese to use in recipes or as a pudding that's perfect paired with fresh berries.
- **Flavor a soup.** Use a basket filter just as you would cheesecloth when preparing a bouquet garni: For a classic mixture, place 1 sprig of parsley, 1 small sprig of thyme, and 1 bay leaf in the center of a basket filter. Gather into a small pouch and tie with kitchen twine or unwaxed, unflavored dental floss. Drop into soup or stew and remove after cooking.

OTHER ELECTRICAL APPLIANCES

Here are some tips about the other electrical gizmos most of us have around the kitchen—from toasters and toaster ovens to electric skillets.

FEED THE DISPOSAL A LITTLE AT A TIME. Saving up for a rainy day is usually a good thing—but not when it comes to garbage disposals. If you let food pile up down there, you increase the risk of jamming the mechanism and encouraging corrosion. So every time you shove food into the disposal, turn on the cold water and give it a whirl.

MAKE IT LAST

GIVE YOUR DISPOSAL LEMONADE. If your garbage disposal is starting to smell like the bottom of an old dumpster, there are flecks of food down there rotting away. Cleaning and freshening your disposal is easy. Toss in a half-dozen ice cubes, add a couple of orange or lemon rinds, and then turn on the cold water and then the machine. Not only will the grinding innards of your disposal be scraped clean, but they'll also be left with a citrus-fresh scent.

DE-JAM A DISPOSAL. If your garbage disposal jams while it's grinding food, turn off the power and grab the little L-shaped wrench that came with the appliance. Fit the tip of this wrench into the hole on the bottom of the disposal's outside housing, and turn it back and forth to shift the blades inside the machine. Use tongs (never your fingers!) to reach into the top of the disposal and remove anything that might be jamming the blades inside. Then turn it on to see whether it's working. If it's not, wait several minutes for the motor to cool, push the reset button, and turn it on again.

SET ASIDE STEEL WOOL. When you're cleaning the outside of a toaster, never use an abrasive metal scrubber on it. If a fiber were to come loose from the scrubber, it could fall inside the toaster and cause a dangerous and damaging short circuit. Usually, all a toaster body requires is a quick wipe with a damp sponge—after you've unplugged the appliance and let it cool, of course.

BE KIND TO THE SELF-CLEANING INTERIOR. A lot of the newer toaster ovens have a continuous-cleaning interior just like some conventional ovens. The walls react to splatters and burn them off slowly without creating smoke. This is a handy feature, but those specially treated surfaces require a gentle touch. To tidy the inside, unplug the toaster oven, remove any of the removable interior parts, and shake the crumbs out onto a spread of old newspapers. Wipe the inside gently with a soft, damp cloth. If you need a tad more cleaning power, dip your cloth in a mixture of warm water and dishwashing liquid and squeeze out the excess before wiping. That's as aggressive as you should get—no abrasive scrubbers and no harsh cleaning chemicals.

POP THE CORN, NOT THE MACHINE. Corn-popping machines are pretty simple and durable, but they're not indestructible. In fact, you can keep those kernels coming longer with a simple precaution: Keep any vents on the housing of the machine free of debris. With all of that heat being generated, the cooling airflow is important to keep your popper from overheating and damaging itself.

SLICE WITH CARE. If your kitchen is blessed with a deli-style food slicer, you need to know that blade sharpness is everything. If you let the blade get dull, you have to buy a new one—it can't be sharpened—so take care of it. A sponge dipped in warm water and dishwashing liquid is all you need to clean the blade. Never use abrasive cleansers or scrubbers. Don't use your slicer on bones, frozen food, or other hard stuff that will dull the blade.

GIVE BREAD AN EVEN TAN. If your toaster isn't browning bread evenly, don't give up on the appliance yet. Sometimes dirt or stains on the inside walls of the toaster can cause heat to reflect back unevenly, affecting the way it toasts. Here's a quick fix for the problem.

FIX IT FAST

1. Unplug the toaster and let it cool. Spread some old newspaper on your kitchen table to catch all of the crumbs that fall out.
2. Turn the toaster upside down on the paper and remove the screws in the base that hold the toaster together.
3. Remove the knob and any end panels. Then remove the guts of the toaster from the shell.
4. Wipe the interior of the shell with a sponge dipped in a mixture of warm water and dishwashing liquid. If you need a little more cleaning power, put a tablespoon of baking soda in a bowl and add water until it forms a paste. Dip a clean, damp sponge into the paste and scrub the interior of the shell.
5. Rinse with water, and towel it thoroughly dry. (You may want to let the unit air-dry for a few hours, as well.) Reassemble the toaster.

SAVE THE BLADE. The twin blades of an electric knife aren't generally serviceable. When they get dull, for instance, you have to buy a brand new set. But if you bend a blade, you might be able to salvage the situation. Here's how: Slip on a heavy-duty work glove and detach the bent blade. Lay the blade flat on the kitchen counter and press down on it with your gloved hand. If the blade straightens, reinsert it for the next round of slicing. If you have to throw away one of the blades, toss them both—don't use mismatched blades.

SIMPLE SOLUTIONS

Transfer Control

Sometimes the only thing wrong with an electric frying pan, or similar heating appliance, is a heat control that's kaput. (The heat control is the gizmo with a selector dial on top. It passes electricity from the electrical cord to the appliance.) Check your other appliances. If your slow cooker has a heat controller that's a perfect match, make the swap. You're back in the frying business.

DISHES, UTENSILS, AND GEAR

Plates; knives, forks, and spoons; and pots and pans: These are the items we rely on day in and day out to put meals on the table. That makes them prime candidates for the Make It Last and Fix It Fast treatment. And since they do eventually wear out, we offer plenty of Pass It Along tips for these workhorses.

MAKE IT LAST

KEEP PLATES IN PLAY. A family of four probably has 10 to 12 dinner plates stacked in the cabinet. However, only the half-dozen plates at the top of the stack get used day in and day out. As a result, several of the plates get the predictable scratches and nicks that come with everyday wear and a few are permanently out of action. After a year or two, the plates look oddly mismatched, particularly when you lay out a large spread for guests. The solution? When you wash a set of dinner plates, put the newly cleaned ones on the bottom of the stack. The plates that weren't used this time will be used the next time. This way, all plates get a piece of the action. Your plates will age more slowly, and they'll do it at the same pace so they'll look like a matched set.

BUCKLE UP YOUR DIRTY DISHES. Dirty dishes and glasses left stacked in and around the sink are vulnerable—they can be tipped over, dropped, or dropped *on*. When properly set into the dishwasher racks, it's as if they have their seatbelts on—as protected as they'll ever get. Make sure that breakable items are firmly supported by the rubber-coated prongs of the interior rack so that they don't get dislodged by the force of rushing water and crash into other objects. The moment a load of dishes is done in the dishwasher, unload them, and make way for the dirty dishes to come so they don't stand around exposed on the counter. Your plates, cups, and glasses will last longer this way.

PREVENT SLIP-UPS. When you're hand washing dishes, always wear rubber gloves. Of course, the gloves will protect your hands from the dishwater. But it protects your plates and glasses, too, because rubber gloves provide a better grip and you're less likely to drop items and break them.

WASH BY HAND. Wash fine cutlery by hand. If you run fine knives through the dishwasher, their handles can loosen. Also, there's a good chance you'll damage them when items bounce around inside the dishwasher. Use a synthetic scrubber and warm water with dishwashing liquid to clean your knives. To avoid cuts, always wipe from the dull side of the blade toward the sharp edge. Don't let your knives soak in water. Dry them with a dish towel as soon as they're clean. With these simple care techniques, a fine cooking knife could last for decades.

HAND WASH FOR A GOOD GRATER. There are two ways that food graters typically fall into ruin: They become dull, and they rust. Both of these maladies can be traced to the same culprit: the dishwasher. In a dishwater, the grater bumps into other objects, dulling its cutting surfaces. Also, dishes often get left in the washer for hours after the washing is complete. That hot, moist environment is a welcome wagon for rust. Wash the grater by hand by immersing it in warm, sudsy water for several minutes. Then gently brush away any remaining food particles with a dish scrubber, stroking from bottom to top—the opposite of your food-grating motion. (This way, you won't shred the dish scrubber.) Towel the grater dry. For extra antirust protection, dry your grater in the oven at 150°F for 10 minutes—unless, of course, it has a plastic handle or any other parts that could melt.

TUNE UP YOUR SHEARS. Your old kitchen shears can become a favorite tool again by sharpening them with a coarse sharpening stone.
1. Lubricate the sharpening stone (check the instructions—use either water or oil).
2. Open the scissors, and then stand one of the blades against the sharpening stone, perpendicular to the surface. You'll notice that one side of the blade has a beveled (angled) edge. Tilt the blade back about 10 degrees toward the beveled side—you're trying to match the angle of the bevel.
3. Draw the blade across the stone, making sure that the entire blade sweeps across the stone at some point. Several strokes should do it.
4. Now switch blades and sharpen again. Snap the scissors open and closed a few times to free up any of the minute metal debris.

For firm cutting action, the tips of the scissor blades should touch. If they don't, use a screwdriver to slightly tighten the screw holding them together until the tips meet. Test them on a sheet of paper and adjust if necessary. When the blades are fastened by a rivet, you have a little less precision in your tightening: Set one side of the rivet on a heavy metal surface and smack the other end of the rivet with a hammer.

BAR RUST. You would think that cookware made of cast iron wouldn't need to be coddled. But rust will eat it up if you're not careful. You can protect iron cookware by seasoning it. Here's how to do just that.
1. Lightly coat a clean skillet or Dutch oven with vegetable oil, lard, or bacon fat.

2. Set the oven at 200° to 300°F, and then place the ironware inside for a half hour.

3. Let the ironware cool, and then use a paper towel to wipe up any remaining oil on the surface.

Cooking fatty foods in a newly seasoned pan will enhance the seasoning. Once the ironware has been seasoned, don't use detergents or harsh scrubbing devices on it. (If you do, you'll have to reseason it.) It will usually come clean with some boiling water and gentle scraping with utensils. Dry it thoroughly by setting it back on the stove on medium heat until it's completely dry. Add a light coating of oil before storing. Especially when it's humid, store your iron cookware with lids off so condensation doesn't form inside and cause rust.

BLOCK THE SAUCE. If you're sick and tired of your plastic storage containers turning an indelible orange after you store tomato-based sauces in them, we have good news: There's an easy way to prevent the stain in the first place. Before you pour in the sauce, just squirt the interior lightly with cooking oil spray. The staining juices won't penetrate the plastic. Mama mia!

MAKE A COOKBOOK SPLATTER GUARD. How many times have you had to buy a new copy of your favorite cookbook because you couldn't read your best recipes any longer through all of the splatters

SIMPLE SOLUTIONS

Spray Reluctant Shears

Your own joints get stiff as you age, and the same goes for scissors. If your kitchen shears are reluctant to open and close, give them a quick spritz of cooking oil spray aimed at the pivot point. Open and close them a few times to work in the lubricant, and then wipe your scissors with a paper towel.

and splotches? Save yourself the money. The next time you open a cookbook on the counter for reference, pull out a piece of plastic wrap long enough to cover it, plus a few extra inches to tuck under the edges of the book to hold the plastic down. You will be able to read your recipe through the plastic, and your prized cookbook will come through even the messiest cooking session with nary a blotch.

If you're willing to throw a little money at the problem, look in your kitchen store for the kind of cookbook stand that includes a see-through plastic shield. Some are free-standing, designed for the countertop, and others are magnetized and can attach to your refrigerator. Aside from the cost, the only downside is that you have yet another object to clean and store in your kitchen.

USE TEMPERATURE, NOT BRAWN. When you stack drinking  glasses in the kitchen cabinet, now and then two of them will get frustratingly stuck together. Careful: Trying to wrench them apart could end in calamity—with broken glass and cut fingers. Instead, simply turn the glasses upright and pour cold water into the top glass, then pour some warm water into a pan and set the bottom glass into that. The top glass will contract from the cold, while the bottom glass expands from the warmth. After a few moments, they'll slide apart. Don't use extremely cold or hot water with this technique—that could cause the glass to crack.

ADD THE AID. If you've been wondering why your glasses are developing a milky crust, you may be derelict in a recurring duty that's all too easy to forget about. Fill that rinse-aid dispenser once a month or so. This is the additive to your rinse cycle that causes water to sheet off and dry without leaving spots.

NEW LIFE FOR MEASURING CUPS. Once you're ready to retire  those old measuring cups, don't throw them out. Instead, give them new jobs in and around the house.

- **Laundry room.** Use the cups to scoop liquid or powdered detergent or softener.
- **Garden shed or garage.** Measuring cups are perfect for scooping potting soil, fertilizer, grass seed, or mulch.
- **Pet supply area.** Use one to scoop dry food, another to scoop clean kitty litter into litter boxes. Use yet another to measure out bedding for pocket pets such as hamsters and gerbils.

- **Freezer.** Keep a plastic measuring cup in the freezer to scoop ice cubes into glasses.
- **Rec room.** Let the kids or grandkids use the cups to mix paints, mold clay, or store small game pieces.

SAUCERS GROW INTO NEW JOBS. A saucer that's chipped and no longer presentable for the dinner table still has plenty of life left in it. Slide it under a potted plant in the living room to catch the overflow of water. Turn the chipped edge to the back, out of sight.

TAKE THE SPATULA OUTSIDE. When it's time to replace a worn-out kitchen spatula, here are two ways to put it to good use.
- Hang the old utensil on a nail in the shed. In late fall, you'll find that it's the perfect size for scooping leaves and other debris out of your rain gutters.
- Drop it into the box where you keep painting supplies. Old spatulas make great long-handled putty knives, and they're ideal for scooping out the last drops of paint from the can.

OLD UTENSILS, NEW USES. When it's time to upgrade flatware, give the pieces new homes all around the house.
- **Send 'em to the garden.** Add an old fork or spoon to your collection of gardening tools. Either can be pressed into service when it's time to transplant seedlings.
- **Hold it!** Set a fork, tines up, in a glass and use it to hold recipe cards while you cook.
- **Create a masterpiece.** Put spoons, forks, and butter knives that aren't sharp into the crafts kit, where they can be used to shape clay.
- **Stir things up.** Take an old butter knife into the garage or workshop and put it to work as a reusable paint stirrer.
- **Beach builders.** Take old spoons to the beach. Kids can use them as construction tools when they build their sandcastles.
- **Take 'em outside.** Wrap full sets (one knife, one spoon, one fork) of flatware and store them in the picnic basket for your outings.
- **Pack 'em with lunch.** Take another set to work and leave them in your desk—no more wasteful use of disposable utensils.
- **Turn 'em into jewelry.** If you're crafty, try your hand at bending fork tines into curlicues or spoon handles into circles to make a one-of-a-kind bracelet, pendant, or ring. Or pass along your fine silverware pieces to a silversmith artisan who will do the same.

7 Uses for
an Old Cutting Board

1. Hang the cutting board on a nail on the pantry wall and screw several small hooks into its surface. Hang spare keys for the doors, car, shed, and neighbor's house on the hooks.
2. Park it in your workshop and let the cutting board take the damage—rather than your workbench—any time you're nailing, pounding, gluing, or soldering.
3. Take it into the garden and use it as a portable, temporary stepping stone for hard-to-reach places.
4. Paint a nice country scene on it, seal the whole thing with polyurethane, and then hang it on the wall.
5. Take an old cutting board camping and throw it in the fire once you've used it to cook the last meal of the trip. No cleanup, and nothing to haul home!
6. Use it as a signboard. Paint your message on it, tie a loop of nylon rope to it, and hang it outside.
7. Stow that old cutting board into the trunk of your car and then press it into service as a portable, all-purpose hard surface. Passengers can use it as a writing, coloring, or crafting surface. Kneel on it when you need to look under the car. Slide it under your jack when you need to change a tire on soft ground.

TRY THESE TRAY USES. Buying a new plastic utensil tray for the kitchen? Recycle the old one! Here are a few ways to reuse that tray.

- **Rinse garden goodies.** If the old tray has slots in the bottom, use it to gather and wash fresh produce, such as green beans and cherry tomatoes. The water and soil clumps will wash right through the bottom.
- **Neaten notions.** Move the tray to the sewing room, where it can keep knitting needles and notions organized.
- **Corral crafts supplies.** Use the tray to organize scissors, hot glue gun sticks, and any number of other odds and ends for crafts.
- **Send it to the office.** Add a utensil tray to a desk drawer to keep pens, pencils, pushpins, and other such items tidy.
- **Organize accessories.** Use a utensil tray to corral combs, brushes, and hair accessories.

SAVE THAT SIEVE. Just because that old colander or sieve is bent, battered, or just plain too ugly to use in the kitchen doesn't mean it's time to retire it. Even a colander with a crack, a missing handle or foot, or a soiled appearance may find a future elsewhere in your home. After all, there's always more life left in every handy kitchen tool!

- **Use it in the veggie patch.** Transfer it to the garden shed, and next time you're picking vegetables use it as your basket. Place your produce inside, give it a rinse outside with the garden hose, and then all you need to do is a final cleaning when you return indoors.

- **Sift sand.** Use the colander in a sandbox for breaking up clumps, sifting out pebbles, or shaking small toys, such as small toy cars, to remove sand.
- **Make smooth gravy.** Instead of lifting turkey, chicken, or pork trimmings after roasting with a slotted spoon, put the colander to good use. Pour the broth and trimmings through the colander, catching the broth in a bowl.
- **Drain bath toys.** Scoop up bathtub toys with a plastic colander and then let them drain. It's a perfect solution to a messy problem.

FIXTURES AND SURFACES

Aside from major appliances, the sink, counters, and flooring are likely your largest kitchen investment, and so it makes good sense to care for them and learn how to fix minor divots, dings, and leaks. Here's all the advice you'll need.

MAKE IT LAST

DON'T GET FRESH WITH YOUR SINK'S FINISH. If you sat down to make a list of the 10 most delicate items in your house, the kitchen sink probably wouldn't come to mind. It seems so durable, after all. But if you want it to keep that smooth and shiny finish, your sink really does require a gentle touch when you clean it. This applies equally to porcelain and metal sinks. Never use abrasive cleansers on your sink—scouring powder, for instance. Instead, clean your sink with dishwashing liquid, an all-purpose cleanser, or a nonabrasive bathroom cleanser.

What you use to apply cleanser is important, too. Avoid abrasive scouring materials like steel wool and scraping devices that will scratch a sink. Instead, use a sponge or a synthetic, nonabrasive cleaning pad made of such materials as nylon, polyester, or polyethylene. This will make the difference between a glimmering sink and a dull, hazy one.

BEWARE ACIDIC TRIMMINGS. When you're slicing fruit or rinsing plates after a meal, it's easy to forget about the scraps and dribbles lying at the bottom of the kitchen sink. But acidic foods lying against the sink for a long time can etch the surface and permanently damage the finish. So make sure to scoop those trimmings out of the sink and toss them in the trash or compost, or put them through the garbage disposal immediately. This advice applies to tea, coffee, citrus fruits, salad dressing, and any other acidic food.

BABY YOUR SINK'S BOTTOM. You use seat belts and bicycle helmets. Your kitchen sink needs a protective device, too—a plastic pad to lay across the bottom when you're hand washing dishes and implements. Not only does this reduce the chance of breaking that drinking glass when it slips from your fingers, but it also protects your sink from chipping and scratching. Look for a mat with holes in it to let water drain through. Mats are available at kitchen stores and discount stores. Don't leave your mat in the sink for extended periods—stains and debris will collect underneath. Pull it out after every dishwashing session and let it dry on a rack. Or buy a wire-coated sink rack if you have a porcelain sink; it reduces the risk of chips if you drop a dish.

SIMPLE SOLUTIONS

Counter-Act Damaging Moisture

Hot, moist air wafting up from your dishwasher door can moisten the wood underlying a laminate counter. To prevent damage to the counter, brush wood sealant onto the underside of the counter's edge where it crosses over your dishwasher.

STEAM VEGETABLES, NOT WOOD. Rice and vegetable steamers emit enough hot, moist air that they can damage kitchen cabinets directly above them. So be sure to set such appliances well away from the woodwork when you turn them on. The same goes for old-fashioned teakettles with a whistle; try to use steam kettles on a front burner so steam doesn't rise up to the wooden cabinets above.

BLOCK OUT TIME FOR WOOD SURFACES. In a busy kitchen, a butcher block can see a lot of action, and it's your job to help it recover from a hard day's work. Some simple maintenance procedures and precautions will help a high-quality butcher block last for decades—knock on wood.

- **Post-prep care.** After you've used a butcher block for food preparation, dip a scrubber sponge in a mixture of warm water and dishwashing liquid. (Never use harsh detergents.) Scrub the wood, rinse the sponge thoroughly in clean water, and sponge the wood again to rinse. Dry the butcher block with a clean towel.
- **Baby butcher block.** To protect a butcher block, oil it once a month. Slightly warm some mineral oil in a pan on the stove. Dampen a clean rag with the oil and wipe the wood to give it a thin coating. Rub the wood in the direction of the grain. If you have a new butcher block, or if you're reseasoning a neglected surface, oil the wood three or four times, waiting several hours between applications.

- **Keep it dry.** Don't allow moisture, or moist foods, to sit on a butcher block table or cutting board any longer than necessary; water can damage the wood.

GET UP THE GRIT. The vinyl flooring installed in kitchens these days comes with a tough, built-in shine. But it still requires your help to make that shine last for years. The grit and grime that gets tracked into your kitchen can act as sandpaper against the floor, eventually dulling it. So protect your floor with simple light mopping once a week.

The two-bucket cleaning method gets up the most dirt. Fill two mop buckets with warm water. Find a floor cleanser that's appropriate for your vinyl and add it to one bucket according to the package directions. Leave the other bucket of water clean for rinsing. Dip your sponge mop into the cleaning water and squeeze out the excess. Mop several square feet of the vinyl. Then dip the mop into the rinse water, squeeze, dip it into the cleaning water, and start moping again. Change the rinse water when it starts to get dark. Using this two-bucket process ensures that your mop isn't picking up dirt from the bucket and smearing it back onto the floor. The less grit you have on the floor, the longer its shine will last.

GET A LEG UP ON SCRATCHES. No matter how tough your kitchen's vinyl flooring is, it can't stand up forever to the scratching and scraping that the bottom of a kitchen chair leg will deal out. Turn your chair upside down and examine the bottom tips that meet the floor. If you find a soft, feltlike surface, great—your floors are protected. If not, visit a hardware store or home improvement store and study the options for a chair of your type. Typically, either cut-it-to-size felt with an adhesive backing or chair leg pads that you tack into the wood will solve your problem and keep that floor shiny.

FIX IT FAST

PATCH A DIVOT. Fixing a chip in a white porcelain sink is easy!
1. Use emery cloth (available at hardware and home supply stores) to sand inside the damaged area to clear away rust and prepare the surface below for bonding.
2. Buy a tube of white porcelain repair paste at your hardware store and squirt a dollop onto a scrap of cardboard.
3. Starting at the bottom of the gouge, paint the patch material onto the damaged spot in layers until it's flush with the surrounding surface.
4. Let the patch dry according to the package directions.

5. Dampen the corner of a clean rag with acetone and use it to smooth out the patch.

TIME TO CLEAR THE AERATOR? If the water is coming out of your kitchen faucet too slowly or in an odd pattern, don't call the plumber yet. The problem might simply be the aerator, that little, round screenlike device at the tip of the faucet. Twist the aerator off with your hands and tap it against the floor to remove any loose debris. Use a straight pin to poke through any clogged holes and other internal nooks and crannies with a buildup of mineral deposits.

WIPE OUT WATER SPOTS. Distressed by milky water spots on your kitchen sink and fixtures? Here's how to mop them up in no time, leaving your sink sparkling clean: Dampen a sponge or cleaning cloth with rubbing alcohol or white vinegar, and wipe all of these surfaces thoroughly. The water spots will break down and disappear, giving you a showcase kitchen sink once again.

BANISH STAINS WITH BLEACH. If a white porcelain sink is looking yellowed or dingy, the solution lies in your laundry room. Cover the bottom of your sink with paper towels, dribble on some chlorine bleach until they're saturated, and let them sit for a half hour. Slip on some rubber gloves, scoop up the paper towels, throw them out, and rinse the sink with water. Then go get some sunglasses—your sink will be that bright. One caution: Don't use bleach on colored porcelain.

One Man's Trash
Mystery of the Vanishing Limestone

It was a lovely addition to the showroom. The staff at DreamMaker Bath and Kitchen in Fallbrook, California, built a beautiful set of columns and a matching fireplace out of sheets of limestone. The extra slabs were neatly stacked off to the side—that is, until the day they disappeared.

Now, when your leftover materials go AWOL, it's hardly the crime of the century. Still, storeowner Jennifer Jones was curious how she had managed to misplace these bulky slabs of limestone. "We asked all our guys," she says, until finally her mind turned to her landlord—a renowned penny-pincher, a renowned recycler, and a genius at finding economical approaches to fixing up his properties. Sure enough, the landlord had moved the errant limestone into a nearby storage structure, thinking that the materials were about to be scrapped.

In retrospect, it all seems so obvious: When materials disappear, first suspect an inveterate recycler. "He finds a purpose for everything," Jones says.

GIVE THE SINK SALT AND SODA. You may find that a dishpan or dish drainer leaves a yellow mark from being in contact with your porcelain sink for so long. Try scouring the yellow marks with baking soda or table salt. Sprinkle the soda or salt on the stain, add a few drops of water to make a mild paste, and then scour the stain.

RESCUE LAMENTABLE LAMINATE. You pulled a pan off a stovetop burner and touched it to the counter for just a second or two, and darn if you didn't scorch the laminate. If the burn didn't go too deep, you may be able to repair the mark. Go to your bathroom and find a gentle abrasive cleaner. Using a damp cloth or sponge, apply some of the cleaner to the burn mark. Use a light touch. You're trying to remove the discolored material without damaging the surrounding counter or digging into the laminate.

If you get a small nick or gouge in your laminate counter, carefully brush some epoxy cement into the gap. In all likelihood, you won't be able to match the color perfectly, but at least you'll seal the hole and restore the smooth surface.

GIVE STAINS THE BRUSH-OFF. If you have a food stain on a Corian-type kitchen sink or counter, squirt a little non-gel toothpaste onto a sponge and rub at the stain gently. The mildly abrasive toothpaste and its whitening chemicals should make quick work of the stain.

PATCH POPPED CORNERS. Don't ignore a vinyl tile that has one of its corners popping up. Sooner or later, it's going to catch your toe and you're going to spill an entire pot roast across the kitchen floor. Here's a quick fix.
1. Spread aluminum foil across the offending tile.
2. Warm up your clothes iron to medium heat and place it over the aluminum foil, until the tile bends more easily and the glue underneath softens.
3. Lift the loose corner of the tile and smear some new tile adhesive underneath.
4. Press down against the tile, pushing from the center of the square out toward the newly glued edge. Wipe up any excess that emerges.
5. Weight the corner down with bricks, wood, or heavy books for several hours to flatten it.

CORRECT A CABINET DOOR'S SWING. The door to one of your kitchen cabinets no longer looks quite straight, or it doesn't fit correctly against the cabinet when it closes. Putting your cabinet door back into the swing of things requires just a minor repair.

First, grab yourself a screwdriver and tighten the screws on the hinges. Doing this will pull the door up into alignment—and it just might be the only adjustment you need. If the door starts to sag again within a couple of days of your handy work, you'll have to put in a little more effort for a longer-lasting solution. This repair is slightly more involved, but still quite easy.
1. Remove the door from the cabinet by unfastening the hinges with a screwdriver.
2. Take a look at the screw holes in the wood, and identify the ones that are large enough to let the door sag.
3. Coat wooden matchsticks, shards from a shim, or some other slender pieces of wood with glue, and slide one into each offending screw hole.

4. Next, reattach the door. With more wood to grip in the screw holes, the hinge screws will set more firmly and should hold the door straight indefinitely.

ORGANIZE SOMEONE ELSE. When it's time to remodel the kitchen, don't just cart the old kitchen cabinetry out to the curb. We'd almost guarantee that someone will want to take (or buy) them from you to use in a home workshop. Advertise in your local paper or, if you live in a larger city, online at www.craigslist.org/about/cities.html. It's a very popular online bulletin board where people buy, sell, and give away items, and it's easy to use. You may just find someone who's willing to pay you for those old cabinets *and* pick them up. Of course, you could put them to use in your own workshop!

CLEANUP TIME

It's a dirty job, but it has to be done—cleaning up, that is. The good news is that with the proper equipment (that's up to you) and advice (we've provided plenty of that below), you can reduce the amount of time and energy you dedicate to the task.

TRY THE TRICKLE-DOWN THEORY. When you're hand washing several items in the kitchen sink, think strategically for a moment before you proceed and you can save a fair amount of dishwashing soap and water. Take all of the container-like items and set them in the sink, nested together. For instance, on the bottom might be a Dutch oven, and inside that you would place the colander, inside that goes a small pot, and inside that goes a measuring cup. Wash any incidental items over this menagerie of containers, dripping the suds and rinse water onto them. Then the measuring cup has enough suds in it that you can just wipe it clean and rinse. Then the pot, then the colander… and so on, until everything is sparkling clean. You got all those dishes done with just one or two squirts of dishwashing liquid, using those same perfectly good suds again and again—and only a bare minimum of water.

LOOK, MOM! NO SCRATCHES. If burned food is clinging to the bottom of a pan, fill it one-third of the way with water and then add 2 tablespoons of baking soda. Bring the water to a boil and simmer. Work at the food gently with a spatula until the food is loosened.

TREAT YOUR TEAPOT. Mineral deposits inside your teapot are unsightly and unappetizing. Before you decide to buy a new one, try this solution to that crusty buildup: Cut up a lemon into chunks and drop it into the teapot. Add several ice cubes, a teaspoon of salt, and a couple of ounces of water. Swirl the mixture around in the bottom of the teapot and leave it for several hours. Pour the mixture down the garbage disposal and rinse the teapot. All clean!

USE BAG-EXTENDING POWDER. How many times have you found yourself emptying the garbage when the bag is only half full because you can't stand the odor of vegetable trimmings festering down there? Here's how to eliminate that odor—and use fewer trash bags. Once or twice a day, sprinkle ¼ cup of baking soda into the trash, grab the edges of the trash bag, and give it a shake to distribute the powder. The baking soda will hold odors to a minimum until the trash bag is full.

MAKE A BAG DISPENSER. When you have used the last can of soda out of that 12-pack box in your refrigerator, you're probably accustomed to folding up the box and sliding it into recycling. Hold up—it can serve a secondary use before you usher it out the door. Pack it full of those plastic grocery bags that are cluttering your pantry. Set the box in a convenient place in the pantry or under the kitchen sink. When you need a bag to line the trash basket in the bathroom, just draw it out of that slot in the center of the box (the hole you're supposed to use as a handle). You'll be able to pluck out bags just the way you pull them out of a box of facial tissues. Think of this as double recycling: You get a second use for the box, and it helps you organize those bags you're recycling, too.

PASS IT ALONG

SIMPLE SOLUTIONS

Rub Out Rust

An unsightly rust mark on your steel or iron sink is no problem as long as you have a common household fluid at hand: WD-40. Just squirt a little onto a cleaning rag, rub at the rust spot on your kitchen sink, and watch the spot fade away. Finish by rinsing with water.

ASSIGN A TUBE TO BAG DUTY. When you have finished a roll of paper towels, don't throw out the cardboard tube. Pack it full of plastic grocery bags, and park your new bag dispenser in a place where you commonly need the bags—for instance, in the bathroom for lining trash baskets or in the garage for quick clean-ups. You'll get about five bags in a paper towel tube—a handy, compact container. To make it easier to use, punch a hole on either side of one end of the tube, run 8 inches of twine through the holes, and tie the twine ends together to make a loop. Now you can hang your dispenser on a hook in the vanity cabinet or off the side of a shelf.

WEAR A TRASH BAG. An extra plastic trash bag, even one you've accidentally nicked or torn, is still perfectly good as an emergency poncho in a downpour. Stash it in your desk at work or in the trunk of your car. When you're caught in a storm without rain gear, cut three holes in the trash bag—one in the center of the bottom for your head, and one on each side of the bottom for your arms. You won't win any awards for fashion, but you will stay dry from your shoulders to your thighs.

FOOD

For best flavor and to maintain its nutritional value, food, whether it's a dry staple or fresh produce, needs to be stored correctly. Keeping foods organized helps you stay on top of what you have, and that prevents you from ending up with three bottles of olive oil or marshmallow fluff. Our tips help out there, but they go a step further, too. On the following pages, you'll find out how to turn old fruit into delicious fruit sauces and make excellent use of that last bit of leftover wine.

MAKE IT LAST

MAKE THOSE SPICES VISIBLE. What's the worst enemy of the spices in your kitchen? Neglect. You pack a cabinet with spice bottles, but the only ones you can see easily are in the front couple of rows. You may not see that poor little bottle of paprika in the back corner for years—when it will be too old to use. And in the meantime, you bought two more bottles of paprika, thinking you were out. With one simple organizational trick, you can get full use of your spices.

- **Spin them.** Buy a tower-style spice rack that spins around on a mini Lazy Susan and sits on your countertop. It takes up only a small amount of space and moves your spice bottles out into the open where you can see them all at a glance. It also frees up cabinet space, of course. Spinning spice racks can be found at kitchen stores and discount stores.
- **Step up.** Buy an inexpensive stair-step shelf for your spices. This sits on the bottom of your cabinet and raises the back rows of spices enough that you can see the labels. These shelves are also available at kitchen stores and discount stores.
- **Box 'em.** Store all of your spices in a shoebox that you can slide in and out of your kitchen cabinet. Smaller-sized shoeboxes that held children's footwear have lower sides and are ideal for this use. Pick up some circular labels at your office supply store and label the top of each spice bottle, so you know what it is at a glance. If you like, cover the box in wrapping paper that fits with your kitchen's décor.

COOL YOUR YEAST. If you buy yeast packets in bulk, some of them could be too old to use by the time you need them. To extend their life by months, store them in the refrigerator or freezer rather than in your kitchen cabinet. Zip them up in a plastic bag while they're in cold storage. When you're ready to use a yeast packet, let it warm up to room temperature first.

WATER YOUR ARTICHOKES. Want your fresh artichokes to last an extra day or two in the fridge? Next time you're at the supermarket, make it a point to seek out the artichokes that have the longest stems. At home, pour a little water in a bowl and place the artichokes stem down into the water, just like freshly cut daisies. Then place the bowl in the fridge, and you'll get the longest possible shelf life out of your fresh artichokes.

WRAP ASPARAGUS. Freshness is the key to good asparagus. To keep it in tip-top shape in your refrigerator, wrap it in a little moisture. Tear off a few paper towels, dampen them under the kitchen faucet, then squeeze to remove the excess water. Lay the towels on the counter, put the asparagus stalks on top, and then wrap them in the towels. Place the bundle in the vegetable bin of your refrigerator. They'll be tasty treats when you're ready to cook them.

FREEZE THE RED BOUNTY. If you find yourself with an overabundance of tomatoes at certain times of year, don't fret: There's no need to toss them away. It's easy to set some aside for the future. Just plop several at a time into freezer bags and put them into the freezer. Later, you can pull out whole frozen tomatoes as needed. Hold them under the kitchen tap for a few moments and the skins will slide off. They're also easy to slice and seed when they're frozen. Thawed tomatoes won't be suitable for serving raw, but they're great for soups and sauces.

TURN LEFTOVERS INTO SOUP. A tasty soup base is yours for free when you use the perfectly good vegetable trimmings you usually throw away. Toss all of your trimmings—from potatoes, carrots, onions, broccoli, bell peppers, and such—into a one-gallon plastic freezer bag and store in the freezer. When it's full, dump it all into a pot, add water, and cook for 20 to 30 minutes. Strain the liquid and use as the starter for a soup. Scrape the remains into the garbage disposal or drop onto your compost heap.

KEEP EGGS FRESH. Unless you're making a large batch of omelets, you won't use an entire dozen eggs at once. To keep eggs fresh, store them in the original carton—not in the door of the fridge. If the eggs were bought from a local farmer, farmer's market, or health food store, they may not have been washed. That's okay—unwashed eggs keep longer than cleaned ones. Eggs have a natural protective coating that keeps bacteria at bay. When you handle or wash an egg, you remove this coating, which allows bacteria to penetrate the shell's pores and degrade the egg. And always discard an egg that's been sitting around cracked—you don't know what kind of bacteria it might contain.

SIMPLE SOLUTIONS

Banish Soggy Cereal

If your boxed cereal goes soft and stale before it's consumed, store it instead in that climate-controlled container you have right there in the kitchen. Take the cereal box out of the kitchen cabinet, pull out the liner bag (cereal and all), and fasten it closed with a clothespin or chip bag clip. Then stick the bag into your self-defrosting freezer. Self-defrosting freezers keep the humidity low, so your cereal will hold its crunch longer.

BAG THOSE MUSHROOMS. You have a hankering for an omelet, so you pull out the eggs, milk, onion, green pepper—and *ugh*, the mushrooms have turned slimy already! To make your mushrooms last longer in the refrigerator, drop them into a paper bag instead of storing them in plastic. The omelet fans in your household will thank you.

SAVE UP MINI MEALS. Save those thin, plastic deli containers that you buy potato salad or guacamole in. Wash them and set them aside to store small amounts of leftover food. (Admit it—you would have thrown out the remaining three raviolis.) Mark each container and put them in the freezer. Once every few weeks, treat your family to a wild leftovers night. Let family members take turns picking out favorite morsels to add to their plates. This is doubly good recycling: Both the plastic containers and the mini meals get a second life.

BAG SOME SANDWICHES. Making up a bunch of sandwiches for the gang to take to a tailgate party? Hang onto the bag that your loaf of bread came in—it's the perfect tote for the sandwiches. Rather than putting each sandwich into a separate plastic bag, just lay the sandwiches, one on top of another, back into the bread bag. It will keep your food clean and fresh. Once you're at the game, each hungry fan can reach into the bag and grab the top sandwich. You've reused the bread bag and saved several plastic sandwich bags to boot.

EAT THE MIDDLE FIRST. The end pieces of a loaf-shaped cake hold in moisture and keep your cake from drying out prematurely. So when you're serving dessert, don't slice the cake from the end. Instead, cut slices out of the middle. When everyone's been served, push the two sides of the cake together. Your cake will still be yummy the next day and the day after that.

SEPARATE CLINGY COOKIES. You know what happens when you stack freshly baked cookies into the cookie jar. When you start drawing out those little delectables, they cling together and break. The cure is simple: First, make sure you wait until the cookies are completely cool. Then place them into the jar in layers, placing a piece of wax paper between each layer. Every cookie will come out of the jar in picture-perfect condition.

GIVE COOKIES COMPANY. As much as the kids might want to, you're not going to let them eat all of the cookies you just baked right now. But wouldn't it be nice if those cookies still tasted freshly baked for the next couple of days? Easy: Drop a slice of white bread into the cookie jar or the plastic bin that you store your cookies in. Cookies will stay moist and fresh down to the last one. This clever trick also works to resoften cookies that have become stale.

SAVE MARSHMALLOWS. On a bone-chilling winter's day, the family decides to warm up with hot chocolate. "Get the marshmallows!" someone cries. So you go to the pantry only to find a bagful of brick-hard white cylinders. Next time you buy a bag of marshmallows, try this trick: Dump them all into a freezer bag and pop them into the freezer. Pull them out as needed, and they'll stay fresh indefinitely.

TURN CONDIMENTS ON THEIR HEADS. The typical home wastes gallons of condiments every year, often because a fresh jar of condiment gets opened before the one in the refrigerator is fully used. Then you have two jars open (needlessly crowding the fridge) and the condiments will go bad before you can use them all. Introduce your family to this simple system for conserving condiments: When a jar of mayonnaise is opened and put into the refrigerator, all of the other jars of mayo in the pantry must be turned upside down. This is a signal to all family members to stop and check the fridge before opening a jar. This approach works for jars of mustard, jelly, peanut butter, pickles, and relish, too.

FIX IT FAST

DRESS UP THE DRESSING DREGS. There are at least a couple of tablespoons of salad dressing left in that bottle, but who has the patience to drain it out—especially when you're hungry? Go to your refrigerator and open up the jar of sweet pickles. Pour a few ounces of the liquid from the pickle jar into the salad dressing bottle, seal the bottle, and shake it vigorously. You'll have enough reinvented dressing to share with the whole family. You can pull off similar salad dressing rescues by dribbling in a little vinegar or lemon juice.

ADD WATER FOR MORE KETCHUP. Wish you could get that last ounce or two of ketchup out of the bottle? No problem. Twist off the cap, pour in a dribble of water, and shake. Now go find one of those oversized souvenir drinking cups—you have a dozen in a dark corner of your pantry. Turn the ketchup bottle upside down into the cup, and set the cup in your refrigerator for a few hours. You'll have the last of the ketchup readily accessible in the bottom of the plastic cup, and the bottle will be ready for the recycling bin.

SHAKE THINGS UP WITH RICE. If the salt keeps clumping up in your saltshaker, an old restaurant trick will save the day: Pour a half teaspoon of uncooked white rice into the shaker. The rice will absorb moisture, which is the culprit that causes the salt to clump. The salt won't be able to get through the shaker's holes, so there's no danger of sprinkling your dinner with uncooked rice.

PROVE YEAST'S WORTH. Picture this scenario: You're about to make some bread, so you reach for the yeast in the fridge. But wait. It looks old—could it be expired? Don't wonder—"proof" it first to make sure it's active. Pour 1/4 cup of warm (not hot) water into a bowl and stir in the packet of yeast until it's dissolved. Wait several minutes. If the solution gives off a breadlike odor and gets all foamy, then the yeast is good to use. Having taken this precaution, you don't have to throw out questionable yeast packets, and you avoid a recipe disaster caused by defunct yeast.

UN-SALT THE SOUP. Oops! You over-salted the soup into a mouth-puckering disaster. But don't toss it. Peel a raw potato and drop it into the soup. It will absorb a lot of the salt and balance out the taste. Remove the potato when the soup is done cooking.

USE A SWEET SOLUTION TO BURNED FOOD. You scorched your sauce, and now you're ready to pour it down the garbage disposal and start over. Wait—all is not lost! Pour that burned sauce, saucy dish, or gravy into a fresh pan. Now sprinkle on a little sugar and taste. Repeat until the burned taste has faded away. (Go slowly—you don't want to make your food too sweet.)

RESCUE THE RAISINS. Your box of raisins has dried up into a brick that any mason would envy. Never fear—they're salvageable. Slide the block of raisins into a pot and add enough water to cover. Put the pot on a burner and bring it to a boil. Turn the burner off, let the raisins cool for a few minutes in the water, and then dump them into a colander in the sink to drain. It's best to use these raisins right away, either as a snack or in cooking.

You may want to try following the tradition of Pennsylvania German cooks. Add the plumped-up raisins (liquid and all) to an unbaked pie crust, stir in some flour, sprinkle sugar over the top, add a hearty squeeze of fresh lemon, and bake until the crust is done and the raisins are bubbly. This simple pie was known as Funeral Pie, because it could be baked at a moment's notice during any season from items already in the pantry.

BAKE STALE CRACKERS. You've discovered a box of crackers at the back of a cabinet that's been absorbing the summer humidity for two months. Don't fret. They may yet get a starring role on your appetizer tray. Place them on a cookie sheet and bake them at 250°F for a few minutes. Once they've cooled, slide these crisp-and-delectable crackers into a ziplock bag for storage.

READY TO BAG THOSE BISCUITS? Biscuits the second time around never taste as yummy as they did when they were fresh out of the oven. Here's how to revive them to near-mint condition: Dampen a brown or white paper bag under the faucet. Put the biscuits inside, and roll up the top of the bag to seal it. Heat your oven to 300°F, and warm your biscuits for 5 minutes. The moisture from the bag will create steam and soften up the biscuits inside.

LABEL THE LABEL. Since early childhood, Mom has been telling us about aging food in the refrigerator: "When in doubt, throw it out." Sure, that's the correct and safe thing to do. But it sure seems a pity to throw out a jar of salsa because you aren't sure whether it's just one day old or two months old. With this simple solution, you'll never be "in doubt." Keep a marker near the refrigerator. Instruct every member of the family to follow this procedure: Whenever a new jar of condiment is opened, mark that day's date on the label. You'll know at a glance how long it's been in the fridge, and never again will you throw out fresh condiments just because you weren't sure.

MAKE AGING FRUIT A FAVORITE. If the apples, oranges, or pears in your fridge have gone a tad soft, don't worry. Unless they're mushy and spoiled, you can still use them in a fruit sauce to pour over waffles or ice cream. You can easily find scores of recipes for fruit sauce on your cookbook shelf or on the Internet. Typically, you'll cut up the fruit, combine it with such ingredients as sugar, jam, juice, and spices, and cook for a few minutes. Store this topping in a plastic container in the refrigerator, and use it to liven up breakfast or snack time.

MAKE A BREAD COLLECTION. Use a 1-gallon ziplock plastic bag to store all bits and pieces of leftover bread and crackers in the freezer. This would include the heel of a loaf of bread, the untouched biscuit from dinner, and the handful of oyster crackers that were going stale.

Anytime a recipe calls for bread crumbs, give your bread bits a whirl in the food processor and you're ready.

CAPTURE THOSE ESCAPING NUTRIENTS. When you boil asparagus, green beans, potatoes, or other vegetables, nutrients are leached from the veggies into the water—and are typically poured down the kitchen drain. If you use that vitamin-laden water as a cooking ingredient, you'll be giving your family an extra nutritional boost. When your soup or spaghetti sauce recipe calls for water, add your veggie water instead.

POURING OUT WINE? FREEZE! If there are just a couple of ounces of wine left in a bottle at the end of your dinner party, don't pour it out. Instead, pour it into an ice cube tray. Your "wine cubes" will be easy to toss into a pot when a recipe calls for wine, or you can use them to chill a glass of wine—without diluting the drink, as would happen with regular ice.

MORE TIPS FOR THE KITCHEN

Here's a roundup of the kitchen-related Pass It Along tips you'll find in the other chapters of *Don't Throw It Out!*

Domestic Challenge

Now that you've read this chapter, test your savvy with this *Fix It or Pitch It* quiz.

Questions

1. Your spouse forgets to clean up the George Foreman Grill after making dinner. You find it in the morning, encrusted with the crisp remains (and odors) of last night's fish. Even though the surface is nonstick, you're guessing that this fish fry lasted for hours because it's reduced the fish to burnt-on charcoal. You know you cannot immerse the grill in water or use a scouring pad to clean the grill because either action will ruin it. Is the grill a lost cause and will it smell forever?

2. You have an old refrigerator that runs well. Unfortunately, a very unpleasant odor has started coming from the appliance. You've cleaned it inside and out and placed boxes of baking soda inside to no avail. Except for the odor, the fridge runs like a charm. Is it worth trying to fix or is it time for a new fridge?

3. The power went off in your neighborhood for a few days and the ice cream you purchased has partially thawed. Now the power is back on. Do you refreeze the ice cream or throw it away?

4. The bananas you bought last week are all overripe. They certainly don't look very good, but are they okay to eat?

5. That restaurant meal you had Monday night was delicious. But now it's Friday and you're wondering whether the leftovers are okay to heat and eat. Do you take the chance?

Answers

1. **Fix it!** Make sure the grill is unplugged, and then place it on the sink drain board so that the bottom of the grill slopes into the sink. Dampen the grill with hot water, and then sprinkle on some baking powder and dish soap. Using a sponge and more hot water as needed, scrub the grill, top and bottom. As necessary, gently pour a little hot water onto the grill surface to wash the grime into the sink. Continue scrubbing and rinsing until the grill is clean.

2. **FIX IT!** The problem may be under, not in, the refrigerator. Under the refrigerator is a receptacle called a drain pan. That's where the melting ice in an auto-defrosting freezer goes once it leaves the freezer. Normally, that water just evaporates, but sometimes, bits of food end up in the pan, too, and after a while, odors and mold can develop. To clean the pan, just remove the grate or panel at the front bottom of the fridge and then reach under and grab the pan. Give it a good washing, and replace it. The odor may also be originating with the rubber gaskets that seal the doors, and you may be able to replace them. If you're unsure about how to proceed, check the owner's manual—or visit the manufacturer's Web site for guidance.

3. **PITCH IT!** It's never a good idea to refreeze ice cream—not only will the texture be off, but there's also a high risk of food poisoning.

4. **FIX IT!** Overripe bananas are wonderful in all sorts of foods. Freeze them and use as an ingredient in smoothies, milkshakes, banana bread or muffins, or mix them into cooked oatmeal for a delicious breakfast.

5. **PITCH IT!** Although foods such as fresh eggs and luncheon meat can last up to 5 days, cooked leftovers are best thrown away after 3 days.

2

FURNITURE

The best furniture has to succeed on so many levels. It can't just look good and suit your decor, it also must provide comfort whether you're dining with the family, reading in an easy chair, or sliding drawers on the buffet to find a clean tablecloth.

That's what makes it so rewarding to invest a little time to make furniture last longer. While you're preserving pieces for later years or even future generations, you're making life easier and more enjoyable right now.

In this chapter, you'll find handy tips on how to find chairs that can stand on their own four legs, couches that may never cushion the landfill, and even candles that won't burn down in a hurry. Oh yes, and find out how to move the big pieces around the house so they live life scratch-free.

Now, kick back and get ready to read lots of great tips. Find a comfortable seat, but keep your feet off the furniture!

WOOD FURNITURE, GENERAL

Solid wood delivers solid service for generations if you treat it right! Plus, there are oodles of quick fixes and nifty new uses for furniture that's worn down.

MAKE IT LAST

MEASURE TWICE, MOVE ONCE. You probably feel pretty good when you remember to measure the space a piece of furniture will occupy before you go out shopping for it. But a few more measurements are in order if you want to avoid scrapes, nicks, and divots before the piece even begins its life in your house. Make sure to measure any doors, halls, or stairs the piece will have to traverse on its journey within your home so you can be sure the piece can be moved to its intended location. Don't forget to account for enough room so the furniture is not in danger of catching corners, banisters, hinges, or doorjambs along the way.

$mart Buys
5 WAYS TO FIND REAL WOOD

You'd think you could determine whether wood-look furniture was solid hardwood with a single glance, but clever manufacturers and retailers go to great trouble to make veneer or laminated pieces look like the real thing. If you're just browsing or buying from a place like a flea market, where the furniture's of unknown origins, do your own sleuthing with these five tests.

1. **Consider the construction.** How have the wood pieces been joined? If you spot dovetail joints, it's probably high-quality hardwood.

2. **Glue that goes on and on.** Continuous glue lines that join pieces of wood from edge to edge or end to end are another indicator of solid wood. Trace one line with your finger, across the top of the piece, around the edge, and all the way to the underbelly. If the glue line stops before you reach the underside, you're probably not looking at a solid hardwood piece.

3. **Get touchy.** Lightly run your fingertips over the piece, feeling for a smooth finish free of drips and bubbles, which indicates quality craftsmanship typical of hardwood pieces. Also make a special point of checking the finish in the hard-to-reach (and sometimes hard-to-see) places near joints or carved molding to make sure they're smooth and don't have globs of dried glue.

4. **Be leery of labels.** Sure it looks like the right color and says "cherry finish," but the wood lurking beneath the finish could be another, softer species or even a veneer that's been reproduced to look like cherry grain on top of plywood or particleboard. If the label says "fruitwood," remember that the term describes a finish meant to resemble certain hardwoods, but is not a type of hardwood itself.

5. **Check the edges.** True hardwood edges look like wood, complete with grain lines. The edges of composite woods, however, look just like what they are—bits of ground wood and sawdust that have been compressed and glued together.

5 Ways to Move Furniture
for Minimal Damage

Even if it is a woman's prerogative to change her mind, all that moving around can take a toll on furniture if you don't take a few straightforward precautions.

1. **Wrap and roll.** Use tissue or pieces of soft cloth to wrap any protruding handles that might catch a wall or railing and any dangling drawer pulls that might swing and slap the furniture's surface.

2. **Damage by accessory.** Check all movers for anything they are wearing (belt buckles, heavy watches, or buttoned cuffs) that may scratch or mar the furniture.

3. **The path of least resistance.** Take some time to clear out the moving route so you don't have to stop, lift, and put down the piece of furniture several times—and so such items as a broom, roller blade, or metal shelf don't scrape the furniture along the way.

4. **Bottoms up.** Lift sofas from the bottom frame and chairs by the seat frame so you don't put any unnecessary pressure on the arms or backs.

5. **Pad the pieces.** If it will fit, place a pad or blanket between the furniture and the opening when passing through doors or windows, so that neither the piece nor the paint gets scratched. And if the space is tight, consider removing doors from their hinges to allow for that extra bit of doorway width.

IT'S NOT THE HEAT. Wood furniture, new or antique, is sensitive to temperature changes and extremes. Too much moisture can cause warping or glue to fail. Hardwood doesn't much care for heat, either, since air holds more moisture at high temps than at low. The ideal conditions are temperatures from 70° to 72°F and relative humidity that's 50 to 55 percent. Minimize radical swings in temperature or moisture in the air by running a small air-conditioning unit where you keep nice wood pieces when you're on vacation in the summer, for example, or using a dehumidifier in those rooms during wet, rainy times.

CENTRALIZE DRY AIR. If you have heavily invested in antiques or expensive hardwood furniture, you may want to add a dehumidifier element to the central air-conditioning or purchase separate dehumidifiers if you use window or wall air-conditioners.

HONE A HABITAT FOR HEALTHY WOOD. Location is everything for solid hardwood furniture you'd like to have around for years to come. To avoid extremes in temperature, arrange furniture away from radiators, heat registers, and air-conditioning units. Keep nice pieces out of strong light, particularly sunlight, which will fade colors, dry out the wood, and deteriorate the finish. No one wants to use the furniture in total darkness, naturally, so rotate pieces to protect any

3 Dusters That Should Bite the Dust

Just because a product will pick up dust or is billed as a duster doesn't mean you should use it to dust furniture. Avoid these products and materials.

1. **Feathers make dust fly.** Feather dusters may look chic, but they only move dust around and send it up into the air to re-settle later. Plus, you can't wash them, and sometimes a feather breaks and the brittle quill below can leave scratches.

2. **Skip the zip.** If you're planning to dust using fabric from old cotton clothing, make sure to remove all snaps (even from recycled baby rompers), buttons, and zippers first—they're sure to scratch or otherwise damage the furniture.

3. **No hanging in there.** If a cloth—commercial or home styled—has threads hanging or edges that are beginning to unravel, either snip them off and seam bind the edges or find another dust cloth. Loose threads will catch on wood slivers, molding, or knobs and pull up a splinter, or scratch or loosen hardware.

one from a disproportionate amount of light exposure. By the same token, rotate accessories such as lamps, clocks, or pillows that rest on the furniture so the whole surface fades at the same rate.

DARE TO DUST. Sure, dusting's a dull chore, but not dusting often enough will dull your wood furniture. Dust is abrasive and can wear down the surface over the years, and it can accumulate in carved edges to make wood look grimy and dark. While running a dust cloth over some wood may seem like a no-brainer, there's a process you should follow to do your wood the most good.

1. Always start with a clean, soft, lint-free cotton cloth. Good choices are dishtowels, clean cloth diapers, or pieces of worn knit sheets or flannel shirts (with buttons removed).

2. If you're not picking up enough dust using a dry cloth, sprinkle just a few drops of water onto the dust cloth (never directly onto the wood surface).

3. Wipe the dust using oval motions and pushing in the direction of the wood's grain.

4. Cup your hand or another cloth at the edge of the wood piece to catch any dust that tumbles off, so it doesn't get on nearby upholstery or the floor.

5. To avoid scratching the furniture, lift any objects you need to dust under—don't just slide them to the already-clean surface.

6. As soon as you can see dust on one side of the cloth, turn it over to the other side, or pick up a clean one.

7. Send the dusty cloths through the wash as soon as possible, so the dust doesn't get back into the air, and no one inadvertently uses one again, which merely moves the dust to a new spot.

WAX THE WOOD, NOT THE TURTLE. If you opt for the professional restorer's choice, paste wax, to create a moisture barrier on hardwood furniture finish, make sure you shop in the right aisle. Waxes for cars, shoes, or other finishes may harm furniture.

STENCIL TO SPRUCE UP SMOOTH SURFACES. Sure, people pay  big money to "distress" brand new wood furniture, but if you've got pieces that are showing wear and tear and shabby chic's not your style, consider painting a stenciled pattern over the offending spot. Here are the basics for stenciling on wood—your choice whether to try it on a mantel, bookshelf, tabletop, wood crate, or on any other wooden furniture that needs sprucing up.

What you'll need:
- measuring tape
- purchased or cut cardboard stencil
- fine grit sandpaper
- tack cloth

Not There! 5 Items to Keep Off Wood Furniture

For a long-lasting finish, limit your wood furniture's contact with the following undesirable objects.

1. **Plastic or rubber knick-knacks.** Their chemical properties will react with the finish of the wood.
2. **Potpourri.** Whether spilled on a wooden surface or still in its paper wrapper, potpourri contains essential oils that can soak into or stain wood so it causes damage similar to a nail polish remover spill.
3. **Plastic pitfalls.** After a few days, plastic will start to react with the finish, so don't use plastic items on wooden tables long term. It's okay to use plastic protectors for meals as long as you remove them promptly afterward.
4. **Hot pots and pans.** Unless you want rings, scorch marks, and spots, keep a metal or ceramic trivet between hot food containers and wooden surfaces. Don't rely on hot pads, tablecloths, or towels for protection, either, because steam can sometimes penetrate them and reach the finish.
5. **Pizza boxes.** Thin cardboard cannot protect a wooden finish from the heat and steam of a sizzling hot pizza. Steam and moisture can do a lot of damage to a table's finish, so keep the pizza box on the (unheated) stove or on a trivet.

- mounting adhesive
- oil or water-based paint, depending on the existing wood's finish
- quick-drying spray polyurethane
- high-gloss polyurethane and a brush to apply it with

1. Measure the space you want to stencil and purchase or cut a stencil in a pattern you like to fit.
2. Sand the surface to prepare it for the paint, working in the same direction as the grain, then wipe off the debris with a tack cloth.
3. Spray the back of the first stencil overlay (or the only stencil overlay if you're working with one color and a very simple pattern) with mounting adhesive and align it on the wood surface.
4. Working with just one color, use a stencil brush to paint inside the stencil boundaries in a circular motion.
5. Carefully remove the first overlay (if you're working with a multi-overlay pattern) and let the paint dry.
6. Repeat with the rest of the stencil overlays, pausing to let each color of paint dry.
7. Once the entire design is dry, wipe the surface with a tack cloth to remove any leftover dust or sanding debris.
8. Apply a thin coat of quick-drying, spray polyurethane on top of the design and let it dry completely, following the manufacturer's instructions.
9. Further seal the stenciling with one more coat of spray polyurethane and let it dry.
10. Use a brush to apply a coat of high-gloss polyurethane.

THE FINE PRINT
Wood Will Never Look Lively

Maybe it's an intentional marketing ploy, maybe not, but the idea that wood furniture is "alive" and needs to "breathe" and be "nourished" or "fed" with oily polishes is 100 percent pure myth. In reality, wood is dead, and underneath the finish, it is extremely dry—and should stay that way. The primary purpose of a finish is to seal the wood so nothing can penetrate it. It is changes in humidity, not any kind of nutrient deprivation, which causes wood to crack.

In practical terms, furniture oil or wax creates a thin barrier that keeps wood from getting scratched as easily, and perhaps improves the shine. But that's it. There's no need to use products to "nourish" your furniture. In fact, most wood furniture experts favor simple paste wax for a thick, hard finish with a soft sheen that will last from 6 months to more than a year. It also helps prevent water rings with its moisture barrier, as long as you mop up the excess quickly.

4 Simple
Shelf Replacements

Got a shelf on a wooden or plywood book-shelf that's bowed, warped or missing? You need not ignore it or remove it and pile lots more junk in the larger spot—not with these far more attractive alternatives!

1. **The bibliophile's solution.** Depending on the size of the missing shelf, find a sturdy coffee table book and place it horizontally over two L brackets attached to the back of the interior bookshelf wall with sturdy screws. That way you can still stack smaller books vertically on top and access the "book shelf" temporarily should you ever want to look at that title.

2. **Shadow box.** You can buy or make a simple wooden shadow box or two, about 3 to 4 inches deep, and then stack them in the space to divide it for storing smaller items and little books.

3. **Potty, not dotty.** Upend two old, clean terra cotta or ceramic pots that are the same height on either side of the shelf below the missing shelf and top them with a thin glass shelf (a cast-off from the medicine cabinet would work great) or a painted 2-by-4 cut to size. Center another upended pot on top of that shelf and top it with another thin shelf, continuing with alternate shelf configurations until the series reaches as high as you would like.

5. **Monopolize the space.** If it will fit nicely, support a board game box with L brackets and stack books on top. If the box is too big, try a discard folded-over game board—think checkers or backgammon—game side facing up. It won't hold heavy stuff but it will have a whimsical appeal with knick-knacks stacked on top.

SEND NICKS INTO HIDING. When an inexpensive tabletop or shelving edge is battered or ridden with pits and holes, consider hiding the whole thing behind decorative fabric trim in a beaded, braided or nail-head pattern. Suede-look trim is a particularly attractive option. Sand the surface lightly first, wipe, and dry, and then glue on the trim with wood glue. This is also a great way to hide dings in metal and high-density particleboard surfaces.  FIX IT FAST

PART THE PAPER. Whether it's a scrap from the morning news or a receipt you were using as a coaster, paper bits seem determined to stick to the surface of fine wood furniture at the first hint of moisture. To solve the problem, raid the pantry. Dampen the paper with a thin layer of salad oil applied with a basting brush. Wait 5 minutes and then rub over the paper with extra-fine steel wool, pushing with the grain. When the paper yields, remove it, and dry any remaining oil with a clean, soft cotton cloth.

STEER CLEAR OF SILICONE. Although ingredients may not be listed on the label, any commercial furniture polish is likely to contain

3 Ways to Shoo That Scratch without Shopping

A scratch or burn on a piece of wood furniture may not require a trip to the furniture store for a commercial solution. Instead, see what you can do with ingredients you have on hand.

1. **Swab it with shoe polish.** Look for a shade of shoe polish that is close to the color of the wood grain, and use a cotton swab to dab a small amount on the scratch. Then, with a soft, dry, cotton cloth, wipe away the excess. Once the polish is dry, determine whether the scratch has been obscured or if you need another coat.

2. **Another benefit of tea.** Use a used tea bag to stain the scratch. Place the moist tea bag over the mar and check back every half hour or so to see whether you're getting results. Repeat with newly used bags until you reach the shade you want, and make sure to dry the surrounding wood thoroughly with a soft, lint-free cloth when you're done.

3. **The soot soultion.** Cigarette burns in wood may succumb to a mixture of lemon juice and ash from the fireplace. Mix together a small amount of each to form a paste and use a cotton swab to dab it directly on to the burn. Rub it off with a soft, clean cotton cloth. Repeat until you like the look of the result.

---

silicone oil. (Contact the manufacturer if you want to be sure.) Silicone oil will make your wood surface a bit shinier, but will also seep into and hasten the deterioration of the seal on even the most lacquered piece of furniture. And if you ever want to refinish the piece later, the years of silicone abuse will make that tough, even for a professional.

If you still want a commercial product that will give your furniture a little shine, opt for a lemon or orange oil-based product such as Howard Products' Touch of Orange, which advertises that it does not contain silicone or linseed oil (which darkens wood with age).

CREATE A COOL FRONT WITH FABRIC. Any piece of upright furniture with a wood surface that's showing signs of its age can get a quick shot of style if you spend an afternoon painting the surface and covering the doors or drawers with fabric. The possibilities are endless, with fabric scraps coming from vintage clothes, old tablecloths, bandanas, or even designer remnants. Here are five easy steps to a cool new front.

THE FINE PRINT
When You Need Wood Glue

There are many, many home repair situations in which you can do just fine with a close cousin of a tool or product specified by the experts, but gluing wood is not one of them. The pores in wood require the special properties of glue labeled "wood" or "woodworkers." Substituting superglue or school glue when working with wood won't get the job done.

FIX IT OR FORGET IT?
6 REASONS TO INVOLVE A PROFESSIONAL FINISHER

When you own solid hardwood furniture, the cost of repair and refinishing is almost always preferable to replacing valuable pieces. However, keep in mind that in the following six instances, a piece that's showing wear and tear won't yield to a do-it-yourself effort. In these cases, you'll need the help of a professional to get the job done.

1. **Persistent peeling patterns.** The surface of the piece is peeling, cracked, or has a deeply scored pattern that looks like a mosaic—but isn't.
2. **Damage runs deep.** The finish has deep gashes, cuts, or burns—more than you can easily disguise with furniture markers or shoe polish.
3. **Polish scars the surface.** You've spilled nail polish or nail polish remover on the surface of the piece.
4. **Paint prevails.** The surface has been splattered with oil-based paint that's accidentally been allowed to dry.
5. **Marred by markers.** A child has drawn on the surface with permanent markers such as Sharpies.
6. **Find the original finish.** You want to refinish but you don't know what the piece was originally finished with—shellac, polyurethane, or some other product.

If you do opt to consult or hire a professional refinisher, make sure to schedule a visit so you can to observe his work techniques firsthand and look over some of his successfully completed projects. Any reputable refinisher should take the time to answer your initial questions and address your concerns during a free session and provide you with a written estimate of repair prices.

1. Choose your fabric. Remove the drawers or doors from the piece of furniture and paint the rest of the piece in a color that complements the fabric.
2. Measure each door or drawer front, and cut a piece from the fabric that is two inches longer on all sides.
3. Place the drawer, faceup, on a steady work surface and center the fabric across the front.
4. Flip the drawer so the fabric is trapped between the work surface and the drawer front. Then use a staple gun to attach the fabric to the underside edges of the drawer front, pulling it taut as you go.
5. Repeat this process for all the remaining drawers or doors. Once the paint on the piece has dried completely, insert the drawers or reattach the doors.

TABLETOPS AND WOOD SURFACES

Don't wait . . . tables need ongoing care to last long and look great—and so they can serve elsewhere when their dining days are done.

4 Ways to Make Sure Table Leaves Aren't Left Behind

A dining table extension leaf is sort of like a right fielder—it doesn't come into play very often, but when it does you want it to be in good shape. Still, you tend to forget about the table leaves until you need them, and like anything else, they can suffer from neglect. Try these tactics to keep your table leaves contributing for a long time.

1. **Try the ins and outs.** When shopping for table leaves, test them out in the store to make sure you can remove and replace them easily. Table leaves for large tables can be heavy and cumbersome; be sure you can insert *and* remove them either by yourself or with another person. Check that the insertion points and holes are aligned, strong, and well designed and that the sliders glide smoothly and easily. No sense spending money on a table with leaves if you end up not using them.

2. **Share storage space.** Store table leaves near the table if at all possible so they'll all benefit from the same cool temperatures and relative humidity. The hot attic or the humid basement may warp or mar the wood, which means the leaves might not fit. Don't forget the convenience factor, either—retrieving them from the far reaches of the house will discourage you from using the leaves regularly.

3. **Wax the runway.** You can make it much easier to insert and remove table leaves with a bit of preventive maintenance. Apply a thin film of paste or liquid furniture wax on both the table runners and the pegs that keep the leaves connected and they'll slide apart—or snap back in place—more readily.

4. **Keep 'em flat.** Store table leaves flat (under a couch, chair, or bed) so they don't warp. To keep them dust-free, insert the leaves into soft-cloth sleeves or bags (you can make them yourself or buy them from a furniture store).

FIX IT FAST

LOOK LIKE YOU TILED THE TABLE. Especially if you're trying to give a face-lift to a low-quality end table or child's play table, you may not want to go to all the trouble of tiling a tabletop. But you can make it look like you did, by using one of the many "tile stencils" available from floor and craft stores to create a faux-tile look on the table with paint. Follow these steps.

What you'll need:
- primer base
- latex paint
- tiles stencil
- central motif stencil
- stencil paint
- stencil brushes
- painter's tape
- measuring tape
- pencil

4 Stylish Ways to Disguise Table Surface Flaws

Whether it's a child's play table, a coffee table, or a traditional dining room table, a worn tabletop can be covered so stylishly that it looks better than it did brand new. Try one of the following for fun and fashion.

1. **Map out a new look.** Simply rest a graphic chalkboard map on top of the table. You can also distress a new map and attach it directly to the sanded tabletop with several coats of decoupage glue, such as Mod Podge.

2. **Be the fairest of them all.** Top a smaller table with a framed or unframed mirror to hide spots or burn marks.

3. **Picture this.** Photocopy old photographs and apply a collage directly to the tabletop. First, brush decoupage glue on the back of the copies and then place them as you like on the surface. Apply a coat of the decoupage glue over the top of the photocopies, let it dry, and then repeat the process according to package directions to seal.

4. **Monopolize.** Use wood glue to attach an outdated cardboard game board to the top of the table, then seal it with a couple of coats of water-based polyurethane or decoupage medium.

---

1. If the table's grimy, wash it with water, and let it dry completely.

2. Prime the whole table. After it dries, add a topcoat of latex.

3. Measure the dimensions of the tabletop, and use a piece of graph paper to determine where you'd like to stencil the faux tiles. It's easiest to do one larger image in the center and then border around it with 4- by 4-inch tile stencils.

4. Use a ruler and square edge to mark where you'll place each of the tile stencils. You can also draw a light border or just mark the corners.

5. Spray the center stencil with adhesive, line it up with the pencil marks, and press it firmly on to the table surface with the adhesive side down.

6. Paint the center pattern through the cutouts in the stencil. Leave the stencil attached even after the paint is dry, a process you can hasten with a air dryer.

7. Starting in the left corner and working clockwise, attach the

4 Substances That Shouldn't Come to the Table

It's ironic that the very surface that's so sturdy in the face of daily family dining can be destroyed by brief contact with seemingly innocuous chemicals. Keep this quartet of oils and liquids away from your wood tabletop at all times.

1. Solvents, such as nail polish remover and paint thinner

2. Alcohol—not just beer, wine or liquor—but also what's contained in colognes, perfumes, mouthwashes, and medications

3. Human chemicals, such as fingerprints, perspiration, and body oil, which can cause harm to a finish over time

4. Sticky residue from plant stalks and flower nectar—either can permanently stain

tile stencil for the "tile border" to the first spot you've marked with adhesive spray. Paint it and then, following the tile stencil manufacturer's instructions, continue with the subsequent overlays. Repeat the process as instructed for each "tile" in the border.

8. To make the tiles look three-dimensional, use a dark paint to darken the lines separating the tiles.

TILE THE TABLE. Whether you're eyeing a tiny oak nightstand, a big round plywood kitchen table, or a 3- by 4-foot solid hardwood coffee table, ceramic mosaic is the crème de la crème method for covering a worn, torn tabletop that wouldn't survive refinishing. Best of all, you can incorporate broken tile pieces into the design, as long as they're all the same thickness (otherwise the tabletop won't sit level). Here's how to proceed.

What you'll need:
- table
- tile pieces, broken into 1- to 3-inch shards with a hammer between a few layers of cloth
- tile adhesive
- flat-sided knife
- grout
- grout float
- sponge
- clean rags
- grout sealer

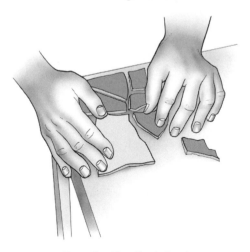

Press the tiles firmly in place.

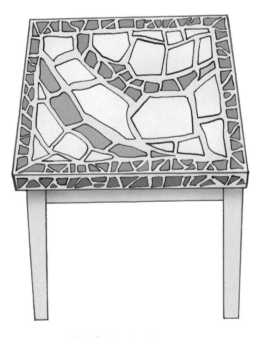

The finished table.

Start a New Top
for the End Table

An end table in the family room or near the telephone will probably wear out fast—or at least the top will start to suffer from water rings, heat bubbles, scratches, and the like. If it doesn't warrant full-fledged refinishing, you can still have a new top without sacrificing the old bottom. Try one of these toppers for size.

- **Bring your board.** If the end table's sturdy, give it a new marble or butcher block top, more commonly known as "that oversize cutting or baking board we never use."
- **The see-through solution.** Use a refurbished and repainted old window on top of the table, attaching it with wood glue along the edges of the window frame. If the surface below the glass isn't aesthetically pleasing, paint or stain it or paint the windowpane itself with glass paint.
- **A corker of an idea.** If you have a cork bulletin board that you don't use anymore, lay it across the end table top, attaching it with wood screws. Use flat thumbtacks to "hang" cardboard coasters on the tabletop.
- **Kitty cushion.** If the end table won't be needed for a lamp or cups, why not make the cat happy? Use Velcro (you'll need both the adhesive kind for the tabletop and the sew-on kind to attach to the fabric) to attach a cushion to the top. Just make sure the cushion has a cover you can take off and wash, Velcro and all, and choose a color that will look good with any nearby upholstery or curtains.

1. Clean and dry the table surface. Spread out newspapers or a drop cloth to rest the piece on.
2. Create a tile design by arranging broken pieces in a mosaic on the tabletop, using pieces with flat edges along the sides of the tabletop so sharp points won't stick out.
3. Once you're happy with the pattern, start removing one piece at a time to reattach to the tabletop. Spread tile adhesive on the unfinished side with a flat-sided or putty knife, then press the tile shard firmly in place, glue side down.
4. Continue gluing one piece at a time until the mosaic is complete. Let dry completely.
5. To grout the tile, mix the grout according to the manufacturer's instructions until it's the consistency of cake batter, making enough to completely cover the tabletop.
6. Pour the grout over the tiles and the entire tabletop, pressing it into place with a grout float. Check to see that grout has penetrated all the cracks between the tile shards.
7. Let the grout dry for 10 minutes. Then use a damp sponge to wipe off any that's still adhering to the top of the tile pieces.
8. Let the grout dry completely, about 24 hours, then buff the filmy haze of grout from the tile tops with a soft, clean cotton rag.

9. Protect the completely dry surface with tile sealer, following the manufacturer's instructions.

10. Allow the sealed surface to cure for three days (longer if indicated in the directions on the tile sealer) before using.

RING OUT THE TABLETOP. Someone's bound to leave a steaming cup of tea or a chilly glass of water on your tabletop at some point, and when that moisture is trapped below the finish, you'll have to contend with a white water ring. Catch it fast and you can usually return the table to its original color just by evaporating the ring using a hair dryer set on low.

If you've let a white ring linger or picked up a used table that already had a few water marks, you'll need to take action—some mild abrasive action, that is. Buff the ring lightly using fine-grade steel wool dipped in lemon oil. Make sure to use a soft, clean cotton cloth to wipe off all the excess oil when you're done. Although the oil won't cause more rings or damage to the table, it will soil or stain any clothing it comes into contact with.

7 Ways to "New" for the Coffee Table

If your low coffee table's too worn to consider refinishing for the living room, move it outside, into the garage, or down the stairs to the basement. With a couple of coats of 100 percent acrylic latex for outside use, or a bit of ingenuity, you can turn that battered coffee table into a handy helper.

1. Use it as a pallet to keep bags of grass seed, birdseed, or potting soil off a damp storage shed floor.

2. Turn the table into a one-shelf shelving unit to keep cardboard boxes off damp basement floors.

3. Keep firewood drier by stacking it on top of the table instead of the ground behind your shed or garage (first position the coffee table against a shed or garage wall for stability).

4. Use it as a potted plant shelf on your deck or porch. Either set the potted plants on the table, or drill through the tabletop and saw large holes for flowerpots.

5. Substitute the table—only if it's rock-solid sturdy and stable—for a step stool to reach rafters or as a bench when painting small items.

6. Turn the table into a beanbag toss game for kids if the table is square or rectangular and leans backward at a slight angle when upended. All you need to do is add stabilizing supports (to make sure it doesn't tip over during the game), and use a saw to cut fun shapes in the table for the beanbags to pass through. Add bright paint and point values for each hole, and let the games begin!

7. If you're really handy, turn the top of the coffee table into a rolling car creeper for undercarriage car repairs. Remove the table legs, then add heavy-duty ball-bearing casters to the bottom of the table. Go for comfort by sewing a vinyl cushion to fit the dimensions of the creeper top then hot glue the cushion to the wood.

CHAIRS

What's the secret to preventing wear and tear on chairs? Care and repair. And when your favorite's on its last legs, it's time to go find it a seat somewhere else.

WRING MORE USE FROM A CHAIR RUNG. A loose chair rung  isn't just annoying; it's a safety hazard that can throw someone off balance and on to the floor. Taking care of the trouble isn't that tough—all you'll need is wood glue, a rope long enough to tie around two chair legs, and a 6- to 8-inch dowel or even a stick from the yard. Then, just follow these steps:

1. While pulling the rung as far out of the loose socket as you can with one hand, squirt as much wood glue as you can fit into and around the hole with your other hand.
2. Pop the end of the rung back into the hole and wipe away any excess glue that remains on the rung or joint with a damp cloth.
3. Prepare the rung so the glue can dry under pressure, first by tying a rope around the two chair legs that house the rung and then jabbing the dowel or stick in the middle of the knot so that it's perpendicular to the rung.
4. Turn the dowel end over end until the rope is taut, then slip the dowel over the exterior side of the chair rung so it continues to keep the rope at that tautness.
5. Leave the rope and dowel in place for at least 24 hours, or until the glue dries completely, and then remove.

WHIP THAT WOBBLE. No need to willingly settle for a wobbly chair, not when a bit of sanding can reestablish equilibrium. After making sure you can't take care of the imbalance merely by flipping the chair over and tightening the bolt, nut, or screw that connects the leg to the piece, follow these steps to put all four legs back on an even keel.

$mart Buys
5 SIGNS A CHAIR WILL WEAR WELL

Whether you're buying a ladder-back or other wooden dining room chair, or trying to figure out which of the chairs you already own should go in high-traffic areas (or under heavyset Aunt Edna at Thanksgiving), look for the following five signs of a sturdy seat.

1. Snug joints with no dribs and drabs of extra glue or filler
2. Parts connected with screws, not nails
3. Slats and rungs that are tightly attached—no rolling or sliding possible
4. The back and leg section made from one piece of wood, ditto the arm-and-leg segment, instead of pieces glued together
5. No wobbles or creaks when you sit

1. Before you begin, cover an outdoor work surface like the driveway or sidewalk with a plastic tarp or old newspapers and upend the chair on the work surface.
2. Measure each leg from base to tip with a measuring tape, and write down the measurements. This should tell you which leg (or legs) is shorter than the others and by how much.
3. Mark the height of the shortest leg on the other legs with a pencil.
4. To make the longer legs the same length as the shortest, gently sand each one down to the pencil mark, beginning with coarse (80-grit) sandpaper and ending with fine (220-grit) sandpaper.

SHOW YOUR STRIPES. Dirt, oil, and sudden splashes of, say, spaghetti sauce can really do a number on painted wood chair legs. But if the rest of the paint job's fine (on that chair and the rest of the set), consider a quirky way to cover the stains. Instead of repainting the whole kit-and-caboodle, paint some strategic stripes only on the unsightly legs—or on just one or two of them. It's a fun look; you can use a color that picks up a pattern in the curtains or the nearby tiled floor. If you like, paint random legs on the entire set of chairs, even some without mars. Here's how:
1. Wash the painted legs with clear water and let dry completely.
2. Use 1½-inch wide painters' tape to mark stripes on the areas you *don't* want to cover, creating any pattern that suits you.
3. Spray or brush the legs with the desired color of paint. If you're trying to cover up a serious stain, opt for a darker color.
4. Let the paint dry and carefully remove the tape to show your stripes.

PASS IT ALONG

TRY A TERRYCLOTH CHAIR COVER. When you have a side chair that's still sturdy but the finish and fabric aren't looking so good, find it a new home in the master bath. If you like, paint the wood with a coat of water-based latex. Then give the seat an appropriate cover with a piece of terrycloth bath towel and a staple gun. Now it can serve as a nice place to sit in the restroom while you perform such tasks as painting your nails or shaving your legs. Or, if you get creative with the paint job, it's a neat alternative to open shelving for storing folded towels. And here's an added bonus: When the seat cover starts getting grimy, or if you just get tired of the color of the terrycloth you originally chose, unscrew the seat, pull out the staples from the terrycloth, and staple another towel in place.

5 Ways to Say "Cheerio" to Chair Pads

Whether they've worn out or you just want a change in decor, tie-on chair pads are the ideal dimensions for lots of other uses. Here are a few nifty ideas to try:

1. **Sit for a story.** If you have more than three or four clean discards, see whether a local day care or church nursery might like to have them on hand for small behinds during story time.

2. **Buffer your bucket.** Drill or punch holes in the rim of the cover of an empty 20- to 30-pound bucket (like the ones birdseed comes in). Thread the ties of the chair pad through the outside of the rim and tie them together under the lid. Place the cover back on the bucket, and you have a makeshift kiddie seat for the garage, deck, or garden—and you can still use the bucket for storage.

3. **Cheer for chair pads.** Take a couple of chair pads along to the ballpark to use as stadium seats. If they're too small for adults, the kids will appreciate them, and you can tie them to a stroller or backpack for easy toting.

4. **Fix a flat in comfort.** Toss a chair pad in the trunk of your car to place under your knees should you need to fix a flat.

5. **Pad a pet bed.** Settle a chair pad in the bottom of a cardboard box or laundry basket, and Fluffy will thank you at bedtime. Small dogs will like this setup, too.

SATISFY SOCIAL CLIMBERS. The seat's sprung, the rungs are loose, the finish is finished . . . who could love a chair like that? Flowering and vegetable vines will overlook the visual flaws. To them, a ladder-back chair is just a great place to climb. Painted in a bright or jewel tone, a discarded-chair trellis can also add a focal point to your landscape or garden. Here's how to transform the chair.

What you'll need:
- discarded wooden chair
- 100 percent acrylic latex paint for outdoor use
- 1 square yard heavy black plastic
- 1 small bag play sand
- 4 six-inch sticks, each about $1/2$-inch in diameter
- 3 feet twine
- 8 to 12 full-sun vine seeds, such as purple hyacinth beans or morning glories

1. Wash the chair and then let it dry.
2. Cut out any spring seats, sand any splinters, and remove any extraneous tacks and staples.
3. Paint the chair.
4. Choose a place for the chair where it will receive full sun and be

protected from harsh winds. That's where vining plants will thrive.

5. Measure the perimeter around the four chair legs and loosen garden soil in a 2-foot ring around the outside.

6. Dig a 4-inch hole for each of the chair legs and line them with the plastic and then the sand.

7. "Plant" the chair in the holes.

8. Push each stick in the ground a couple of inches from each chair leg. Tie an 8-inch piece of twine around the end of each stick, draw it over to the leg at a diagonal, and use a thumbtack or small finish nail to attach it to the leg. This will help the new vines start their climbing journey.

9. Plant three to four vine seeds in the soil near each stick and a couple of inches apart. You may need to loosely wind the new vines around the strings when they're 5 to 6 inches tall to get the plants climbing in the right direction.

UPHOLSTERED FURNITURE

Forget plastic slipcovers and sofas no one's allowed to sit on! With these tips and tricks, upholstered furniture will deliver cushiony comfort for years to come.

MAKE IT LAST

UPHOLSTERY THAT UPHOLDS. Durable leather is the clear choice for long-lasting upholstery, but if your budget or taste dictates fabric, you can still look forward to long wear—just make sure to select a piece with a durable weave. Here's a simple test you can use to rate the strength of the weave: hold the fabric sample tight in one hand and pull with the other, then reverse directions. The threads should stay tightly woven. Polypropylene or nylon will be a winner every time. The traditional formal sitting room fabrics, like satins and brocades, aren't the best bet unless only dainty folks will occupy the couch and only a couple of times a year.

HOLD BACK ON H_2O. Cleaning upholstery is beneficial only if you don't get it so wet that the fabric stretches or gets soiled and spotty—or the fill or padding beneath mildews from the moisture. Make sure to keep upholstery fabric as dry as you possibly can when you're shampooing. If necessary, you can speed up the drying process by opening a window or turning on a fan, dehumidifier, or central or window unit air-conditioner.

$mart Buys

7 WAYS TO SPOT A LONG-LASTING COUCH

Landfills are chock-full of couches that lasted mere seasons. For upholstered furniture with staying power, follow these guidelines.

1. **Kick in for kiln-dried.** A solid hardwood frame made from kiln-dried hardwoods such as oak, birch, or maple, will hold pegs, screws, and nails secure for years.

2. **Fancy the frame.** Look under the sofa for joints strengthened with blocks or dowels, and blocks further reinforced with extra glue or screws—but no staples.

3. **Look at those legs.** On the sturdiest couches, the legs are an integral part of the frame, not glued on.

4. **Be firm with springs.** For firm seats, ask whether the couch has sinuous S-shaped springs or drop-in coil springs—either attaches directly to the frame and supports the seat deck to provide firmness.

5. **Be crazy for 8s.** Eight-way, hand-tied springs are considered the hallmark of a top-quality couch and provide the most comfort and durability, accompanied, of course, by the highest price tag.

6. **Can your fanny feel the frame?** Whether a cushion contains down, cotton, polyester fill, or foam, the stuffing should be evenly distributed, and you shouldn't be able to feel springs or frame when you sit.

7. **This is a test.** Before investing in a sofa, always try it out in the store. Sit on it and try bouncing a bit to make sure it doesn't creak or thump, which may indicate springs that are hitting the frame.

SCREEN TEST THE VACUUM. The best way to lengthen a sofa's upholstered life is with frequent vacuuming, but even the upholstery attachment can fray or loosen fabric. So, set up a screen . . . a 12- by 12-inch piece of vinyl screen, that is, duct taped along the edges and placed on top of a section of upholstery. Hold the screen firmly in place with one hand, run the upholstery attachment across the top with the other, and you'll suck up the dust without disturbing or damaging the fibers of the fabric. When you're done with one section, move on to another.

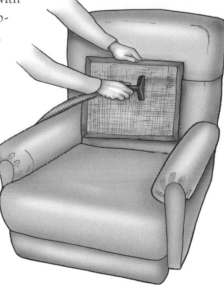

LET THERE BE LITTLE LIGHT. Public Enemy Number 1 for upholstered couches and chairs is sunlight, which fades and wears the fabric. When you can, keep upholstery away from sunlight and when you can't, consider using cloth slipcovers.

6 Ways to Keep Pets off the Sofa

Whether Fluffy simply must sharpen her claws on the futon couch or Fido's decided the arm chair is his new dog bed, pet scratching, hair, and odor will inevitably hasten the demise of upholstered furniture. But several strategies and products on the market might help, and none requires declawing or listening to your pup howl for hours on end.

1. **Divide and conquer.** Rearrange furniture so that all your good upholstered pieces are in one or two rooms with doors that shut, even if you have to switch a bedroom and living room.

2. **Do fence me in.** Indoor wireless fences, such as the one manufactured by PetSafe, require a few weeks of training. Although they don't work for all dogs, they are definitely worth a shot if you don't have suitable interior doors.

3. **Cat, scratch hither.** For cats that are particularly susceptible to catnip, a catnip-scented scratching board, like the ones sold at CatClaws.com, is sometimes enough to keep them away from other furniture.

4. **Fido's bitter about them apples.** Dogs hate the smell and taste of a product called Bitter Apple, available at most pet stores.

5. **Felled by Feliway.** Feliway works to keep cats from scratching and urine marking. It works on the principle that a cat thinks an area marked with Feliway has already been marked by him. The liquid can be sprayed directly on some furniture (test it first) or dispensed from a plug-in, both available from DrsFosterSmith.com.

6. **Soften the claws.** Definitely a last resort due to the cost and the agony of getting them on the cat—and maybe impossible if your cat's temperamental—but Soft Paws nail caps attach to your cat's nails with medical superglue. They last a month or two to keep kitty from sharp scratching. And consider this: They're cheap compared with the cost of replacing upholstered furniture!

FIX IT FAST

BABY YOUR LEATHER. Even modern-day leather can develop fine cracks or fade as it ages. Come to the rescue, not with a pricey leather upholstery restorative, but with plain old baby oil (available at your local drug store). Apply a fine film to the leather with a soft cloth and let it soak in. After an hour or so, buff off any extra oil so it won't stain clothing. The oil seals fine cracks, restores the leather's luster, and also lets it breathe—a good selling point since moisture trapped in upholstery can make it mildew and deteriorate.

PAY THE PIPING. You can make frayed piping on seat or couch cushions—or the couch itself—look sharp again by threading a heavy needle with the same color yarn or embroidery floss and encircling the piping anew.

RE-LINE IN NO TIME. Haven't you always wanted to buy a couple yards of wild, flamboyant trim or delicate lace from the remnant bin at your favorite fabric store? Well, here's your chance to indulge while disguising any rips or dangles in the bottom lining of your sofa or chair. To start, thread elastic or elastic cord through a piece of wide lace, trim, or beading from a fabric store so you can gather it. Then, simply use upholstery tacks to pin the gathered fabric in place to disguise any trouble spots.

UPHOLSTERY CLEANSERS—SKIP THE COMMERCIAL. Far more important than purchasing a water-based retail upholstery cleaning product is making sure you don't damage the upholstery by getting it too wet during cleaning. In fact, a simple solution of dishwashing liquid or liquid laundry detergent and warm water will work just as well, if you follow these steps.

1. In a large mixing bowl, use a hand mixer to whip one cup warm water with 1/4 cup dishwashing liquid (such as Ivory) or liquid laundry detergent until the suds resemble whipped cream.

2. Test the foam on an inconspicuous patch of upholstery. Start by dabbing 1 teaspoon of whipped suds onto the fabric with a dry, soft cloth or soft brush.

3. Use a plastic spatula to gently lift the dirty suds from the fabric. Repeat if necessary (that is, as long as the foam you're removing contains more dirt).

THE FINE PRINT
Clean by the Code

Even with the proliferation of off-the-shelf upholstery cleaning products, you run the risk of staining or fraying upholstered furniture if you wash it improperly. The good news is that certain manufacturers have voluntarily complied with uniform cleaning standards and marked the furniture with a code that declares precisely how the fabric can be cleaned. You might find the code on fabric samples at the store (it's good to check before you buy so you don't end with a "vacuum only" fabric) or on a label under the seat cushion. If it's available, here's what it means.

- **W** Water-based cleanser. Spot clean with the suds from a mild detergent or commercial upholstery shampoo, used sparingly.

- **S** Solvent cleanser. Clean the fabric section by section with a mild, water-free dry-cleaning solvent used sparingly in a well-ventilated room with no potential for sparks or flame. Note: If you use a water-based solvent cleanser on a product labeled "S" it will probably spot and shrink. Also be aware that solvent cleansers will not remove water stains.

- **S–W** Solvent or water-based cleanser.

- **X** Vacuum only. Clean fabric using a vacuum cleaner or light brushing to prevent the accumulation of dust and grime. Using water-based foam or solvent-based cleaning agents will likely cause excessive shrinking, fading, or spotting.

4. Dip a soft, clean cloth in clear water (not too much, just to dampen) and wipe any remaining soap and dirt from the area.

5. Allow the test spot dry completely. If it looks cleaner but undamaged, proceed with the rest treating no more than a square foot of fabric at a time.

PASS IT ALONG

SEND COUCH CUSHIONS TO THE DOGS. It's a sad fact of life that upholstered furniture is not a welcome contribution to thrift stores and other charities unless it's in exceptionally good condition. The stuff's just too darn hard to restore and hygiene is an issue. Also, the agencies are overrun with sofas and love seats that were made to last only a couple of years.

There's another group, though, that's not nearly so picky. Consider donating the detachable cushions from your sofa or stuffed armchairs to a pet shelter, where they can be used for bedding and to comfort frightened animals. If the covers come off, give them a wash first (even the ones that are dry clean only, and use cold water, since you're not worried about fraying or wear at this point). If the covers can't be removed, send the cushions through an oversized commercial washing before passing them along to the pound.

I Can See Myself!
5 No-Harm Ways to Clean Mirrors

Wander through any antique store and you're bound to see many examples of mirrors that were poorly maintained and have aged prematurely due to improper—and infrequent—cleaning. Those flakes and black edges are usually the result of bleach and ammonia causing the silver to oxidize. Still, streaks keep the mirror from doing its job, so compromise by cleaning the glass regularly, but carefully, following these guidelines:

1. **All the news that's fit to clean with.** Use a little bit of water and some newsprint paper to clean simple water marks; also try a little dirt or oil on the glass without harmful chemicals.

2. **Rub, don't spray.** When you do use glass cleaner for stubborn spots, spray it on a soft, lint-free rag or towel and not directly on the mirror.

3. **Start in the middle.** Here's another simple precaution you can take to prevent cleaning fluids from reaching the mirror back or edge: start by wiping in the center of the mirror and gradually work your way to the borders, stopping at least a half inch from the edges.

4. **Watch the back.** Never apply any type of cleaning product to the back of the mirror. Why? Because the cleaning solutions can interact with the silver—and no one sees the back anyhow!

5. **Let sheep inspire you.** If a splatter, caked on blob, or odd splotch is particularly stubborn and simply won't yield to any of the softer measures listed above, it's time to enlist the help of some #0000 steel wool and gently rub the spot off—working only on the glass, naturally.

MIRRORS

Fight mirror flaking with softness and prevent falls with fortified fasteners. And a new use for shards is a stepping stone's throw away.

WATCH YOUR MIRROR'S WEIGHT. Even if you don't believe the old saw about seven years of bad luck, no one wants a broken mirror on their hands. One of the best preventive measures is hanging the mirror with an anchor or wood screw designed to support its weight. But no guesstimating how heavy your mirror is, not when errors can spell disaster! Instead, climb on the bathroom scale, first by yourself and then with the mirror, to determine its exact weight.

MAKE IT LAST

MIRROR, MIRROR ON THE TABLE. When a black-edged or flaking mirror is no longer suitable for high-profile areas, it need not end its reflecting days. Consider laying it flat and moving it to the center of the dining room table, where it will add a beautiful reflective element to a centerpiece or bowl of flowers. Or, send it to the fishes by turning it on its side and sliding it between the aquarium and the wall. If it has any big ugly spots that would attract from the view inside the fish bowl, use two-sided cellophane tape to cover them with undersea pictures, first.

PASS IT ALONG

CANDLES

Candles are a quick and inexpensive way to create a romantic atmosphere. These down-to-earth strategies will keep the flames burning longer . . . and let you repurpose the stubs.

HELP WAX STAY COOL. If candles are the sorts of things you tend to buy on sale and forget all about, spend a few minutes moving them to a suitable storage space and they'll still be colorful and straight when you need them. Plus you'll add hours of burn time when you stash candles in a place that's cool and dry and out of direct sunlight, which quickly causes the colors to bleach out.

MAKE IT LAST

LIGHTS OUT AFTER AN HOUR. Although it's absolutely counterintuitive, the fact is that burning a pillar or jar candle for at least an hour per inch of diameter each time you light up will give the candle many more burning hours over time. This way, the flame has enough time to melt the wax all the way to the outer edges so the whole candle burns down efficiently. Each time you cut short a burning session, the flame only burns the wax in the center, which wastes the outer wax at that level.

KEEP CANDLES OUT OF THE WIND. Sure, the flame looks dramatic dancing and casting shadows, but you should still make every attempt to burn candles, particularly the wider ones like pillars and votives, away from drafts. Moving air makes a candle burn unevenly across the top, which wastes a lot of wax.

DON'T CRACK YOUR CANDLE JAR. If you'd like to end up with a holder you can refill and use again, stop burning a jar candle when there's about 3/4 inch of wax left in the bottom. If you forget and let the candle burn all the way to the bottom, the jar could crack and break—leaving you no jar for the next time, plenty of melted wax to clean up, and a fire hazard.

FIX IT FAST

SHRINK WAX. Unless you're going in for that Italian bistro look, candleholders look better without wax drips. Of course, wax seems determined to cling, and chipping with a sharp object is a no-no. Instead, put the holders in the deep freeze—but just for an hour or so. When the wax gets cold it shrinks, and you can pop it right out of all those nooks and crannies in a snap.

Vote for Long-Lasting Votives

Okay, so they're tiny, but why should you suffer the inconvenience of replacing votive candles and those adorable little holders any sooner than you absolutely have to? Maximize the life of both wax and container with the following tips.

- **Keep it contained.** Always burn a votive inside a holder to keep the flame from encountering so much air it burns too quickly and wastes wax. A votive burned in a particularly drafty room won't last very long without a holder.
- **No knifing, please.** If you can't stand the sight of wax drippings on the votive holder, work with hot water and restrain the urge to use a sharp object to pry the wax loose— that will only scratch and weaken the glass, increasing the likelihood of breakage.
- **Use votive holders.** Burn votives in glass that's designed for them specifically. Ordinary glassware won't withstand the temperature changes that occur when a candle burns.
- **Water your holder.** Glass votive holders will clean in a snap and be ready for the next occupant when you add a few drops—just a few!—of water to the glass before inserting the candle.

SEW, TRY THIS PINCUSHION TIP. Believe it or not, a half-used votive, taper stub, or any candle missing a wick can actually do more good in the sewing box than the trash can. Once you've trimmed off any visible burnt wick, you can use the wax chunk as a pincushion. And there's even a bonus: Pins with a bit of wax on them slip through fabric more easily.

MELT AN ANNIVERSARY GIFT. It seems a shame to toss all the stubs from a group of tapers you use for a special occasion—so don't. Instead, melt the leftovers from candles featured in, say, the sconces at Thanksgiving or the centerpieces at a wedding reception, and make one large candle to be burned a year from the day. It can become a family tradition, or you can mail the big candle to a loved one who was not there to share the big day.

To melt the wax, place the candle stubs in an empty non-aluminum food can and set the can in a pan with two inches of boiling water over low heat. Once all the wax is melted, use a hot pad to remove the can and then fish the wicks out using a disposable spoon. Now you can mold the wax into a new, huge candle using an empty potato chip can and a wick purchased from the craft store.

5 Off the Wall Uses for Old Frames

Whether you've upgraded to fancier frames for your treasured mementos or the old models can't get the job done anymore, there are five fun ways to reuse old frames instead of sending them to the Salvation Army.

1. **Covered with candles.** Lay a glass-topped frame flat and top it with pillar candles in various colors and sizes for a dresser or bath counter display. Glue felt on the underside to make sure the tabletop doesn't get scratched.

2. **Framed for storage.** Awards or mementos that you've tired of displaying but would still like to keep will stay in better shape if you store them in frames, particularly if the frames have archival-quality windows. Several documents will slide into a single frame, though you may want to place a sheet of acid free paper between them. Stack the framed keepsakes on shelves or in boxes, or hang them on the wall in the storage area for safekeeping.

3. **Guard the recipe.** If you've ended up with a spare easel-style frame, consider keeping it in a kitchen drawer and pull it out when you need a way to prop up a recipe card—just slip the card behind the glass and it will stay clean, too.

4. **Coast on old photos.** Any old wallet-size or 3" by 5" frames can have a second career as coasters. If you like, leave a photo or color copy of some artwork inside.

5. **At your service.** Larger frames with ornate edges at least an inch deep can come in handy for parties or coffee breaks. Cut a piece of press-on cork or a vinyl placemat to fit the inside and you've got a nifty serving tray.

ARTWORK AND FRAMES

Protect hanging treasures from the sun and safeguard against gravity—just a few of the colorful tips and tricks you can use to keep your artwork looking priceless for years to come.

MAKE IT LAST — **SPRAY THE CLOTH, NOT THE SOIL.** Ammonia glass cleaners are an enemy to wood frames, but it's easy enough to avoid spraying the outer edges when you clean the glass. Just spray the cleaning cloth out of range of the delicate frame edges and wipe the glass clean, instead of spraying the glass itself and risking stray spatters on the surrounding wood or lacquer finish. This also keeps liquid from seeping under the edges to hurt the mat, art, or photo.

FIX IT FAST — **STOP THE SUN FROM SHINING.** One of the worst wears on artwork, posters, and framed photos is sunlight, so it's always advisable to display pieces on walls that don't receive a direct dose. If you've already hung artwork in a sunny spot, consider altering the window. You can obtain a static cling ultraviolet window film at a home store

---

5 Ways to Keep Frames Free of Falling

A few falls from the wall can damage the sturdiest frame or artwork, not including the inevitable breakage to the glass fronts. Follow these tactics so your frame will stay put (though in earthquake territory, the results aren't guaranteed!):

1. **Weighty matters.** Always weigh whatever you're hanging before you purchase any wall fasteners, and read the package to make sure the hanger you choose can sustain the weight of the artwork.
2. **Light work for nails.** If you're hanging something really light and feel confident using a nail, still angle the nail at 45 degrees to increase the weight it can support and reduce the chance of the picture falling.
3. **Nailing no-nos.** Heavy material, such as mirrors or curio shelves need wall fas-

teners (anchors or wood screws) that distribute weight evenly—they won't stay up with ordinary nails or screws.

4. **Anchors away for plaster walls.** If you plan to hang something heavier than a poster on a plaster wall that's 2-3 inches thick, use an expansion anchor or a lead shield with a No. 6 wood screw.
5. **The demands of drywall.** A spreading anchor is the logical pick if you're working with a drywall or plaster and lath wall. Read the package to make sure its length matches the thickness of the wall and that it's long enough to pierce both the drywall and the object you're hanging. You can also use No. 6 wood screws to mount anything that weighs 10 pounds or less, screwing them at least one inch into the wood stud behind the drywall.

and place it yourself to block 99 percent of the UV rays that age art. If you like, you can buy a "privacy" film that makes it difficult to see in your windows while you can still see out, or a film in any number of designer colors or patterns.

MORE TIPS FOR YOUR FURNITURE

Here's a roundup of the furniture-related Pass It Along tips you'll find in the other chapters of *Don't Throw It Out!*

CHAPTER	TIP	PAGE
1	Reuse the Racks	7
1	Try these Tray Uses	25
3	6 Ways to Draw a New Plan for Dressers	84
3	Table an Old Sheet	87
3	Try a Tie Seat	101
4	Close the Book on Safety	122
5	Rock Around the Clock	131
7	Bowl Them Over	212
8	6 Uses for an Old Tennis Ball	259
9	Shelve Unusable Terra-Cotta Pots	279

DOMESTIC CHALLENGE

Test your furniture know-how by taking this true and false quiz.

Questions

1. The best way to maintain your upholstered furniture is to wipe it with a clean damp cloth once a week.

2. When durability is your primary consideration when shopping for upholstered furniture, synthetic fabrics including rayon and nylon are the best bets.

3. You've come home with a terrific flea market find: A very old but very beautiful wood table. The best way to clean it is by wiping it with a warm soap and water mixture.

4. In a pinch, you can launder the cushion covers on upholstered furniture. Just undo the zippers, and then toss them in the wash on a gentle cycle.

5. It's a good idea to protect the surface of wood furniture, but not with plastic place mats.

Answers

1. **FALSE.** Regular vacuuming with a brush attachment is the best way to maintain your upholstered furniture. That prevents dirt and dust from getting worked into the fibers of the fabric, which not only soil it, but also abrade the upholstery, causing it to wear out more quickly. Always make sure that the brush attachment is scrupulously clean so that you don't end up brushing dirt on, rather than off, the furniture.

2. **FALSE.** Wool is one of the most durable fibers and leather can wear like iron. And although some synthetics wear well (polyester, for instance), other, such as rayon, rate poorly when it comes to durability.

3. **TRUE.** Use a vegetable oil based soap, such as Murphy's, and then rinse and dry well. If the furniture is still dirty, try using a very fine steel wool (#0000) dipped in wood furniture cleaner.

4. FALSE. Always follow the cleaning and care guidelines that came with your upholstered furniture. And keep in mind that the zippers on the cushions were put there so that the covers could be put on-—and not to make them easy to remove.

5. TRUE. Chemicals in some plastics can react with and damage furniture finishes. Avoid putting any plastic items on wood furniture.

3

THE BEDROOM

On the following pages you'll find tips for umpteen ways to maximize the value of every object in the bedroom. For instance, you'll find out how an hour with a few hand tools can keep your bedstead from ever going bump in the night again. Ideas for better bedding are also a few tips away, including a way to "see the light" on bargain sheets, and how to choose the best feather down for the dollar.

No one can give you more space in the closet, but the advice on these pages will teach you how to select and maintain the clothing inside so that it fits well, wears hard, and sticks around for a long time. Even long-gone canvas shoes, straw hats, and stretched-out sweaters can make it back from the brink with a little TLC and our ingenious ideas. As for sheets, panty hose, boots, and the like that have outlived their usefulness, all of them will find new life—in your home and in the homes of others. So go ahead and take in all this info on buying the best and fixing the rest—it will help you rest easy.

MATTRESSES AND BED FRAMES

Better sleep is the reward when you buy the best (not necessarily the most expensive) mattress and tweak the squeaks. Turn worn frames to new tasks—no tossing!

MAKE IT LAST

TOSS AND TURN. A high-quality mattress will last much longer if you even out the wear by flipping it about once a month: side to side one month, top to bottom the next. This is most important when the mattress is brand new (particularly if it is high plush), because that's when the cushions are still spongy enough to form lasting indentations of your body contours. After the first 4 to 5 months, you can reduce flipping frequency to once every couple of months, because the cushion top is no longer as susceptible to impressions. To flip a larger

5 Ways to Maintain Mattress Value, Starting at the Store

Here are five strategies to bear in mind as you shop for a new mattress.

1. **Buy bigger for little kids.** A twin mattress may seem like a bargain for a child's bedroom, but if you plan to get the full 10 to 15 years of use from it, consider the fact that a grown teenager is likely to be uncomfortable in such a small bed. And if you start with a full-size bed, you won't have to replace all the sheets and comforters when the child is older and needs a bigger bed.

2. **Royal beds need center support.** If you're purchasing a bed frame and mattress together, make sure that king- or queen-size frames have a center support so the mattress won't develop a sag prematurely.

3. **Punt the pillow top.** That extra layer of padding sewn to the top of a mattress doesn't necessarily add value. It costs more, and it also tends to compress and develop ruts from use, and you can't replace it. Instead, buy a separate replaceable waffle or featherbed pad.

4. **Find a mattress you can flip over—literally!** The newly popular "one-side" mattresses are impossible to rotate for more even wear, which means your mattress wears out faster, because you'll compress the same section every single night.

5. **Read the label.** Federal law requires that any mattress containing used stuffing—which simply does not wear as well as new stuff—must carry a tag or label with that information. Also take a long, hard look at the label on a box spring, particularly if the pattern of the box spring is different from the mattress it's been paired with. The labels should indicate whether the mattress or box spring have been "disinfected," which means someone else has already used it for a trial period and sent it back under one of those liberal discount mattress store return policies. There are serious health risks to consider before deciding to sleep on mattresses treated with pesticides and cleaning agents.

mattress, enlist a friend's help and follow these steps:

1. Pull the bed away from the wall so you'll have a place to stand to maneuver the mattress.
2. Strip the mattress and vacuum the top.
3. Slip a large plastic garbage bag under one end of the top mattress, leaving several inches hanging out to use as a handle.
4. Stand on the end opposite the plastic bag and, with a mighty heave, pull the top mattress toward you and away from the plastic, easing it to a standing position on top of the plastic.
5. With a helper (if the mattress is too much for you alone), lower the mattress to the flip side, work the plastic out, and then push the mattress into place.

FIX IT OR FORGET IT?
REPLACING A MATTRESS: MAKE IT A PACKAGE DEAL

When your mattress is past redemption, it's probably time to replace the box spring too, even if it's not as noticeably worn. The two pieces are designed to work together, and a new mattress will soon conform to the weak areas of an old box spring. That will substantially compromise the support and comfort of the entire unit and wear out the mattress that much faster.

RESET YOUR SLATS. When the slats on your wood bed frame tend to slip from the cleats on the rails and send the mattress and box spring plunging, it's time for a more lasting attachment. Usually the problem is caused by the rails bulging, which they can't do if the slats are drilled right on to the cleats. Here's how to make that fix.

FIX IT FAST

1. Remove the box spring and mattress from the bed frame.
2. Place the slats on the cleats along the rail, leaving equal spaces between them.
3. Pull in each side rail and hold it straight with a pipe clamp.
4. Bore pilot holes in two spots about an inch from each slat edge with a drill.
5. Fasten the slats to the cleats with screws.
6. Once all the slats are attached, remove the pipe clamps, or work one at a time if you have just one clamp.

After you've drilled pilot holes in the cleats, fasten the slats to them with screws.

Pump It Up

No one is pretending you can get a great night's sleep on an air mattress, but they are handy for overnight guests or sleepovers. Of course, if the mattress wasn't stored in the box or had a rough time at the last campout, it's a sure bet that you'll discover a couple of little leaks when your guests are on the way. Don't despair—simply head to the toy store. The same kits that are sold for patching bicycle tires or kiddie wading pools work just as well on an air mattress.

RUB OUT URINE SMELLS WITH BORAX. Let's face it: Accidents can happen—to both man and beast. To remove the urine stain and the odor, strip off all the bedding, slip on some plastic or rubber gloves, and wet the area with a damp sponge. Then sprinkle on some borax and rub it in with your hands. Once the spot's dry—and you may have to speed the process with a hair dryer—you can vacuum up the residue and the odor. If the urine scent is old or especially persistent, repeat the process. To protect the mattress next time, cover it with a moisture-proof mattress protector, available wherever bedding is sold.

PASS IT ALONG

PARK YOUR BEDSTEAD FOR BIKE STORAGE. If you're lucky enough to have an antique iron bed with rails on the headpiece but unlucky enough to have broken or worn out the rest, you're in luck! You're just six easy steps away from a sturdy bike rack.

1. Remove the headpiece from the rest of the bed and lightly sand and paint the iron to retard rust.
2. Remove the casters from the legs.
3. Measure the space between the two legs on the headpiece. Once you locate the spot where you'll install the bike racks, mark the same distance on the site with a string between two nails. (It's easiest to find a site with a soil base, like a space in the yard a few inches from the driveway.)
4. Dig a hole that's 8 inches deep and 6 inches in diameter at each end of the string. Make sure that the center of the hole lines up with the end of the string.
5. Pour quick-setting cement, such as Quick Crete, into the holes. Then place the headpiece in an upright position, with each leg resting in the center of one of the two holes. Be sure that the legs go at least 4 inches into the concrete and that the rack is high enough for you

to easily pick up the front wheel of a bike to slide it between the rails. Just use whatever you have on hand, such as a sawhorse or some bricks, as a support to keep the headpiece propped up until the cement hardens.

6. Let the concrete dry for 48 hours before removing the supports, and then allow it to cure for another week or two before using the rack.

SPRING INTO A PEA PROP. That battered box spring may look like it's ready for the landfill, but lurking below the worn batting is a handy helper for vegetables that grow on the up and up. Once you unwrap the batting and cotton covers on the box spring coils, you can use wire cutters to sever off any number of handy plant stakes and trellises. You can jab the bottom of each coil right into the ground and gently train trailing peas, beans and even morning glories to grow on it. If the coil isn't tall enough for the job, connect several together with florist wire. Or, you can use it to extend the height of a tomato cage or teepee trellis—just wire it to the top.

BED DOWN THE FIRE. Any solid, modestly sized wooden headboard may need to head for the fireplace . . . Not to become wood ash for radishes, but to serve as a novel mantel surround. After a good washing, you can use wood screws to attach it to the wall. Or, you can transform the headboard by sanding and painting it, or even using it as a base for a beautiful mosaic—just make sure to consider fire safety first in your choice of materials.

THE FINE PRINT
Check Out the Down

Buying a new comforter? Before you buy, take a good look—at the label, that is, if you want a down comforter that will perform best over the long haul.

The label will list a "loft" number that describes how fluffy the down clusters are. Higher numbers mean more fill with less weight (in other words, a longer life without the clumping and condensing that decrease warmth and comfort). Keep in mind that the fill power rating applies only to down products, not to synthetic-fill comforters.

A fill power rating of 800 is the most luxurious, but products with that rating usually cost about as much as a good used car. Buy the highest fill power you can afford (any number higher than 550 is considered good). Avoid products that don't have fill power listed on the label. If you're in the market for a discount comforter, spend your bucks on the highest loft available and never mind the cover material. Remember that a down comforter should always be covered by a duvet, which you'll need to purchase separately.

TURNING INTO A TREE. If a worn wooden bed frame has sturdy posts that are at least 4 by 4 inches, they need never leave the bedroom. Instead, they can take on the new job of organizing clothes as a clothes tree. Here's how to do it. Drill holes in the post and then attach 5-inch wooden dowels or metal clothes hooks at intervals. To anchor the post at the bottom, screw it into a 12-inch diameter block or cylinder of wood, or "plant" it in a 16-inch plastic pot full of Quick Crete.

CRIBS

With cribs, safety is all that's important, so shop smart and don't try refurbishing. Older models can start anew in the garden or on the wall.

FIX IT FAST **CURB THE TOO-HIGH CORNER POST.** Corner posts should protrude no farther than 1/16 inch above the end panels on a crib, or your baby can get injured from getting her clothing entangled with the post. If the posts on your crib are too long, saw them off and sand down the edges. This rule does not apply to posts 16 inches or higher if they'll be used to support a canopy.

FIX IT OR FORGET IT?
CRIBS: ONLY FAIRLY NEW WILL DO

Although it's tempting to eek every last bit of use from an heirloom crib or to purchase a quaint antique, it's far better to acquire a newer one for the safety of the baby. How new? In September 1995, the U.S. Consumer Product Safety Commission (CPSC) announced a roundup to crush and destroy used cribs, because it estimated about 50 babies were tragically suffocating or strangling each year in older-model cribs with broken parts or unsafe designs. No matter what the crib's age, though, you should still scrutinize it looking for these safety features.

Yes
• A firm, tight-fitting mattress and a mattress support that does not easily pull apart from the corner posts. If you can fit more than two fingers between the mattress and the side of the crib, move on.

• A strong headboard and frame. Give the assembled crib a strong shake to make sure.
• Slats that are no more than 2⅜ inches apart. If a 12-ounce soda can fits easily between slats, the spaces are too wide.

No
• Cribs made before 1973, when federal guidelines went into effect
• Missing or cracked slats
• Peeling paint, splinters, or rough edges
• Missing, loose, broken, or improperly installed screws, brackets, or other hardware on the crib or mattress support
• Fancy decorations that can break off and pose a choking hazard, decals that are cracked or flaking, or painted designs on the inside of the crib
• Cribs with cutout designs along the rail that could trap your baby's arm or neck

---

BABY, HANG THOSE QUILTS! If you have an old a crib, consider turning it into a homey quilt rack. You can make two, because each rack takes just one of the long sides. Here's how to proceed.

PASS IT ALONG

1. Remove every other upright post from one of the sides of a crib.
2. Cut four 5-inch "legs" from the removed posts.
3. Place the side that faces the inside of the crib on a work surface; use wood glue or screws to attach the legs to the four corners of the crib rack. They'll keep it from banging the wall and leave space for the quilts to drape over the individual rungs and behind the rack.
4. Now you're ready to hang the quilt rack on the wall from two evenly spaced L-brackets.

NIGHTSTANDS AND DRESSERS

An ironing board? Glue and pressed flowers? Read on to find out how these (and other items) can protect bedroom furniture from clutter and things that go bump in the night.

IRONING BOARD ON DUTY. Ever think about how much stuff you need when you're sick in bed? One of the ways an otherwise functional nightstand can become worn and weak is when someone adds

MAKE IT LAST

All flannel sheets look about the same, so make sure to read the label before buying. If it doesn't say "preshrunk," count on your sheets to shrink when you wash them the first time, enough so that your fitted sheet will stop fitting.

30 pounds of flu-relief paraphernalia during days of bed rest. Take it easy on the nightstand by moving it out of the way when someone's bedridden and replacing it with an adjustable ironing board with its waterproof cover. Swing the pointed end of the board over the covers to form a tray that's within easy reach, making it the ideal place for steamy mugs and the remote. Another advantage: While sick-bay items might linger on to damage the nightstand over a period of weeks, you'll have to clear the ironing board ASAP once the sick person's well—because you'll need it to press clothes.

FIX IT FAST

MAKE A BLEMISH BEAUTIFUL. The top of a nightstand is bound to get lots of nicks and watermarks since it holds items ranging from nail scissors to cups of warm milk. Disguise wear and tear marks with something tiny and pretty, like decoupaged pressed flowers. The process is surprisingly straightforward and should yield a beautiful and refreshed surface in a day if you follow these instructions.

What you'll need:
- drop cloth
- wood putty
- sandpaper
- découpage glue
- pressed flowers
- water-based polyurethane

1. Clear the table and dust it completely. It's best to work outdoors where there's good ventilation. Set the table on the drop cloth.
2. Repair any deep dents or nicks on the table top with wood putty. Let dry and then sand until smooth.
3. Brush the area you want to hide with a coat of quick-drying decoupage glue such as Mod Podge.
4. Use tweezers to set a pressed flower while the glue is wet.

5. Let the glue dry 15 to 20 minutes, and then add another coat.

6. To achieve a uniform look, seal the entire stand with a coat of water-based polyurethane.

CLAP ON. The objects in your bedroom will be less likely to get broken or marred if you'll just see the light—one that's equipped with a clap-sensitive on/off switch, that is. Devices such as The Clapper (a sound-activated on/off switch), available at most home improvement stores and on the Internet, will allow you to turn on or off a bedroom light remotely. That's great if you want to turn off the overhead light when you're done reading, but even better if you wake to a threatening sound or child's cry in the middle of the night. You signal with a clap, and the light comes on so you won't need to fumble around in the dark looking for the light switch.

KITTY IN THE CUPBOARD. If you're ready to give away a standard nightstand with a drawer up top and a cupboard in the bottom, pass on the old piece of furniture for your cat's amusement. You'll need to make a few modifications: Simply remove the lower door or doors and repaint the piece (if you'd like). Staple or use upholstery nails to attach two tea towels side by side below the drawer to act as curtains, set a comfy pillow inside the cupboard, and wait for Fluffy to discover the hideaway. Include two other fabulous upgrades in kitty's new hideaway: Store cat toys in the drawer, and tack an old piece of carpet to the back as a scratching post.

MOVE IT TO THE BATHROOM. Tired of your old dresser? Don't send it to the Salvation Army just yet. If it's the right size, you may be able to turn it into a new bathroom vanity. All you need: A one-piece basin countertop or a drop-in sink basin with a self-sealing rim (available at most home improvement stores) and some basic plumbing skills. Once the sink is installed, and before the water is turned back on, repaint or refinish the new vanity. Everyone will think you spent big bucks on the upgrade!

MIRRORS

Old-fashioned mirrors can be the fairest of them all for decades—as looking glasses, or in new roles in the garden or on the dining room table. Just check the tips on the following pages to find out how.

6 Ways to Draw a New Plan for Drawers

Even the least expensive wooden or plywood drawers can take on a new job when their nightstand, end table, or dresser has retired. These ideas go from smallest to largest.

1. **Play with display.** A smaller nightstand drawer can become an open wall-mounted shadow box with very few simple alterations—just choose one with a face that's flush with the rest of the drawer (overhanging edges will make it hard to hang straight on the wall). If the drawer is taller than 16 inches, make sure to add a painted plywood shelf to break up the space, or just place an open wooden box within the box.

2. **Baby your dolls.** Small to medium drawers can make a handy baby doll or stuffed animal bed. Put rollers or rocker rails on the bottom to make them that much better.

3. **Wow 'em window box.** Narrow or rectangular dresser drawers that are 12 to 18 inches wide and 12 to 14 inches deep, make a nifty window box, inside or out. Just make sure to line it with heavy, dark plastic for insulation and consider whether you want to drill the drainage holes directly into the discard drawer or place

separate pots with saucers in the "box" with moss or mulch between them.

4. **Sliding storage.** Shallow, wide drawers (say 24 to 60 inches on any side and 4 to 8 inches deep) can be used to make simple, open, under-the-bed storage for sweaters, extra sheets, throw pillows, and the like. All you need to do is install rolling casters on the four corners and they'll slide right out when you want them.

5. **Sleep space for kitty.** Adopt the same strategy without the rollers to make an under-the-bed kitty resting place. Make sure to leave enough space for the cat to climb in between the underside of the bed and the top of the storage drawer, and glue felt to the bottom of the drawer so it won't scrape the floor.

6. **Raised to be a garden.** Deep or semi-deep drawers that are larger and wider, say 24 to 60 inches can make satisfactory raised flower beds. Sand and paint or seal them with polyurethane first if you'd like them to last more than one season, then either mount them on cinderblocks or several stacked wood pallets or nail on legs (no taller than 24 inches) made of 2-by-4s.

MAKE IT LAST   **TURN BACK THE BLACK.** A mirror is most susceptible to damage while it's being cleaned. Protect your mirror from flaking or turning black at the edges by wiping it with a lint-free cloth dampened with plain water, and then drying it. Most commercial cleaners, including ammonia-based Windex and bleach, will cause the silver in the mirror's backing to oxidize and turn black and also causes the silver layer to gradually become brittle and eventually flake. If you must use a commercial product, make sure to use a rag sprayed with the cleaner to wipe the mirror—start in the center, leaving the outer edges alone so the fluid won't seep into the backing accidentally.

FIX IT FAST   **WOOL WON'T SCRATCH.** When a mirror gets a grease mark or stubborn bit of debris on it that won't yield to rubbing with a soft cloth, haul out the strong stuff—but only the most delicate grade. Of steel wool, that is. Using very little pressure, gently work over the trouble spot with #0000 steel wool, and it should disappear without scratching the rest of the surface.

PAINT THOSE POCKMARKS. It's a shame when a gorgeous mirror gets tiny pits (usually where the silver backing has flaked), scratches, or even cracks. Turn flaws into fine art by disguising them with glass paint. If the mirror has a frame, take one element from the texture or pattern and reproduce it on the marred area. If not, try whatever will suit the style of the mirror or the room it rests in, using a stencil or cling decals as a guide if you're not handy with freehand. All you need to turn your old mirror into a brand new showpiece is Relief outliner paint (such as Cerne Relief) from the craft store or Internet suppliers, glass paint in desired colors, and brushes that are slender enough for your design. Once you've got your supplies, here's how to proceed.

1. Use plain water on a lint-free cloth to wipe the mirror clean. Allow the mirror to dry completely.
2. Outline the pattern using a relief outliner paint; allow the paint to dry completely.
3. Using a brush and working with one color and a couple square inch sections at a time. Fill in the outline with glass paint and allow to dry thoroughly between colors or you risk leaving painted fingerprints on other parts of the mirror.

BED LINENS

No short-lived bed sheets here, not with better buying tactics and some TLC. You can even change flat to fitted, without a magic wand.

TIE-DYE FOR A ZIPPIER LIFE. Detergents can fade even the lightest color sheets, but fret not because there's lots of life left in those cotton threads, especially if you consider this colorful solution: Channel your inner flower child and tie-dye the sheets to cover faded spots and light stains. You can find tie-dye kits, regular dyes, and vegetable dyes available in craft stores and fabric stores. Wherever you shop, just be sure the dye you choose is nontoxic. Follow the instructions on the dye, then wash the dyed sheets separately from other laundry the first time around, adding a cup of white vinegar to the load to set the dye.

MAKE IT LAST

You should also dry the sheets on the medium or hot setting of your clothes dryer to help set the dye.

 **FIX IT FAST**

FROM FLAT TO FITTED. Adding a cushion top to your mattress adds comfort, but it also adds height, which may mean your old fitted sheets don't fit anymore. Luckily, most flat sheets for full-size or larger beds have quite a bit of extra fabric enough to accommodate any extra height, and it's easy to turn these flat sheets into fitted ones.

1. Measure the mattress's length, width, and depth, including the cushion top and/or mattress cover.
2. Add twice the measurement of the depth to the measurement of the length, plus another 4 inches for the casing and for necessary ease.
3. Mark those measurements on the flat sheet, and then cut to fit.
4. On each corner, cut out a square the depth of the mattress (including any add-ons like a mattress pad).
5. Place the outsides together and sew the cut edges of the square together to create a pocket on each corner.
6. Use a serger to sew around the outer edge of the entire sheet to finish it, or turn under a 1/4-inch hem and machine-sew it.
7. To make the elastic casing that will hold the sheet in place, measure and mark 6 inches on either side of the bottom of each corner seam. Press under 1 inch along the bottom edge, then sew along the top edge of the casing to create an area for the elastic. (The casing will be twice the length of the elastic piece to allow for gathering.)

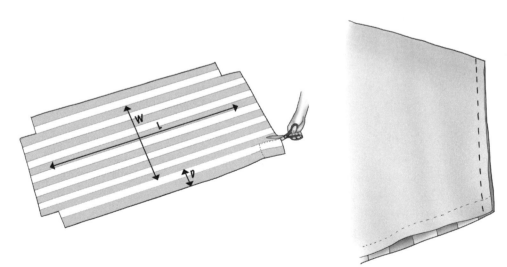

Mark the measurements and cut to fit.

8. Cut four pieces of ¾-inch-wide elastic into 6-inch lengths.

9. Insert a piece of elastic into each casing, then sew through each end of the casing and elastic to secure it in place.

A MITEY END. If dust mites put your allergy symptoms into overdrive, you probably already know how to banish them from your bedding: washing in very hot water with detergent. Some pillows and blankets won't stand up to such rigors, though. But that doesn't mean you have to surrender to the little critters and their droppings (the actual allergy trigger). Give your blankets and pillows a spin in your dryer on high heat for 10 minutes. A good number of those pesky mites will be killed—or loosened and blown out the vent.

A SHEET FIT FOR FIDO. An old sheet makes a fun and inexpensive temporary dog house, which is especially nice when it's a bit hot out. Just fold the sheet in half lengthwise, and double it over a clothesline or a rope between trees or two chairs, outdoors or in. Weight the ends with cans of food or bricks or stake them down.

PASS IT ALONG

TABLE AN OLD SHEET. A designer or decorative flat sheet can easily be transformed into a fantastic tablecloth. Just make sure to sew (or fabric glue) a small pocket into each corner, so you can slip small rocks or weights inside to weigh the tablecloth down if you'll be using it outdoors.

FROM BED TO BATH. Some folks buy a new sheet for the express purpose of turning it into a shower curtain, but a previously used version is just as suitable (and more cost-efficient). There are lots of ways to effect the transformation, but the one that will assure your sheet will last longest in its new role is sewing ribbons along the top in intervals and then tying the curtain to the shower rod or curtain hooks. Ribbons are much less likely to rip a fragile old sheet as you hang, remove, or wash it than grommets, hooks, or buttons.

> ## $mart Buys
> ### HIGH-QUALITY SHEETS:
> ### SEE THE LIGHT
>
> When you shop for sheets, stick to stores where you can see and feel the samples, or ask to unwrap a package before you buy. That will give you two sure-fire ways to determine whether the linens are of good quality. First, hold up the sheet to a light, which will not shine through a sheet with a high thread count. Second, you'll be able to scratch the sheet with your fingernail to see if any pill comes off—a sure sign a sheet is of lesser quality.

TAKE SHEETS TO THE BEACH. As long as it still has the elastic, a worn fitted sheet makes a great beach companion. You can use it to sunbathe on and it will dry super quick—and for once, the bunched edges are an advantage since you can fill them with sand to keep the sheet from blowing away.

SCRAP BAG TO SCRAP BOOK. It seems just awful to let those bits of embroidery or vintage vat-dyed patterns go to waste just because the sheet or pillowcase they're decorating can no longer make the grade. So . . . don't! Clip the scraps, hem the edges or starch whole pieces to keep them from fraying and then use them when you can to liven up scrapbook pages, the fronts of journals, stamped greeting cards, cardboard frames—the possibilities are endless.

KID CRAFTS FOR OLD SHEETS. Whether that old sheet has become too thin, too torn, or just lost its sense of style, give it renewed life as the main prop in these projects and activities for the young as well as the young at heart.

- **Looks like an angel.** For the start of a sparkly angel outfit, put a light coat of clear spray paint or spray glue adhesive on an old white sheet. Then toss glitter over it before it dries.
- **Hot day watercolors.** As an antidote to summer boredom, hang an old white sheet from the line or a fence, soak it with the hose, and let young artists paint all over it with tempera. Don't like it when you're done? Hose it down and start over.
- **Fly me through the sheet!** Cut 8 to 10 holes of varying sizes big enough for a paper airplane to sail through in a bedsheet. Label each opening with a point value or a reward like "choose dinner tonight." Suspend the sheet from the clothesline or a couple of strings in the house, and let contestants (or teams) take turns trying to fly homemade airplanes through the holes to score.
- **Sled indoors on hardwood floors.** This is a great activity for a rainy day. Let kids take turns sitting on one end of the sheet while someone else pulls on the other end around on a hardwood floor.

SOCKS

Mind and mend to help any socks the dryer does spare wear a lot longer. And find umpteen uses for the worn ones, starting with dog beds and dusters.

4 New Uses for Old Pillowcases

A pillowcase that can no longer stand up to the rigors of daily use on a bed (or to the scrutiny of the fashion police) can still function quite well in one of these four roles.

1. **A chew toy with bite.** Your small dog will thank you for giving up on a polyester pillowcase when you roll it lengthwise into a thin "snake" and tie three knots in it, one at each end and one in the middle. Now you have a chew toy that's suitable for a game of tug of war, too.

2. **Wrap it up.** If the pillowcase is still in decent shape, tie-dye or stamp an old plain cotton case and use it to wrap oversized gifts. It's reusable, too!

3. **Pillowcase prints.** Use a plain cotton pillowcase as a canvas and have family members make their hand- or footprints on it with tempera paint. Use a laundry marker to write the date and names. Then frame or mat the whole thing as a piece of memorabilia.

4. **News-in-a-bag.** If a polyester pillowcase is still strong but looks stained or out of fashion, keep it on hand for stashing recyclable newspapers. The pillowcase is the perfect size, and you won't get newsprint on your hands when you drop the papers at their final destination—you can just shake them out of the cases.

PROTECT THE PROTECTOR. Using an old Mason jar to cover frost-threatened plants at night is a time-honored tradition, but it's much more effective if you cover the jars with old socks. Doing this not only protects the jar from breaking should it accidentally get knocked over in the garden, it also keeps the glass from getting too hot and burning the plant if you don't remove the jar right away when the sun comes up the next morning.

PASS IT ALONG

SOFTEN WITH STRAY SOCKS. Hang on to a few of those stray socks you find in the dryer in the laundry room—not because you have any hope that the dryer will eventually cough up the mates—but to replace dryer sheets with a less expensive, environmentally friendly option. Make a "fabric softener sock" of sorts by pressing the mouth of a jug of liquid softener against the sock and turning it over until you have a thin rim of fabric softener on the sock. Put the sock in with a load of laundry in the dryer, and remove it when your soft, sweet-smelling clothes are dry.

SOCK IT TO DUST MITES. Dust loves to settle in some awfully tricky places—between banister posts, for instance, in the grooves of molding, or between the slats of a dining room chair back. No problem: Just slide an old sock on each hand, reach into those little crevices with your fingers, and wipe out the dust.

SOCK AWAY A DOG BED. If you have an endless supply of orphan socks, use them to do a good turn for your loving doggie pal. With just a bit of time but not much skill, you can stuff the individual socks, sew them into a coil of sorts, and then make the coil into a cushioned dog bed. Here's how.

1. Start with 8 to 10 clean, discarded socks all about the same size. Using all the same fabric is nice, too (like all sweat or dress socks), but your dog probably won't be picky since with his sensitive nose they'll all smell like the family.

2. Stuff the first sock loosely with polyester fill, recycled nylon panty hose, or a mixture of the two.

3. Start sewing a larger coil by bending the toe of the first sock back on itself and tacking it down securely with needle and thread. Keep winding the sock around itself, pecan roll-style, tacking as you go and ending with the open cuff.

4. Stuff the toe of the next sock into the open end of the first sock, and stitch it into place through the cuff of the first sock.

5. Fill the second sock with polyester or panty hose and continue on, adding socks, stuffing them, sewing them together, and wrapping the tube around on itself to continue the spiral. Make sure to sew the toe of each additional sock into the open end of the proceeding sock.

6. Once the spiral is large enough for use as a dog bed, flip it over, and sew the coils together on this side with a running stitch.

FOOTWEAR

Walk more miles in your shoes and have healthier feet, to boot, with tactics from freezing odors to spraying starch. And when your favorites just don't cut it anymore, reuse them as planters.

MAKE IT LAST

MARCH LONGER WITH MORE STARCH. Canvas shoes are tough to clean and prone to mildew, so try a preventive measure to extend the time between cleanings. Spray a coat of starch over the entire surface of the clean and dry shoe, then let it dry completely. That's it! The protective layer will keep dirt from clinging to the shoes as quickly and make it easier to brush off the stuff that does accumulate.

FIX IT FAST

GO AHEAD AND LITTER! Have you reached the point at which you're willing to throw athletic shoes away because they smell bad?

One Man's Trash
The Darnedest Thing to Collect

It's only fitting that a tool once used to recycle billions of socks has itself been recycled into a hot collector's item. At one time a staple of the sewing box, stocking darners have gone the way of the buttonhook and the horse and buggy, but darner historian Wayne Muller has done his part to put them on the comeback trail as a highly sought collectible.

The U.S. Patent Office issued more than 100 patents for the humble stocking darner (also known as darning eggs or balls) between 1865 and 1956. While most every household had at least a basic model, fancier models were made from materials ranging from glass to wood to sterling silver, and in patterns from blue willow to glass eggs painted to resemble tiny dolls. Still, all had the same purpose: to hold fabric taut so a seamstress could darn a hole handily.

Muller began his collection accidentally in 1977, when his wife Mary suggested he purchase some little thing to disarm a coastal California antique dealer who was trying to close shop. The two came across two more darners the very next day, and that fledgling collection somehow burgeoned into more than 500 examples from 21 countries, and is now considered the largest collection in the world. Muller also went on to write the definitive darner guidebook *Darn It! The History and Romance of Darners* in 1995. Filled with vivid photos and darner lore, trivia, and a price guide, it's still in print and available from Amazon.com.

You may be able to salvage them. All you need is a pair of socks and some kitty litter to solve the problem.

1. Turn the socks inside out and pour ¾ cup of clean clay cat litter into each. Tie a knot in the ends of the socks.
2. Slip the litter-filled socks into the shoes, and let them sit overnight to absorb moisture as well as odors.
3. Air out the filled socks for another 24 hours or so if you want to reuse them. If you're done, empty out the kitty litter, turn the socks right-side out, brush any remains into the compost, and send them through the wash.

FREEZE OUT THE FUNK. If you're dedicated to keeping odiferous sneakers out of the landfill, here's a tip that will help you maintain that dedication. Pour ½ cup of baking soda in each smelly shoe, place it in a ziplock freezer bag, zip it shut, and place the bagged shoes in the freezer for 24 hours. The combination is particularly effective because the baking soda takes care of the odor and the cold air thwarts bacterial growth. Take the shoes out, dispose of the baking soda, give them an hour or so to thaw, and you're back in business.

HEAL LEATHER WITHOUT THE HYPE. Don't sacrifice the shine just because your old leather shoes are dried out and in need of rejuvenation. Lots of products on the market will restore the leather but leave the finish dull. Instead, rub the shoes with a soft cloth doused in about a tablespoon of castor oil. The leather will look healthier and give off a glow.

USE PUTTY, SILLY! Reclaim those ailing canvas shoes left in the back of the closet for years, even if they're so dirty you can no longer tell what color they are. But never mind the fancy products from the athletic shoe store, scope out the home store instead. That's where you'll find putty-type wallpaper cleanser, which cleans up canvas in a hurry without a lot of scrubbing on your part.

PASS IT ALONG

FETCH STUFF IN OVERSIZED SLIPPERS. Big, floppy slippers are unsightly enough when they're practically new. Who would want to wear them when they're all stretched out? You, that's who! Keep them on hand in a spot near the back door, so you can step into them with your outdoor shoes still on any time you barrel back into the house in wet or muddy work shoes. When your indoor chore is done (with no wet or muddy tracks to show for it), head back out, but leave the

5 Ways to Delay the Departure of Panty Hose

If you wear them at all, you doubtless (pardon the pun) run through dozens of pairs of panty hose every year. It's frustrating (and it gets expensive), but you can soften the blow by keeping clean pairs of unwearable panty hose on hand for the following purposes.

1. **Keep broom bristles in shape.** Cut a 5-inch band from one panty hose leg and slip it over the business end of a broom, leaving 3 inches of bristles free at the bottom. This band of nylon will prevent the broom straws from bending out of shape, even if they're synthetic.

2. **Lengthen onion life.** Onions will stay fresh longer if you drop one at a time down the leg of some clean, dry panty hose, tying a knot at the top of each. Hang the holder from a hook on the kitchen wall and air can circulate to keep the onions fresh. Snip the end off with scissors to free each onion as you need it, starting from the bottom. Works great for potatoes, too.

3. **Make a scrunchie.** Need a hair holder in a hurry? Tie a 3-inch section of panty hose leg around your ponytail like a scrunchie.

4. **Belly band to bedroll.** Need to roll up an old sleeping bag? Cut the waistband from a pair of panty hose, and slip it around the bedroll to keep it together.

5. **Wrap it up.** Once you've opened a roll of wrapping paper, slip the excess into a sleeve made from one leg of panty hose. No more tears or unraveling! For two or more rolls, leave the pair of panty hose intact, slip a roll in each leg, and hang it from a clothes hanger.

oversized slippers inside for the next time. Some catalogs sell wool or fleece "scuffs" for big bucks; your worn-out slippers offer the same dirt protection for free.

THESE BOOTS ARE MADE FOR PLANTING. Just because old work boots are too worn to wear doesn't mean you can't take advantage of all that sturdy leather or nylon and waterproofing. Let the plants benefit from a boot-shaped planter you can make in a half hour or so. Here's how to proceed.

1. Remove the lace from one of the boots, and then pull the tongue all the way forward.

2. Start by pouring 2 to 3 inches of aquarium gravel into the boots for drainage.

3. Scoop about 2 inches of potting soil mixed with a half cup of composted soil or manure on top of the gravel.

4. Gently slide an annual, such as a marigold or impatiens, out of its 4-inch pot, loosening the

An pair of old boots can make delightful planters.

7 Steps to Buying the Best Shoes

Maybe you wear out a few favorite pairs of athletic shoes, but you'll never wear out some footwear because it doesn't fit properly. So, you give it away long before it's worn. Or you have to buy new shoes fairly often because the ones you have in the closet hurt your feet. To find shoes that will wear well because they fit well, follow these seven simple steps.

1. **Don't wait.** Unless the shoe is rigid leather, it shouldn't require "breaking in," so don't buy a pair if they're not comfortable when you put them on in the store.
2. **Walk to the store.** Go shopping for walking shoes right after a long walk, which is when your feet should be the most swollen. That will ensure you won't buy shoes that are too small.
3. **Don't have a seat.** To get the most accurate measurement, stand while your feet are being measured.
4. **Toe the line.** While standing in a new pair of shoes, you should have about a finger's width of space between the tip of your longest toe and the top of the shoe's interior, and be able to wiggle all your toes comfortably inside the shoe.
5. **Never mind last time.** The size of your last pair of shoes is an okay starting point, but never base a shoe purchase on just that. Sizing varies among manufacturers and even styles. Try on shoes to make sure this pair fits, despite what the label says.
6. **Two feet, one shoe size.** Keep in mind that your right foot is not always the same size as the left, so you'll have to try on both shoes in a pair and pick a pair that fits the largest foot.
7. **BYO socks.** Most shoe stores offer only thin slip-ons if you're not wearing socks and want to try on shoes. Don't bother—you need to try on shoes with exactly the same type of socks you intend to wear them with, so bring along a pair or wait until next time.

compacted roots with your fingers, and then dipping the bottom in water. Another good choice: the succulent hens-and-chicks.

5. Place the plant in the center of the soil. Hold it straight while you gently pack more soil around and on top of the roots to within 3 inches of the top of the boot.
6. If you like, plant a second, trailing plant like a wave petunia, philodendron, or creeping thyme to one side of the annual.
7. Place the planter in full sun on a site in the garden, porch, or deck that's protected from strong winds. Water it thoroughly and regularly, keeping in mind that annuals need lots of water and that these plants won't be able to spread their roots to draw it from the soil.

SWEATERS

Whether wool or modern weave, help sweaters hold their shape and their value with a tactic used by crime scene investigators and some neat needlework.

KEEP SWEATERS SHAPELY. Old sweaters usually stretch out before they wear out. Help your sweater avoid that fate by taking its measurements when it's brand new, or if it's too late for that, when it's fitting really well. Trace the outline of the sweater directly onto an old framed screen, marking it with white chalk. Ever after, when you wash the sweater "block" it into the pattern on the screen so it will dry into its proper shape. This works exceptionally well for cotton sweaters that seem to hang low at the hem or sleeves; the blocking "lifts" those areas back in place after washings.

MAKE IT LAST

HEAT SHABBY CUFFS. Ribbed cuffs and waists on knit or wool sweaters look worse if they stretch on a regular basis. Return them to tautness with a hot water bath. Microwave a 1-quart bowl of water until it's just below boiling point, and then dip just the cuffs or waistband into the bowl. Blot the excess water with a towel and then place the sweater on another towel to blow-dry the wet spots. Soon enough, the ribbing will shrink back into a springy state.

FIX IT FAST

KEEP STAINS SECRET. If a sweater has a pull or a soiled area that can't be fixed, just disguise the trouble spot and give your garment a new look. Using fabric glue or needle and thread, glue or sew buttons, bows, or embroidered patches in a symmetrical or random pattern that suits the style of the sweater; visit your local fabric or craft store for ideas. Appliqué, using felt or wool, is also popular. You can create "patches" for your damaged garment (and a custom-look, to boot!) with a few small scraps of wool or felt and some embroidery floss.

Still Working After All These Years
HONEY, I SHRUNK THE SWEATER

Sue Burns learned the benefits of having a husband who did laundry back in 1994. That's when husband Ken accidentally shrunk two of her wool sweaters at their Leland, Michigan home. Instead of throwing them away, Sue decided to reclaim the wool and make jackets for her tiny daughters . . . and a cottage industry was born.

Burns' friends quickly took notice of the wool jackets and soon she was making more for them, then for customers, and soon baabaaZuzu (www.baabaazuzu.com) became a formal company that leaped from the couple's living room to a store in the village of Lake Leeluanau, Michigan.

These days the business makes much more than reclaimed wool children's clothes, including adult jackets and vests, scarves, hats, and mittens. All the materials are 100 percent recycled, most of them purchased from local secondhand stores. Today, the couple so despises wasting wool that they've started using scraps from larger products to make Christmas stockings for sale.

WEDDING ATTIRE

You'll only wear it once but preserving wedding attire is a labor of love—and a great way to pass along tradition and help low-income wedding parties.

PASS IT ALONG

DONATE YOUR DRESS TO A DREAM. If your old bridal gown doesn't have any wedding prospects within your own family, why not share your legacy to make the Big Day better for a bargain-seeking bride-to-be, and generate some funds for a great cause at the same time? Brides Against Breast Cancer is the Making Memories Foundation's number one fund-raising event across the nation. It's made possible by women who donate their wedding dresses to be re-sold at substantial savings through a "nationwide tour of gowns" that makes more than 32 stops across the country. Money earned is then earmarked to grant wishes for women and men who have been diagnosed with terminal breast cancer.

Making Memories, based in Portland, Oregon (see Resources), sells dresses from size 4 to 44; slips, veils, shoes, and other accessories are also available in some cities. The nonprofit also accepts complete sets of bridesmaid dresses from weddings held since 2000, along with veils, slips, shoes, mother's dresses, and flower girl gowns. Other items specific to weddings, including jewelry, books, ring pillows, wedding purses, and the like are gladly received.

NOW STARRING . . . Did you know that an average wedding gown often contains 10 or more yards of fabric and lace in large swaths that can be readily recycled by a performing arts troupe or a local theatre? If you aren't interested in hanging on to your dress after the wedding, consider passing it along to costumers who may be able to use the dress in its original style. Crafty costumers may also be able to dye the dress or disassemble it and repurpose the fabric lengths.

ALWAYS A BRIDESMAID. Don't despair—someone will love that peach chiffon gown with the drop-waist bow you wore in a wedding 20 years ago! High school drama clubs, local theatre groups, day care centers, and sometimes little girls in your own family may find ways to breathe new life into your formal frock. Bridesmaid's dresses can also be passed along or donated to charities that collect used clothing, especially near Halloween.

9 Something News from an Old Wedding Dress

Whether your wedding dress was a bargain from the Salvation Army or you just no longer have a sentimental attachment to it, there are loads of ways to use the expensive fabrics, lace, and sequins to jazz up other household items or even to create new heirlooms. Of course, you have to be willing to put scissors to fabric, or have an experienced tailor do so. Once you cross that threshold, here are nine fantastic projects you can try.

1. **A tree skirt for Queen Victoria.** Use material from the waist down and add fringe at the bottom—perfect for a Christmas tree decorated Victorian style.

2. **From wedding to christening.** This is a particularly appropriate idea in families where the marriage didn't work out, but you'd still like to keep that lavish material in the family. A tailor, seamstress, or home-sewing enthusiast can do the honors.

3. **Trim for the next bride's toes.** Decorate a pair of plain white tennies with lace from the wedding dress that the daughter or next family bride can wear to the rehearsal or reception.

4. **Wrap for a wedding album or frame.** This is a particularly nice idea if you have an old dress that can't be worn by a modern bride but you'd still like to pass it along somehow.

5. **Ornamental ideas.** Use the sequins, lace, or even satin to concoct one-of-a-kind Christmas ornaments.

6. **Dress up a bridal bear.** Use the material scraps to create a dress for a child's favorite bear—a cute and cuddly keepsake for a flower girl or new stepchild after a second wedding.

7. **Hankies are handy.** Hem a little patch from the dress into a handkerchief ideal to carry to the next wedding . . . or to keep on hand when the wedding bills start pouring in.

8. **Then comes baby.** Sew or glue part of the train or skirt to make a festive skirt for a bassinet.

9. **Bag it.** Use the laundered fabric and lace from a special dress and veil to sew gift bags for a new bridal party or for favor bags at the reception.

CUT—THAT'S A WRAP. If you've kept that pricey bridesmaid dress, consider this: In a smaller dose, that silky pastel material might make a very nice shoulder wrap or cover-up for a formal or semi-formal dress or silky black pants worn with a plain T-shirt.

1. Determine how large you want the wrap to be by using a scarf, shawl, or other wrap, or use a length of rolled wrapping paper to test fit the wrap. (A good starter size is 30 inches high by 60 inches long.) Allow an extra inch in both directions for a hem. Make a paper pattern, if desired.

2. Mark and cut the wrap out of the dress, placing dress seams or features strategically on the wrap.

3. Hem all the edges using fusible, double-sided hemming tape and an iron by turning up ½ inch on all sides, or sew a true hem by turning under ¼ inch, then another ¼ inch on all sides and sewing along the folded edge.

4. Sew or use hemming tape to add fringe or ribbon to both short ends of the wrap for a more sophisticated version.

TEEN DREAM COME TRUE. Fashionable and mint-condition gowns and cocktail dresses are sought after by a variety of prom-night charities. These organizations collect prom dresses from individuals, manufacturers, and bridal shops and pass them along to teens who can't afford prom attire or who have experienced hardship. Glitter-and-glam giveaways are a huge hit with teens each year. Go online and type in "prom dress donations," and you'll find organizations with names such as The Glass Slipper Project and The Princess Project. You may be delighted to find a collection site in your local area.

HEART AND SOLE. Donate your once-worn bridal shoes (from the bride or bridesmaids) to organizations that lend professional outfits to unemployed women trying to reenter the workforce. Low-income women can borrow—at no cost—clothing, shoes, and accessories for interviews and the first few weeks on the new job. Call your local Chamber of Commerce, women's shelter, or family service organization to get information about a lending service in your area. And don't think that men can't get a piece of the action, too. Spit-and-polish dress shoes are always welcome at clothing distribution centers and homeless advocacy locations.

Say Your Vows, Store Your Dress

You'll have a lifetime to enjoy wedded bliss, but to preserve a wedding dress worthy of the great granddaughters, it's essential to get the gown cleaned no more than 6 months after the wedding before any stains, grime, or body oils set. To protect your dress during the grace period, though, follow these tips.

- **Consider your closet's climate.** Keep the gown in a dark, dry place, such as a closet. The attic is probably too hot (or cold), the basement too humid.
- **No hanging around.** Store the gown flat, not hung by its shoulders or dress loops.
- **Dress your dress in white.** Protect the wedding gown by covering it in a clean white sheet before placing it on a closet shelf—plastic is a no-no because petroleum's off-gassing can cause yellowing. Put the sheet on a flat surface like the bed, lay the gown on top, and fold the sheet over the top. Then fold the sheet-wrapped gown in thirds from top to bottom, once at the waist and once at the train.
- **Reason to refold.** If your dress still hasn't made it to the cleaners after 3 months of storage, it's time to do a little preventive maintenance. Remove the gown from the shelf, and refold it so the creases don't form indents in the material. Keep the clean sheet on the whole time, though.

DELICATE AND ANTIQUE CLOTHING

Preserve the look from bygone eras with some silky strategies and a few snaps—and remember that vintage picks really do run smaller than today's clothes.

SNAP TO IT! You won't be able to wear a silky shirt or dress more than a few times before it loses its shape or forms tiny runs if it's bunched in a drawer or collapsed on the closet floor. Most wire hangers only add to the problem because silky items slip right off. The solution? A needle and thread, two ordinary snaps, and a padded satin hanger. Here's what you do: Sew a socket from one snap to the seam allowance on the inside of each shoulder seam of the shirt or dress, then stitch the matching ball part to corresponding ends of a padded satin hanger. When you take off the blouse, snap it into place and it will stay wrinkle free until the next outing.

MAKE IT LAST

PREVENT MESS WITH MESH. Sweaters, lingerie, other delicate clothing, and long items can take a lot of beating and stretching from a washing machine's agitator. The simple way to protect such items: Pop them into a mesh bag and then wash as usual. Mesh laundry bags are available at fabric and discount stores.

SIZE UP VINTAGE CLOTHING. Whether it's a 1960s psychedelic shirt or a flapper dress from the 1920s, always try on a piece of vintage clothing if you expect it to fit for even one wearing. Old clothes frequently have no label, and due to improved nutrition (among other factors), women have grown bigger and taller, and old sizes no longer correspond to our modern notions.

HEMS

Drop the droops! Help your hem stay put with a catchy sewing stitch, and see that no one sees it with a tool you borrow from a grade-schooler.

MAKE IT LAST

SEW STOP-AND-GO HEMS. No amount of rigging will keep hand-stitched hems from occasionally breaking or working loose, but you can stop one little tear from destroying the entire hem on a skirt or

Keep Buttons Hanging by a Thread

When there's no time to sew, but you can see a button's getting ready to work its way loose, dig through your makeup drawer and come up with some clear fingernail polish. A couple of dots on the thread right in the center of the button should delay the button from popping off until you can sew it on more firmly. It will even last through one wash in warm water.

shirt. It just takes a few extra minutes when you're stitching to tie off the thread every 5 inches or so, instead of waiting until the hem is complete or a longer length of thread gives out. That way one loose or broken stitch only takes a few others with it, and you'll never have to resew the whole hem.

ADD SOME ART. Don't give up your floodies just yet. If the hem of your pants is a little too short from repeated washings or a slightly expanding waistline, or from being paired with higher heels, just turn to your creative side. Add a coordinating edging (made from lace, patterned bias tape, or fabric) to lengthen the pants legs, or add one of the special beaded or balled upholstery trims made for pillows and furniture to make your too-short pants into one-of-a-kind wearable art.

FIX IT FAST

CRAYOLA COVER-UP. People can get very attached to their favorite blue jeans, so it pays to be able to let hems out if a child gets taller or you want blue jean shorts to become a little longer. Problem is, the crease from the previous hem tends to show up as an obvious white line in the lengthened clothing. Iron out the problem with the help of a blue crayon. Literally color over the hemline until it's the same color as the rest of the material, then iron the color into the jeans by pressing them, wrong-side out, on an ironing board protected with newspaper. If you wash in cold water, the wax cover-up should survive seven or eight trips to the laundry.

NECKTIES

The guy may resist wearing the tie, but it will still look great for decades with tying tactics and savvy storage. As for retired ties, make them take a seat.

MAKE IT LAST

TAKE A DAY OF REST. While no one would ever object to your wearing a tie two days in a row on fashion grounds, the practice won't prolong its life. To keep the fabric in good shape, a tie needs at least a day left unknotted to return to its normal shape after each wearing.

5 Quick Costumes from the Bedroom

Most anything that can be recycled from the bedroom can be transformed into a last-minute getup for a costume party. Try a few of these on for size.

1. **Chew a Chiclet.** Cut a place for your head and armholes in a plain white pillowcase.
2. **Tacky tourist.** Wear that loud shirt in the back of the closet and array yourself with cameras, shades, maps sticking out of pockets, and a reluctance to speak anything but English!
3. **Show your Freudian slip.** Wear a full-length slip (over some other undergarments, please) and draw a beard and mustache on your face with eyebrow pencil, a lá Sigmund Freud.
4. **Ghostly glam.** Why not dress up the typical plain sheet ghost costume with a bit of makeup. Include the standard cut holes and slits for eyes and mouth—but add eye shadow and false lashes on the eyes, lipstick on the mouth, blush on the cheeks, and costume earrings or a necklace glued onto the appropriate ghostly spot—you get the idea!
5. **Static cling.** First, get dressed in all one color, like white or black. Then, use safety pins to attach socks, a pair of underwear, a dryer sheet, or a pair of panty hose. To cinch the outfit, tease your hair using hair spray to add some static-inspired volume, or if it's short, comb it straight up.

UNTIE THAT TIE. Once you've mastered the lost art of tying a necktie, put it in reverse to keep your tie in good shape. The healthiest way to remove a tie—for the tie—is to work backward through the tying steps. Pulling the smaller end through the knot is much quicker, but it might make the tie stretch out of shape.

ROLL AGAINST WRINKLES. There are so many "don'ts" surrounding  **FIX IT FAST** the care of wrinkled ties: Don't dry clean silk ties or they'll lose their luster. Don't wash a tie in water because it will shrink unevenly. Don't iron a tie or it may harden and get shiny. So what can you do if a tie gets mussed or wrinkled? First, try rolling it, beginning with the narrow end. Leave it like that for a couple of days and see whether the wrinkles go away.

If not, think steam. Close the door and hang the tie in the bathroom during a long, hot shower or hold the hanger over the steam from a boiling kettle for a few minutes.

TRY A TIE SEAT. When you've amassed dozens of ties over the years,  **PASS IT ALONG** use the ones that have outlived their purpose to give a new life—and a fresh look—to a ladder-back chair with a broken seat. You may like the technique so well that you'll start using it to replace seats on chairs that don't need fixing—or buy a bunch of thrift store ties to redo a whole set of chairs.

What you'll need:

- 10 to 14 men's ties, no knits, and preferably narrow styles
- staple gun
- tack hammer
- scissors
- decorative upholstery tacks

1. Remove all the woven fabric from the seat of the chair. Wipe it clean, sand, and then repaint or restain the chair, if desired.

2. Make a template for the tie seat by cutting a piece of poster board to the size of the seat.

3. Arrange the ties on the poster board by alternating wide and narrow ends for a tight weave. You can see how many you'll need and which ones look pleasing next to each other. Leave 4 inches of tie extending beyond each edge of the chair seat template.

4. Turn the chair over on a flat, sturdy work surface (a patio or kitchen floor, for example) covered in newspaper.

5 Tactics for Tie Storage

Whether you wear a tie every day or just need it for the occasional wedding or church service, you can extend its life by decades with proper care. Ties are cut on the fabric's bias, which gives them stretch for knotting, but it also makes them susceptible to lumps and bumps. Follow these *tie*dy storage techniques for long-lasting neckwear.

1. **No hanging.** Hang ties up on a tie rack that keeps them hanging vertically, rather than bunched at one end of a wire hanger.

2. **Knit, roll, and stow.** Knit ties may stretch if they're stored on a rack. Instead, roll your ties and put them in a dresser drawer.

3. **Don't light the way.** Store all ties, whether they're constructed of natural or synthetic fabrics, away from direct light to prevent fading.

4. **Cardboard care.** Flat storage is another safe way to give your ties a long life. Cut a piece of acid-free cardboard to fit inside your tie for flat storage. Or ask for the cardboard that the department store uses to keep ties neatly displayed.

5. **Traveling tie tactics.** To keep a tie in good shape inside a suitcase or carry-on bag, roll it up, narrow end first, and slip it into a sock or tie case.

5. Following the pattern you laid out on the poster board, use a staple gun to attach the ties, one at a time, to the underside of the seat frame, first working from left to right. Staple one end of a tie to the underside of one of the sides of the seat frame, and then draw the tie over the frame and across the seat. Pull it tight and loop it over the opposite side of the seat frame so you can staple the other end in place under the frame.

6. Continue until you have a row of attached ties that covers the seat frame from left to right. Tap in any staples that aren't secure with a hammer.

7. Weave a second group of ties through the first row from front to back, one at a time, working under and over. Leave 4 inches of tie dangling on either side.

8. Attach the front-to-back ties to the chair seat frame in the same manner used in Step 5.

9. When you've stapled all the woven ties into place, cut off any excess tie fabric, then fold under each cut edge and staple it in place on the wooden frame.

10. For added strength, push decorative upholstery tacks through the ties along the front and sides of the chair seat.

MISCELLANEOUS CLOTHING

Ward off closet clutter by creating new and better stuff with castoffs. Was that designer handbag once a leather jacket?

ADD SALT TO RESHAPE STRAW. That misshapen straw hat doesn't have to go out on the trash heap. Restore it as much as possible to its original shape with a good dose of salt water. If the ocean's not nearby, dissolve ½ cup of salt in a gallon of hot water, and then refrigerate the mixture until it's cold. Soak the hat (minus any decorations) in the water for a few hours or as long as it takes to get soft and pliable. Then, with the help of an overturned plastic bowl, clay pot, bowling ball, or whatever matches your head's shape, remold the hat and brim. When the hat dries completely, it should hold its shape for many months.

BAG AN OLD LEATHER JACKET If you really love that leather jacket but its wearing days are done, keep it around—but in a different, much more usable form—as a leather pocketbook. Plain is fine, of course, but if you have a creative bent, try your hand at decorating it with some acrylic paint. Here's the plan, which doesn't take a lot of skill, but does require a leather hole punch.

What you'll need:
- old leather jacket
- very sharp scissors
- leather glue
- acrylic paint
- craft paint brush
- leather hole punch set
- clear spray paint
- 3 yards leather lace

1. Cut two 8- by 8-inch leather squares from the jacket.
2. If you're using paint, coat both sides of the leather with a base coat of acrylic. Let it dry, and then use other colors of acrylic to paint a pattern.
3. Squeeze a bead of glue around three edges of the wrong side of one of the squares. The glue should be 1/4 inch from the edge. Press the two squares together, wrong sides facing.
4. Use a leather hole punch to make holes 1/2 inch apart along the left and right sides of the purse, about 1/2 inch in from the sides.
5. Spray clear varnish on both sides of the pouch.
6. Tie two knots 1/4 inch apart in one end of the leather lace. Spray some clear varnish on the knots to secure them.

7. Starting from the bottom on the right side, lace up the side with the leather lace. Tie a knot in the leather lace after the top hole on the right side.

8. To leave around 38 inches of leather lace free to serve as a strap, tie another knot 38 inches from the knot on the top of the right side.

9. Pull the free end of the leather lace all the way through the top hole of the left side of the bag, until the knot you tied earlier halts it.

10. Thread the remaining lace through the holes on the left side of the bag, continuing to work from the top down. At the bottom, tie two more knots in the lace about ¼ inch apart. Cut off the excess.

11. Spray clear varnish on all the knots in the lace to strengthen them. If you like, tie a knot in the top of the shoulder strap to make it stronger or shorter.

MORE TIPS FOR THE BEDROOM

Here's a roundup of the bedroom-related Pass It Along tips you'll find in the other chapters of *Don't Throw It Out!*

CHAPTER	TIP	PAGE
1	Transfer Trays to Another Room	7
7	Bust Dust with Dryer Sheets	216
7	Freshen Your Dresser	216
8	Serve up a Picture Frame	259
8	Slap Shot for Spiders	261
9	12 Ways to Reuse and Old Garden Hose	284

Domestic Challenge

Before you fall for an urban myth or unfounded rumor about reuse or donations, take this true–false test!

Questions

1. It's illegal to remove the tag from bed pillows, so you can't remove the stuffing and use it to make other pillows thicker.

2. Your dry cleaner would probably welcome your extra metal clothes hangers.

3. You can cut the elastic bottoms from old sweat pant legs and use them as hair scrunchies.

4. You can tell if it's time to re-purpose your bed pillows by having someone else tuck you in.

5. Hats for Hope will take donations of used baseball hats to pass along to cancer patients in treatment.

6. Nike accepts only its own brand for the Reuse-A-Shoe program that gathers, separates and grinds old athletic shoes into Nike Grind material to use in athletic surfaces and fields.

7. You can reuse a large purse as an unusual and artistic hanging plant holder.

8. You can cut up an old mattress pad to use as a pot holder or placemat.

9. Most modern-day sheets have been treated with chemicals that make them impossible to pleat or starch for use as curtains.

10. You should always tie a pair of shoes together before donating it to a thrift store or homeless shelter.

Answers

1. FALSE. The warning tag applies to retailers, not the pillow's owner, and re-using the stuffing is a great idea as long as you launder it first (inside a tied-shut pillowcase) if needed.

2. **TRUE.** Yes, they can reuse them if they're in very good condition. And if your cleaner doesn't want 'em, offer them to the local thrift store.

3. **TRUE.** Just make sure you cut above the seam that holds the elastic in place.

4. **TRUE.** A pillow should bring your head and neck into alignment, so lie on the bed in your typical sleep position and ask someone else to see if your spine is straight. If not, time for a new pillow! It's best to toss that flat pillow completely rather than trying to reuse it.

5. **FALSE.** This worthy organization accepts cash donations only and provides brand-new hats, but the local thrift store, particularly at Halloween, pre-school or drama club usually welcomes extra hats.

6. **FALSE.** Any brand athletic shoe is fair game and the playgrounds, called NikeGO Places, help kids get exercise and have fun.

7. **TRUE.** Plastic and vinyl purses are ideal plant holders; just make sure you line the inside with a cut-down heavy plastic garbage bag, though, and instead of planting directly use the purse to hold an ordinary pot and saucer.

8. **FALSE.** The pad will unravel after just a couple of uses and it's not all that attractive, so it's best to keep a used mattress pad away from food prep. It would work great as a packing blanket if you move though.

9. **FALSE.** Sheets are just good old-fashioned cotton and can be recycled into curtains. But if they're worn and soft, they'll probably work better as an unstructured swag, or if you line the curtains (with more sheets!)

10. **TRUE.** This is a great way to keep the pair together. Shoes for donation should be in excellent or good condition with little or no noticeable wear. It would be extra generous if you replaced the laces so everything looked as new as possible. When shoes don't have laces, slap a masking tape label on each shoe with its size, description and "right" or "left."

4
THE REC ROOM

Relaxing is serious business. There's precious little time left after family, work, and the rest of life's responsibilities to spend it looking for a lost knitting needle or running to the store for a container to hold your beading supplies. And it shouldn't take building an extension on the rec room (or cost as much) to keep it all corralled.

And it won't—after you read our ingenious ways to keep your home hobby center organized, functional, and well . . . more relaxing. We start by offering advice that will help you maintain your hobby supplies (and the fruits of your labors). Next, we'll help you solve some common crafting problems. You wouldn't believe how many inexpensive alternatives there are, using items that you probably already have sitting around, to costly craft store items.

And of course, when it is time to pass on a treasured heirloom like your old bowling ball bag, or even one you wouldn't dream of giving away like your Grandmother's own scrapbook, we'll show you the way.

With these tips up your sleeve, you may actually find a little more time for your hobbies.

KNITTING AND CROCHETING

Suddenly, everyone is knitting or crocheting—these are the hottest new pastimes. Of course, our experts didn't just hop onto the bandwagon. Their time-tested advice will see you through any project, from making sure your creations enjoy a long life to helping you pass on the leftover bits and pieces you no longer want.

MAKE IT LAST

INCLUDE INSTRUCTIONS. When you've taken the time to knit or crochet a gift for a friend or family member, you want that item to last for as long as possible. Before you hand it over, be sure to include the care instructions from the skein of yarn you're using (usually printed on the inside of the label). That way, the gift's new owner will know exactly how to clean it, and the sweater, scarf, hat, or blanket will last and last and last.

CRAFT HOLES THAT HOLD. Making buttonholes that hold can be quite tricky when you're knitting or crocheting a garment. Experienced fiber artists know that making horizontal (rather than vertical) buttonholes not only hold buttons more securely, but are far less likely to cause gaps in a garment.

FIX IT FAST

BURN YOUR YARN. Have you come into possession of some yarn but aren't sure whether it's made from a natural or a synthetic fiber? Here's a sure-fire way to find out: Snip a small piece of the yarn and use a match to burn one end. Let it burn for a second or two, and then blow out the flame. After it cools, feel the burnt tip. If it feels hard, like melted plastic, then it's synthetic. If, on the other hand, it simply crumbles or crushes easily between your fingers (like ash), it's cotton, wool, or another natural fiber.

STOP THE STICK. Under certain conditions, metal or wooden knitting needles can become sticky. Maybe your hands are dry, perhaps the needles are new or just dirty. To eliminate the stickiness, rub the needles with just a little Butcher's wax (available at hardware stores) or waxed paper, and then buff well. The needles will be as smooth as silk.

KEEP TRACK OF MATES. Keeping your knitting needles organized in a clean oatmeal carton or a box from a bottle of liquor is a terrific idea, but if you have a lot of needles, pairs easily become separated, and that's inconvenient. To keep needles together, wrap a twist-tie around each set, near the top of the needles. Then, when you need a pair of needles, you'll be able to quickly grab the ones you want.

MARK THE MEASUREMENTS. Knitting a pattern almost always requires some amount of measuring. Now, you could keep a ruler or measuring tape with you, but if you want to reduce the number of items in your work space, simply turn your needles into rulers: Use two colors of permanent markers to mark inch and half-inch increments on your knitting needles, for instance using black for inches and green for half-inches. You'll have a ruler on hand at all times. Of course, this tip works best on light-colored needles.

SAVE SCRAPS. Most knitters and crocheters tend to hoard yarn scraps, but after they sit around for a while, some of us get fed up and toss them out. Don't. Next time you're pressed for an idea about how to use those bits of leftover yarn, check this list for inspiration.

PASS IT ALONG

- **Add edging.** Use yarn scraps to give your next project a colorful embellishment: the turtleneck and/or cuffs of a sweater, the cuffs of mittens or gloves, the fingers of gloves, the edge of a blanket or afghan.
- **Hold on!** Use a crocheted strand of yarn as a handle for a small knitted or crocheted coin purse.
- **See stripes.** You don't need much yarn to add a colorful stripe or two to almost any project.
- **Get fringe benefits.** Use leftover yarn to make pom-poms, tassels, or fringe for use on scarves or ponchos.

GIVE A PUPPET SOME HAIR. You may have neither the space nor the desire to store leftover yarn, but that certainly doesn't mean it belongs in the trash. Check with local schools, libraries, day care

Advice from the Pros

The International Quilt Study Center at the University of Nebraska–Lincoln is dedicated to researching the ways in which quilts—yes, quilts—reflect many complex factors about a society, including its attitudes about class, gender, and politics. In addition to studying old quilts, the Center is often consulted about quilt care, maintenance, and storage. Here is some of the staff's general advice about measures you can take when storing a quilt, whether newly made or a family heirloom, to ensure it has the longest life possible.

- **Mind the climate.** Store quilts and other valuable textiles in a room that has a steady temperature of 65° to 70°F and a level of humidity that ranges between 40 to 50 percent. These conditions prevent the quilt's fibers from drying out because of excessive dryness, and the growth of mildew from too much moisture.

- **Avoid the light.** Both natural light and artificial light cause the colors in a quilt (and any other fabric) to fade.

- **Clean carefully.** If a quilt is very old, very delicate, or very valuable, consult a fabric conservator before attempting to clean it. (You can find a fabric conservator by calling a local art museum.) Otherwise, vacuuming may be the safest cleaning method. Use a vacuum with a weak suction to remove dust and discourage insects and mold.

- **Store it right.** Ideally, quilts should be stored flat, with nothing on top—not even other quilts. Since that's rarely possible, the Center stores most of its quilts in archival boxes. The quilts are first folded, with sheets of acid-free tissue between the layers. You can find these materials by looking online using the search term "archival storage." If you choose this storage method, be sure to refold the quilt once in a while so that the same fibers aren't always subjected to the tension of folding.

For more about The International Quilt Study Center—and more quilt care tips—log onto www.quiltstudy.org.

centers, and day camps, any of which may be willing (and grateful) to take the yarn off your hands for crafts projects.

SUPPLY SWAPPING SOIREE. Next time you find yourself with a bumper crop of leftover yarns—or fabric, or any other crafts supply, for that matter—organize a swapping party with friends or family who enjoy the same hobbies. Ask everyone who plans to attend to bring their leftovers (neatly packaged and labeled, please) to the get-together, and then invite your guests to browse what others brought and take what they want. At the end of the swap, you'll end up with a whole new batch of crafting goodies.

FEATHER A NEST. If you're a bird lover, consider giving your leftover yarn scraps to the local birds as a sort of housewarming gift. Cut all of the yarn into 3- to 4-inch pieces, stuff it into a mesh bag (like the kind that onions come in), and then just hang it from a tree or bush in a protected area.

QUILTING

Quilting may not have originated in the United States, but the art form does seem to have a distinctly American quality about it—as does good old Yankee ingenuity. You'll find plenty of *that* evident in the following tips.

HANG IT UP. If you're like many quilters, purchasing fabric is something of a happy addiction, which means you have lots and lots of it to store and keep track of. Keeping it all organized neatly and conveniently is a snap, if you have some spare trouser or skirt hangers around. Use the hangers to organize fabrics by color and/or pattern (or whatever works for you). Hanging the fabrics allows you to easily see what you have—no more pulling cloth out of drawers. To make the system work even better, record how much yardage you have of each kind of fabric on a small piece of paper and use a pin to attach it to the where it will be visible.

BAG IT. Constructing a quilt often involves cutting and organizing hundreds of pieces of fabric and keeping the pieced blocks (or other shapes) organized while you're assembling the quilt top. The best way to keep all of those fabric pieces neat, clean, separated, and organized is with ziplock plastic bags. The smallest snack-sized bags can be pressed into service to hold cut shapes; the largest bags (usually 2-gallon) keep pieced blocks together and protected.

ALTERNA-TEMPLATES. In the old days, quilters used cardboard to make their templates. The downside of this method was that cardboard wasn't very sturdy and had to be replaced after just a few uses. We've come a long way since then, and today's quilters can purchase rolls or sheets of template plastic that come complete with grid lines. Those templates are very useful, but they can get pricey. Here are some far less expensive options to consider.

SIMPLE SOLUTIONS

The Online Swap Meet

You have a big box of supplies leftover from your crafting adventures: half skeins of yarn, small bags of glitter and sequins, some felt, and a stack of foam core. You can't find anyone nearby to take it off your hands, but you can't bear to throw it away, either.

We have the perfect solution for you: It's called Swap-Bot, a Web site that allows members to swap nearly anything—including bits of crafts supplies—with other members all across the country (and all over the world). Signing up is free, just log on to www.swap-bot.com to get started.

- **Check the fridge.** When you've finished with a tub of margarine, a can of coffee, or a large tub of yogurt or ricotta cheese, go ahead and recycle the container, but hang on to the plastic lid and use it to make sturdy templates.
- **Get to the heart of the mat-ter.** Next time you're out cruising yard sales, keep an eye out for plastic placemats. Take them home, clean them up, and—*voilà!*—sturdy plastic template material.

BE A BIT ABRASIVE. When you're tracing shapes for quilting, it's important that both the fabric and the pattern template remain firmly in place. And it can get tricky to keep everything from moving around, especially if you use slippery plastic templates.

Fortunately, there's a very simple way to make sure everything stays where it should. Head to your local hardware store and purchase some adhesive-backed, fine grit sandpaper. Start by cutting small pieces from the sandpaper, then remove the backing and place a piece or two on the backside of each of your templates. The sandpaper won't harm the fabric as long as you press gently, and it prevents the plastic shape from sliding as you trace around it.

TAPE MARKS THE SPOT. Do you sometimes have trouble finding where you left off quilting when you return to a large project? That is a frustratingly common problem—especially if you're working on a large quilt. You can eliminate that issue with this quick and easy solution: Just place a small piece of blue painter's masking tape where you've ended each time you wrap up a quilting session, and you'll know exactly where to start next time. Blue painter's masking tape is available anywhere house paints are sold.

BANISH BLOOD FROM A QUILT. It's almost inevitable for hand-quilters. You prick your finger with a needle and next thing you know, a drop or two of blood drips onto the quilt. To prevent a permanent stain, you need to act quickly: Gently dab the stain with a little of your own saliva and then dab again with a dry paper towel, but don't rub. Saliva works because the enzymes in it actually "digest" the protein in the blood. Repeat as necessary.

If the stain is stubborn, treat it with a little 3 percent hydrogen peroxide (available from the first-aid section of any drugstore), but be sure to test it on an inconspicuous spot first to make sure it doesn't affect the color.

SEND FABRIC TO CHURCH. If you find yourself with excess fabric that you know you won't use, consider donating it to a local church. Many have organized quilting bees, in which members come together to make quilts for charity. Those groups often accept donations and other quilting supplies.

PASS IT ALONG

COME ON, GET SCRAPPY. If you're considering getting rid of bits and pieces of fabric because you don't have enough of any one style or color to make a highly designed quilt, consider making a scrap quilt. Scrap quilts are just what they sound like: A quilt constructed of left-over fabric scraps.

And if you're not happy with the outcome, someone else surely will be. Check with local churches, many of which may accept a donation of a completed blanket or quilt.

DONATE A COMPLETED QUILT. So many charitable organizations—in your own neighborhood and across the country—gratefully accept donations of completed quilts (or other blankets). Check with the following two organizations, both of which accept quilt (and other blanket) donations for various causes. Please check each organization's Web site for specifics.

- **Binky Patrol** (www.binkypatrol.org) accepts donations of blankets for "children and teens in need of comfort."
- **Project Linus** (www.projectlinus.org) seeks to "provide a sense of security, warmth and comfort to children who are seriously ill, traumatized, or otherwise in need through the gifts of new, handmade blankets and afghans, lovingly created by volunteer 'blanketeers.'"

SCRAPBOOKING

These days it seems like everyone is into scrapbooking—and for good reason. After all, who doesn't enjoy taking a stroll down memory lane once in a while. The following tips will help you put together a scrapbook that will last generations, help you solve some common dilemmas, and provide ideas about how to reuse and recycle some of your scrapbooking leftovers.

SAVE THOSE SHARPIES! Buying lots of markers and pens in beautiful colors is a waste if they just dry out before you get a chance to use them to decorate your scrapbook. To give them a much longer life,

MAKE IT LAST

store them flat in a bin rather than standing up on either end. Stored flat, the ink in the pens will stay fluid for a lot longer.

BACK UP YOUR SCRAPBOOK. This tip may seem like an extreme measure, but if your scrapbook features one-of-a-kind items, it may be a good idea. As you complete each page, take it to the local office supply store and make a color copy. Place all the color copies in a separate binder. Then you can choose whether to store the original or the copy someplace safe (a fireproof storage box, for instance, or even off-site). That way, you'll always have at least one copy of your precious memento book.

FIX IT FAST

GIVE FIRST-AID TO AN OLD SCRAPBOOK. Scrapbooking was a popular pastime long before archival methods were invented. If you come across an old memento book while looking through the attic, take care. It may be very delicate, requiring a bit of maintenance before it can be enjoyed. Here are some ways to protect and preserve those memories.

- **Give it a new home.** If the binding or cover of the book, or both, are so tattered that they're not worth saving, your best bet is to move all the items to a brand-new, archival scrapbook, available at larger crafts stores such as Michaels.
- **Cut 'em loose.** If you don't feel comfortable removing items from the scrapbook's pages, remove the pages completely with a razor and transfer them to archival sleeves.
- **Or scan 'em.** You can also salvage pages by scanning and printing them. Then you can display the full-color print of each page instead of the delicate original.
- **Show the photos.** Take photographs of very fragile items and place those in the scrapbook. Transfer the delicate mementos to archival storage boxes.
- **Keep it in the dark.** If you decide to keep the old scrapbook as is, transfer it to an acid-free conservation slipcase. Store it flat and out of direct sunlight.

SHARPEN YOUR TOOLS. Over time, the paper punches, pinking shears, and shaped scissors you use for your scrapbooking (and other) projects will become dull. Luckily, clever crafters have come up with an ingenious solution. Grab some aluminum foil from the kitchen and fold it in half once or twice. Punch or cut through the foil a few times, and your tool will sharpen right up. Test it on some paper or light card stock and repeat if necessary. Do not use this sharpening technique on fabric shears—always have those professionally sharpened.

STOP THE STICK. Oftentimes a new hole punch sticks because the joints are tight. Although they generally loosen over time, there is a way to loosen them lickity-split: Just punch through a sheet of waxed paper a few times—the wax lubricates and loosens the punch so it'll be easy to use right out of the package.

STOW YOUR SCISSORS. If you have more than one or two pairs of scissors, keeping them organized can be a challenge. Here's how to keep them corralled: Find or purchase a hatbox, one with tall sides if you have scissors with long blades. Next, start saving the empty tubes from paper towels. Place tubes, on end, in the hatbox (trim them if necessary), using enough tubes to fill the box. Slip your scissors, pointed end down, in the tubes. If you do trim the tubes, leave them long enough so that the scissor ends do not touch the bottom of the box. This technique works best when there are enough tubes to fill the box. Otherwise, they'll topple. So if you don't have enough pairs of scissors, just select a smaller box.

FRAME IT! When you use a die cutter to make shapes for your scrapbook, you're left with the "negative"—the sheet of paper, felt, thin metal, and the like, out of which you've cut the shape. Sure, you can use that scrap to make "punchies," but why not try putting those pieces to work as picture mats for your scrapbook? To do this, cut around the cut-out shape to make the frame into a shape you're happy with. Next, place the image you've selected on the paper you're using. Finally, position your new picture mat so that the image peeks through the cut-out frame.

PASS IT ALONG

HOME-GROWN HISTORY. Do you have a scrapbook that belonged to Grandma, one that you like to pull out during the holidays to share with family and friends? Why not share it with an even larger audience the rest of the year?

You see, that old scrapbook is more than just a personal history; it's a mirror that reflects what the rest of the world was like at the time the book was created. Contact your local library or historical society. Staffers are often interested in personal historic memorabilia to include in exhibitions, and may jump at the chance to display your scrapbook, on temporary loan, of course.

GENERAL CRAFTING

Wrestling with an unorganized crafting space? Trying to get oil paint off your hands? Sorting through leftover supplies? Just refer to the following tips for instruction and inspiration.

FIX IT FAST

TAKE INVENTORY. If your crafts room or closet is an unorganized mess, you have a twofold problem: (1) You'll likely end up buying supplies you don't need because you don't know what you have; and (2) crafting will simply stop being enjoyable—who wants to have to wade through piles of stuff just to have a little fun? But the first step to getting organized is not spending money on fancy organizing accessories. Start by making a list of what you have on hand and where it's stored. You may be surprised (and inspired) by what you already have. Before you start a new project, check your inventory. And when you do purchase new supplies, be sure to add them to the list. This inventory will keep you from wasting money and help you begin to get organized.

CRAFTS STORAGE IS A SHOE-IN. If you like to have all your crafting tools visible and at hand rather than organized (and hidden) in drawers, a clear vinyl shoe bag just might be the answer. Hung on a wall, a shoe bag—which usually keeps 10 to 12 pairs of shoes organized—can hold your scissors, glues, glue gun, brushes, markers, and the like. Not only is everything neat and tidy, it's in full view.

HOPE FOR SNIFFLES. Is trying to keep your craft supplies neat and organized driving you nuts? Don't flip your wig. Start saving tissue boxes. Cut off the tops and use the bottoms to sort and contain supplies ranging from needles and hooks to bits of fabric and yarn.

USE THE PILLBOX SOLUTION. One of the pesky issues home jewelry makers have to contend with are all the tiny items to keep track of: beads, loops, clips, clamps, and clasps, to name but a few. Of course, there are lots of specialty containers available at beading and crafts stores, but those can be *very* pricey.

Some folks like to use ice cube trays to keep it all organized, and that works fine, as long as the trays don't get knocked around; otherwise, pieces go everywhere. A better, and more economical option is large pill organizers—the type with lids that snap closed. The lids keep tiny bits from spilling should the container be knocked over.

MAT, HEAL THYSELF. What did crafters do before the invention of the self-healing cutting mat? Unfortunately, these mats are prone to warping, but there is a quick and easy fix. Fill the kitchen sink or bathtub with enough hot water to cover the mat and then set it in the water. Once the mat is pliable, remove it from the water and use paper towels to dry it thoroughly. Next, place the mat on a table or desk, cover with more dry paper towels, and then put a cookie sheet on top. Lay some heavy books on the cookie sheet, leave the whole thing overnight, and in the morning, the cutting mat will be as good as new.

OIL ON, PAINT OFF. You've just completed your paint-by-numbers masterpiece, but now you have oil paint on your hands. Don't cancel the opening! Instead, reach for the baby oil and rub it on your hands vigorously. The paint will come right off.

If you don't have baby oil on hand, no problem—mayonnaise will do the trick, too!

SIMPLE SOLUTIONS

No Scissors? No Problem!

I really enjoy doing needlepoint. My great aunt taught me when I was a kid, and now I like to carry a project with me almost everywhere I go—including during my subway commute to work. It really helps the time pass more quickly.

These days, I don't feel comfortable taking scissors on the New York City subway, which made working on a project kind of tricky. I was lamenting this fact to my boyfriend John one day. The next day, he surprised me with a really clever solution. He wrapped some of my crewel yarn around the spool of an empty Glide brand dental floss cylinder and pulled the end up through the hole the floss usually comes out of. The small razor on the floss lid works like a charm to snip the yarn!

—Myrsini Stephanides
Astoria, New York

ORCHESTRATE A SOLUTION. When you're trying to follow a pattern or directions of any sort while you're knitting, crocheting, doing needlepoint or anything else, it's incredibly frustrating to have the book close or flip to the wrong page. And it's a literal pain in the neck to read directions on a pattern that's laid flat on a table. Is there a solution? Yes, indeed—we have two:

- **A note-able idea.** Is there a musician in the family? A music stand will hold a book or loose pattern open and at a comfortable angle while you work.
- **Raid the kitchen.** Do you have a cookbook holder—the kind designed to keep a cookbook open to the correct page while you cook? Then you have a pattern holder.

PASS IT ALONG

DON'T SCRAP THE SCRAPS. Small leftover felt or woolen scraps almost never belong in the trash. Here are five ways to put them to use around the house.

1. **Give it an inside job.** Trim the felt to fit inside small lidded containers and use the containers to store jewelry.
2. **Stop scratches.** Glue the felt (cut to fit) onto the bottom of knickknacks, lamps, and vases to protect shelves and furniture.
3. **Decorate a card.** Cut small shapes from the felt and use the pieces to decorate homemade greeting cards.
4. **Give it to the kids.** Save your assorted scrap stash for a crafting session at a children's party.
5. **Decorate!** Create flowers or other designs from various pieces of felt, finish the edges with a blanket stitch to prevent raveling, and then

---

Raid the Toy Chest

Long after the kids have grown up and gone, the toys often linger on. If you find yourself tempted to throw away boxes of small toys and doodads—stray game pieces, doll house accessories, gumball machine trinkets, plastic beads, jacks, and the like—pause and think before you toss. Those assorted bits and pieces can be put to great use in the creation of a crafty gift for a child. All you need are an inexpensive picture frame, acrylic paint in a color—or numerous colors if you're feeling particularly inspired—of your choice, enough toys to completely cover the frame, and a glue gun.

1. Paint the frame; let dry.
2. On a sheet of paper the same size as your frame, arrange the toys and other bobbles in a pattern that you like.
3. Using the glue gun, attach the toys to the frame using your pattern as a guide. Leave the frame flat until it is completely dry.

use a glue gun to attach the shapes to throw pillows, a tote bag, or a plain lamp shade for a quick and easy spruce up.

TIE A YELLOW (OR RED, OR BLUE) RIBBON. Leftover ribbon has so many uses, you may find yourself actually collecting scraps!

- **Watch it!** Leftover scraps of heavy, ribbed ribbon (such as grosgrain) make cheery watch bands.
- **Add some trim.** Use fusible web to attach leftover ribbon to the bottom edge of a skirt, the sleeves of a shirt or blouse, or to a fabric tote bag as an embellishment.
- **Add class to a vase.** A plain glass vase can be transformed with a little scrap ribbon. Wrap ribbon around the top and bottom of the vase and secure it with a little white glue.

GIVE THEM A HEADS UP. Even though they usually wear heavy gloves, the indispensable folks who deal with our trash can always use a little extra protection. So do those pickup people a favor by labeling any potentially dangerous broken stuff as such. After you carefully bag the shards of any broken porcelain or glass collectible, write "glass" or "sharp" in red or black magic marker on a piece of masking tape, and tape it across the bag.

BOOKS

Lend your library a longer life—it could be as simple as restacking or debugging. Then borrow some of these clever ideas for making old books into new treasures.

GO BACK TO STACKS. Although it might seem like the height of sloppiness, stacking leather-bound or vintage hardback books on their sides is actually a smart move. When you store them on edge, the weight of the book can damage the binding.

MAKE IT LAST

SPINE-SAVING SOLUTIONS. Vintage books have vintage glue in their bindings that will crack and maybe even free a section of pages if you continually open the book to a flat position. (Hear that spine pop?). If you intend to actually read your antiques, make sure you do so with two small pillows or clean foam wedges at the ready. Place one on either side of the open book and it will stay open—but not all the way, which will make the binding last a nice, long time.

BAG BOOK BUGS. Roaches simply adore the glue in book bindings, while silverfish are attracted to natural fibers and starchy materials. To keep a valuable leather-bound book from being consumed by bugs, wrap it in an acid-free paper book jacket (available at most stationery stores and online). Then slip it inside a gallon-size plastic ziplock bag for protection. But don't zip that zipper! Leave the bag open so the air will circulate and you won't trap book-damaging moisture inside.

FIX IT FAST

SHOO THE SILVERFISH. If the bugs have already started chewing on an antique leather-bound book you'd like to keep in good shape, meet them with mothballs. To start, put the book in a ziplock plastic bag and set a few mothballs inside, too, placing them near the opening without letting them touch the book since they'll stain the leather. Lay the book in the bag in a cool, dry place, and keep it sealed for a week. When you open up and carefully remove first mothballs, then book, the bugs should all be dead.

PASS IT ALONG

CLOSE THE BOOK ON SAFETY. If a favorite hardback has irreparably gummed pages or a not-so-favorite one isn't in good enough shape to donate to the library, think about the bank . . . making a bank from the book, that is. A hard-bound book "safe" can rest right in the bookshelf without encouraging any curiosity, and it's a great place to store sentimental, as well as valuable, keepsakes. These are the basic steps for creating the safe, which you can decorate however you want or leave plain.

What you'll need:
- 1 hardcover book, at least 2 inches deep, jacket removed (if there is one)
- ruler
- pencil
- craft knife
- 8½- by 11-inch piece of felt, for lining
- glue gun and glue sticks
- scrap cardboard

1. With the book closed, measure and mark a spot on the side of the pages 1 inch up from the back cover.
2. Open the book at that spot, placing another book or a paperweight over the left side to keep the book open flat while you work.

3. Make a pattern to cut the "secret compartment" from the pages by measuring and marking a rectangle that's 2 inches inside the perimeter of the right-hand page.

4. Using the ruler as a straight edge, cut the rectangles from the marked page and those below it with the craft knife, cutting through 10 pages at a time. Remove the paper cutouts and discard. Trace the inside of the rectangle with a pencil to make the same template on the first uncut page and then repeat the cuts on that page and the nine below it.

5. Continue repeating this process until you reach the back cover of the book. When you come to the last 10 to 20 pages, insert a piece of cardboard over the back cover to protect it from the knife's blade.

6. Measure, mark, and cut pieces of felt the same size as the bottom and sides of the rectangular secret compartment.

7. Line the insides of the secret compartment with the felt, using the glue gun to apply enough glue for the felt to hold the pages in place from the inside, while from the outside, the pages look like those of an ordinary book.

8. Attach the pages of the "secret compartment" block to the back cover, using a bit more glue between the cover and the last page.

9. Let the glue dry completely. Your book safe is now ready, with the first few chapters containing pages that flip freely and the remainder staying immobile and housing a secure spot for valuables.

COLLECTIBLES

Whether you like to collect plates, figurines, or bobble head dolls, you'll find plenty of good advice below to help you care for and fully enjoy all your goodies.

MAKE IT LAST

JUST IN CASE. To prevent your precious collectibles from being knocked over by cats, dogs, children, or visitors, keep them in closed cabinets or high off the ground. And make sure the display case is well secured to the wall behind it—this will ensure that the whole cabinet won't be accidentally overturned.

IT IS THE HEAT . . . Keep collectibles away from sources of heat, including fireplaces, radiators, floor heaters, stoves, and even high-wattage light bulbs. Heat can cause finishes on ceramic to discolor.

. . . AND THE HUMIDITY. Choose a display area for your collectibles that is well away from water sources such as water pipes, fish tanks, and sinks. If the collectibles are particularly valuable, you may want to invest in a dehumidifier for the room they're in.

IT'S IN THE LIPS. To prevent collectible plates from sliding forward and off a display shelf, install a lip at the front of the shelf. A strip of molding or a dowel from the lumberyard or hardware store glued to the front edge of the shelf, and then stained or painted to match, will provide some unobtrusive security.

FIX IT FAST

WORK WITH THE BEST. If the worst happens and you decide to take your piece to a restorer, be sure he or she is a member of the American Institute of Conservators (AIC). Members follow specific professional protocols about performing repairs that can be 'undone' if necessary and about causing minimal damage to the item, both of which are vital to protecting the value of your collectible.

Avoid a Breakup

Larry Vescera has repaired more than a shattered dream or two in his day. He's a restoration specialist who works at Pick Up the Pieces in Costa Mesa, California, one of the country's oldest and largest art restoration companies. The experts at Pick Up the Pieces have worked with countless piles of broken porcelain and restored them into the treasured collectibles they once were.

According to Vescera, many people are unsure of what to do with damaged collectibles, and in some cases have even thrown away expensive porcelain figurines that have suffered damage. "They simply don't know about the new technologies that exist which allow almost every type of material to be restored. No matter what the material, or the extent of the damage, it can almost always be restored to its original condition," he says. But as we all know, an ounce of prevention is worth a gallon of superglue.

Vescera encourages collectors to become experts in the proper care and maintenance of their pieces. "About 35 percent of items brought in for repair were damaged during cleaning," he says, offering these tips on how to properly clean collectibles to avoid damaging or breaking them.

- **Do it yourself.** Do not allow anyone other than yourself to dust or clean your collectibles. That means you'll need to find something a little less delicate for junior to do to earn his allowance.
- **Porcelain pieces prefer alcohol.** The most efficient and effective way to clean your porcelain collectibles is to spray them using a solution made of equal parts rubbing alcohol and water. Then hold the piece upside down over a sink or bucket until it stops dripping. A hair dryer set on low and cool can also be an effective way to blow dust off delicate pieces, but don't forget to hold on while you blow.
- **Skip the vacuum.** Never, ever, vacuum porcelain collectibles. You could accidentally remove a small part.
- **Use a mini DustBuster.** To dust delicate pieces, wipe with a small, soft cloth wrapped around one finger. And do not use a paper towel, which can scratch the finish.
- **Make sure the soap is soft.** If you absolutely must wash a collectible plate or figurine, always use warm water and a mild soap. As you wash, make sure to rinse off the soap thoroughly to prevent the buildup of a dull film on your pieces.

MAKE MEMORIES OF MEALS PAST. Breaking an heirloom plate can be kind of like losing an old friend. But it doesn't have to be the end of the relationship. If you are into crafting or know someone who is, your loss can turn into a gain. That's because shards of broken porcelain can be used to create beautiful mosaics. If you don't have a crafty pal, check with a local school to see whether the art classes might be interested in taking the shards off your hands.

PASS IT ALONG

BOWLING

You don't have to be a professional bowler to want to get the most out of the sport. Of course we offer tips to help you care for your shoes and ball, but we'll even tell you how your old bowling balls can keep zoo animals entertained!

A CLEAN BALL ROLLS TRUE. Clean your bowling ball after every session to remove excess oil and grit picked up from the lanes. Rub the ball with a dry washcloth and Windex, 3M Finesse-It II (available at auto-body shops), or specialized ball cleaner. Some cleaning substances, including denatured alcohol, gasoline, acetone, and other solvents, are banned in competitive bowling because they may soften the ball and help it track better as it rolls down the lane. Not sure what's legal? Inquire at your local lanes before experimenting.

BUFF YOUR WAY TO A SCRATCH-FREE BALL. To restore a scratched bowling ball to its original finish and performance, wet-sand the ball with 220 or 320 grit wet/dry sandpaper and then again with 400 or 600 grit wet/dry paper. Finally, polish the ball with 3M Finesse-It II (available at auto-body shops).

KEEP THE BALL LOOKING STRIKING. A scratch on the surface of a bowling ball isn't just unsightly, it can sabotage your score by causing the ball to roll unpredictably. Scratches that are not too deep can be sanded out with extra fine grit (400 grit or finer) wet or dry sandpaper. Finish the repair by polishing the ball with buffing compound (available from auto parts stores).

SPARE THE BALL BAG. So, you no longer bowl; that's no reason to toss out that bowling bag. An old bowling ball bag makes a good carrying case for lawn bowls, horseshoes, or a bocce ball set. The bags

One Man's Trash
Bowling for . . . Bears?

Bowling balls are constructed of plastic, resins, rubber, or urethane, or a combination of those materials, which means they are not biodegradable. So what can an environmentally conscious consumer do with used bowling balls? Here's a solution that's eco-friendly—and animal-friendly, too.

If you're the Family Sports Center in Asheboro, North Carolina, you donate 155 of them to the North Carolina Zoological Society—and not because the zoo opened a bowling alley.

Animals, including black and grizzly bears, cheetahs, lions, rhinos, and some primates, love to play with bowling balls. Play enriches their lives; that in turn, encourages more natural behavior. Add to the mix that the zoos receive the balls at no cost, and it becomes a win–win situation for everyone involved.

Many zoos around the country incorporate bowling balls (and other donated items) in their "behavioral enrichment" programs. If you're interested in donating an old ball, contact a local zoo for more information.

are usually made of durable material and are designed to tote around heavy-ish sporting goods.

MUSICAL INSTRUMENTS

Heed the sage advice in the following tips and you'll get the most out of your musical instruments.

KEEP GUITARS MOISTURIZED. An acoustic guitar (and, in fact, any fretted instrument) can represent a hefty investment, so it's important to store it correctly. That includes controlling the humidity in the room where you keep it. If the humidity dips below 45 percent—as it often does during the autumn and winter in four-season parts of the country—the guitar's wood can dry and split or crack. Invest in a humidifier to prevent this. One popular model, called a Dampit or green snake, is an 8-inch flexible rubber tube. The tube has small holes on its sides and contains a sponge. Just soak the snake in water, wring it out, and wipe it off—there should be no water dripping from it. Then place one end of the snake in the sound hole of the instrument. The sponge slowly releases moisture into the hollow of the instrument, maintaining the humidity inside the piece and keeping it from cracking. Dampits, which cost around $15 and are available from music stores, are made for guitars, upright basses, cellos, violas, and violins.

MAKE IT LAST

BUST THE DUST. Have dust bunnies invaded your guitar? If you see them floating around inside the body of the instrument, grab the vacuum cleaner and, using the smallest tool on it, get rid of that dust. It can trap moisture and cause the growth of mildew.

STOP A CLOG. Ploink! Have you broken a steel string on your guitar? Don't sing a sad song—instead, set that broken string aside. The next time there's a clog in your kitchen or bathroom sink, use it as a mini snake to clear the clog away.

PASS IT ALONG

SHARE YOUR LOVE OF MUSIC. Old sheet music—for any instrument—doesn't belong in the recycling bin; it belongs in the hands of someone who can use it. To find that someone, contact music teachers in your neighborhood. Most would be happy to take the sheet music to distribute to students. You can find studios by looking in the Yellow Pages under music instruction.

Pickin' and Grinnin'

One Thanksgiving at my mother's house, I was rooting around in the attic and found my old guitar: an acoustic Suzuki student model from the 1960s. The strings were missing, but otherwise it wasn't in too bad shape. I never actually learned to play, but seeing it reminded me of my teenage rock star dreams. I decided to take it home and tune it up. Not really knowing much about guitars, I did some research on the Internet and discovered that all it would take to get this old instrument back into playing shape was a new set of strings and one missing part: a saddle.

The strings on a guitar are attached to its body at the bridge. The saddle sits atop the bridge, and the strings pass over the saddle. It's usually made of wood, bone, or plastic, and it affects the guitar's tuning and intonation.

Now you know as much basic guitar anatomy as I do.

I set off to the local mega-guitar store to buy a replacement saddle. The not-so-young man, in the leopard-print jeans, was eager to sell me a package of four toothpick-sized sticks for just over $2.

"They're kind of a specialty item," he said. "They're smaller than the saddle on a full-sized guitar, and you need more than one because kids lose them all the time."

Well, I'm not a kid, and even if I did lose them, I wasn't going to pay that much for four toothpick-sized sticks when I could buy a hundred toothpick-sized toothpicks for a buck. I spent the savings on a better set of strings and found a toothpick.

It fit perfectly, and soon my old "ax" was tuned up and ready for rocking again.

—Tony Santoro
Forest Park, New York

AUDIO AND VIDEO

Audio and video gear tends to be expensive, and so it makes sense to treat it all with tender loving care. From headphones to vinyl albums, CDs to DVDs, the following tips show you how to do just that. And of course, we've included some ingenious ways to pass along what you no longer need or want.

MAKE IT LAST

STORE 'EM IN THE SHADE. Whether you paid $3 or $300 for your audio headphones, you can extend their life by keeping them out of direct sunlight. The heat and light damages the magnets in the equipment, causing them to wear out a lot more quickly.

KEEP YOUR EAR (PHONES) CLEAN. When you're not using headphones, hang them up so that the earpieces are facing one another. This protects them from dust that can muddy the sound.

VIVA LA VINYL. Just when you thought it was safe to throw out that turntable, you learn that vinyl is making a comeback. Here's how to make sure your old and new album purchases last a good long time.

- **Keep it cool.** The ideal temperature for the storage of vinyl record albums and 45s is between 65° and 75°F. If you have a particularly valuable collection, consider investing in a humidifier or dehumidifier to maintain humidity at 45 to 50 percent. Excessive moisture can cause mold growth on record sleeves. In any case, make sure to keep the albums in a room where the temperature doesn't fluctuate drastically. That usually means keeping the collection out of the basement, attic, and garage.
- **Don't stack 'em.** Store albums on end, like books—never stack or store them flat.
- **Consider recovery.** Albums come wrapped in plastic called shrink wrap. Remove this covering immediately; it can trap moisture and encourage mold growth. For the safest storage, slide each album (cardboard sleeve and all) inside a Mylar sleeve, available from retailers such as Archival Methods (www.archivalmethods.com), University Products (www.universityproducts.com), or Metal Edge (www.metaledgeinc.com).

USE SAFE STORAGE. Experts say that music (and photographs) saved to DVDs and CDs can last for up to 50 years. We can't guarantee that lifespan, but we can tell you that the material will definitely last longer if you store the devices correctly, in plastic (not paper) cases designed specifically for those disks.

Still Working After All These Years
SPEAKERS OF THE HOUSE

I've had the same pair of bookshelf speakers for over 20 years. Before that they were my father's, and he had them for 15 years before that. Although they're large by today's standards, I use them regularly, and can even plug my MP3 player into them.

It hasn't taken much to keep them sounding great, but they have been repaired from time to time. The list goes something like this:

I've resoldered a few connections inside the speaker. (One good thing is that the cabinets are made of solid wood, and it takes only removing a few screws to remove the fronts.)

I've replaced the jacks where the speaker wire plugs in. (It helps to own basic tools like screwdrivers and to have an acquaintance with an electronics store like Radio Shack.)

Once, a curtain rod slipped off its brackets and poked through the fabric on the front of the speaker. No worries: I replaced the fabric with a remnant from the local fabric store that matched the original pretty closely.

With advice from the guys at the electronics store, I've kept the speakers in great working order. These days, it's a little furniture polish on the outside now and then, and a touch-up with a brown crayon when they get dinged. I think they may last another 20 years.

—Joe Dortene
Cambridge, Massachusetts

KEEP THEM ON EDGE. To prevent scratches, always store CDs and DVDs in their cases on their edges, the way you store books. Never stack disks; it makes them more prone to damage.

SKIP THE STICKERS. Most office supply stores these days sell blank CD and DVD stickers that you can design and decorate on your computer, and then print out and place on your homemade CDs and DVDs. They may seem like a good idea, but some experts advise steering clear of them. If the label pulls up and gets caught in your computer or CD or DVD player, you could have a major repair on your hands. Your best bet is to use a non-solvent based marker to label CDs and DVDs.

COVER ALL THE BASES. A well-cared for VHS tape can certainly last for decades. The question is whether VHS players will be widely available in the future—anyone who has 8-millimeter movies knows how difficult it is to find a rental projector. A smart course of action for valuable material (wedding day, baby's first step) is to hold onto the videotapes, take good care of them, *and* transfer the data to DVDs.

KEEP TAPES COOL. And dry. Just like most other items, it's important to store videotapes in a cool, dry environment. To really prolong tape life, storage at 40°F is best. But not many of us are willing to set the thermostat that low. In most cases, around 70°F is fine.

AND AWAY FROM THE TELEVISION. If you store videotapes on top of the television, you should know that you're significantly reducing the lifespan of those tapes. The heat and dust that accumulate there can ruin the tapes. Move them to a cooler spot.

STOW IT UNDER COVER. Although most blank videotapes are sold in cardboard sleeves, those containers will not fully protect the tapes from dust—which can degrade the image. Store important tapes in polypropylene cases.

START FRESH. To make sure your recordings last a long time, start with a brand-new tape rather than one that has already been used. The image quality will be much better and the tape will last longer.

DON'T PLAY IT HOT OR COLD. Sometimes you can't avoid a videotape getting very cold or hot (for instance while being transported in a car). In those cases, make sure to allow the tape to come to room temperature before popping it into the VCR and playing it. This will prevent damage to the tape.

CLONE IT. Whether it's a home movie or a rerun of a favorite program, a tape that will be played frequently will wear out more quickly than one viewed infrequently. To make sure the tape lasts, make a copy right away and play that—store the original in a safe place. When and if the copy wears out, you can make a new one from the original.

GIVE YOUR TAPES A WORKOUT. Once or twice each year, full fast-forward and then rewind your video tapes. This prevents a tightly wound tape from sticking to itself and ruining the images.

WARM IT UP. Before you record on a new tape, pop it in the VCR, fast-forward it to the end, and the rewind it again completely. Taking this step before you record will result in a better quality recording because the fast-forward/rewind evens the tension on the tape.

DOCTOR THAT DISK. Trouble reading a CD or DVD? Don't trash it  just yet. First, use a bulb blower (available at camera shops or online— search for "bulb blower") or a can of compressed air (available from office supply stores) to rid the disk of dust. If you're still unable to read it, use a clean cotton cloth and a little isopropyl alcohol to wipe the disk in straight lines from the center to the outer ring. Never wipe a CD or DVD in a circular motion—with the grain, so to speak—because if you create any new scratches they will likely make the disk unreadable.

You'll likely spot the scratch and now know where to direct a little extra cleaning action, as explained above. When dealing with a music or movie disk, here's a hint: If the skip occurs soon after hitting play, then the scratch is closer to the disk center; if the problem occurs later on, the scratch is closer to the disk's outside perimeter.

ROCK AROUND THE CLOCK. If you're getting ready to toss your  old vinyl albums because they're no longer playable, think about transforming one or more into wall clocks. It's a perfectly ingenious way to create a gift for yourself or any music lover. Just be sure you're not using an album that's still a valuable part of someone's collection. (If you don't have a record handy, you can get one very cheaply at a local Salvation Army or thrift shop.)

What you'll need:

- 1 twelve-inch vinyl record album or EP (the label should be in good condition, because it will show on your finished clock
- 1 clock movement kit, available at most crafts stores, including Michaels
- adhesive numerals (these may come with the clock movement kit; if you prefer a different style, they're available at home decorating, crafts, and hardware stores)

Directions are simple: Just follow the instructions in the clock movement kit and—voila!—you have a brand-new clock, for under $10! The bonus: This technique works with CDs and DVDs, too.

GIVE THE GIFT OF GAME. So you've beaten that computer game and have no more use for it. Don't throw it away. There are several ways to pass it on to benefit someone else.

One Man's Trash
Re-Disk-covery

What's round, made of vinyl, has a groove, and can hold fruit? A recycled album that's been turned into a bowl.

Brooklyn artist and designer Jeff Davis turns literally tons of old 45s, LPs, and vintage album covers into bowls, clocks, coasters, snack trays, sketchbooks, and note cards, and sells them through his company Vinylux— Vintage Vinyl Design (www.vinylux.net).

Using heat and pressure, Jeff transforms old, unwanted records into usable objets d'art. The record labels are laminated to protect them from moisture and to seal the spindle hole.

According to Jeff, there seems to be no end in sight to the number of records lying dormant in the basements, attics, and garages of America. Over the course of four years, Vinylux has recycled about 175,000 vinyl records and album covers. That's nearly 50 tons of plastic and cardboard that might have otherwise just gone into landfills.

- **Donate it.** Check your local library, Boys & Girls Clubs, community center, or YMCA. Such organizations often accept donations of computer games.
- **Swap it.** Organize a computer game swap with friends or family, or swap the game online through a site such as Swap-Bot (www.swap-bot.com).
- **Sell it.** Visit a game store. Some now buy and sell used games. An account with Web sites such as half.com (www.half.com) allows you to sell games (and just about anything else) online.

TWINKLE, TWINKLE, LITTLE . . . CD. When a CD or DVD is damaged beyond repair, you could toss it in the trash, but here's a craftier idea: Give it a dazzling new life. Here are two fun and easy ways to recycle your old discs.
- **Make a mini wreath.** Use a drill to make a hole in the CD, close to the edge. Use hot glue to attach bits of decoration—bulky yarn wound in a spiral, dried greenery from the crafts store, beads, buttons—to the CD to turn it into a miniature wreath to hang on the wall or the Christmas tree.
- **Coast along.** Use the CD to make the base of a knitted, crocheted, or woven coaster. Use hot glue (white household glue isn't moisture proof) to attach your crafty creation to the CD, and you have instant drink coasters.

SAY SO LONG TO YOUR TV. If you've decided it's time for a new television, think twice before carrying the old one out to the curb. Here are four ways to pass it on to a new home.
- **Keep it.** If it still works, why not turn the old TV into a monitor for computer games?
- **Donate it.** Check with local community organizations, churches, YMCAs, or the Salvation Army to find out whether it would accept a used but working television.
- **Sell it.** For a small fee, you can place an ad in a local Pennysaver or newspaper—not only will someone come to your home and take the television away, you'll make a buck or two in the bargain!

DON'T CHUCK THAT TV. Here's a shocking statistic: An old television's cathode ray tube (CRT) can contain up to 4 pounds of lead, and so anything consumers can do to keep their old TVs out of landfills is a smart move. Luckily, there are resources that provide information about how to get rid of the old television in an environmentally friendly way: *Consumer Reports* magazine's Greener Choices (www.greenerchoices.org); the EPA's Plug-in to eCycling (www.epa.gov/epaoswer/osw/conserve/plugin/); and eBay's Rethink Initiative (http://rethink.ebay.com). Each of these Web sites offers lists and links to local organizations that will take an old television off your hands.

DIGITAL CAMERAS AND PRINTS

The advent of digital print cameras and digital camcorders has changed the way we record our memories. Read on for our expert advice about saving and storing your images.

MAKE IT LAST

MIND YOUR MEMORIES. Storing photographs and home movies so that you can enjoy them in the years to come isn't as easy as it once was. These days, you have to work to keep up with hardware and software advances.

- **Lucky number 8.** Projectors for 8-millimeter and super-8 home movies are nearly impossible to rent and quite expensive to purchase. And so it's wise to transfer movies on those media to DVD. A local camera store or an online service such as Home Movie Depot (www.homemoviedepot.com) can do these transfers for you. (This isn't to say that you should throw away your super-8 or 8mm films. After all, vinyl record albums are making a comeback.)
- **Refresh the disks.** To ensure that you'll be able to read image files (and thereby your precious photos), make backups to CDs or DVDs and then resave them to fresh CDs or DVDs every couple of years.
- **Outsource the printing.** A photograph that you print at home from a digital camera might not last as long as one developed from film. In fact, it may not last even 3 years. For images that you do want to preserve, experts recommend having them professionally printed. Otherwise, using the ink and paper recommended by your printer manufacturer is the best bet.

DOMESTIC CHALLENGE

The rec room's all about fun, but extending the life of your games and hobby equipment is much more enjoyable when you keep things simple. Take this quiz before taking up a new hobby—or to help you decide which of your existing stuff could be preserved, fixed or passed along with the least effort.

Questions

1. Which media is easy to borrow elsewhere before buying—even if you like the most up to date stuff?

   A. Music
   B. Books
   C. Magazines
   D. All of the above

2. What's the easiest place to store DVDs if you don't like to dust?

   A. Plastic shoebox underneath the player
   B. Wooden shelf over the player
   C. Archival photo box across the room from the player

3. Which craft requires the least amount of start-up equipment for beginners?

   A. Crocheting
   B. Quilting
   C. Sewing
   D. Scrapbooking

4. Which craft is just as manageable when you're on the go as it is in your own rec room?

   A. Rag rugs
   B. Needlepoint
   C. Knitting
   D. None of the above

5. Which type of craft makes it easiest for a pack rat to avoid impulse purchases?

   A. Quilting
   B. Needlepoint
   C. Découpage
   D. Scrapbooking

6. Which craft or hobby relies on materials you can easily purchase at the thrift store or a flea market?

   A. Quilting
   B. Rag rugs
   C. Knitting
   D. All of the above

7. If you're forever losing components, which type of craft kit is easiest to complete with stuff you can find around the house?

   A. Photo albums and scrapbooks
   B. Découpage
   C. Needlepoint pillows
   D. None of the above

8. Which board game has pieces that are easiest to replace?

   A. Scrabble
   B. Yahtzee
   C. Monopoly
   D. Chess

9. If you give up half way through a craft project, which materials will be most welcome as giveaways?

   A. Paint by numbers
   B. Knitting
   C. Beads
   D. Découpage

(continues)

Domestic Challenge

10. Which type of toy is easiest to clean?

    A. Cotton stuffed animals
    B. Small plastic toys
    C. Traditional wood toys

Answers

1. **A.** Music. You can listen to the latest on the radio, particularly on Internet stations, and wait for the CDs you really like to reach the record store bargain bin, Amazon's used item list or the lending library. Books are harder to borrow brand new, especially from the library, and magazines are usually hopelessly out of date before you can check them out of the library (though you can go there to read them).

2. **C.** The static from the TV attracts dust that will get all over the DVD cases, so the best bet is storing them away from the TV and the second best bet is putting the cases in a closed container.

3. **A.** Crocheting. With a single ball of yarn, a crochet hook, and a pair of scissors, you're off to the races while the others require an outfitted sewing box and a hoop and sewing machine or glue, scissors, book and papers—not to mention mementos.

4. **C.** Knitting. No need to make eye contact for knitting and sweaters, socks and scarves are easily toted around in a bag. Needlepoint, on the other hand, requires nice strong light and rag rugs tend to get too large to carry after a point.

5. **B.** Needlepoint. Since most projects are sold in complete kits, it's much easier to limit yourself to finishing one before purchasing another, while acquiring material for potential quilting, découpage, or scrapping projects can become a hobby unto itself—and fill bin after bin, closet after closet with material.

6. **D.** All of the above. You can find loads of material for quilts or rag rugs already in the proper format at a thrift store, or still part of worn clothes. Just make sure to note fabric content before you start cutting stuff into fat quarters or lengths for rugs. Yarn, too, may be sold in unopened packages or unraveled from knitted items.

7. **B.** Découpage. You can use three parts Elmer's glue to one part water in place of pre-packaged finishes like Mod Podge. The needlepoint, though, will need the same texture of embroidery floss or it will stick out, and any photo albums and scrapbooks should be compiled with only archival quality, acid-free materials.

8. **C.** Monopoly. Any of the board pieces can be replaced with, say, a button or an eraser without distracting. For chess, though, it can affect smooth play to have one piece you can't easily determine the role—if you speak up to ask, you've let your opponent in on your thinking. Yahtzee's the next simplest, you can buy new dice or type up new score cards. Scrabble's impossible—everyone will know which letter is on the flip side of the substitute block.

9. **B.** Knitting. Many individuals and charities welcome yarn and needles, even if the yarn has to be picked out to start again. It's much harder to work up enthusiasm for someone else's half-painted creation, particularly as the paints are bound to be dried out, and beads and decoupage glues have safety issues that make them unwelcome at kiddie drop-off sites like day cares.

10. **B.** Small plastic toys can just take a turn through the dishwasher, while stuffed animals can't be soaked in water if they have natural fiber filling, mechanical parts, or torn seams. Wood toys are just like wood furniture—no abrasives, no submerging in water and no bleach or ammonia cleaners.

5
HOME OFFICE

Your home office is always a work in progress. It has to morph from a place of business to a space where loved ones connect with one another through e-mail. To keep it all running smoothly, we offer the following tips that will help you maximize efficiency, repair exasperating problems, and reuse and recycle wisely.

Top priority is maintaining home office tools—computers, scanners, printers, fax machines, phones, and even office furniture—so that they last a long time; you'll find plenty of hands-on advice about that here. You'll also learn how to troubleshoot some minor (and a few potentially disastrous) problems, including slow computers, staticky cell phones, and sticky keyboards. Finally, when the items in your home office can no longer do the job for which they were intended, turn to our suggestions for moving them along, and check out our recommendations about how to destroy or donate dated gear that you really don't need, such as cell phones, disks loaded with personal information, or computers. Ready? Let's get to work and make your home office hum.

COMPUTERS

These days, when almost everyone keeps in touch by email, it pays to stay tech savvy. In this next section you'll learn what to look for when buying a new system, how to get the most out of that older machine, and what to do when it's time to retire it.

MAKE IT LAST

BUY NOW FOR THE FUTURE. To purchase a computer with technological staying power (and get the biggest bang for your buck), consider more than just price. For several years now, basic desktop computer prices have stood firm between $1,000 and $1,500, largely because computer manufacturers are maintaining prices but adding technology and software to newer models. So, even though it's generally true that high-tech equipment drops in price as the technology becomes more common (remember when desktop calculators cost $350?), this does not necessarily hold true for computers. The smartest move is to compare prices and technology as you shop. You may discover that this year's model is indeed a better deal than last year's.

REVAMP AN OLD COMPUTER. If your computer is two or fewer years old, you should know about the three different upgrades that will make the machine last longer and bring its capabilities closer to newer, more advanced models. Any one of these upgrades should be less expensive than buying new—even after paying a computer expert or computer service department to install the upgrade. If, however, you need all three upgrades, then it's best to buy new, since your total cost will likely come close to the price of a new machine. To find an expert in upgrades, start with the store where you purchased your computer. Larger electronics stores that include computer departments, like Best Buy, also provide upgrade services. Here are the details.

1. **Maximize memory.** Adding random access memory, or RAM, will allow your computer to process data faster. It'll also boost your machine's stability so that it won't crash when opening several programs simultaneously. The ideal amount: 512 megabytes of RAM. Averaging in cost from $50 to $125, this is an economical way to juice up your computer's performance.

2. **Make room for media.** Your machine may play DVDs, but wouldn't you like to store all those vacation photos on a DVD of your own? While recordable DVD drives are standard on many higher end computers, a machine more than a couple of years old may only

have a CD-ROM (read only memory) drive. A relatively inexpensive way to give yourself a more versatile—and economic—computer is to add a better removable media drive. For less than $100, you can add an internal or external DVD+/-RW (read/write) drive. Recordable DVDs are inexpensive, and DVD storage is currently the most economical way of storing data off your computer.

3. **Upgrade the hard drive.** Taking this step will provide more storage capacity, so your computer can hold more photos and music (the largest data files). Your computer will also open these files more quickly. The cost, somewhere between $80 and $160, is an economical trade-off if you've suddenly started downloading music and storing digital family photographs.

RUN A CLEAN MACHINE. Keeping the exterior of your computer clean is one way to sidestep potential problems. Why? External grime can block airflow in and out of the machine's vents. This could cause your computer to overheat, which in turn can damage the machine.

To keep your computer's outside spotless, get yourself a pack of lint-free antistatic wipes, swabs, or both, available for around $10 wherever computers are sold. Read package instructions before using.

Wipe down all parts that open, such as the disk tray. If you spot a dust bunny and you're without the right wipes, slightly dampen a paper towel with room temperature tap water and use that to wipe down your computer. This process lacks the handy antistatic element, but it works in a pinch. Before cleaning with a dampened cloth, always turn off and then unplug the computer from the main power source.

BEAT THE HEAT. When a computer is exposed to extreme external heat, you risk damaging the computer's internal chips, which in turn might necessitate either an expensive repair or replacement. If at all possible, place your computer in a spot away from direct

---

$mart Buys

MAKE A DATE FOR A GOOD BUY

Planning a new computer purchase? Here are the best times of year to buy.

- **New year.** Early January is typically when new computer models come out, and by February, these new computers have worked their way into computer retail stores. That means prices for last year's "leftover" models drop.
- **Overstock options.** Prices may also plummet in February as retailers look to get rid of overstocked computer inventory brought in for the December holiday gift-buying season.
- **Summer sales.** July is another good time to find computer bargains; it's after the prime selling season ends for Father's Day and graduation gifts. Again, retailers will be placing good stuff on sale to unload overstocks.

sunlight and try to keep your home office on the cool side—although there's certainly no need for frigid temps. It's really more of an issue during hot, sticky summer months if you don't have air-conditioning. A desk fan beside your computer does the trick.

WATCH THE JUICE. Power surges—sudden increases in the amount of power coming into your home—can wreak havoc on your computer and result in total data loss, even if your computer is plugged in but turned off. This sort of "phantom surge" is a common occurrence when the power comes back on after a neighborhood blackout. That makes a surge protector one must-have piece of equipment. How much should you pay? Models that cost less than $20 won't provide the kind of protection you need, and those over $40 are probably more than your home office requires. That's a small price to pay to protect a large investment.

FIX IT OR FORGET IT?
KNOW WHAT YOU NEED

Should you upgrade your current computer or buy a new machine? Sometimes it's tricky to know. Here are some guidelines to help you decide when you're faced with this decision.

Upgrade if:
- You spend most of your computer time sending e-mail, surfing the Web, or keeping track of household expenditures.
- Your computer is less than 5 years old, and your primary complaint about it is that it's too slow.
- You have reliability issues, such as frequent crashes, and your computer is less than 2 years old.

Buy new if:
- The children in your life want to play the latest, most sophisticated computer games. These require speedy processors, a lot of memory (RAM), and powerful hard drives.
- You enjoy working with and manipulating images from a digital camera.
- You want to be able to edit video from your digital camcorder.
- The price to upgrade (including the upgrade service cost) is more than 50 percent of a new computer.

BYE-BYE BATTERY. After about 1,000 charges, or 2 to 4 years of regular usage, your laptop's battery will expire and need to be replaced. Thankfully, there is a straightforward way to extend a battery's life span, or help it come closer to the outside 4-year mark—and maybe even exceed it. Simply remove the battery from the laptop when you're not using it. If the laptop is your primary computer (you use it a few times every day) and you need to keep it plugged in, slip out the battery and store it in a cool, dry place, like a desk drawer. Before removing the battery and putting into storage, experts recommend that you check to make sure it is approximately 50 percent charged, since this keeps it stable and allows for some naturally occurring self-discharge.

BATTERY BASICS. Has your laptop battery run out of juice at an inopportune moment? You can extend the time between necessary laptop battery charges by following a few simple tips.

- **The drain game.** Let the battery drain completely, and then let it charge completely before using it. This means that you hit the road with a maximum charge. The time it takes to fully charge a battery varies by model; consult the owner's manual.
- **Pay for more power.** Regardless of what kind of battery came with your laptop, upgrade to a nickel-metal-hydride (NiMH) battery or a lithium-ion battery. This is not an option for every model, but it's worth investigating since these types of batteries are more powerful than the nickel-cadmium (NiCad) battery that often comes with less expensive laptops.
- **Plug and play.** Because playing DVDs and CDs drains your laptop's battery quickly, plug into an electrical outlet if it's available.
- **Mind the monitor.** Reduce the monitor's brightness level so that it uses less power. Just be careful not to dim the screen so much that you risk eyestrain.
- **Computer catnaps.** If you know ahead of time that it will be a while until you can recharge your battery, use the laptop's power-management feature. This generally means a faster segue into sleep or standby mode, which is sort of like your computer taking a snooze after a certain amount of inactivity.

GET ON ITS CASE. Sometimes the case that comes with a new laptop is not the best way to carry it around—if the laptop even comes with a case. To get the most bang for your buck when shopping for a laptop case, here's what you need to consider.

- **Sturdiness.** Gently, yet firmly, tug at all the major seams to verify quality construction.
- **Waterproofing.** Make sure the case is water-resistant.
- **Padding.** All case sides should be well-padded, top to bottom.
- **Weight.** Slip your laptop inside any case you're considering to gauge total weight.
- **Comfort.** Try out several strap choices to determine what feels most comfortable before you commit to purchasing a particular style of laptop case. You'll find plenty of options—shoulder straps, backpack-style straps, and longer straps that criss-cross your body. Some of them are padded; others are not. There are also traditional suitcase styles, including the rolling laptop case on wheels.

UNDERCOVER CASE. You bought that laptop to give your home a little mobility. But ever since hearing about the high incidence of laptop theft, you never take it anywhere. That makes no sense. One way to deter thieves is to purchase a laptop case that doesn't look like a laptop case, perhaps choosing something from the luggage department. Really, who wants to steal your underwear? This is a great option for anyone especially interested in a case with wheels. If this is your chosen route, however, you will have to add foam padding, available in any craft or fabric shop, to all sides of the suitcase!

GET OFF ITS CASE. Never use your laptop while it is in the case. Operating it while it's so insulated could cause serious overheating, which can irreparably damage the machine.

FIX IT FAST

DEFEAT DUST BUNNIES. If it's been a while since you cleaned your computer's exterior, dust clumps may be clogging the air vents. When the vents are clogged, the machine can overheat. That can cause software and hardware problems. A can of compressed air, available for around $5 wherever computers or photography equipment are sold, is the solution. Here are some tips to keep in mind.

- **It's a blast.** Spray the grimy area with 1-second air blasts, pointing the nozzle so it sprays parallel to the vent's surface. In other words, don't blast air (and dust) directly into the vent.
- **Tipping point.** Hold the can in an upright position, perpendicular to the floor. If you allow the can to tip while spraying, it may release damaging condensation into your computer.
- **Selective suction.** *Never* use a household or shop vacuum to clean the computer's vents (or keyboard); their suction may loosen internal parts. Those tools also emit a magnetic field that often creates static electricity, which in turn might damage electrical components within your computer.

CLEAN THE DRIVE FOR SPEED. Bits and pieces of previous communication between software programs accumulate in your computer's hard drive. Over time, this assorted junk causes your computer to slow down. To speedily clear this worthless material from a PC, you can download free software from Microsoft. To find it, point your browser to http://safety.live.com. From this home page, click Clean Up, and follow the directions. In addition, the site offers two additional free programs that improve PC performance.

- **Tune Up** defragments the hard disk, which makes the computer function more efficiently. It will able to find all the pieces of a previously saved file more easily, and that increases the computer's speed.
- **Protection** scans your computer for most viruses and then removes them. This program also identifies and eliminates potential vulnerabilities.

Although no free programs exist for Mac users, two highly recommended options for optimizing hard drive space are Disk Warrior, at around $40, and Norton Utilities, at around $80. The latter costs a bit more because it includes additional troubleshooting options, which a salesperson should be able to explain. In fact, don't be timid about asking for a demonstration when considering a purchase costing $80.

GIVE PROBLEMS THE BOOT. Computer experts say that in most instances, a frozen or crashed computer is due to confusion between software programs. In other words, your computer is multitasking to the point of shutdown. Many times the solution is to restart, or reboot, your computer. Here's how to proceed.

1. To reboot the machine when it is frozen, press the main on/off power button, hold it down for about 10 seconds or until the machine shuts down, and then release.
2. Before restarting the computer, double-check wire connections. If something feels loose, pull it out and plug it back in. Wait 30 seconds or so, and then turn on the computer again.

All the work you did since your last save will be lost, but rebooting is always the first step to fixing a crashed computer—and also the first step an expert would take. By the way, now would be a good time to mention the merits of saving your files frequently.

SETTLE SOFTWARE DIFFERENCES. Sometimes software that's already on your computer won't work with a new program, especially if the existing software is more than 2 years old. If you've been humming along without frozen screens or crashes, but soon after loading a new program experience problems, try running the new program with no other software programs open. Conversely, when you open any older software programs, make sure the newer program is closed.

If this doesn't solve the problem, your next best bet is to uninstall the new program. Insert the suspicious software program's disk and click the uninstall option that comes up on the screen. The operating system probably can't handle the new program without an expert's input.

CLEAN THE SCREEN. When it comes to desktop and laptop computer screens, you can look but don't touch. Many have what's called liquid-crystal displays (LCD), which are very susceptible to vision-blurring fingerprints. However, if your screen does get grimy there are two speedy cleaning procedures you can try.

1. In a bowl, mix one part distilled water to one part isopropyl alcohol with 50 percent or less alcohol. *Never* use 70 or 90 percent alcohol (more common rubbing alcohol) because it's too harsh for LCD screens. And don't use tap water, since it could leave mineral spots.

2. Moisten, but do not drench, a clean lint-free cloth with the mixture. Wipe the screen by moving from one side of the screen to the other. Don't stop in the middle or you may leave a new smudge.

LCD screens are sensitive, and if your homemade brew is too harsh, you risk damaging the monitor. So, if your measuring skills are unsteady, purchase a special cleaner created specifically for LCD screens. Available wherever computers are sold and starting around $10, these products come in single-wipe packets and in spray bottles.

PASS IT ALONG

ELIMINATE E-WASTE. In many places, it's illegal to toss computers in the trash (the same holds true for TVs, monitors, laptops, cell phones, stereos, fax machines, and computer keyboards). There's even a name for such unlawful garbage: electronic waste, or e-waste for short. Luckily, there are many safe and legal ways to discard this garbage.

• **Recycle golden oldies.** If your computer is more than 5 years old, the bad news is that it's probably obsolete. The good news is that it's easy to properly dispose of the machine. Visit www.earth911.org, find the Information section, and then click on Electronics Recycling to find out how to dispose of a computer in your town.

• **Refurbishing rules.** If your machine is 2 to 5 years old, everyone wins, because computers in this age range are still new enough to refurbish and pass on. The Web site www.earth911.org offers lists of organizations that accept computers.

MAKE A CLEAN BREAK. When it's time to retire an old computer, don't pass it along until you've obliterated all sensitive personal information from the hard drive. Even a social security number in the wrong hands could lead to identity theft. You need to overwrite the hard drive; here's how.

- **Use the system disks.** One way to overwrite the hard drive on PCs and Macs is to insert the original install CD or DVD (the disk with the operating system on it), and follow the directions in the owner's manual to wipe the hard drive clean. Or visit the computer manufacturer's Web site for directions.

- **Download a disk eraser.** PC users can also choose from several free downloadable programs that will thoroughly clean a hard drive. One such program can be found at www.pcinspector.de. The site initially shows up in German, but it's easy to switch to English. Carefully read all of the instructions and then download the professional data deletion program, which, by the way, meets U.S. military standards. Eraser, from Heidi Computers, is another free program. It's available at www.heidi.ie.

- **Enlist an expert.** If you're running an older Mac operating system (anything prior to OSX), you will probably need to enlist help from a computer expert or purchase a data deletion program. One such program is SuperScrubber, available from www.jiiva.com. At around $30, this program will erase any Mac hard drive—and also meets military specifications.

COMPUTER ACCESSORIES

The central processing unit (CPU) may be the brains of a computer, but peripherals—keyboard, printer, scanner, and mouse—are just as important to keeping your office running smoothly.

MAKE IT LAST

MAKE A MOUSE HAPPY. If you use a roller ball mouse—one that has a ball that you can see when you turn the mouse upside down—then you need to clean the inner workings at least every month to keep it working smoothly. Otherwise, you'll be paying for replacements more frequently. Here's how to clean it.

1. Unplug the mouse and then turn it over. You will see the tracking ball as well as a round ring that holds the tracking ball in place.
2. Remove the ring by pressing down and rotating it counterclockwise until you can lift it off.

3. Flip the mouse over so that the ball drops out. Wash the ball with warm tap water and mild dishwashing liquid, then thoroughly dry it with a lint-free cloth.
4. Before replacing the ball and ring, look for three small rollers (each about 1/16-inch wide) inside the mouse cavity where the ball sits. They're likely covered with built-up dirt. Use cotton swabs or a toothpick to scrap off the dirt. Gently knock the still-open cavity down into the palm of your hand to get rid of loose particles.
5. Replace the ball and ring cover.

PICK PROPER PAPER. Using the right paper for your printer can actually make your printer last longer. Paper that's too heavy or too thin can cause jams that can break the printer. If you have an inkjet printer, buy inkjet paper. If you have a laser printer, buy laser paper. The exception to this rule is paper identified as everyday paper, general all-purpose paper, or copy paper. These papers are designed to work with all printers, fax machines, and copiers.

BUY THE BEST. You may have heard that it's a waste of money to purchase a scanner that has greater resolution capabilities (picture clarity) than your printer. False! Although it is true that high-resolution scanners are pricier than low-resolution models, it's not a waste of money if you own an old printer that you'll likely replace before the new scanner wears out. After replacing that printer with new technology, you'll be able to scan and print photos like a pro.

FIX IT FAST

MINT CONDITION MOUSE PAD. If you find that your mouse isn't tracking smoothly, accumulated dirt on the mouse pad fabric may be the problem. Take a look at the pad, and if it looks soiled, toss it in the washing machine whenever you wash a load that requires cold water, the gentle cycle, and a gentle detergent, such as Woolite. Let the pad air-dry before using it again.

TROUBLESHOOT YOUR PRINTER. When your printer jams with regularity, it's either broken for good or it may just need a little help.
- **Single-serving solution.** If you're printing on heavy paper or card stock, you may need to feed it one sheet at a time instead of loading up the paper tray.
- **Beware of lingering labels.** If you've recently printed labels of any kind, open the panel that accesses the ink and look for a stray piece.

If you spot one, unplug the printer, grab a pair of tweezers, and gently pick the misplaced label off and out.

TAPE MARKS THE SPOT. If you've ever unplugged peripherals from your computer and then felt lost when it came time to replace the cords again, we have a tip for you: After you unplug each item, place a small piece of masking tape over the plug—so you remember where to replug it later. If you need to unplug several cords, tear off a small piece of masking tape, write a 1 on it, and wrap it around the cord of your first unplugged item. On a second piece of tape write the number 1 and put it over this item's plug. Write a 2 on the next set of masking tape markers, and continue accordingly with each item unplugged.

DOWNLOAD DIRECTIONS. Often the best way to troubleshoot problems with a scanner, printer, or fax machine is to read the device's owner's manual. If you misplaced this valuable handbook or you never received one, here's how to get a copy: Log onto the product manufacturer's Web site. Ninety-nine percent of all manufacturers make their manuals available for download, usually in a section of the site called "support" or "downloads." Barring that, check the CD that came with the device; you'll likely find a user's manual there.

CLEAN THE KEYBOARD. Have you ever typed "cat" but it came out "caaaat"? A dirty keyboard was probably the culprit. Grit and grime can get caught under the keys, causing them to stick. Fortunately, cleaning a desktop computer keyboard is simple. You'll need a lint-free cloth, rubbing alcohol, cotton swabs, and a can of compressed air.

One Man's Trash
Safe Sipping

I have a confession to make. I drink at my computer. So right about now you're either reprimanding me or nonchalantly saying something like, "So, who doesn't?" The simple truth is, sooner or later we all give in and want water, soda, or iced tea enough to risk spillage. Fortunately, necessity being the mother of invention, I found a solution to the drink-spilling worry. It's a Rubbermaid 16-ounce Sip Bottle. I had this cup from the days when I picked my friend's young son up at school and always had juice for him. One day it struck me that if it was designed to be spill proof I could bring it into my computer area. When the straw is down (and the lid is on correctly), nothing can spill. What to do with a hot drink? Use a travel mug. Not the cardboard kind with the flimsy plastic lid, but the heavy-duty ones with a handle you press to temporarily open a small sipping opening.

—Deborah Shadovitz
Los Angeles, California

P.S. You'll find spill-proof cups for hot or cold drinks at grocery and discount stores and now even in computer stores.

1. First, unplug the keyboard from the rest of the computer.
2. Hold the keyboard upside down and gently shake it to release loose debris between the keys.
3. Spray the upside down keyboard with compressed in 1-second blasts, moving the nozzle to a new location with each blast.
4. Set down the keyboard, right-side up. Place a drop or two of rubbing alcohol on a cotton swab and swipe the key sides and top. If your keyboard is very dirty you may go through quite a few swabs.
5. Finally, wipe the keyboard surface and around each key with a lint-free dry cloth. (Never pour liquid directly on the keyboard—you knew that, right?)

DRIP-DRY. If you happen to spill liquid on your keyboard, don't panic—yet. Here's what you should do.
1. Immediately unplug the keyboard, and then save your work if you can do so with just the mouse and without touching the keyboard.
2. Turn off the computer and then unplug it.
3. Sop up as much liquid from the keyboard as you can, then flip it over so the keys face down and let gravity pull out more. As water drips out, sop it up, then put the keyboard back in place upside down.
4. Wait 48 hours before plugging everything back in. Cross your fingers and turn on the computer. The keyboard should work. If, however, the keyboard's still not working, sorry... it's a goner.

PASS IT ALONG

EMPTY, NOT USELESS. Did you know that empty laser and inkjet printer cartridges are recyclable? Well, they are, and there are plenty of online resources available to help guide you every step of the way.

$mart Buys
UPGRADING A MOUSE

A new mouse is relatively inexpensive, as computer purchases go. Here's what you need to know about the three available mouse styles.

- **Roller ball mouse.** It works off an internal rubber ball that moves against three internal rollers. This type of mouse is the most "old-fashioned" and least expensive option, but it also needs frequent cleaning.
- **Optical mouse.** It uses a beam of light to track the position of the cursor on the screen and costs slightly more than a rubber ball mouse, but it's maintenance-free.
- **Wireless mouse.** This priciest option works with optical technology, but there is no wire connecting it to your computer. It runs on batteries that need to be replaced occasionally. If you're sitting close to someone else who's using a wireless mouse, their mouse movements may show up on your screen. Best to be at least 5 feet apart.

So, before you toss another empty cartridge into the trash, pause and consider the following.

Some cartridges can be re-filled and reused up to five times, which means a significant reduction in plastic trash dumped into landfills. Even better, you may be able to make some money for your good deeds. To find ink cartridge recycling resources, begin with the instruction sheet tucked inside the box that the cartridge came in. Many companies offer cartridge recycling programs, even covering mailing costs. Here are some of the best Web sites.

- **www.hp.com.** Search for "product reuse and recycling" on the Hewlett-Packard Web site.
- **www.freerecycling.com.** This Internet-based company offers cash payments for empty cartridges, with paybacks ranging from 30 cents to around $2.
- **www.emptysolution.com.** After signing up online for the program, Empty Solution sends you prepaid UPS labels. Once you collect at least 10 laser or 20 inkjet cartridges, use a label to send in the empties. After your cartridges are inspected, a check is mailed to you.

CDS AND DVDS

They may seem almost indestructible, but CDs and DVDs still require some care to get the most out of them. In this section you'll find clever ways to organize, care for, and when the time comes, properly and securely dispose of the shiny disks.

ID THE DISKS. It's easy to mistakenly toss valuable data when unlabeled disks pile up around the home office. Labeling your disks is the best way to keep track of your data. But labeling incorrectly can actually ruin a disk. Here's the right way to label.

MAKE IT LAST

- **Look before you stick.** Never write or place labels on the data side of the disk. (That's the shiny side opposite the one with the manufacturer's information.)

- **Peeling with problems.** Whenever possible, avoid using adhesive labels directly on your CDs and DVDs. If they peel, those labels can ruin your disk drive.
- **Pass on pressure.** When writing directly onto a disk, use a felt-tip marker and never a ballpoint pen. The latter requires too much pressure and pressing down on the disk could damage it.

FIX IT FAST

SMOOTH A SCRATCH. If you suspect a scratch is rendering a disk unreadable, don't panic right away—all is not necessarily lost. You may be able to buff the scratch out and resurrect your disk.

All disks have a clear protective coating on the data side, and a visible scratch sometimes affects only that coating and not the layer that contains data. If you smooth the edges of that scratch, the disk often becomes readable again. Here are two ways you can approach that scratch. Both require a soft, clean, lint-free cloth. In either case, always gently wipe in a straight line from the disk center to the outer edge, being careful never to wipe in a circular motion.

1. Sparingly dampen the lint-free cloth with plain, room temperature water and wipe the disk. Repeat the wiping process with a dry section of the cloth.
2. Squeeze a dot (about the size of half a pea) of plain white toothpaste or metal polish on the cloth. These are abrasive cleansers, so be gentle—you don't want to create new scratches. Dampen a fresh section of the cloth with room temperature tap water. Repeat to remove all buffing paste. With a dry section of your cloth, wipe dry.

SEE THE SCRATCH. When you're trying to buff out a scratch, it helps to know exactly where it is. Hold the disk under a bright desk lamp and tilt it at various angles. The scratch will be very apparent.

SEND THE SOFTWARE, TOO. When you donate your old computer, don't forget to pack up your old software programs and manuals and bundle them along with the machine. That way, whoever gets the computer can benefit fully from your generosity. Of course, it also gets the old software out of your home.

PASS IT ALONG

DESTROY THE EVIDENCE. If you need to destroy a disk that contains sensitive data, such as tax information or your social security number, you may be able to slide it through your home paper shredder; many newer models can tackle disks. Check the owner's manual to find out whether yours can.

4 Tips
to Protect Disks

Despite their 1.2-millimeter thickness, CDs and DVDs are amazingly durable. They are not, however, impervious to damage. By taking a few precautionary measures, you can give the disks an even longer life.

1. **Handle with care.** Touch only its outer edge or only the side with no recorded information. This prevents fingerprints or dust particles from damaging data.
2. **Serve disks data side up.** Never place a disk's data side on a hard surface. This keeps dirt from scratching the disk.
3. **A case for cases.** Store each disk in its own protective case. Office supply stores carry paper, soft plastic (often made of Tyvek), and hard, high-impact-resistant plastic versions. For long-term storage, hard plastic cases are best. Stack disks on their edges (like books) and keep them in a dry, cool spot away from direct sunlight.
4. **Dust can do damage.** Remove spots, dust, and fingerprints by gently wiping the disk using a soft, clean, dry, lint-free cloth in a straight line from the disk center to the outer edge. Avoid wiping in a circular motion as this could drive dust particles deeper into the disk and create scratches that may damage your data.

If your shredder isn't able to handle disks or you don't own a shredder, simply grab a dishtowel and a hammer. Place the towel on a cement surface (an outdoor stoop or sidewalk), fold the towel in half, place the disk inside your "wrapper," and use a hammer to smack the towel five or six times. The disk should now be in many hundreds of unreadable and irretrievable pieces and is ready for the trash.

DISKS REDUX. In most cases, CDs and DVDs are recyclable only in bulk, which means you can't just set them out for curbside pickup. Fortunately, there are lots of ways to give those old CDs and DVDs a second, third, even fourth life around the house. Here are just a few.

- **Fly-swatting fun.** Use a hot glue gun to attach a CD or DVD to a dowel or an old ruler, and use it as a make-do flyswatter in the backyard, basement, or workshop.
- **Decorative disks.** Attach dried greenery and small ornaments from the crafts store with a hot glue gun to make mini Christmas wreaths and gift tags.
- **Bye-bye birdie.** Some gardeners hang CDs on fruit trees to keeps birds from eating their crops.
- **Clever crafts.** If you have a stash of unwanted CDs or DVDs, put your crafty cap on and give an old disk a new life as a coaster, a base for a glass votive (apply felt to the back of the CD), a model of the planet Saturn (cut a ball in half and glue it over the hole on both sides of the CD), or an ice-skating rink for a miniature Christmas village. If you're feeling particularly adventurous, crack, cut, or smash CDs in a towel, then decorate a mirror, picture frame, or flowerpot with the pieces.

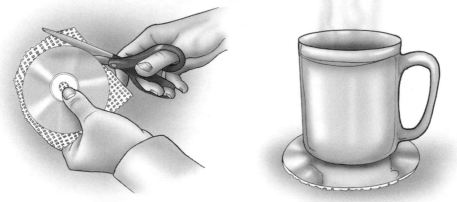

Don't throw away an old CD. Use a hot glue gun to attach some felt to one side and—voilà!—you have an instant coaster.

CORDLESS PHONES

Except for the fact that we occasionally misplace the handset, we love cordless phones. In fact, they're a multitasker's dream come true. Here are a few tips to keep this essential device in perfect working order, day after day, call after call.

TOP TIPS FOR CORD-FREE SUCCESS. Keep your cordless phone working like a charm with these tips.

MAKE IT LAST

- **Interference intervention.** Place the phone's base at least 20 feet from microwave ovens, television sets, radios, and any other electronic products that cause radio-frequency interference.
- **Channel surfing.** If you're not already familiar with the channel button, consult the phone's instruction manual and learn about it. When you push this button, the handset looks for a clearer signal from the base, reducing static.
- **Sayonara to static.** Static can also be caused by another electrical device in the room; sometimes wandering to another room clears up the problem.
- **Better battery behavior.** To significantly increase the life of your phone's battery, place the handset in its base only when the battery is completely empty. Most cordless phones beep when it's time. Some newer batteries, however, do not require this precaution, so consult the owner's manual for specifics about your phone's battery.

READY! SET! CHARGE! To keep a cordless phone juiced and always ready for business, it's important to provide the charging hardware with a little TLC.

- **Contact cleanings.** Once a month, use a pencil eraser to clean away dirt from between the charge contacts on both the base and the handset.
- **Beep. Beep. Beep.** When it comes to a cordless phone's battery, the question isn't *if* it will die, but *when.* The average life span is one year. You'll know

SIMPLE SOLUTIONS

Organize by the Book

If you have a lot of CDs and DVDs but not a lot of storage space, we have the solution for you. All you need is a 3-ring binder, CD/DVD sleeves or photo album refill pages for 5- by 8-inch images, and just a little bit of shelf space. Slip each disk into a slot (of the sleeve or photo page) and then place in the binder. No doubling up, please, since this could cause one disk to scratch the other. Organize your disks as you would photographs—by year or by subject. Place the photo album refill pages in your binder, place your binder on your bookshelf, and step back to admire your newly organized information center.

that it's time to replace the battery when the phone's low-battery warning is constantly going off (sometimes a beep, sometimes a message in the receiver's viewing window). But if this happens several months before a year is up, consult your phone's owner's manual for battery-charging tips you haven't yet tried.

- **Dating dos.** Before replacing your phone's battery, use a permanent felt tip marker to write the installation date on the battery. When a year's almost up, buy a new battery and keep it on standby.

CELL PHONES

Whether you consider it an ever-ready emergency communications device or an electronic leash, the cell phone is one of those everyday items we can't imagine living without—even though a decade ago, few of us even owned one. In this section you'll find advice about how to keep your mobile up and running so it's there when you need it.

MAKE IT LAST

A SLICKER FOR YOUR CELL. Water can ruin a cell phone, and most warranties don't cover phones damaged by water. In fact, some phones have a smearable ink inside the case that indicates whether the phone

---

$mart Buys
WIRELESS WINNERS

Many variables affect a cordless phone's range capabilities (in other words, how far you can wander from the base unit and still enjoy a clear connection). Claims made by manufacturers are based on optimal conditions, so heed promises with caution.

- **Cost of quality.** For ultimate sound quality and range, shop for a 2.4-GHz cordless phone. Depending on other features, these phones start at around $150. A less expensive 900-MHz phone, which will cost around $40, offers decent sound quality and range. If you don't want to spend that much, look for a 46- to 49-MHz phone that has noise reduction circuitry.
- **Standby stats.** Consider a phone's battery standby time, which is the amount of time,

usually between 7 and 30 days, a phone will stay charged when it's unused and out of the base. This is important information to have if you like to keep the cordless phone beside your desk, but the base is in the kitchen. Longer standby times usually work off a nickel-metal-hydride (NiMH) battery.

- **Oodles of options.** As for must-have features, this could be a chapter unto itself. Your best bet is to clear a good hour to review the selection at your local electronics superstore. Here's an additional hint: Call waiting, three-way calling, and caller ID are pretty standard phone options, but for these features to work they must be included in the contract with your phone service provider.

---

has had water damage. But you can't put your life on hold just because the skies have opened up. Next time you know you'll need to make or take calls outdoors on a rainy day, slip your phone inside a ziplock plastic bag and seal it shut. You'll be able to push the buttons through the plastic and hear your caller through it, too.

To protect your cell for the long haul, it's a good idea to invest in a water-resistant cell phone case. Usually made of a microfiber fabric, these covers need not be removed to use the phone—you can speak, hear, and dial as usual. While water resistant cases won't allow you to pocket your cell while scuba diving, they do protect against splashes and minor spills. At an average cost of around $30, that's way less expensive than the price of a new phone. And remember, even if your service provider gave you the phone for free with your contract, you will be charged for a replacement.

SCRATCH-PROOF THE SCREEN. Even if you keep your cell phone in a case, the screen can still get scratched. Scratches make it difficult to read, especially in bright light. And if you have a camera phone, a scratced screen makes all your pictures look like they've been taken in fog. But you can keep the screen scratch-free by taking one simple precaution: Covering it. Companies such as Belkin, ScreenGuardz, and WriteRight have been making nonadhesive, clear vinyl screen protectors for personal digital assistants (PDAs) for years, and now sell a similar product designed to protect the faces of cell phones and camera phones. You'll find them at chain stationery stores; many phone retailers carry them, as well. If you cannot find small-sized covers, buy the larger ones, and cut them to fit.

USE IT OR LOSE IT. It takes longer to recharge a completely drained phone battery, but here's why you should run it down totally every so often before you recharge it. If your phone's battery is a nickel-metal-hydride (NiMH) or nickel-cadmium (NiCd) type, then it's prone to the dreaded "memory effect." These kinds of batteries are made up of cells, and if those cells aren't fully discharged and recharged on a regular basis, the battery stops making use of them. This happens when you place the phone in the charger to "top it off" every night, whether or not the battery is fully drained. Sooner—rather than later—the battery's capacity to hold a charge diminishes. To avoid the memory effect, make sure you discharge and recharge the battery fully every three to five charge cycles.

CHARGE IT THREE TIMES Another way to prevent the dreaded memory effect (see previous tip) is to treat a new battery right, right from the beginning. Condition it by making sure you fully charge and then completely discharge the battery the first three times you install a new battery or use a new phone.

AVOID BATTERY BURNOUT. Overcharging can be worse than undercharging a battery. Never leave one charging for more than 24 hours straight. Not only will the battery overheat and possibly malfunction, but the excess heat can damage the phone as well.

 **FIX IT FAST** **STIFLE STATIC.** Cell phones: We can't live with them, and we can't live without them. When yours acts up, try these quick tricks to correct annoying static.

- **Move around.** If you're indoors, move to a spot near a window or go outside.
- **Check your chip.** If your phone is troubled by static both indoors and out, an internal memory chip upgrade may solve the problem. In many cases this upgrade won't cost a cent, so call your service provider for more information.
- **Look for a landline.** Cell phone reception often improves if at least one person is on a landline; it improves even more if the call is initiated from the landline.

TRY THE OLD SWITCHEROO. If your cell phone suddenly won't hold a charge, the battery may be dead, or the charger may be busted. But how can you know which component is the issue? Does a friend have the same phone? Borrow her charger and see whether this fixes the problem. If yes, then call your cell phone service provider to find out about buying a new charger, which, incidentally, is far less expensive than a new phone or a new battery.

CAN YOU SEE ME NOW? Should your cell phone's display window quit displaying, it may be because you had the cell in a pocket while taking a brisk walk

---

SIMPLE SOLUTIONS

5 Improvised Cell Phone Cases

Your cell phone will last a lot longer if you keep it protected in a case. Here are five "cases" you probably already have around the house that will do the job in a pinch.
1. Change purse
2. Drawstring jewelry bag
3. Eyeglass case
4. Pocket protector
5. Small padded mailing envelope

---

in the cold outdoors. A cell's display functions best at room temperature. Place the phone on a table (indoors, of course) and wait for about an hour. After the phone warms up, you may be back in business.

MAKE CONTACT. If the power on your cell phone cuts out unexpectedly, it may be because the battery isn't making good contact with the phone. Don't throw it out: Grab a pencil eraser and rub the little metal strips on the underside of the battery as well as the corresponding terminals on the phone. Often, dust can get under the battery cover and accumulate under the battery. Use a squeeze bulb or a puff of breath to blow the dust and eraser rubbings away.

CALL FOR HELP. It's estimated that more than 150 million cell phones have been discarded in the United States, and that's a shame, because your old phone can help save a life.

PASS IT ALONG

Charitable organizations including The National Coalition Against Domestic Violence (www.ncadv.org), Phones 4 Charity (www.phones4charity.org), and the Wireless Recycling program (www.wirelessrecycling.com), as well as local groups and some of the major service providers, will accept used cell phones and redistribute them to those who can really use them.

If the phone doesn't work anymore, they'll still take it. Broken phones can be refurbished and donated (or at least recycled and disposed of in an environmentally safe way—and that benefits everyone). Ask your service provider whether it accepts donations, or visit the aforementioned organizations on the Internet.

CLEAR THE CHIP. Before donating your phone, make sure your service provider has deactivated it—and clean out your address book and any other stored information. Go to www.wirelessrecycling.com, and look for the big pink eraser on the home page. Click it. After entering your cell phone's manufacturer and model number, you can download step-by-step instructions to erase your phone's saved data. You could also go to a free-standing cellular phone retail shop and ask the salesperson to clear out your personal information.

RECHARGEABLE AND RECYCLABLE. Nickel-cadmium (NiCd), nickel-metal-hydride (NiMH), and lithium-ion (Li-ion), are rechargeable batteries commonly used in cellular and cordless phones. When their time has come and they're ready to be pitched, don't throw them out with the regular trash; their chemical components are poisonous and don't belong in a landfill.

Some major electronics, household, and discount stores have joined with The Rechargeable Battery Recycling Corporation (RBRC) to help consumers recycle their portable rechargeable batteries. Participating retailers will take the batteries off your hands and recycle or dispose of them in an environmentally safe manner. Go to the RBRC's Web site at www.rbrc.org to find a complete list of participating retailers.

OFFICE SUPPLIES AND EQUIPMENT

They're the kinds of items you don't think about until they begin to pile up, run out, or quit working. The next section will give you a few ideas about how to manage some of those doodads—batteries, business cards, and paper shredders.

MAKE IT LAST

GIVE BATTERIES STAYING POWER. Batteries are not cheap, so when you find them on sale, it pays to stock up. Of course, if you don't store them properly, or buy so many that they expire before you can use them, your savings go down the drain. Keep these guidelines in mind so that your money-saving purchases stay fresh until you've used every last battery.

- **Use 'em for years.** Alkaline batteries have a 7-year shelf life.
- **Avoid extremes.** Store alkaline batteries at room temperature—and *not* in the refrigerator, as some people do. Refrigerators are damp, and dampness shortens battery life. Conversely, heat may also shorten battery life, so keep batteries away from hot or sunny areas.
- **Preserve the packaging.** Avoid carrying loose batteries in a purse, pocket, or briefcase. Contact with metal, like keys or coins, may short-circuit a battery and render it useless. Leave the batteries in their original packaging as long as possible.

THROW A PARADE. You've finished shredding lots of paperwork with your cross-cut shredder. But don't put it in the recycling bin just yet. Give all that paper a second life. Here are four ideas.

- Add white paper (with no colored ink) to your compost pile.
- Use the paper as packing material when you have to ship or store delicate items.
- Check with your local Humane Society or other animal shelter; the organization sometimes collects shredded (and unshredded) paper to use as bedding for animals housed there.
- Use it (indoors, so it's easy to sweep up and toss) as confetti at a kid's party. They'll have a grand time tossing it about.

KEEP CARDS IN BUSINESS. The last time you switched jobs, you probably left with more than photographs from the company picnic and your "Employee of the Month" plaque. Most likely you had an almost full box of business cards, too. Pitch them? Not on your life! Even if you weren't particularly fond of the old place, put those old

$mart Buys
SHOPPING FOR SHREDDERS

Before purchasing a paper shredder, identify your needs and expectations. Here are some guidelines to help you out.

- **The ways of waste.** Integrated shredders come with their own waste receptacle. Stand-alone shredders expand to fit over almost any waste can. Integrated shredders are generally more expensive than stand-alone models.
- **Vertical strips stack up.** Strip-cut shredders, also called straight-cut or spaghetti-cut, slice paper vertically into long, thin strips. Strips don't compress as well as smaller pieces of paper, so be prepared to empty the waste receptacle frequently if you do a lot of shredding.
- **Serious security.** Cross-cut shredders slice paper vertically and horizontally, providing the ultimate security. The resulting confetti does compress well, so there's less bulk to dispose of. Of course, these models are

more expensive than their strip-cutting counterparts, and they do generate some dust and lint.
- **Paper check.** The shredder's throat, either large or small, is the opening where you feed the paper. The average home office requires a throat measuring 8¾ to 9 inches, so be sure to know the size of the paper you'll be shredding.
- **Favorable features.** Safety and convenience features that may be worth an extra buck include a light or buzzer that indicates a paper jam; a reverse feed, which helps to clear paper jams; an auto-off feature that turns the machine off when paper isn't being fed into the shredder; and a transparent waste receptacle that allows you to see when it's time to empty the bin. Avoid using mesh receptacles; tiny bits of paper and lint can be pushed through the mesh as the bin fills, creating a cleaning challenge.

cards back to work as note cards. Keep a few tucked in your wallet or purse to jot down a note when there's no paper handy.

FILE UNDER "CLEVER." If you find yourself with a stack of old business cards—yours or someone else's—think twice before throwing them out. With just a little trimming, a card fits into the label holder on the front of a filing cabinet.

OFFICE FURNITURE

What's an office without furniture? A store room? A maze? Certainly, not a place to get any work done. Read on for ways to furnish and maintain a home office—without going out of business.

MAKE IT LAST

LIKE A COASTER FOR YOUR DESK. Newer optical mice may not need a mouse pad to perform well, but don't toss your pad quite yet. Using a mouse on a bare desk surface can mar the desk's finish. Although a pad may not be technologically necessary, it is essential—if you want your desk to remain in tip-top shape.

GO TO THE MAT FOR YOUR CARPET. If you've recently set up a home office area in a room with carpeting, there's one simple and inexpensive step you can take to make the carpet live a long life: Purchase an office chair mat from an office supply store. These vinyl mats prevent a rolling office chair from causing permanent ruts in the carpet (and the padding beneath) and destroying the pile. Prices start at around $25—a small price to pay compared with having to replace an entire room of carpet.

LIGHT UP. If you buy one item for your home office, make it a high-quality desk lamp. Why? First, when you buy the right lamp the first time, you won't need to spend your hard-earned money buying replacements, and second, your eyes will forever thank you.

- **Be flexible.** Shop for a lamp with an adjustable arm, often called a pliable gooseneck, so you can redirect the light source as you move about in your chair.
- **Use natural light.** Choose a lamp that can handle a full-spectrum fluorescent bulb or a full-spectrum fluorescent tube. Here's why: The standard fluorescent or indoor incandescent bulb produces a predominantly yellow-orange glow, which in tests has been shown

to make us anxious or irritable. A full-spectrum bulb shines with yellow and orange but also green, blue, and violet, creating a more natural light source—like the sun—which is not only better for your eyes, but also for your mood.

GETTING ORGANIZED

There's an old saying that a clean desk is the sign of a sick mind, but the truth is, it's hard to get anything done if your work space is disorganized. Here are some ways to get organized and stay that way.

NO DRAWERS? NO PROBLEM. Just because your home office desk  **FIX IT FAST** is a table with no drawers doesn't mean you can't have a completely organized space. Here's how.

- **Just jar it.** Stow small supplies in small jars, like those that baby food comes in. To keep the jars organized, purchase shallow picture ledges at your favorite home improvement store. The shelves are shallow enough to be unobtrusive, but wide enough to hold the jars and other office necessaries.
- **Press and hold.** Press an unused napkin holder into service as a holder for bills, checkbooks, or credit cards.
- **Cubbies galore.** To instantly create a dozen or more small storage cubbies, hang a shoe bag with pockets beside your desk. Use the cubbies to organize your scissors, rulers, staplers, a stash of envelopes, and even receipts.

LIGHTEN YOUR PAPER LOAD. Did you know the Internal Revenue Service accepts scanned and printed receipts? If your office is shy on storage space, scan and save those tax deductibles as jpg files in a folder called IRS receipts. Now toss the paper ones.

Nearly Free Furniture

Outside of hand-me-downs, free home office furniture is pretty hard to come by. Almost free, however, is another story. Here are two quick tricks to help you locate good deals.

1. **See the signs.** Keep your eyes open for smaller commercial building "For Sale" signs. It often means that the inhabitants will soon be moving… but not necessarily with their desks and chairs. It's worth 15 minutes to pop into the building, ask for the office manager, inquire as to whether they're planning on moving once the building is sold, and, if so, will they be lugging office furniture with them. If not, the company may offer gently used merchandise for great prices.

2. **Check out closing sales.** Don't discount the closing sales of retail stores for great bargains beyond merchandise. Once all the shoes, housewares, and whatever else have been sold, store fixtures often go next. Tall shelving units that display shoes are great for organizing books, magazines, or files. A large table that previously held dinnerware easily becomes a roomy desk.

SHARE AND SHARE ALIKE. Let's say you decided to turn a now-grown child's bedroom into a home office. Okay, now you have an extra bed but no desk! The solution? Announce to your circle of friends that you have a square deal—one free bed for one free desk. Swapping furniture is a win-win for everyone...fast, free, and fun.

INFORMATION GATHERING

Want to get off the automated menu merry-go-round? This section offers ways to cut to the chase when you need to know *now*, and you want to speak with a real person on the other end of the telephone line.

FIX IT FAST
PRESS "1" IF YOU'RE TICKED. You're in your home office with a fresh cup of tea. It's time to address that unknown charge on your phone bill or electric bill or statement from your investment broker. You call the appropriate 800 number, but soon find yourself caught in a maze of automated phone menus. The quickest trick in the book to reach a live customer service rep: Visit http://gethuman.com/us/. This Web site features a list of more than 500 companies, with each company's toll-free phone number and a shortcut to reach each company's live customer service department. You can search for a company by alphabetical listing or by category.

FIND FACTS FAST. Need to call a company or service but aren't able to lay your hands on the toll-free number? Here are three ways to find the number you need in a flash.

1. For U.S.-based companies, call 1-800-555-1212. This is directory assistance for toll-free phone numbers. It comes with a charge, just as 411 does, but sometimes a fast fix is worth a small fee.
2. EDGAR (Electronic Data Gathering, Analysis, and Retrieval system), sponsored by the U.S. Securities and Exchange Commission, is located at www.sec.gov/edgar/searchedgar/companysearch.html. Use this Web site to locate the number of a public company.

WORKING IN COMFORT

Let's face it: Work, whether it's paying bills or checking homework, isn't always fun. But it shouldn't hurt, either. The following tips will help you fix all sorts of office problems, from tired eyes and aching backs to annoying distractions.

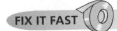

ELIMINATE MONITOR GLARE. Glare from a computer screen can cause eyestrain, but it's easy to remedy the problem. You'll need a monitor glare screen endorsed by the American Optometric Association (AOA). It's also sometimes called an anti-glare filter. The AOA Seal of Acceptance, which will be displayed on the screen's packaging, means the filter passed specific tests. To purchase the proper size, measure your monitor viewing area diagonally. There are different styles from which to choose, but overall, the following features are most important.

- Optical glass, which is more effective than plastic or micromesh
- Antireflective coating that provides up to 99 percent glare reduction
- A transmission level that reflects your needs—this number, ranging from about 35 to 65 percent, represents how light or dark the filter is, and how much it reduces glare from ambient light, or light coming from all directions in the room. Lower transmission levels reduce high glare levels; a higher transmission level is fine for less glare.
- Static reduction or elimination
- An easy-to-clean feature that requires only water and a soft cloth

SEE? NO EYESTRAIN. There are several reasons not to place your desk in front of a window, even though the idea of a view may appeal to you. Desk location can create a sharp contrast between the light in front of you and a computer monitor's brightness level. When this disparity occurs, your eyes have to work hard to adjust each time you look up, and the result is often eyestrain. Ideally, you want to place your desk to the left or right of a window. If this is impossible, invest in a room-dimming shade to quickly fix the problem.

PUT UP A SCREEN. Are your eyes feeling tired and sore? Excessive hours spent in front of a monitor—whether for work or enjoyment—may be the culprit. Computer Vision Syndrome, or CVS, causes tired or sore eyes, periodic blurred vision, headaches, dry or red eyes, contact lens discomfort, and excessive tearing. The simplest way to combat CVS and preserve your eyes' health is to follow the 20/20/20 rule: Look away from your computer and take a vision break every 20 minutes; look away for at least 20 seconds; and focus on an object that's at least 20 feet away.

GAZE IN COMFORT. A perfect computer is useless if monitor-gazing makes your neck sore, strains your eyes, and causes your shoulders to ache. Here's how to position the monitor to fix the problem.

1. Position your monitor directly in front of you, so you're looking dead center at the monitor when seated comfortably.
2. Your monitor should be at arm's length (20 to 25 inches) from the tip of your nose when you are seated. Increase this distance to 25 to 30 inches if your screen (measured diagonally) is 20 inches or larger.
3. Tilt the monitor or adjust your chair height so that your eyes are level with an imaginary line drawn horizontally across the center of the screen. This imaginary line may need to be lowered if your wear bifocals, trifocals, or progressive lenses.

SAY GOODBYE TO GLARE. Pay atention to your back for eye health. When seated at your desk, you do not want overhead lights or lamps behind you to contrast too sharply with your monitor's brightness level. This creates a glare on your monitor that can provoke eyestrain. To check this balance, turn your monitor off and place the backside of a mirror against your monitor. If you see direct-light bursts hitting the mirror, then it indicates that they're also hitting your screen. You may be able to move the light source, or scoot the desk left or right until the glare's gone.

GET INTO POSITION. How and where you place your keyboard can significantly reduce—if not completely remedy—shoulder and arm strain. Position the keyboard so its center is lined up with the center of your body, and it's at the same height as your elbows. While typing, your upper arms should rest naturally and comfortably at your sides and your elbows should point neither inward nor outward. To see whether your keyboard is at the right height, turn your chair sideways 90 degrees and place your hands in your lap. Your elbow should be level with the keyboard.

DISPENSE WITH DISTRACTIONS. When it's time to get down to work, here's a quick trick to keep communication lines limited but open with family members in the other part of the house. Tell them they may use the home phone to call you on your cell phone. Since it takes more time to punch in your number than barge into your office, there will likely be fewer disruptions.

SITE IT WISELY. Where you place your desk can mean the difference between a lasting, productive home office and a makeshift, chaotic space. Here are three places *not* to site your home office.

- **Bedroom.** This is where you want to experience peaceful thoughts and restful sleep. Ruminating about your investments or the phone bill you forgot to pay is not how you want to spend your nights.
- **Kitchen.** This is the busiest room in the house and not a good place to try to get work done.
- **Family room.** This room tends to house the television and games, so you may want to set up your office in a less-used room.

MORE TIPS FOR THE HOME OFFICE

Here's a roundup of the home office-related Pass It Along tips you'll find in the other chapters of *Don't Throw It Out!*

CHAPTER	TIP	PAGE
1	Brew Up Clever Uses for Filters	16
1	Try These Tray Uses	25
8	The Puck Stops Here	261
9	They Won't Fly, But You Can Recycle Potted Plant Saucers	281

DOMESTIC CHALLENGE

Odds are good that many supplies from your home office can be put to good use somewhere else, but there are a few surprising truths about reusing and donating discards.

Questions

1. If you want to donate a PC to a non-profit and still protect your privacy, prepare to pay at least $12 for a program to clean your hard drive.

2. You cannot donate bad phones or vehicle-installed models to most organizations like the YWCA that refurbish the phones for domestic abuse victims.

3. If you have an old cell phone you don't need, rest easy knowing it might help a victim of domestic abuse dial 911 if you donate it to an organization such as the YWCA.

4. The local elementary school will enthusiastically accept those bundles of old pens from trade shows and service businesses that seem to accumulate in your desk drawer, as long as you make sure they work first.

5. An old bulletin board can be converted into a handy serving tray if it's no larger than 18 inches on any side.

6. Manufacturers such as Apple, Minolta, and Hewlett-Packard provide pre-paid return labels or envelopes to return their toner or ink cartridges for reuse or recycling.

7. Printer fuser cords, iPods and palm pilots are just a few of the items accepted by the Recycle for Breast Cancer organization.

8. Any senior citizen center or veterans hospital will welcome a donation of an old-fashioned rotary phone—after all, that's what most of those folks grew up with.

9. If one side of a printed page only has a few lines of ink on it, you can flip it over and reload it for new printing jobs.

10. You can't recycle shredded documents unless your program accepts "mixed paper."

Answers

1. **FALSE.** There are several programs online you can download

for free that still thoroughly purge any personal info from your hard drive.

2. **TRUE.** They're not appropriate for most of the intended recipients and are too costly to re-program.

3. **FALSE.** It varies from group to group, and some generate funds for domestic abuse programs by recycling the components of old phones. If it makes a difference to you how your old phone will be used, make sure to ask before parting with your property.

4. **FALSE.** Most elementary school students are still working with pencils. Try a local women's shelter or donate extras to the thrift store, instead.

5. **TRUE.** Any wider or longer and the tray will be too flimsy. Use the larger versions to mat larger prints (spray paint the cork in a suitable color, first) or to refurbish the top of an end table or TV tray.

6. **TRUE.** Lexmark, Xerox cartridges, and Arista Business Imaging Solutions are a few others.

7. **TRUE.** The organization benefits Susan G. Komen Breast Cancer Foundation and will send free prepaid shipping labels, envelopes, collection boxes or send a truck for items ranging from printer cartridges to televisions.

8. **FALSE.** While some organizations may indeed welcome the vintage items, they can be difficult for people with arthritis or other limited dexterity issues to use—and they make it impossible to access automated phone services. Instead, look into donating the phone to a local drama group, or see what it will bring from an antique dealer.

9. **FALSE.** Unless you're set up for two-sided printing, ink jet printers in particular suffer when already-inked paper comes in contact with the rollers, and you may be messing up your entire operation if you do it often enough.

10. **TRUE.** The rag and pulp content of the paper is what matters, and that doesn't change just because it's been shredded. Even if you can't recycle mixed paper in your area, you can use the shreds as a great addition to the compost pile.

6

THE BATHROOM

Okay, we agree that you shouldn't talk about the toilet or the bathroom in polite company. But we're making an exception for these bathroom tips, because they'll help you make items last in the room where every square inch is subject to wear and tear on a daily basis, and remodeling costs are at a premium.

All aspects of the "room behind the closed door" are considered, from floor tiles to exhaust fans. You'll learn how to make a bathtub seal last longer, how to keep your lip gloss fresh, and how to extend the life of your shower—with items from the automotive supply store.

Is your powder room already showing its age? Discover sticky tips for mending snags in the shower curtain, find a sour solution to hard-water stains, and use this sneaky method to get the curling iron to stop smoking.

Did you know that there is a Web site devoted entirely to the relocation and replacement of toilet tank lids? That and so many other ideas for bathrooms are on the following pages . . . you'll agree they're "flush" with possibilities!

BATHTUBS AND SHOWERS

Whether you're a soaker or a sprayer, these tips will help you to tend to the bathing area for years of low-cost use—and save water and prevent germs, too.

MAKE IT LAST

CAULK WITH CARE. Whether you're putting in a new bathtub or just sprucing up an old one, there's a trick to caulking it so the seal will last for a long time. Start by completely filling the tub with water. Allow the water to settle for a few minutes, and then seal the gaps anywhere the tub meets the walls, floor, and shower doors with silicone caulk. Let the caulk set for a half hour before emptying the tub. Then allow the caulk to cure for at least another hour before filling the tub again. Most bathtubs expand somewhat when filled or when someone stands in them to take a shower. When you start off with a tub full of water, the caulk sets at the point when the tub is the most

---

BACK FROM THE BRINK
Old Tub, New Finish

My husband and I moved into a recently vacated apartment. It was in good shape, but the bathtub's finish was a mess (it had been painted by hand). We had to refinish the tub; the trick was figuring out how. We didn't want to go more than a long weekend without the bathtub and shower, and we couldn't afford to spend much on the project.

First, we removed the caulking around the tub and fixtures. Then, with the window open, we used paint remover jelly and a plastic spatula to scrape off the old paint. Now the tub had to be refinished. Epoxy paint was our first choice, but it was too expensive and complicated to use. Our next choice was spray enamel. Why? It's inexpensive, it would work, and it would cut the project time in less than half.

We gave the tub a thorough cleaning and removed all the hardware. Next, we treated all the surfaces that would be painted with muriatic acid from the hardware store so that the paint would adhere. Before you work with any harsh chemicals, make sure you have plenty of ventilation, wear rubber work gloves and eye protection, and plug the drain so as little as possible gets into the water supply. If you don't like harsh chemicals, you can achieve the same results by rubbing the surface with very fine (#000 grade) steel wool.

We soaked up the remaining muriatic acid with some old rags and rinsed the tub once again and allowed it to dry. Then we covered the walls, floor, and showerhead with plastic drop cloths and masking tape.

We applied several light coats of the paint to the tub. After each coat dried, which took about an hour, we gave the tub a light sanding. With the final coat dry, the fixtures replaced, and all the joints re-caulked, it looked like a brand new tub. To dispose of the rags we soaked in harsh chemicals, we placed them in a can filled with water and threw them away during our neighborhood's hazardous waste pickup day.

—Betsy Reynold
Summit, New Jersey

---

expanded. Emptying the tub before the caulk fully cures allows the flexible silicone to seep into the smallest spaces. This way, as the tub expands and contracts with regular use, the caulk is securely set and less likely to work loose.

HOW HOT IS TOO HOT? Let 'em read it in red. One small bottle and brush can save gallons of water every week and prolong the life of your bathroom faucets and dials. Who hasn't spent a few moments with the water running while trying to figure out which positions on the faucet handles will yield the desired water temperature—and maybe gotten a shocking blast of cold or hot water in the bargain? And if you have one giant dial for both tub and shower that rotates to different settings, all the experimenting makes it wear out more quickly or even break.

The solution? Nail polish. Paint a bright red (or any color you like that's also easy to see) slash right on the chrome or tile to indicate where the dial or handle should be for optimal shower or bath temperatures. If preferences vary in your family, note each one with a nail polish symbol or initial—for a colorful and functional end result, ask each family member to choose their own color of nail polish. And don't worry, you should be able to easily remove most polish marks on bathroom surfaces: Scrape the polish with your fingernail, or apply a drop of nail polish remover to a cotton swab and very lightly touch the polish mark, swiping away the color with the dry end of the swab.

SLIP OFF NONSLIP STICKERS. Those nonslip safety decals are great when they're brand new, and they keep you from slipping in the shower. But after a while the edges start to lift and become yet another hiding place for soap and other slippery scum to build up on the bathtub or shower floor. Unfortunately, trying to peel off an old one usually leaves some part of the rubber appliqué stuck to the tub. Here's how to dissolve the glue and leave the tub's surface squeaky-clean and scum free.

FIX IT FAST

Keep in mind that when you're working with lighter fluid, you need to make sure there's plenty of ventilation. In addition, wear rubber work gloves and eye protection, plug the drain so as little as possible gets into the water supply, and (of course) don't smoke. To dispose of the soaked rags and any paper towels, place them in a can filled with water, and throw the can away during your next local hazardous waste pickup day.

1. Close the bathtub drain.
2. Soak a rag in lighter fluid and lay it over the remnants of the decal for a few minutes.
3. Remove the rag and use a thin, plastic spatula or an old credit card to pry the edge up. Squirt a little more lighter fluid under the decal as you lift.
4. Once the sticker is fully removed, squirt a little more lighter fluid on the sticky residue and rub it off with a paper towel.
5. Use another rag to soak up the remaining lighter fluid, then rinse out the entire tub with warm, soapy water.

   If any of the glue from the decal remains, use a slightly abrasive product such as Ajax Scouring Cleanser and a scouring sponge directly on the spot.

   A final note: The lighter fluid shouldn't harm plastic or fiberglass surfaces, but test it out on an inconspicuous area first, and skip the abrasive cleaner altogether.

WHIRLPOOL TUBS

The ultimate treat tub needs a little tender loving care to give you years of bubbly fun. This down-home remedy will preserve your uptown investment.

MAKE IT LAST

GIVE YOUR JACUZZI JETS A WHIRL. If you have a whirlpool bathtub, you may not know that the jets need to be cleaned. You may think, all that water is always rushing through them, so they stay clean, right? Wrong. Mold can grow in the jets, especially if you don't use the sprayers with some regularity. Paying attention to them by performing some quick and easy maintenance moves will keep the jets clean and flowing—and make the whole system last longer.

Commercial products, such as Whirlout, are available for this very purpose; they're sold in the plumbing aisle of home supply stores and online. But if you don't want to make a special trip or spend the money, here's are two trusted home remedies that work just as well and costs less: Add 1 cup of chlorine bleach to a tub filled just above the jets with hot water. Run the jets for about 20 minutes. Do this once a month and you'll keep your Jacuzzi mildew-free. The other trick that works for some people: Add a scoop of non-sudsing automatic dishwasher detergent to a tub full of hot water. Let the jets run for about 20 minutes.

SHOWERHEADS

Our solutions for leaky showerheads rain down! Read on to find out how dental floss can repair a leak and how to move that old shower into the yard and transform it into a greenhouse.

TAPE A LEAKY SHOWERHEAD. Sometimes, the only way to fix a leaky showerhead is to replace it. But don't be surprised if the new one drips at the joint where it threads onto the shower body. That can happen when worn threads on an old pipe don't make a completely watertight fit with a new fixture.

MAKE IT LAST

Taking a little extra time to make a watertight seal with the new fixture will keep the head from leaking—and wasting a significant amount of water—for years to come. To start, remove the old showerhead. You'll need to clean the old pipe joint compound from the pipe threads: To do this, dip an old toothbrush or some heavy grade (#4) steel wool in mineral spirits or paint thinner and scrub the threads. Next, wipe all the threads with an old rag or paper towel to remove any trace of the mineral spirits or thinner. Then, to make the new seal watertight, apply a fresh pipe joint compound, Teflon tape, or both, to the pipe threads before attaching the new fixture. You'll find pipe joint compound and Teflon tape at most hardware and plumbing supply stores.

SIMPLE SOLUTIONS

Floss to Stop the Flow

I woke up one night to the drip–drip–drip of a leak in my bathroom. The leak was coming from where the showerhead attached to the rest of the plumbing. The last thing I was going to do was make a late-night trip to a hardware store for plumbing supplies. Fortunately, I had enough of the raw materials right in the bathroom to fashion a stopgap solution, and I didn't have to go out after all. Although the showerhead was screwed on pretty tight, I was able to remove it with just a pair of pliers, after wrapping the showerhead with a rag to protect it.

I took a few minutes to clean away any old pipe joint compound from both the pipe threads and the threads on the inside of the showerhead with an old toothbrush dipped in all-purpose household pine cleaner. When finished, I wiped the threads with a paper towel to remove any traces of the cleaner. Then I smeared both sides with a finger full of petroleum jelly. Finally, I wound some waxed dental floss around the threads before replacing the showerhead.

I knew this wouldn't stem the leak permanently, but it did stop the leaking long enough for me to get back to sleep and go to the hardware store the next day.

—Connie Hatch
New York, New York

"HANDLE" THE LEAK. A constantly dripping shower doesn't always mean there's something wrong with the showerhead. In fact, if water continues to drip long after you've finished showering, it often means that a washer in one of the faucet handles leading to the head needs to be replaced. You'll have a pretty good idea which one needs to be replaced just by feeling the temperature of the dripping water. If the water feels cold, chances are it's the cold-water faucet that needs to be serviced; if the drip is warm, then it's probably the hot. To change the washer:

Remove the handle.

The washer is below the nut.

1. To start, turn off the water at the supply valve leading to the offending faucet.

2. Unscrew the faucet's handset; you may need to pop off the little cap that says "hot" or "cold" first. On common shower faucet handles, the washer is located below the packing nut, at the bottom of the spindle that fits into the fixture.

Replace the washer.

3. Remove the worn washer and replace it with a new one.

Occasionally, when you disassemble and reassemble the handles, you may need to use a wrench on a polished surface. If that happens, put a few layers of masking tape over the decorative part first to prevent scratches.

Replacement washers are available at most hardware or home supply stores. Several varieties are usually packaged together, ensuring that one of them will fit.

One Man's Trash
From a Hot Shower to Hothouse

When my aunt decided to remodel her bathroom, she asked me to help remove her two-sided glass shower enclosure so she could replace it with a more traditional bathtub. Since it was in good shape, I decided to save the parts and erect them in my mother's backyard as a mini potting shed and greenhouse. Here's how:

First, I spread construction gravel over a 5-foot-square patch of ground and then built a low platform of exterior-grade 3/4-inch plywood and 2-by-4s. I drove some rebar into the ground vertically all around the platform and used U-bolts to secure the rebar to the platform, so the whole thing wouldn't blow over in a strong wind. I reinstalled the bottom tracks of the shower enclosure on the platform's south side so that the greenhouse would get the most sun during the day.

After placing the glass panels in the tracks and temporarily supporting them with additional 2-by-4s propped up against them, I built the side and back walls of the enclosure out of 3/4-inch exterior-grade plywood. Then I attached the enclosure to the platform and reinforced the structure at the corners with galvanized angle brackets.

The corrugated plastic roof was laid across the top and screwed into the plywood walls and glued with silicone to the upper rail of the glass enclosure. It was slanted slightly so the rain could run off. After some adjustable shelves were added to the inside, nonglass part of the structure, my mother was ready to start her growing season earlier than usual.

Caulking all the joints and corners and adding a few coats of exterior paint made the greenhouse practically impervious to the elements and kind of homey, as well. My niece contributed to the effort by painting a garden mural on one of the outside walls.

All the materials, save the shower enclosure itself, were bought at the local home supply store, and all of them were pretty inexpensive.

—Tim Tucker
Long Beach, New York

SHOWER CURTAINS

It's curtains for you! Shower curtains, that is. These tips will help you put a stop to mildew, tears, and sags, then recast worn curtains to new roles at home or play.

BID ADIEU TO MILDEW. Nothing ages a shower faster than trapped moisture—it mildews caulk and grout, makes the air musty, and starts that never-ending cycle of bleaching and scrubbing, which, in turn, ages scrub brushes and cleaning cloths in a hurry. One simple tool can stop mildew in its early stages: the humble squeegee, available in the automotive section of any discount department store. Wipe down the walls and shower door (if you have one) after every shower; it takes just a minute once you have the habit of doing so. It beats the heck out of inhaling bleach fumes and scraping caulk after mildew's gained a stronghold.

MAKE IT LAST

FAVOR FABRIC LOOPS. When you're starting fresh with shower curtains, try to purchase the ones with fabric loops that fasten with buttons instead of those with ring holes for metal or plastic rings or hooks. You'll avoid the inevitable holes that hooks poke in vinyl, and you won't have to replace or ignore broken plastic hooks or malfunctioning or rusty metal hooks. And you simply unbutton the fabric loops to remove the curtain from the rod for washing, which means you're much less likely to have to reinstall the rod because you once again pulled it down with the curtain!

 FIX IT FAST **DUCT TAPE TO THE RESCUE.** If it seems like you rip one ring hole every time you put up or take down your vinyl shower curtain, don't be resigned to living with a perpetually sagging gap. Instead, get out the duct tape and cover the entire hole on both sides, then use a hole punch or craft knife to re-create the ring hole. In the old days, this idea would doom your curtain to looking patched together, but today, duct tape comes in loads of colors and even patterns. You may even want to reinforce the entire top strip of an aging vinyl curtain with a bright color or design and redo all the holes, not just the torn one.

PASS IT ALONG **KEEP VINYL IN YOUR VEHICLE.** An old vinyl shower curtain with a few tears or missing grommets may no longer make the grade in the bathroom, but it sure is helpful to keep in the car. Use it to line the trunk before transporting messy items, from Christmas trees to potluck dinner entrees, or keep it folded in there to serve as an impromptu picnic tablecloth or to line the car floors if everyone shows up with muddy shoes. Be sure to wash it one last time before sending it off to its new job: Just toss the curtain in the washing machine with a little white vinegar and liquid laundry detergent. To remove all the soap, add a little fabric softener during the appropriate cycle.

---

5 Uses for an Old Shower Curtain

Think you've already heard of a million uses for that old shower curtain? Think again. Here are five additional ways to give it another life.

1. Use it as an off-season cover for stored patio furniture or barbecues. Lash it with bungee cords.
2. Keep it in the trunk as a tarp for roadside emergencies if you have to sit on the ground to change a tire or make a quick underbody repair.
3. Put it to use as a lightweight ground cloth for under a tent.
4. Turn it into a leakproof drop cloth for home-painting projects.
5. Transform it into a banner directing folks to your garage sale or family reunion. Use paint to write your message.

TOILETS

Toilet tanks and lids will stand the test of time with these long-wear strategies and quick fixes. We've even included advice about the proper way to plunge.

CREATE A CAULK CUSHION. A loose toilet tank lid makes an irritating scraping noise that's particularly embarrassing if it's a guest who's, er, taking a seat. Annoyance aside, the sliding also grinds down the porcelain on the tank rim more quickly, necessitating a replacement or possibly setting up a disastrous crash scenario. Even fix-it novices can take care of the problem with some good old silicone caulk. Essentially, you create a cushiony gasket by removing the lid, applying a bead of caulk around the top of the tank rim, and letting it dry for at least 24 hours before replacing the top. The effort should pay off for years, but the best part is that any time the gasket slips or breaks, you can just lay down another bead of caulk—no one will ever see it if it gets caked up.

FIX IT FAST

SOLVE THAT SWEATY TANK. Sweating toilet tanks can do more than surprise you when you're half-asleep. The constant dripping can also cause the floor underneath the tank to rot—and that can quickly lead to some very expensive repairs. But here's a quick solution to end the tank sweats.

Tank water that's cooler than the ambient air in the bathroom causes moisture to condense on the outside of the tank and sweat to form. Installing a toilet tank liner (available at any plumbing supply or home improvement store) will insulate the tank's walls. It will also keep the outside temperature from having much of an effect on the water within the tank. Before you can insert the liner, you'll need to shut off the toilet's water supply, completely empty the tank (flush it a few times and then bail out the rest of the water), and allow the interior dry thoroughly. Then, just glue (kits come with adhesive) the foam liner to the inside walls of the tank. Make sure the liner doesn't interfere with the flushing mechanism.

Polish the Posh Fixtures

Have you decided to splurge a bit for those really expensive sink fixtures in your newly remodeled bathroom? Here's how to keep them looking exquisite. Once a month or so, wipe them down with a rag sprayed with a wax-based furniture polish. That will keep mineral deposits from building up and staining or pitting the surface.

Still Working After All These Years
IT'S GOOD TO BE THE KING

The Palace of Knossos, on the Greek island of Crete was, according to myth, the home of King Minos and the Minotaur.

It seems that when the old king had legendary builder Daedalus construct the labyrinth to contain the fearsome bullheaded creature, Minos also had Daedalus do a little side job and install some innovative indoor plumbing.

Visitors to the present-day site can see for themselves among the ruins, beautiful frescos, and giant pithoi (large storage jars), the remains of one of the world's oldest working flush toilets, circa 1600 B.C. Located adjacent to the queen's private bathroom, the toilet is fitted with an overhead reservoir and a running-water drainage system of cone-shaped terracotta tiles to prevent clogging. The ancient bathroom is still functional after almost 4,000 years, though it's no longer in use.

Give the glue an hour to set, then open the valve, and refill the tank.

If you don't want to buy the kit, use some flat pieces of packing Styrofoam about ½-inch thick, and attach them to the sides of the tank with silicone adhesive.

EASY FIX FOR HARD STAINS. Even though porcelain is a pretty tough material, it's not impervious to stains, such as those caused by hard water in the toilet bowl. To remove hard-water stains, pour 1 cup of white vinegar into the toilet each week, and let it stand for 5 minutes before brushing and flushing. The mildly acidic vinegar will neutralize the alkaline salts that build up on the sides of the bowl and make cleaning hard-water stains a breeze.

GIVE THE TOILET A FACE-LIFT. One question many folks face when they spruce up their bathroom is what to do with the toilet. Replacing it may not be an option for the do-it-yourselfer because the cost alone can be prohibitive. But there's a relatively inexpensive and easy way to change the look of your toilet. Most of the hardware on the toilet—including the tank and even the flushometer—can be replaced. You can purchase hardware sets at any plumbing supply store or home remodeling center. Be prepared to describe the type of toilet setup you have; bringing a photograph will help. Simply changing the handle on the tank from, say, chrome to brass can make your toilet fit better into your bathroom's decor. A new toilet seat and new bolt covers will add to the rejuvenation.

PASS IT ALONG

REPLACE A TOILET, MAKE A BUCK. When it's time to get rid of your old toilet in favor of a newer model, check with your local sanitation department about how to properly dispose of it. But first, remove the internal metal parts—they can often be recycled or even

Everyone has a "plumber's helper" in the bathroom, but many people don't know how to use one properly. Here are a few pointers to keep in mind that will make your plunging experience much more productive.

- **Bell-shaped for suction.** A good plunger has a bell-shaped attachment (for use on toilets) that you can fold up into the head of the plunger when not in use. The bell-shaped attachment is molded specifically for dislodging toilet clogs.
- **Just add jelly.** A plunger can only do its job when its mouth forms an airtight seal around the clogged drain. One way to achieve a seal is to apply a little petroleum jelly to the lip of the plunger before you take the plunge.
- **Watch the water level.** Plungers work best if the water level in the sink, tub, or toilet covers the head of the plunger. Sometimes you'll need to add water to the fixture.
- **Precision plunging.** While the mouth of the plunger is sealed over the drain or in the toilet, pump it rapidly in sets of 10 to 12 small plunges, interspersed every so often with one powerful plunge.
- **Chemical caution.** Do not use a plunger if you've already used a chemical drain cleanser. This can cause the caustic cleaner to splash on you and your floor.

sold (!) as scrap metal. Ask a local plumber (check the Yellow Pages under plumber) about how to cash it in. To find the number of your local sanitation department, search online using your town's name and "sanitation department," or check the local government listings (the blue pages) of your local phone book under sanitation.

DO TRICKS WITH TOILET TUBES. No matter what, you're going to generate some toilet paper tubes—might as well make use of them. Here are four clever ways to put them to work.

1. **Coiled cord case.** Use a tube to stash the extra length of an extension cord in use. Simply "fold" the excess cord (that would otherwise trip you on the floor) into an 8-inch accordion and slide it into the tube, which then rests on the floor and out of sight.

2. **Better battery behavior.** If your flashlight takes DD batteries, slide a clean, dry toilet paper tube inside before inserting the

One Man's Trash
Flipping for Toilet Tank Lids

The folks at www.ToiletTankLid.com have devoted their entire site to the most humble of bathroom fixtures—the toilet tank lid—be it chipped, cracked, broken, or missing. The site is an exhaustive clearinghouse for people who want to buy a particular obsolete, used, vintage or old porcelain china toilet tank lid—and those who want to sell the same (yes, that could mean you). Browsing the Web site, you'll see how far people will go to keep toilet tank lids out of landfills, including using a grouping of them as an impromptu wall sculpture.

batteries. The tube will keep the batteries snug and the terminal connections in place. That means no more shaking and cursing before the light comes on.

3. **Great in the garden.** Believe it or not, toilet paper tubes can make growing carrots a piece of cake. The tubes will protect against cutworms in the soil (which can kill a plant overnight), make pulling carrots easier at harvest time, work well in container gardens, or help import loose, rich soil just for the carrots. At planting time, upend the tubes in an empty shoebox and fill them with potting soil or compost. Plant four carrot seeds in each tube, leaving about an inch of space at the top; transplant the plants when the taproots grow out of the bottoms of the tubes. At that time, make sure to give the tubes a thorough drenching so they'll eventually disintegrate, and leave a half inch of the tube rim above the soil to discourage cutworms.

4. **Makeshift maracas.** Need a way to keep a child entertained while you're busy fixing the toilet? Glue heavy-duty cellophane wrap over one end of a tube, fill the tube one-quarter full with dried beans, then cover and glue the open end closed for a quick-to-make percussion instrument.

CEILINGS, WALLS, AND FLOORS

Don't let humidity and tight space get the upper hand! It's time to reclaim your bathroom surfaces with smart shopping and a whole lot of common sense.

MAKE IT LAST

PICK PAINT WISELY. Believe it or not, when you're painting or repainting a bathroom, choosing the right kind of paint for the job, and not just the right color, is one of the most important decisions you make. Why? Because it can determine how long the paint job lasts.

Any room in your house that experiences frequent high humidity and temperature changes, combined with poor air circulation, becomes a fertile breeding ground for mold and mildew—and that can cause the paint to peel.

Start with a paint designed to prohibit the growth of mold and mildew. Plenty of these kinds of paint are available in home improvement stores and paint stores. Major paint manufacturers make universal bases that are tintable, along with titanium white, which is an ideal choice for ceilings.

STIR UP A BREEZE. Anyplace in your home where there's high humidity, poor ventilation, and warm temperatures, there's likely to be mold and mildew. That's why the tropical atmosphere of a steamy bathroom is so attractive to fungi. And mold and mildew, besides being unhealthy, can stain the paint in your bathroom.

Unless you and your family are willing to take cold showers and baths, the bathroom is always going to be steamy, but you can do something to promote better ventilation. Most modern homes, because of too-efficient weatherproofing, have poor air circulation. If your bathroom has a window, the simplest way to improve airflow is to leave it open at least an inch during, and for a few minutes after, you finish a hot shower or bath. This may mean it's a little cooler when you step out of the water, so keep an extra bath towel or a warm bathrobe nearby.

BE A FAN OF FANS. If you're planning a new bathroom or remodeling an old one, consider installing an exhaust fan. An exhaust fan in the bathroom will keep excess condensation from building up on the walls—which can destroy paint, wall coverings, or decorative pieces—and prevent mold from forming on moist surfaces. Most fans need to be vented to an attic or to the outside, so make sure to consult with an electrician before installing an exhaust fan.

$mart Buys
NATURAL LINOLEUM WAS GOOD ENOUGH FOR GRANDPA

If you're putting a new floor down in a bathroom or kitchen, you may be considering vinyl tile, but you might want to give some thought to natural linoleum instead. Natural linoleum has been a flooring mainstay for more then 100 years because it is made primarily from natural raw materials: linseed oil, pine resins, and jute. It was used for decades before inexpensive vinyl flooring became available. Due to its environmental advantages and durability, it's making a comeback. The raw materials used to make natural linoleum are minimally processed from commonly available, rapidly renewable resources, making it much more environmentally friendly than vinyl. It generally wears longer and requires less maintenance than its less expensive vinyl cousin. Comparable in price to high-end vinyl flooring (about $4 per square foot), natural linoleum can be purchased at almost any flooring or home improvement store. But be aware that sheet vinyl flooring is often generically referred to as "linoleum," so make sure you ask for "natural linoleum."

PROTECT PLASTER WALLS. If your bathroom has half-tile walls—walls on which the tiling starts at the floor and ends halfway to the ceiling—you may find yourself painting the areas without tiles more often than you'd like. Moisture plays havoc with paint, especially in the places most exposed, like directly behind the shower. After only a short time, this leads to peeling paint and exposed wallboard. Wet wallboard will eventually disintegrate and need to be replaced, and that can be an expensive and troublesome repair.

An inexpensive and easy-to-install alternative to constant re-painting, and a nip-in-the-bud to rotting plaster, is polymer plastic sheeting from the home improvement store. It's available in a variety of colors and textures and is easy to apply to the wall with construction adhesive. The plastic panels come in 4- by 8-foot sheets, about $1/16$-inch thick. They're also easy to custom fit: To cut, just score with a utility blade and snap along the straight edge, or cut with a jig saw. Seal the seams between sheets with lengths of plastic channeling of the same color and thickness of the sheets.

Once the wall covering is installed and you've sealed the corners with silicone, you'll have an easy-to-clean, but otherwise mainte-nance-free, shower wall for years to come.

THE FINE PRINT
Trisodium Phosphate

Available at most hardware and home improvement stores in white powder form, trisodium phosphate (TSP) is a well-known powerful cleaning agent and degreaser. It's also commonly used to prepare household surfaces for painting.

TSP is pretty strong stuff and the usual precautions—wearing rubber gloves and eye protection, and making sure there's plenty of ventilation—apply when using it. But compared to other harsh chemical- and petro-leum-based cleaners, it's relatively safe for you and the environment. For instance, TSP is commonly found as a food additive and is also typically used as an emulsifier or thick-ening agent. In this form, it's listed as sodium phosphate on the label.

TSP and other similar compounds were once common in laundry and dishwashing de-tergents. But the phosphate part, being a fer-tilizer, causes the overgrowth of algae blooms in some bodies of water (especially ones fed by public sewer systems). In the early 1970s the use of phosphate-containing products was prohibited. The good news is that there are now substitute products sold as TSP Substitute or TSP–Phosphate-Free (TSP–PF), containing 80 to 90 percent sodium carbonate.

TSP–PF makes a very strong cleaning agent when mixed in a solution of $1/4$ cup of TSP to 1 gallon of warm water. For cleaning a greasy or stained surface (like a kitchen wall be-hind the stove) before repainting, cook up a stronger solution, say 1 cup of TSP to 3 quarts of warm water. To kill mildew, add some chlorine bleach to the TSP/water solution: $1/4$ cup of chlorine bleach to $1/4$ cup of TSP and 1 gallon of water.

$mart Buys

TOILET PURCHASE PRIMER

It's been lingering in the back of your mind for a while and now the time has come—to say goodbye to your old toilet, that is. Here are some expert tips that will help you make the smartest, most economical choice.

- **Color.** You may be enticed by the thought of owning a cherry red toilet, but make sure the color can cut it for the long haul. White may be a better choice. It's more versatile, like an empty canvas, and you can dress it up with a toilet seat cover, which is a lot less expensive to replace should you get bored with the look of it.
- **One-piece or two-piece.** Most toilets come in two pieces—the tank and the bowl. One-piece, also called low profile, toilets are available in more contemporary styles, but are far more expensive. The only benefit of a one-piece toilet? No chance of leakage between bowl and tank.
- **Gravity-fed or pressure-assisted.** Gravity-fed toilets are more common that pressure-assisted systems. When you flush one, water travels from the tank down into the bowl below by means of gravity. Water then builds up in the toilet and the pressure forces it through the S-shaped trap. A siphoning action completes the flush into the waste pipeline.

  Pressure-assisted systems are completely sealed in the toilet housing. This means that when the tank fills up, it traps and compresses the air within. The pressure-assisted flush is also more powerful than the unassisted gravity flush, allowing toilet manufacturers to design bowls with larger water surfaces that require less cleaning.

Although a more powerful flush might seem like the way to go, there are a few drawbacks to keep in mind: Pressure-assisted systems are often louder than their gravity-fed counterparts and tend to be more complicated when it comes to repairs (especially for do-it-yourselfers) when things do go wrong.

- **Round or oblong bowl.** Round bowls, which are more common in households, save space because they're generally 2 inches shorter than elongated styles. Oblong bowls tend to have a larger water surface, and consequently a larger, and more comfortable, seat, than round models.
- **Tanks.** All tanks have a similar capacity, and all are mandated by federal standards to use no more than 1.6 gallons of water per flush (compared with the 3 to 7 gallons used by the models of yesteryear). Tank choices include handle placement (either side, front, or top) and flush valve size. The flush valve, located at the bottom center of the tank, is activated by the flush lever and releases the water held in the tank into the toilet bowl. The larger the flush valve, the higher the rate of water flow.
- **Rough-in.** When shopping around for a new toilet, make sure to look for one that matches the rough-in of the toilet you're replacing. Rough-in is the distance from the finished wall behind the toilet to the center of the gasket where the toilet is bolted to the floor. The standard for most installations is 12 inches, but if you're replacing a very old toilet, the distance could vary from 10 to 14 inches.

BLEACH MAKES GROUT GROUCHY. It's mighty tempting to try to whiten grout between tiles with bleach, but the chlorine is so harsh it will make the grout deteriorate much more quickly. Instead, mix 1 cup of baking soda, 1/2 cup of borax (you can find it in the laundry aisle at the grocery store), and 1/2 cup of hot water. Brush the mixture over the grout and tile, scrub it lightly, and then rinse with hot water (and a clean cloth if the grout's on the floor or counter). After the grout's dry again, follow directions to seal it with grout sealer, available at any home improvement store.

FIX IT FAST

KILL STAINS AT THE SOURCE. The high level of moisture in a bathroom leads to one of the most common household problems: stains on walls and ceilings. You might try to cover a stain by applying a fresh coat of paint, but chances are the stains will bleed right through the new layer. Also keep in mind that painting right over the stain can create an ideal environment for the growth of mold and mildew—a warm and snug spot under the new layer of paint. If you want to cover up a water stain, make sure you properly eliminate the stain first. Here's how.

1. Wash the surface with a solution of bleach and water. In a bucket, combine 1 gallon of water and 1 cup of chlorine bleach. Use a spray bottle to apply the mixture, and a scrub brush or abrasive scrubber to clean the stain. Rinse the area with clean water, but be careful not to soak the surface.

5 Uses for Extra, Chipped or Broken Tiles

Whether you end up with five extras from a carton of the tiles you're installing in the shower or some chipped and broken pieces, you have to consider them as a hot craft possibility, not potential trash, when there are so many projects like these just waiting for you to put on your creativity cap.

- **Splash the back.** Create a horizontal backsplash behind the kitchen sink. Use four or five plain tiles interspersed with a few decorative tiles that are the same size.
- **Handprints that protect.** Have a child (or a pet!) make a hand or paw print with ceramic paint on a whole tile. After it dries, glue felt on the back and you've got a personalized trivet, hot pad, or coaster to use anywhere in the house.
- **Archaic mosaic.** More colorful tile pieces can be used in any number of mosaic/concrete crafts, like stepping stones, birdbaths, or concrete planters. Just press them in while the concrete is still wet, and wipe or sand the film that forms on top when the concrete is dry. If the tile shards aren't small enough, place them in a paper bag and gently pound them into smaller pieces with a mallet or rock, wearing safety goggles as you do this.
- **Vote votive.** This is a fun project to do with a kid: glue pieces of ceramic tile to a clean, empty can (like the one tomato paste comes in) and then grout over the surface to create a quick—and surprisingly durable—candle or pencil holder. Follow the directions on the grout as if you were applying it to another vertical surface, like the wall.
- **Bingo!** If the extra tiles are tiny, say about 1-inch square or a little larger, glue a bit of felt on the back and keep a dozen or so around to use as game markers for bingo, replacement checkers or game pieces for Monopoly and the like.

2. Dry the area to be repainted with a hair dryer, dehumidifier, heater, or a fan, and be sure the surface is completely dry before priming.

3. Prime the surface with a shellac-based primer-sealer such as B-I-N, and use a topcoat that contains a mildewcide to prevent the growth of mold and mildew.

FIX A LEAK TO STOP A STAIN. Not all stains on the bathroom walls or ceiling are caused by mildew. Many are caused by leaking or sweaty pipes. Before you repaint a water-stained area on a wall, make sure you know what caused the stain in the first place.

If there is a pipe in the wall, you'll have to remove some of the wallboard to expose the faulty pipe and repair the leak. This may present a challenge for many do-it-yourselfers, so if it looks like a major leak, be prepared to call a plumber. If the culprit is a sweating water pipe or steam riser, wrap it with foam insulation, sold in hardware and home improvement stores, before repairing the plaster or wallboard, and repainting.

CHECK THE BACK UP FRONT. Before you refasten a loose tile or replace a broken one, check underneath the tile and examine the surface of the wall. A common cause of loose tiles is moisture under the tiles. Cracks in the grout or a leaky pipe can allow water to get behind the tiles and soften the subsurface. Be sure to correct the source of the problem and check that the backing is in good condition—dry and solid—before attaching a new tile. Otherwise, the repair will be a temporary one.

DIG THROUGH THE BONES. When installing replacement tiles, the challenge is to find ones that match your existing tiles. Tile dealers often have "bone piles" of rejects and seconds that may contain just what you're after.

MIST THE GROUT. So you need to replace several tiles on the bathroom wall. Actually placing the tiles is only half the battle. After setting the grout, you need to allow 72 hours for it to dry fully before you can seal it. The tricky part is keeping the grout from drying too quickly, because if it does, it can shrink or crack. Here's what to do: Twenty-four hours after you set it, mist the grout lightly with water from a spray bottle. Mist it again after another 24 hours. Seal the grout on the third day.

SMALL APPLIANCES AND GADGETS

Grooming or primping? Either way, grab a vacuum, baby oil, and cotton swab to extend the life of your gizmos.

MAKE IT LAST

VACUUM YOUR BLOW-DRYER. The intake area of a blow-dryer does more than draw in air to cool the heating element. It also sucks dust, hair, makeup, and powder into the motor, causing it to overheat and possibly burn out. And when the motor burns out, you'll have to go out and buy a new hair dryer. To keep your blow-dryer working for years, make sure to vacuum the holes at the back of the dryer periodically—whenever they look clogged. Also, you can help keep the holes clear between vacuumings by cleaning them with a straight pin—while the dryer is unplugged, of course.

BATHE YOUR BLADE. Most electric shavers will cut less efficiently after a while, no matter how diligently you pop off the screen and brush out the blades. That's because the tiny spaces in the screen and between the blades get clogged with hair and dead skin (yuck!) and need to be replaced sooner or later. But not so fast. Before you spend your hard earned money, try this trick: Soak both the screen and the blade assembly for 1 hour in enough rubbing alcohol to cover them. Then allow both pieces to air-dry for a few minutes. When the alcohol evaporates, it will dry up the stuff that collects on the blade and screen, and then you can blow the dried up gunk away with a blast of air from a hair dryer. Do this once a month or so and your razor, and your beard, will thank you.

DEFEND AGAINST DULLNESS. A couple's arguments about unauthorized razor sharing may go on forever, but you can extend the life of a twin blade or cartridge razor in just a few minutes. Find a plastic container or jar that's tall enough to hold the entire razor, but narrow enough that it doesn't take up too much space (a large plastic spice jar is the perfect size). Keep the jar on the bathroom counter or edge of the bathtub and put enough mineral oil in the jar to cover the head of the razor if you drop it in blade first. The mineral oil prevents the blade from corroding, which hastens the dulling process. Rinse the razor after every use and store it inside the covered jar.

You can usually double, or even triple, the number of quality shaves from one of those pricey twin blades or cartridges, while you cut down on nicks—and fights about who dulled the razor.

SMOKE SIGNALS. If your curling iron is smoking, it may be time for you to step in and clean off hair spray and oil that have accumulated on the metal. This simple act can help extend its life for at least a few more months. Here's how to do just that on a cool curling iron: Dampen a cotton swab with rubbing alcohol and run it over all the metal surfaces and perforations, repeating as many times as necessary to remove all the built-up grime. Then allow the iron dry for a few minutes to make sure all the alcohol has evaporated before revving up for curls once more.

FIX IT FAST

STUD-SEEKING SHAVER. If that old electric shaver just doesn't cut it anymore, don't toss it in the trash—put it in the toolbox. An old trick for finding studs behind wallboard is to run an electric shaver along the wall (it doesn't matter which part of the shaver touches the wall). The sound the shaver makes will change when it passes over a stud (it'll be less "echo-y").

PASS IT ALONG

One Man's Trash
A Toothsome Rug Business

Reusing an old toothbrush to scrub grout is one thing, but Phyllis Hause of Denver has based an entire business on recycled toothbrushes for the better part of 20 years.

As one of 12 children growing up on an isolated farm in Nebraska, she wanted her mother, who was part Native American, to teach her how to make rugs. "But the nearest town was 10 miles, and it didn't have a place to buy needles anyhow," she remembers. After trying to make do with bobby and safety pins, an old toothbrush that had a hole for hanging caught her eye. "I cut the bristles off with wire cutters, and filed the other end to a point with my father's treadle grindstone. That's what we used to sew rugs from brown bags of skirt bottoms we bought at Goodwill for a dollar."

In 1986, many years and many, many rugs later, Hause began Aunt Philly's Toothbrush Rugs with a mere $100. In its early days, the company sold kits and patterns and even allowed customers to bring in their old toothbrushes and exchange them for filed-down toothbrush needles.

Wouldn't you know? The very same year that Hause founded her company manufacturers stopped making the toothbrush models that had a hole for hanging. Hause responded by learning to mold her own needles. Two decades later, the business is still going strong and the needles still look precisely like filed-down Pepsodent toothbrushes from days gone by.

The Web site for Aunt Philly's Toothbrush Rugs is located at www.auntphillys.com.

A hair dryer that works only on one setting (whether it's too hot or too cold) need not be banished from the household. Instead, use it for jobs for which the single setting won't matter, such as one of the following:

- **Workshop workhorse.** Use it to quickly dry small amounts of glue, shellac, or paint in the workshop.
- **Hair dryer becomes nail dryer.** Dry freshly painted fingernails with a few short blasts.
- **Antagonize adhesives.** Remove shelf paper, stickers, or decals more easily by warming them with a hair dryer first to loosen the adhesive.
- **Dish dryer.** Use it to dry hard-to-reach spots on hand-washed dishes, such as the bottoms of muffin pans or the interiors of small vases or screw-on lids. You'll never want to do dishes again without it.
- **Heat for a gelatin mold.** Warm the outside of the bottom of a gelatin mold with 30 seconds or so of hair dryer heat. The molded recipe should slip right out—neater than dipping in warm water!

TOOTHBRUSH TACKLES GUNK AND GRIME. Dried-on toothpaste and soap can be difficult to clean off textured faucet handles in the bathroom and kitchen, unless you use the proper tool—the toothbrush that's ready for the trash bin. Keep an old toothbrush on hand to clean out the gunk and grime that tends to get stuck in the recesses of carved fixtures. Better yet, have you upgraded your battery-powered toothbrush? Use the old one to power clean tough stains on and around the faucet and handles.

SAVE A TOOTHBRUSH, CELEBRATE A FRIEND. If you really re-place your toothbrushes every three months, as recommended by the American Dental Association, you'll end up with far more plastic cast-offs than you could ever use for cleaning, or that you can feel good about sending to the landfill. But there's a fun alter-native. You can re-form the plastic handles into "friendship bracelets," a great project to try with a young relative or maybe a Girl Scout or church group. The colorful circles make great throw toys for pets, too.

You'll need as many old tooth-brushes as you can rustle up, a saucepan, tongs, oven mitts, a towel on which to drain the toothbrushes, and a glass jar of the same diameter as you'd like the bracelets. Here's how to proceed.

1. Start by removing the bristles from all the toothbrushes, either by pulling them out or by cutting them off with wire cutters.

2. Bring water to boil in a saucepan wide enough to accommodate the longest of the brushes you'll be working with.

3. Use tongs to carefully dunk one toothbrush handle at a time into the boiling water, immersing it until the plastic becomes pliable, usually about 1 minute.

4. Remove the handle from the water using the tongs. While wearing oven mitts, bend the handle into the desired shape by wrapping it around a clean glass jar the diameter you'd like the ring or bracelet.

5. Slip the jar out of the ring. Leave the ring on a towel to cool and harden. Then it's ready to wear, give as a gift, or throw for Fido.

MEDICINE CABINETS

With these handy hints you can streamline your medicine cabinet in no time—or find it a new storage job.

PICTURE-PERFECT FRAME. Just because it has rusty metal trim or yellowing paint doesn't mean your medicine cabinet is ready to be thrown out. Whether it's mirrored or plain, wood or metal, you can make the front a lot more appealing just by adding a frame or framed color copy of a photo or artwork. Here's how.

1. Measure the perimeter of the cabinet door.

2. For the mirror front, choose a lightweight vinyl, wood, or particleboard picture frame with the same dimensions as the cabinet door plus an extra half inch on all sides. The frame boards should be at least 1 inch wide. For solid or glass doors, choose a frame with the same dimensions as the door, but don't worry about how wide the frame boards are, since the artwork will cover the door.

3. Stain or paint the frame, if desired, and let it dry. Insert a color copy of the desired photo or artwork. (Don't use an original since it might suffer from prolonged exposure to bathroom moisture.)

4. Remove the cabinet door. Clean and dry it.

5. Measure and cut strips of strong self-adhesive Velcro to outline the edges of the door front, then apply one side around the edges of the front of the door.

6. Apply the corresponding side of the Velcro strips to the back edge of the frame.

7. Replace the cabinet door.

8. Line up the Velcro strips and attach the framed photo to the cabinet.

PASS IT ALONG

CABINET BECOMES CRAFTS CONTAINER. When it's time to replace a medicine cabinet, don't throw the old one in the trash. Instead, transfer it to the hobby room or the home workshop where you can use it to store supplies, from small tools, needles, and pins to screws, washers, and drill bits.

PILL BOTTLES

If you take prescription medications, you also have a ready supply of crafty storage containers. Read on to learn more.

PASS IT ALONG

STORAGE SOLUTIONS GALORE. If you regularly take prescription medications, eventually you'll have lots of empty pill containers. And that's great because it means you have lots of air- and watertight, re-

"Safety first" is the motto when you vet your medicine cabinet—some outdated meds and ointments can actually be harmful. But aside from that, if you get the stuff that's no longer effective out of the cabinet, you'll be able to keep and organize the items you use at least once a week, which guarantees you'll get a lot more use from them before they go out of date. And the exercise can serve as a reminder to buy smaller quantities of items that do expire, such as cold medicines and sunscreen. Finally, it's satisfying to spend a half hour pitching these items.

1. Any medications that have expired. Do not reuse the containers for other purposes without removing the labels and washing thoroughly.
2. Any tablets that are cracked or discolored
3. Liquid medicine that has separated
4. Any bottles without labels
5. Any antibiotics you're no longer taking, even if they haven't yet expired. They're not as effective over time, and some can even be harmful after the expiration date.

6. Expired antibiotic ointments
7. Expired vitamins
8. Gauze bandages and adhesive strips that are beyond the expiration date—not only are they less effective, they're probably no longer sterile.
9. Sunscreen past its expiration date—it won't protect you against the sun's rays. (You may have to check the packaging carefully to find the date—but it's there.)
10. Any container whose lid no longer works correctly. It's an open invitation to spills, and many tablets don't do well in open air. If the contents are still fairly fresh, transfer them to small plastic apothecary bottles you can purchase at the drug store, or use a pill bottle from an old prescription—give it a good wash first, of course.

It's best to return expired medications to the pharmacy for disposal. Don't wash medications down the drain or flush them, because they end up in the water supply. And don't toss medications in the waste can if you have children or pets in the household.

liably closing, versatile, and nearly indestructible storage containers right at your fingertips.

There are countless varieties of small items that you can store inside these small jars: beads, jewelry (great when you're traveling), sewing needles and pins, paperclips, screws, seeds, tacks, and washers, to name just a few. You can even fill the bottles with child-resistant caps with potentially messy stuff like petroleum jelly or spackle, and they won't accidentally open in your purse, toolbox, backpack, or portable first-aid kit.

RUGS, TOWELS, AND OTHER LINENS

Keep the bath linens cozy, soft, and tough—or let some deserving charities soak up any remaining goodness.

Take to the Tea Trees for Antiseptic Ointment

An antibiotic cream is the very thing you need to have on hand for emergency cuts, but the creams do eventually expire, just as any antibiotic does. To avoid being caught with a cut and an outdated package, keep some tea tree oil on hand. This oil, which is available at some drug and discount stores, most health food stores, and on-line, acts as an antiseptic when dabbed on a wound. Some folks also swear by it for insect bites and blisters. But what makes it really handy is that it won't lose its effectiveness over time, which means a tiny bottle can stay in the medicine cabinet for years.

MAKE IT LAST

DON'T THROW OUT THE TOWEL. You can almost be guilt-free when you purchase those expensive lush, cottony, zillion-loop towels and washcloths if you can make them last 10 years, which is the estimated shelf life of a well-made towel, according to Cotton Incorporated. Of course, there's a catch: You need to invest a little extra time and effort in order to care for the towels properly, which is surprisingly more about what not to do than what you should do. Follow these five simple steps to keep luxury towels luxurious well into the next decade:

1. **Clean with care.** Wash towels whenever they're soiled, using detergent. Soft water is preferable.
2. **Beware of bleach.** Never bleach colored towels.
3. **Stay away from softeners.** To keep towels absorbent, avoid fabric softeners, which contain silicones designed to repel water.
4. **Keep whites bright.** Always wash your white towels separately, or they'll gradually pick up a bit of color from other wash items and start looking dingy.
5. **Shake and snap.** If you're going to line dry terry towels, you'll need to poof up the loops. Shake each towel with an authoritative snap once before you hang it, and again after it's dry.

FIX IT FAST

PICKLE STIFF TOWELS. Should your cotton towels become stiff, sweet talk them back to being soft and absorbent with a tart vinegar treatment. Here's how.

1. Run your washer on the hot-water setting until there's enough water to cover the towels.
2. Add 4 cups of white vinegar to the hot water and then place the towels in the washer.

3. Soak the towels overnight or for 8 to 10 hours.

4. Spin off the vinegar water, add detergent, and run the towels through an ordinary cycle, adding ½ cup of vinegar to the final rinse.

TOWELS FOR TOTO. When you get a look at your dingy, worn towels, you might think they're too old to even donate to Goodwill—and most thrift stores would probably agree with you. The local animal shelter, on the other hand, willingly accepts even the most worn towels for cleaning purposes, bedding, and even security blankets for its four-footed residents. Worn fabric shower curtains, toilet covers, and bath mats may also be welcome additions. To find a local animal shelter, look up humane society in the Yellow Pages, animal control in the local government listings (the blue pages) of your phone book, or consult a nearby pet store or veterinarian.

SHOWER CURTAIN CLEANERS. Think twice before tossing those old towels into the trash. Put a few aside in the laundry room. Throw several towels into the washing machine along with your plastic or vinyl shower curtain and they'll behave like agitators, scrubbing the curtain clean as it launders.

BATHROOM RUGS ON THE MOVE. The old bathroom rug may not be bright enough to decorate your bathroom anymore, but that's no reason to toss it out. Stash a couple in the cleaning closet and then, next time you need to move a heavy appliance like a stove or fridge or a piece of furniture and don't want to break your back or scratch the floor, call them into service. Just place a couple, upside down, on the floor, under the edge of the piece you want to move. The rubbery part on the rug's bottom won't slip out from under the appliance as you move it around, and the fuzzy part on top slides like silk along a smooth floor.

HAIR CARE

One or two simple techniques will keep your hair care items around for hundreds of hairstyles.

GIVE YOUR HAIRBRUSH A LITTLE TLC. Even an item as mundane as a hairbrush can live a longer life if you care for it properly. Treat it with kindness and it'll last up to twice as long. Here's how.

3 Ways to Make Shampoo and Conditioner Last Longer

Whether you're fond of $40 salon shampoo or the $2 drug store version, these tips can make your favorite products last longer.

1. **Dry scalp savior.** To get more washes from expensive dandruff shampoos, treat dry scalp with a "gold" type medicinal mouthwash (yes, mouthwash) in addition to your usual medicated shampoo. Every couple of days (and when you're not planning to go out for a few hours) rub a couple of tablespoons of Listerine or a generic equivalent into your scalp and leave it until the odor dissipates. It treats dry scalp so well you'll need to use dandruff shampoo only every third hair wash or so.

2. **Don't banish empty bottles.** Instead, keep it in the shower where you can use it to mix a small bit of shampoo and a squirt of water before applying to your hair. You'll be able to see just how much foam you have before applying it to your hair, so you'll use less.

3. **Detangle dry hair.** If you tend to use a lot of conditioner trying to smooth unruly hair, try detangling it with just a touch of conditioner while it's still dry. Recycle a pump hair spray bottle, and fill it with homemade detangler consisting of one part conditioner and 10 parts water. Spray it on dry hair, comb it through, and then leave it there throughout the day. You'll use a lot less conditioner during your morning shower and find that your hair will be easier to tame.

- **Be kind to bristles.** When removing hair from a brush before washing, avoid rough handling as it can damage the bristles and reduce the life of your brush.
- **Warm water bath.** Wash nylon and acrylic brushes in warm water with a mild detergent. Rinse well and let air-dry
- **Clean without harsh cleansers.** Wash natural bristle brushes with a mild shampoo in warm (never hot) water. Never add harsh cleansers such as bleach to the water; they can permanently damage delicate natural bristles. Let air-dry.
- **No washing wood.** Never submerge or soak wooden brushes in water. Instead, use mild soap and water to clean just the bristles. Rinse and shake dry.

A COOL BLAST SAVES SPRAY. Even a fairly carefree hairstyle can eat up hair spray and styling gel. But there is one clever way to make your gels and sprays last longer. You can actually use less product if you have a hair dryer with a "cold-shot" button. Exposing your hair to a blast of cold air toward the end of drying actually sets the style. That means you can use far less gel and spray.

PASS IT ALONG

GIVE YOUR PETS THE OLD BRUSH (OFF). Just because your old hairbrush has lost a few bristles doesn't mean it's a lost cause. Wash it in some pet shampoo and then use it as a pet brush. Neither Fido nor Fluffy will care that it's one of your old cast-offs, and it'll save you a trip to the pet store.

COSMETICS

Put on a happy face with these ideas for making even the most expensive cosmetics last longer.

MASCARA—DO THE TWIST! Do you find yourself pumping the mascara wand in and out of the tube before you apply it? You're inadvertently pumping air into the wand, too, which makes the mascara dry up prematurely. Make your mascara last a lot longer by simply twisting and turning the brush in the tube rather than pushing it in and out.

MAKE IT LAST

BRING OUT THE BABY OIL. If your mascara seems to be dried out, but you need to get just a few more uses out of it, trickle just a drop or two of baby oil on the wand and then mix it well. It should yield a few more coats of eyelash enhancement. (If your mascara is more than six months old, it should be replaced.)

GIVE LIPSTICK THE BIG CHILL. Warm weather can play havoc with lipstick. It can cause it to soften to the point that it's nearly impossible to apply, with clumps breaking off and smearing. The solution? When the temperatures start to soar, just transfer your lipstick (and eye pencils, for that matter) to the refrigerator for day-to-day storage. Take them out as you need to use them, and then just return them to the fridge until more temperate weather returns. You'll get clean lines over and over again.

ICE YOUR SMILE. Always running out of lip gloss? Try running an ice cube over your lips to "set" the stuff after each application; you'll have to replenish only half as often.

BATHE YOUR BRUSHES. Before your makeup brushes get completely gooked up and unusable, give them some tender loving care. Start by dipping them into a small paper cup or empty yogurt container filled with two parts water and one part fine-fabric cleanser such as Woolite. Rinse the brushes in clean water. You can also restore the bristles to their nearly original pliable state by submerging them in a fresh

Makeup Expires, Too?

No matter what the cost, makeup eventually stops doing its job and needs to be tossed. Along with keeping the following guidelines in mind for cleaning purposes, let them inspire you to get rid of the unopened makeup that's the wrong color or that you'll never use right away. There's always a YWCA, battered women's shelter, or even a high school drama group that can use the (new and unopened) stuff. Remember: The clock starts ticking when the product is sold, not when it's opened! And regardless of how long you've had the makeup, remember celebrity stylist Bobbie Brown's advice: "Anything that smells funny or has changed color or dried out goes in the trash."

ITEM	LIFE EXPECTANCY
Mascara	3 to 6 months
Cream blush	6 months to 1 year
Concealer, eye cream, eye shadow, pencils	1 year
Foundation, lipstick, moisturizer	1 to 1½ years
Face powder, powder blush	2 years

mixture of one part baking soda and two parts water. Rinse again in clean water and allow the brushes to dry before using them.

FIX IT FAST

WHEN LIPSTICK CAN'T CUT IT, CUT IT! When the end of your lipstick gets flat or overly rounded, don't make do with the smears. Instead, dig up a straight razor or craft knife and slice the end diagonally (like on a new lipstick). You'll be able to create sharp outlines and smoothly fill in the centers once more. Make sure the lipstick isn't so soft that it breaks when you try to slice it; popping it in the fridge for a minute or two should do the trick.

PASS IT ALONG

BRUSH YOUR BROWS. Next time you run out of mascara, save the brush. Wash and dry it, and then toss it into your makeup case. To give your look a finishing touch after applying makeup, neaten your eyebrows with the mascara wand.

MOVE THAT COMPACT MIRROR. Once the pressed powder runs out in your compact, there's no need to toss the compact and its mirror in the trash—instead, pack it in your camping first-aid kit. Not only does it come in handy for checking your look while you're on the trail, it can double as a signal mirror—just in case.

TOILETRIES

When you work out ways to preserve powder and stretch soap, everyone wins—including those who get the extras!

THE WAY TO HOLE-Y CELLOPHANE. You can make face powder and powder puffs last longer by simply keeping the cellophane that covers the powder in place. To avoid small rips where you want small holes, soften the wrap with a warm towel fresh from the dryer. Then use a large needle to poke 8 or 10 holes in the top. That way you can shake just a dusting of powder into the lid of the container and mop it up with a powder puff from there. You'll cut down on the amount of powder wasted every time you wash the puffs, you'll keep the oil from the puff from touching and matting the "new" powder in the box, and you'll eliminate spills.

MAKE IT LAST

SCOTCH THE SLIMY SOAP. If you have an old-fashioned ceramic or porcelain soap dish that doesn't have air holes, your soap doesn't really have a fighting chance at a long life—it gets soft and slimy, you use more than you need, and half of it gets left behind on the dish. Give the bar better odds of survival by slipping the leftover plastic ring from an exhausted roll of Scotch tape between it and the soap dish. That way, air will circulate around and beneath it, so it dries and hardens more quickly. That's much better than sloughing off into the sink or coming apart in your hands during the next wash.

CRAFTY SPRINKLE SHAKERS. Powder manufacturers have spent millions and millions of dollars designing shakers that dispense evenly and keep moisture locked out. That's what makes an empty plastic baby powder shaker an ideal tool for crafters: These containers will sprinkle anything from glitter to tiny confetti dots evenly, and they won't let moisture gum up the materials in between projects. Just make sure to take apart and wash and thoroughly dry the whole empty container, using cotton swabs and a hair dryer to get at the threads for the screw-on lid and the small holes. Then fill it up to be ready for the next time you want to make a scrapbook page or painting project glitter.

PASS IT ALONG

MORE TIPS FOR THE BATHROOM

Here's a roundup of the bathroom-related Pass It Along tips you'll find in the other chapters of *Don't Throw It Out!*

CHAPTER	TIP	PAGE
1	New Life for Measuring Cups	23
1	Try These Tray Uses	25
1	7 Uses for an Old Cutting Board	25
1	Assign a Tube to Bag Duty	33
2	Try a Terrycloth Chair Cover	60
3	Move it to the Bathroom	83
8	6 Uses for an Old Tennis Ball	259

Domestic Challenge

If you're always on the lookout for innovative bath products, you're in luck. The products below are currently on the market or still on a designer's sketch pad. You'll need to decide which products are real and which are fictional—there are three imposters on this list of products.

Questions

1. Scale Blaster will keep tubs and showers in action for a long time—it removes calcite in pipes and around fixtures with an inaudible sonic impulse. Imposter or not?

2. Stop scrubbing! The All Aluminum Shower is rust proof, stain proof and antibacterial. Imposter or not?

3. The Foot Flush foot pedal extends the life of an older toilet with hands-free flushing, particularly helpful for folks with limited mobility. Imposter or not?

4. A cracked or peeling toilet seat gets a new look with a peel-and-stick Soft Seat patterned or solid cover. Imposter or not?

5. Give the medicine cabinet a makeover with a Mirrormate peel and stick frame—you don't even have to take it off the wall first. Imposter or not?

6. SpectraLOCK Grout won't crack, fade or powder out like the ordinary stuff and it even comes in glow-in-the-dark and metallic colors. Imposter or not?

7. E-Z Faucet saves water and wear and tear on existing faucet handles by using infrared hands-free technology to control water temperature and flow. Imposter or not?

8. A sleek Allure-and-Away Faucet Cover retracts into the wall after the water is drawn to protect kids from bumping their heads and makes your finish last loads longer without sacrificing style with brushed nickel and brass-look designs. Imposter or not?

9. The Chem-Free toilet tank cartridge is fabricated with an antimicrobial agent so that it not only keeps the bowl clean for 50,000 flushes but the enclosed Mineral Magnets themselves won't ever get moldy or mildewed. Imposter or not?

10. The overhead Bathtub Blow Dryer releases a giant blast of dry heat once you've drained the tub, preventing mildew, mold, and scale build-up and caulk deterioration. Imposter or not?

Answers

And the imposters are:

2. However, Frigo Designs does make an All Stainless Shower that's rust-proof, stain proof and antibacterial.

8. Nothing like this is on the market yet, but there are plenty of unsophisticated faucet covers for sale: hippo-, elephant-, and frog shaped designs, for example, if you'd like to protect yourself from an angular faucet.

10. No one's invented a bathtub dryer just yet, but maybe the time has come!

7

THE LAUNDRY ROOM AND CLEANING CLOSET

When you treat your laundry and cleaning tools with loving care, they repay you tenfold. This is as true for your clothes dryer as it is for hammers and saws. For one thing, well-treated cleaning supplies save you money because you don't have to keep buying new gear. But that's not all—they do their cleaning job better and more quickly than neglected equipment. So let's take a look at some ingenious ways to get the longest life and the best performance out of all of the items that make your home sparkle and shine—

washing machines and clothes dryers, irons, vacuum cleaners, mops, brooms, cloths, sponges, and more. And after you have squeezed, scrubbed, and polished the last ounce of cleaning goodness out of these materials, we have some clever uses for what's left.

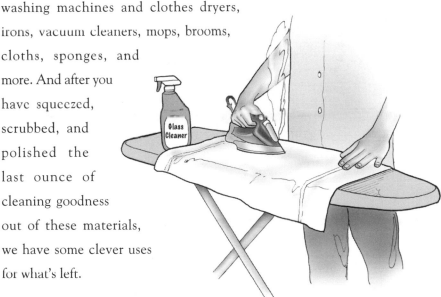

THE WHOLE LAUNDRY ROOM

In this section we take a global approach and consider the laundry room as a whole and how to protect it so that a major overhaul or construction project won't be necessary.

MAKE IT LAST

TEACH KIDS RESTRAINT. Children don't always appreciate the labor, materials, and equipment that are wasted when clothing gets washed unnecessarily. They may try on a shirt, decide not to wear it, and then toss it in the laundry hamper instead of hanging it back up. If there are children in your household, teach them some habits that will reduce the regular laundry load. First, many articles of clothing don't have to be washed every time they're worn—pants and skirts, for instance, particularly if they received only light wear during a school day. Also, play clothing can be worn multiple times. After all, in the backyard, who's going to know whether those grass stains are today's or yesterday's?

GET "FLOOD INSURANCE." Is your washing machine working with a safety net? A drip pan under the appliance can save you grief if the machine should spring a leak—particularly if the washer is on an upper floor, where a flood would endanger expensive carpet, flooring, walls, and the ceiling of the room below. Make sure the drip pan you buy has an outlet—a way to connect a hose that will carry water away to a drainpipe, a floor drain, or a sump pump. When you install a drip pan, get a friend to help so you can set the washer on it gently without breaking the pan. Drip pans also are a good idea under water heaters. You can buy drip pans for around $30 at home improvement and plumbing supply stores. Consider it inexpensive flood insurance.

TURN OFF THE TAP. Look around the laundry room. What would happen if one of the hoses supplying water to the washing machine burst when you weren't home? How much damage would a foot of water do to your house? Take one simple precaution, and you'll never learn the answer to those frightful questions: Get in the habit of turning off the supply valves that feed water to the washing machine and turning them back on only when the washer is in operation. This will take the pressure off the hoses when they're not in use, so they'll last longer, and will ensure that if they ever do burst you will be around to notice the problem. Tape a small sign beside the washer's controls, to remind yourself to open the valves before washing clothes.

SWAP OUT THOSE HOSES. To prevent damaging leaks in your laundry room, change the supply and drain hoses every 5 years. Replacements are available at plumbing and home improvement stores and are easy to install. Wrap a piece of duct tape around one of the new hoses and mark the date on it in indelible marker, so you'll know when it's time to change the hoses again.

Here's an alternative idea if you're not a do-it-yourselfer: When it's time to change washer hoses, wait until you're in need of a plumbing repair elsewhere around the house, and ask the plumber to change the hoses at the same time. The cost will be minimal, and you'll be saving yourself the cost of an extra service call.

CUT UP THE SHEETS. Here's a simple way to make your dryer sheets last twice as long: As soon as you open a new box, snip them all in half with scissors and then use only one of the halves in each load. Your clothing will still come out of the dryer with that fresh smell and no static cling—they'll just have a little less chemical on them. Or save yourself the task of cutting the sheets in half and use each sheet for two dryer loads instead of one.

ADD SOME WATTAGE. You step out into the daylight in your newly laundered clothes, and to your horror you discover spots that you thought had been washed away. Time for a new washer? Time to switch detergents? No, it's time for an astoundingly simple fix in your laundry room: Add some good, bright light. Why? The best way to fight clothing stains is to catch them early and treat them before you wash. And if a stain doesn't come out in the wash, you want to treat it again and wash the item before drying. (Sending it through the dryer will set the stain.) Seeing those stains on your family's clothing requires good light—particularly on wet clothing, which can turn darker and hide the stain you're trying to remove. So add a lamp or increase the wattage in the lighting you already have in the laundry room. Your wardrobe will thank you, and in the long run you'll have less wear on your equipment from washing and rewashing.

FIX IT FAST

WASHERS

We've come a long way from the old scrub board. And in some ways, that's too bad, because you can be sure that old washing tool was easy to use, easy to maintain and relatively inexpensive to replace.

Not so today. A washer is a major investment and so it makes sense to maintain it and make repairs when necessary. Of course, when it does finally give up the ghost, it's also smart to put its parts to good use.

MAKE IT LAST

WASH THE WASHER. Detergents and hard water can combine to build up deposits in your washing machine's tub and elsewhere in the machinery. This milky-looking crust causes your machine to run less efficiently—meaning it will wear out faster. The deposits also act like sandpaper against your clothing, abrading the fibers and making your duds wear out faster, too. So it's doubly important to take care of a mineral deposit problem.

The best time to clean the inside of your washing machine? Right after you have run a full load of laundry using hot water. The built-up grime inside the tub will be at its softest then. Here's how.

1. Pull out any removable interior parts from your washer, such as the lint filter, bleach dispenser, and fabric softener dispenser.
2. Pour 1 tablespoon of laundry detergent into a bucket. Drop those items you've removed from the washer into the bucket, and fill it with hot water to cover.
3. Now for the washer itself: Squirt down the interior of the washer with all-purpose cleanser and wipe it with a sponge, a cleaning cloth, or paper towels. Make sure that you clean the upper rim and the underside of the compartment, where grime likes to collect and hide.
4. Clean any intricate parts with an old toothbrush or a cotton swab.
5. Retrieve the machine parts that have been soaking in the bucket, wipe them, and reinstall them.
6. Now run the machine through a full-tub hot cycle again with no clothes inside.

BANISH BUILDUP. Now that your washer has been washed, you want to prevent that mineral deposit from ever again building up in the tub and inner workings. So once a month run it without clothing through a full, hot cycle with 1 cup of white vinegar added to the wash. That milky crust will be a thing of the past.

POLISH MAKES PERFECT. If you're constantly sliding the laundry basket back and forth between the washer and dryer, you may want to take a precaution to prevent scratches. Just polish the machines with good old car polish or even wax paste, such as Butcher's wax paste, available at hardware stores.

FINE-TUNE THE LAUNDRY.
Wouldn't it be nice to reduce the volume of clothing that has to go through the washer–dryer cycle in your home? This would translate into less water and energy expended, fewer chemicals used, and less wear on your washer—not to mention enormous savings in time. You can do all of this by buying easy-care clothing. When you're out garment shopping, choose the new stain-resistant items, which are common now for casual wear in particular. Check the clothing labels for a fabric treatment such as Nano-Care. Other good bets include microfiber (wrinkle-resistant materials that have a nice drape), cotton-polyester-spandex knits, and polyester-cotton blends (which stand up to wrinkling situations—even in your suitcase). Keep high-maintenance fabrics such as silk, acetate, 100-percent cotton, and velvet to a minimum. Set them aside for board meetings or a special night out.

MINIMIZE THE CYCLE. Most "dirty" clothing only requires a little freshening and doesn't need the entire, package-recommended amount of detergent. Unless you're cleaning particularly grimy clothing, use only half the recommended amount of detergent, and set your washer on the shortest wash cycle. Your clothing will still get perfectly clean, and both your washer and your clothing will last a lot longer because they'll be subjected to less wear and tear. Of course, you also will reduce your consumption of detergent and energy, and that adds up to more money in your pocket.

CHECK THE DOSAGE. Here's a simple test you can conduct to find out whether you're using too much laundry detergent. Throw a small towel in with your routine laundry. Once it comes out of the dryer, drop the towel into a sinkful of water and squeeze. If it emits a cloud of residue, cut back on the amount of detergent you put into the washer. Your clothes will feel better when you wear them, and your laundry detergent will last much longer.

HOSE DOWN MUDDY KIDS. You say one of your youngsters was playing football on a muddy vacant lot, and now his jeans are caked with brown mess from belt loops to cuffs? Do not put those muddy jeans in with the routine laundry—some percentage of that dirt will just get distributed among the other garments. If it's a warm day, take your child into the backyard and hose him down thoroughly (he'll love it) to wash away as much surface dirt as possible. If it's cool out, strip the jeans off him and hose the jeans down without the wriggling youngster inside. Then those pants should be ready for the regular wash. Using a less-vigorous wash cycle—or washing those pants once instead of twice—means less wear on your washer.

FIX IT FAST

GIVE FILTERS THE BRUSH-OFF. If your washer fills too slowly, the little screens that filter the water may be clogged with deposits—a simple problem to fix. Turn off the valves that supply water to the washer, and unplug it from the electrical outlet. Working over a pan or bucket, use a pair of adjustable pliers to disconnect the two hoses from the back of the washer. You'll see little round screens set just inside the two intake fittings. (While you're at it, detach the other end of the feeder hose from the water supply, just in case there are similar filters there.) Pull the filters out with a small screwdriver, taking care not to damage them. Use an old toothbrush to clean them. If they are crusted over with mineral deposits, soak them for several hours in white vinegar, and then brush them clean. Push the little filters back into place and reattach the hoses, making sure that you match up the hot and cold hoses correctly. Turn the supply valves back on, and plug the washer into the electrical outlet.

STOP FEEDING IT GARLIC. Does your washing machine have bad breath? We're just kidding about garlic—mildew is probably causing that musty odor. To fix the problem, run the washer empty on the large-load setting, using hot water, and add two cups of bleach. When the washer is not in use, leave its door open, so it dries thoroughly.

LET IT GARDEN IN RETIREMENT. When an old washing machine  dies, remove the interior tub from the defunct washer, take it into the backyard, and use it as a planter. It's already nicely perforated for drainage. If you like, dig a round hole the width of the tub and sink

---

BACK FROM THE BRINK
The Wring of Truth

Lee Maxwell knows a thing or two about old washing machines. Over the last 20 years, he has restored more than a thousand of them for his Washing Machine Museum in Eaton, Colorado. And the barn is chock-full of old washers he hasn't gotten around to yet.

What makes the old machines last? Mostly, the manufacturer's pride in workmanship and dependability. He's seen washers that were still working after 45 years—and had never needed a service call. "The old adage that they don't make things like they used to is true," says Maxwell, age 75, who roams the U.S. and Canada collecting machines. "We live in a throw-away society. Ask any washing machine repairman, and he'll tell you the same thing."

He has noticed that washer owners in days of yore found clever ways to extend the lives of their machines. For instance, now and then he finds an old wringer-washer that has dishtowels wrapped around the rollers that were used to press water out of the laundry. What were the towels for? After years of use, the rubber rollers had worn down and lost their pressing power. So the clever owners bulked them up again by adding the dishtowels and stitching them into place—squeezing (so to speak) more life out of their equipment.

What kind of washer does Maxwell have in his own home? Although he won't reveal the brand name, he will reveal that it's the modern front-loading variety. He notes that front loaders use less water and energy, but overall he's doesn't think they're any better or worse than top-loading machines.

Let's just say he calls it a wash.

So you're thinking of buying a new-fangled washer that spins the laundry faster than a tornado? Unless you're going to park that washer on solid concrete in your house, pin the salesperson down on this crucial issue: How much will it vibrate on a wood-frame floor? Placing a washing machine—particularly a vigorous front-loader—on the upper floors of a house often invites a vibration problem; in some cases, a vigorous, dish-rattling, wall-cracking vibration problem.

If the washer you already have vibrates too much, make sure it's level. Place a carpenter's level on top of the machine and adjust the feet of the washer until it is level front to back and side to side. Then run a load of laundry and watch the washer's feet to see whether any are leaving the floor (use a flashlight, or try sliding a sheet of paper under each foot). Readjust and tighten the feet against the floor as needed.

If the washer still rattles your dentures, head to a hardware or farm supply store and purchase a heavy-duty mat manufactured out of recycled tires. Cut it to match the "foot-print" of your washer and place your appliance on top of it. The mat will absorb both the vibration and sound of the appliance.

it partway into the ground. Depending on the material, you might be able to spray paint the outside of the tub in a color that's consistent with your landscape.

BOWL THEM OVER. If you have a front-loading washer that's ready for the junkyard, spend a minute retrieving a particularly useful piece of it—that round window. In most front loaders, the concave window is made of super-strong glass called Pyrex. Loosen the screws that hold the window in place and carefully remove it from the door. Wash the piece thoroughly, and now you have a remarkable serving bowl that also will be a great conversation piece. You could also use the window as a garden cloche on those nights when the air temperature drops too low for tender plants.

SHOW THAT BASKET THE DOOR. Old laundry baskets that you have retired can still see plenty of active duty as an outdoor carryall.
- **Corral cans and bottles.** On recycling day, use one to haul your cans to the curb.
- **Tote weeds.** In the garden, toss weeds into one as you move from between garden beds.
- **Use it as a ball basket.** On the tennis court, use one to hold all of those old tennis balls when you're practicing with the kids.
- **Send it to the pool.** Use an old laundry basket as a support chair for toddlers in a backyard kiddie pool. Even though you're right at pool-

side, the basket sides offer support for splashing children and saves you from bending over the side of the pool for long stretches of time.

- **And then take it out again.** Speaking of pools, you can use an old basket to keep pool toys tidy. Drill drainage holes in the bottom of the basket so pool water drains out when kids toss in toys after use.

- **Organize the car.** Corral necessities in your car trunk in one—car blankets, flashlights, first-aid kits, and ice scrapers can be stored in a laundry basket. And don't forget how handy baskets can be to support grocery sacks on the way from the store—it's much better than scooping up the bag of apples that spilled.
- **Pick a peck of veggies.** Old baskets on the small side make great bins for scrubbing garden vegetables. Place veggies in the basket, and then dunk the basket into a large sink of water to wash away soil. Lift the basket from the sink, and let the veggies drain.

DRYERS

Read on for plenty of hot tips that will keep your dryer in ship shape year after year and explain how to make simple repairs that will save you cold hard cash.

EVICT THE FLUFFY STUFF. When your clothes dryer was new, it dried a normal load of clothes in a half hour. Now it takes an hour or more to completely dry a load. Is it time to junk that dryer and invest in a new one? Maybe not. First, take a few minutes to consider the following questions: Does the bin spin inside? Is it hot to the touch when the dryer has been on? If both answers are "yes," then your dryer is working. The real culprit: Lint blocking the flow of air that dries your clothing. Take this problem seriously, because the extra drying time puts needless wear on your dryer and costs more in energy (and therefore money), too. Also, lint is so flammable that Boy Scouts and Girl Scouts use it to start campfires—so obviously it's a fire hazard wherever it builds up.

MAKE IT LAST

You probably already know to pull out your dryer's lint filter after every load and scrape the lint into a trash can. But that doesn't totally eliminate the lint problem. Every few months, slide a long-handled tool down into the slot where the filter goes and pull out any loose lint. A large bottlebrush will do a nice job of this, or use your vacuum cleaner's crevice tool. Then go to the back of your dryer and pull off the ventilation duct. Slip on a work glove, scoop out whatever lint you can from the hole on the back of your dryer and also from the vent itself, then push the vent back into place.

FIX IT FAST

BRUSH UP ON VENT CLEANING . . . You say you've been faithfully removing the lint from your dryer as described above, but it's still not drying a load of clothing in a half hour? Then the lint blockage is not in your dryer—it's in the vent that carries hot, moist air from your dryer to the outside. If you have the kind of duct that's not built into a wall, pull it away from your dryer on one end and from the vent that leads to the outside on the other. Take the duct into the backyard, shake it over a garbage can, and brush out the interior. (Don't use water, which will reduce lint to an unmanageable mess.) You can also use the vacuum and brush attachment to remove any pockets of lint.

. . . OR MAKE IT AN INSIDE JOB. If you need to clean lint out of a dryer vent that is built into a wall of your house, you'll have to brush it out where it stands, of course. To start, pull the clothes dryer away from the beginning of the vent. Then pull the hood off the other end

SIMPLE SOLUTIONS

Lint Removal: When You Can't Get There from Here

Cleaning lint out of your dryer vent can be quite a chore, whether your vent is removable and can be transferred to the backyard for cleaning or it's permanently ensconced in the walls of your house. At a minimum, dryer vents are several feet long, and they often have elbow joints that further complicate reaching the lint inside. Of course, you could invest in a dryer vent brush from a home improvement store, but why shell out good money for a tool that you will use only infrequently? You probably can improvise a perfectly suitable vent-cleaning tool from materials around your house, says Alisa LeSueur, a vent and rain gutter expert based in San Antonio, Texas.

Start by identifying your stiff-yet-flexible "rod," or reaching device. Good candidates: a garden hose, a heavy rope, a cable, or an extension cord. Make sure it's longer than your vent. Now find a "lint brush" to attach to the end. Good candidates for a brushing device: a toilet brush, knotted socks, or rags. When you attach the brush to the rod, secure it firmly with wire, cord, or duct tape. You don't want it to come loose inside the vent.

of the vent outside (it should be either on the side of the house or on the roof). You'll need a blowing machine stationed at the beginning of the vent inside the house. This will force the loosened lint out of the vent. Either use the dryer itself as a blower, an electric (not gasoline) leaf blower, or a shop vacuum set on "blow." If you use your dryer for this, cover the opening at the back with metal screening so your vent-cleaning tool doesn't poke inside and damage it. When you stand at the end of the vent outside, wear safety goggles, since you'll get blasts of high-speed lint in your face.

Measure the length of a vent, and then mark that length on a cleaning rod so you'll know when you have poked through. (Check out *Lint Removal: When You Can't Get There from Here* for information about how to make your own dryer vent brush.) Inside the house, turn on your blower and direct the air into the vent. From the outside, feed your rod device (hose, cable, or extension cord) into the vent without the brush attached. You might need to poke, prod, and twist when you hit elbow joints. When your rod emerges from the other end of the vent in your laundry room, move your blower aside and fasten your brush to the end of the rod. Return the blower to its position at the start of the vent, and from the outside pull the brush through to dislodge any remaining lint. Before reconnecting the duct, put on a work glove and brush the lint out of the short vent running through the wall of your house and out of the duct cover on the outside.

TOSS IN THE TOWEL. When you have just a few items spinning in the dryer, they often cling to the sides of the bin and fail to tumble. That means they take longer to dry—causing more wear on your dryer—and are more likely to come out wrinkled because they stayed bunched up. To cure this problem, add a heavier item—a dry towel, for instance—that will knock the little items around and help them dry more efficiently. Use a towel that's in the same color range to reduce the chances of a noticeable lint problem or dye transfer.

MAKE A BOY SCOUT HAPPY. We're warned that dryer lint is highly flammable, so it seems a shame to just throw lint away when its sole "talent" could be put to use. Lint makes a swell fire starter in a fireplace or campfire. Here's how to prepare it: Rip off the lid from a cardboard (not foam) egg carton and toss the top into the recycling bin. Stuff a tight ball of lint into each of the 12 "buckets" in the bottom of the egg carton. Light a candle, and drip the wax over each ball of lint until

PASS IT ALONG

it's thoroughly coated. (Or do the same with melted paraffin.) Let the wax cool, and store the carton in a safe place until you're ready to use the fire starters. To start a fire, tear off two or three of the wax-covered lint balls (cardboard and all) and place them under the kindling. Set a match to them, and your fire will be roaring in no time.

BUST DUST WITH DRYER SHEETS. Used fabric softener sheets usually still have traces of their static-decreasing chemical on them. When you use the sheets to wipe down dust-prone objects, items won't attract dirt so easily. Use used dryer sheets to clean your computer screen, your television, and your window blinds.

FRESHEN YOUR DRESSER. Rather than throwing away all of those used dryer sheets, stuff each one into a mesh laundry bag, the kind you use to protect delicate clothing in the wash. Once you have collected several, tuck the bag into the back of a clothing drawer to keep your dresser smelling fresh.

GET ON THE STICK. Here's how to get a little more cleaning out of a used dyer sheet: Wrap it around the mop head of your disposable mopping-cloth system. Let it scoop up some dust and debris from your floor before you throw it out for good.

$mart Buys

IS YOUR DRYER VENT DANGEROUS

Dryer lint is extremely flammable, and any vent that may collect it must be made of the safest material, says Alisa LeSueur, a vent and rain gutter expert based in San Antonio, Texas. Make sure your dryer vent is made of smooth, round aluminum or steel—not ridged metal and not plastic. Screws should not be used to hold the sections of your vent together. If there is any tape on the vent, make sure it's 2- or 3-inch aluminum tape, not duct tape or masking tape, both of which are flammable. A 4-inch-wide vent is ideal. The 3-inch variety, sometimes used to fit inside walls of a home, will reduce airflow and so reduce your dryer's efficiency. Make sure, too, your vent carries your dryer's exhaust to the outside, not into the laundry room, into the attic, or into a garage.

TAKE A TIP FROM TISSUES. With all of your newfound uses for used dryer sheets, just how are you going to store them without creating a cluttered mess? Easy: through even further recycling. Park an empty facial tissue box in your laundry room, and tuck your used dryer sheets into the box until you need them.

MAKE YOUR OWN DRYER SHEET. Have a clean rag that needs a new job around the house? Drizzle a tiny bit of liquid fabric softener on it, let it set for about 15 minutes, and then toss the rag instead of a dryer sheet into the dryer with your next load of clothes. The rag will last through several loads. When it loses its static-busting power, sprinkle it with a little more fabric softener. Make sure your rag is clean at the outset, of course. Also, it helps to choose a rag that has a distinctive look, so you won't confuse it with the regular laundry.

IRONS AND STEAMERS

It's a great feeling, donning a crisply ironed skirt or shirt. Learn to maintain and use your iron correctly, and you'll never be rumpled again.

MAKE A HEAT SHIELD. A lot of the heat generated by your iron gets absorbed by the ironing board and is wasted—meaning your iron has to work longer and harder than necessary to do its job. To make more efficient use of the heat generated by your iron, wrap your ironing board in aluminum foil, shiny side up, underneath the cover. This will reflect more heat back onto the clothing you're ironing. Your ironing will go more quickly, meaning less wear on your equipment.

MAKE IT LAST

CALL FOR BACKUP. Over months of ironing, an ironing board cover can develop a coating of starch and other laundry products. This residue can transfer to your clothes and get them dirty before you've even worn them. So buy a backup ironing board cover. Whenever you notice a little deposit building up on the cover, drop it into the washing machine, and use the spare in the meantime. This will keep your clean clothes clean, saving time, supplies, and equipment.

IRON THEM DAMP. Doesn't it feel silly to dry a shirt and then, when it's time to iron it, squirt it with water all over again? This is not only extra work for your dryer, but for your iron, too, since it has to smooth out all of your shirt's baked-in wrinkles. The solution: Pull items that you need to iron out of the dryer while they're still a little bit damp. Your clothing will start out with fewer wrinkles, so the ironing will go more quickly, which means you'll get more mileage out of your

When you're browsing for a new clothes iron, expect to wade through a baffling array of features, gizmos, and add-ons that may or may not be useful to you. Don't let them distract you from core issues, however. Conduct this simple test before you make any final decision: Pick up the iron by its handle. Is the weight too light or too heavy? Is the handle a perfect fit for your hand? If your ironing sessions tend to be more than 10 or 15 minutes at a stretch, the fit of the handle and the weight will become crucial factors.

equipment. You won't have to sprinkle the garment. You'll also reduce the energy consumption of both your dryer and your iron.

PRESS WITH A BOTTLE. Find yourself firing up the iron for just one or two items of clothing? Save yourself the bother—and the electricity. A relatively new arrival on the shelves at your discount store is a product called wrinkle-release spray. The night before your big presentation, put that wrinkled blouse on a hanger, shoosh it with this spray, and smooth it with your hands. In the morning it will be dry and smooth. Wrinkle-release spray can't compete with an iron if you're looking for board-stiff starching or razor-edge creases, but it's awfully handy when ironing is impractical. Travelers find that they can pack small bottles of wrinkle-release spray and leave their steamers behind. Use it for casual clothing at home, too, and you'll put less wear on your ironing equipment.

FIX IT FAST

RUB OUT STARCH DEPOSITS. To clean built-up starch from your iron, lay an old towel across your ironing board, and spray the towel very lightly with glass cleanser. Let your iron heat up, and then iron the sprayed towel until the deposit is gone. Wipe the iron down with a towel dampened with fresh water, and you'll be ready to iron again.

COOK AWAY RESIDUE. The inside of your iron can get caked with mineral deposits from tap water. To keep it steamin' along, clean it periodically with this technique: Fill the iron with a mixture of half distilled water and half white vinegar. Turn on the iron to high for 15 minutes, let it cool, and then pour out the solution. To rinse, refill the iron with distilled water, heat it again, and pour the water out.

PASS IT ALONG

TRY A LITTLE WICKET WIZARDRY. Have you lost a croquet wicket? With a quick snip of wire cutters and a bend here and there, you can quickly transform an extra wire coat hanger into a croquet wicket. A white coat hanger is the best choice because it stands out better against the grass than the usual brown metal ones.

Grandma's old ironing board is making a comeback—newly promoted to the role of hot decorator item. So go to the shed, dust off that old board, and reuse it. If it's wood, apply some furniture polish or stain to make it presentable. Here are three ways to use it.

- **Add it to your decor.** Arrange an old wooden ironing board in a stair landing, and use it as a display table. Drape some antique linen fabric across it, and add a few framed photographs and dried flowers.

- **Table it.** Use a wooden ironing board as a sofa table; its long, narrow shape is perfect for the space between your couch and a windowed wall. Your houseplants will most certainly love it.

- **Send it to the shed.** Strip all board covers and padding off of a metal ironing board, and use it as a potting bench outside or in the garden shed. The metal mesh top means any soil that's spilled can fall right through to the ground.

TAKE THOSE HANGERS "HOME." Got a mountain of wire hangers taking over your closet? Drop a few dozen into a shopping bag and take them back from whence they came—the dry cleaner—the next time you have some laundry to drop off. Many dry cleaning businesses are happy to reuse wire hangers. Many second-hand stores and organizations sell used clothing and may accept hangers in good condition as well.

VACUUM CLEANERS

If you've purchased a new vacuum cleaner lately, you know what a dent it can make in your wallet. The tips below will help you get the most out of this cleaning machine and tell you how to make simple repairs that will save you a little cash.

UPRIGHT OR CANISTER? If you're thinking of buying a vacuum cleaner, first think about how you will use it the most. These rules of thumb will get you started.

MAKE IT LAST

- **Uprights rule on carpet.** Upright vacuum cleaners are best for homes that have a lot of carpet. They're less expensive and are easier to store, since they don't take up much floor space.

- **Canisters are better for bare floors.** Canister vacuums are better on bare floors and in homes where you'll do a lot of reaching—to clean stairs and curtains, for instance. Storing that long hose can feel like wrestling a python, though.

CHECK THE BAG. Is there a "change bag" indicator light on your vacuum cleaner? Keep in mind that those little gizmos can't always be trusted. Get into the quick and simple habit of popping the lid on the vacuum cleaner every time you're about to use it. If the dirt collection bag is three-quarters or more full, change it. A simple poke with a finger will give you a good idea of how full it is. If you wait until the bag is jam-packed and nearly rock hard, the machine is working too hard (which in turn means needless wear and tear and perhaps the need for a premature replacement) and not creating enough suction to clean—so you're wasting lots of effort.

SPRINKLE AT THE RIGHT TIME. If you like to sprinkle a powdered freshening product on your carpet and then vacuum it up, consider your timing. Some fine powders can actually block the pores that allow airflow through a vacuum cleaner bag. That reduces the machine's suction, defeating the whole purpose. Not only that, but the vacuum will have to pull harder to do the same amount of work, so the motor will wear out faster. So freshen your carpet when you're about to change the vacuum's bag anyway—when it's between half and three-quarters full. Throw the bag out afterward and insert a new one. Your vacuum will work better, and you won't go through bags as quickly.

Still Working After All These Years
A PRESSING SITUATION

Would a clunky old warm-it-in-the-fire iron do a reasonable job of de-wrinkling a modern person's shirt? Sure it would, says Bill Heyman of Marlborough, New Hampshire, who speaks from personal experience.

"Irons last an awfully long time," says the co-owner of the Shaker Brook Farm Antique Pressing Iron Museum. "They're pretty much indestructible."

Now, museum owners don't normally throw their display treasures into active duty. But Heyman once found himself stuck. He had flown from New York to his home (at the time) in Switzerland, where he was scheduled to make his first appearance as a square dance caller (another personal passion). He had a pair of new, suitcase-wrinkled Western shirts for himself and his wife. But his steam iron was nowhere to be found.

In a near panic, he pulled an antique iron out of his collection—a simple brass "slug" iron from the early or mid-1800s. It was the kind with a metal block that you heat in a fire and then slide into a handled ironing frame. Heyman polished the bottom of the iron, heated the device on his stove, and did the ironing. Then he rushed through a shower and slipped the shirt on—only to discover that he had ironed his wife's smaller shirt by mistake.

So he called the square dance in a wrinkled shirt after all. But he knows first-hand that his prized irons could be "pressed" into service in an emergency.

FINE DUST MIGHT SPELL TROUBLE. Fine debris such as spackling dust or sawdust may damage the ball bearings in your vacuum and cost you an expensive repair. It's always best to use a workshop vacuum for remodeling debris and dust.

SIMPLE SOLUTIONS

Instant Carpet Freshener

Is your carpet or rug smelling a little musty? No need to buy one of those powdered carpet fresheners. Pull that box of baking soda out of the kitchen cabinet and sprinkle it on. Give it 10 minutes to do its odor-absorbing job, and then vacuum it up.

BABY YOUR INDOOR VAC. Don't drag your indoor vacuum cleaner out to vacuum your car's interior. Instead, use your shop vac, or drive to the carwash. Your indoor vac will live a longer life.

WITH HANDHELDS, KEEP THE CORD. If you're tempted to buy a handheld vacuum (good move—they're a time-saving tool), do your consumer research first and cast a skeptical eye on the cordless variety. You don't want a rechargeable battery that's going to give up the ghost after several months—which happens with some units. A more cautious approach: Choose the kind of handheld vacuum that plugs into an outlet and attach it to a long extension cord, so you can get a lot of housecleaning done without changing outlets frequently.

PREVENTIVE MEASURES ARE A SNAP. Do you think the belt driving your vacuum cleaner's beater bar has been snapping way too frequently? Carpet fringe or the edges of throw rugs could be the culprit. When the brush gets snagged on fringe or a loose throw rug, it stops spinning, but the belt keeps trying to turn it. The resulting friction will wear out the belt in no time. A simple adjustment might be all you need: Just raise the height setting on your vacuum. And, of course, take special care when you're vacuuming at the edges of rugs.

NEW BELT IS A CINCH. One of the most common "breakdowns" on a vacuum cleaner is a snapped belt—the little band that spins the machine's beater bar. This simply won't do, because that brush has to spin in order to lift dirt off your carpet. But don't trash the vacuum yet. A broken belt is easy to fix, and you'll feel like a hero if you save yourself a trip to the repair shop. Models vary, but in general you'll need to remove a guard plate with a screwdriver, pop out the beater bar, remove the broken belt, and insert a new one (available at home improvement and discount stores), and then reassemble the machine. (Check

FIX IT FAST

the owner's manual for specifics.) To help the vacuum cleaner's belt last longer and work better, inspect the underside of the machine now and then, and pull out any thread, string, long hair, wire, or other debris that might be interfering with its operation. If necessary, snip this debris with scissors or a razor blade to free it.

USE DIFFERENT STROKES. Each time you vacuum a carpet or rug, vacuum in a different direction than you did the last time. This will help the carpet or rug fibers from getting matted and trapping soil in the carpet.

PASS IT ALONG

VACUUM GOT A FLAT? You might be ready to give up on an old vacuum cleaner not because the motor dies, but because other peripheral parts break. What are the chances you can (or would even want to) get the wheels on an old canister vacuum cleaner fixed, for instance? If your vacuum has lost its mobility, but still has plenty of air-pulling power, park it permanently where it can still perform a needed service: in the shed, by a workbench, or near a crafts table. In these locations, a vacuum hose can make quick work of sawdust and other small-scale messes.

TRY A TOOL WITH TEETH. Stick an old hair comb in your cleaning caddy or in the attachments compartment of your vacuum cleaner. It makes a handy tool for quickly lifting up lint, dust, and thread that's become ensconced in vacuum cleaner brushes and in hook-and-loop fasteners. Just make sure it doesn't wind up back in the bathroom.

CLEANING PRODUCTS

It's a dirty job, but someone has to do it—clean the house, that is. The tips below will help you make those cleaning products last a bit longer and offer advice about the only cleansers you really need.

STRETCH THAT LIQUID SOAP. Sure, liquid hand soap is meant to pour down the drain—it would just be nice if it didn't go so fast. When you're refilling hand soap dispensers, fill them only three-quarters of the way and top them off with water. Gently shake the dispenser for a few minutes to blend. The soap will still be thick enough for washing your hands, but it will last longer.

MAKE IT LAST

SAVE YOUR STRENGTH. That super-strong, grime-busting general purpose cleanser you bought at the supermarket is overkill for many of the cleaning tasks around the house. To make that tough cleanser stretch further, save it for the nasty cleanup jobs only. For lighter duty, whip up this inexpensive, gentle, neutral cleanser: Fill a 32-ounce spray bottle with water, add a squirt of dishwashing liquid, and label the bottle. Spray it on hard surfaces and wipe with a damp sponge or cleaning cloth, then follow up with a dry cloth.

DIGESTION TAKES TIME. There are few odors that are harder to eradicate than what can be politely called organic mishaps (pet accidents, vomit, and little boys with bad aim, for instance). Enzyme digesters fall into a special category of cleanser that is a godsend for cleaning and deodorizing organic material. Enzyme digesters work slowly, however—often over hours or days—and the spot needs to stay moist for the enzymes to do their job. To make sure the spot you're cleaning doesn't dry out prematurely, cover it with a sheet of plastic wrap (or even a plastic grocery bag) and weight the plastic down at the corners. Follow the product's directions, of course, for application, time to wait, and rinsing.

FIX IT FAST

SHINE FOR LESS. If you're short on metal polish for spiffing up brass and copper items in your house, some common sources of mild acid will stand in just as well. Just dampen a cotton cleaning cloth with some white vinegar or lemon juice and buff the metal to remove tarnish. Afterward, rinse thoroughly and wipe the metal dry.

CHECK THE DATE. If you've just discovered a long-forgotten bottle of cleanser that's been gathering dust in a dark corner of your cleaning closet, your frugal nature may tempt you to put that cleanser back to work. Not so fast. Consider this: Time and temperature extremes can alter the chemistry of a cleaning product. (Has it been languishing in that unheated shed, for instance? Or in a very warm spot in the house?)

Sure, you need a few special-purpose cleansers in your cabinet for narrowly focused tasks, polishing brass, for instance. But for everyday cleaning around the house, you need only five crucial bottles on the shelf.

1. **General purpose cleanser.** This spray cleanser is good for a multitude of surfaces around the house (although it will probably be a tad smeary on glass).

2. **Glass cleanser.** These cleansers are are typically ammonia or alcohol based and are designed to dry quickly and streak-free.

3. **Disinfecting cleanser.** This one both cleans and kills germs, making it ideal for sinks, kitchen appliance handles, food preparation areas, cutting boards, toilet exteriors, phones, and other hard, germy surfaces.

4. **Toilet bowl cleanser.** Yup, you could call this a narrowly focused cleanser—but it's one you want to use frequently.

5. **Floor cleanser.** Read the fine print to make sure you're mopping with a cleanser that will get the dirt up without causing damage to your floor.

In general, cleaning pros expect a cleanser to have a shelf life of one year—if it remains unopened. If you don't know how long you've had the cleanser, look for a date that has been stamped on the container by the manufacturer. If the cleanser is too old, check the label for disposal instructions. You may need to contact your local hazardous waste agency or your municipality.

CLOTHS AND SPONGES

Remember the days when the only cleaning cloths you used were some ratty old t-shirts or cloth diapers? Some of today's cleaning tools are high-tech, made from material such as microfiber. But we still use the old stand-bys—sponges and gloves, for instance. In the tips below, we cover the old and the new.

MAKE IT LAST

BABY FURNITURE CLOTHS. Rags that you use for general-purpose cleaning can actually damage furniture if you switch them to wood-polishing duty. That's because cleaning cloths can cling to traces of cleaning chemicals and smear these chemicals around where you don't want them. So here's the best approach for keeping your cloths in productive service longer: Store cloths for polishing furniture separate from other cleaning cloths, to make sure chemicals that aren't meant for furniture don't get transferred there. Clean your furniture-polishing cloths by simply rinsing them in warm water or running them through the washing machine all by themselves—warm wash, gentle cycle. Don't use laundry detergent, fabric softener, or other cleansers on these cloths. The wood in your house will thank you, and your cloths will be usable for a lot longer.

GO MICRO. You're understandably suspicious of the hype surrounding new products, so perhaps you've been avoiding the next big thing: new-fangled microfiber cleaning cloths. But consider this: These high-tech cloths are so good at cleaning that you often don't need to use cleaning chemicals at all (that's cash in your pocket and fewer chemicals is a win–win for everyone), and they last a long time, to boot. Breakthrough science has allowed the manufacture of fabrics made up of microscopic, wedge-like fibers that pull up dirt into the cloth rather than just pushing it along the surface that's being cleaned (as with cotton). Microfiber cloths can be used damp or dry. With a quick rinse under the faucet, they release all of their dirt and are ready for use again. They can be laundered 500 times, while cottons cloths typically fall apart after 50 to 100 washings. There's one caution, however: When you wash your microfiber cloths, don't use fabric softener on them—the chemical will reduce their effectiveness.

SANITIZE THE SPONGE. To get more life out of your kitchen sponge, drop it into the upper rack of your dishwasher when you run a load. This will clean it, and kill the germs that lurk in kitchen sponges. Just make sure that you secure the sponge so it doesn't get caught in the dishwasher mechanism inside. Germ-killing alternatives: Put your wet

$mart Buys
POINTERS ON POLISH

Some furniture polishes that are designed to provide a quick-and-slick shine actually will damage your furniture in the long run, says fine-furniture expert Michael Carter, who is an advisor to Steinway and Sons for its furniture care products. Although polishes containing silicone are popular, he says, they only provide a "fast and false finish." The silicone looks shiny, but it will actually penetrate the finish of your furniture and cling to the wood. Ultimately, it will make any future refinishing and repairs impossible.

Carter avoids polishes that contain citrus, too, because the acid will break down a finish and darken wood over time. He steers away from wax and benzene (toluene) as well.

Treat your furniture to a high-quality polish, Carter says (he likes the cream form of polish), and don't be tempted to dilute it. Many people try to add water to their furniture polish to make it go further. The added water doesn't help your furniture any more than licking helps your chapped lips—both do more damage than good.

sponge in the microwave and zap it for a half minute (careful—it will come out steaming hot). Or use it around the kitchen to mop up after you use a spray disinfectant.

PREVENT PUNCTURES. If you have long fingernails, you probably go through a pair of rubber gloves quickly, poking holes through the fingertips. To make your gloves last longer, stuff little bits of material into each fingertip—snippets of old cloth, pieces of cotton balls, or even tissue paper will do the trick.

FIX IT FAST

GLOVES RAISING A STINK? The inside of a rubber glove is a closed, dark, and often moist place—meaning that it can easily develop a musty odor. To get the upper hand, turn your rubber gloves inside out when you're done with them to let them dry. Then turn them right side out again and sprinkle some baking soda inside, which will absorb odors and will feel comfy the next time you slip on the gloves.

COLOR-CODE THE SPONGES. When you're covering more than one room during a cleaning session, it's only natural to use those same tools from one area to the next. But don't forget that sponges are notorious for picking up bacteria and harboring them in their moist recesses. To prevent spreading contamination from one room to the next (in particular between the bathroom and the kitchen), assign a color of sponge to each room. Green may be reserved for the bathroom alone, for instance, and blue for the kitchen. You can take it even further in the kitchen, assigning one color sponge for wiping tables and countertops and another for washing dishes.

PASS IT ALONG

SET IT LOOSE IN THE WILDS. A sponge that's too grungy looking for kitchen duty probably still has plenty of water-sopping talent left in it. Stow it with your camping gear or hand it over to an outdoors enthusiast you know. When a puddle develops inside a leaky tent, a sponge is a mighty welcome tool. Or collect several sponges in a mesh bag and drop the bundle into a canoe to sop up the inevitable puddles that form in the boat's bottom.

FIND A JARRING NEW JOB. Holey rubber gloves may be useless for dishwashing, but it can still help out around the house. Park them in the pantry or anywhere else you're likely to need to open stubborn jars. Rubber gloves will give you just the nonslip grip you need for the job.

MOPS AND BROOMS

Whether it sweeps or swabs, you'll find tips below that will help you make it last, fix it fast, or pass it along.

HANG UP THE MOP. A mop stored incorrectly is more likely to become misshapen and develop mildew—moving it quickly toward the trash heap. To get the most mileage out of your mop, rinse it well and make sure it dries thoroughly before you store it in an enclosed space, so it's less likely to develop mildew. When you're finished with a mopping job, first prop it, with the mop head up, in the shower stall or tub to let it dry. When you put it away, hang it with the mop head down—but not against the floor, which would compress the head. For longer storage, hang it from a coat hook or nail in your cleaning closet. If necessary, drill a hole in the mop handle to hang it from.

MAKE IT LAST

FLIP-FLOP THE MOP. Have you fallen in love with those disposable mopping-cloth systems? That's fine, but don't be too quick to throw out that mopping cloth. Before you do, remove it from the mop head and reinstall it with the clean reverse side showing. You'll get double the use out of those disposable cloths.

HANG THE BROOM, TOO! When you simply lean your broom bristle-end-down in the corner to store it, its weight pushes down against the bristles. Over time, the broom's fibers permanently bend out of shape, and some of their sweeping action is lost. Brooms, like mops, will give you longer service if you hang them on a nail or a hook rather than standing them on their heads.

DIRTY BRUSH? BAG IT. Your dustpan and brush can get pretty unsightly when they've seen a lot of grimy duty. To keep them clean during messy jobs, cover each in a plastic grocery bag and secure the bag with a rubber band. They'll still do their sweeping job perfectly well. When the mess is swept up, turn the dustpan's bag inside out to contain the dirt, remove the bag from the brush, and drop it into the bag that's holding the dirt, tie the bag off, and drop the bundle into the trash can.

PASS IT ALONG

SWEEP ELSEWHERE. A tattered and soiled broom may not be welcome in your home's cleaning closet anymore, but that's not to say it's useless. Keep your worn brooms in the shed to help with such nasty cleaning duties as freeing up the caked-on grime at the bottom of a garbage can or sweeping cobwebs from a shed or garage.

SAVE THE STICK. Got a broom whose bristles are scattered to the four winds? It can still help out around the house—this time in the laundry room, basement, or garage.

- **Hang 'em high.** Install hooks or other mounting hardware against the ceiling or between rafters, and use the broomstick as a hanging rail for clothing. Extra hanging space is always welcome on laundry day as clothing comes out of the dryer and needs to be hung up immediately, or when you want to rotate clothing out of your closet and into seasonal storage.
- **Make an arm extender.** Store a broomstick with your painting gear and duct-tape it to a roller when you need extra reach.
- **Stake your claim.** Use a hatchet to (very carefully) whittle one end of a broomstick to a point, and then use the handle as a garden stake or as a hose guide around delicate plants when you're dragging your garden hose from bed to bed.

LET YOUR BOOTS KICK THE BUCKET. If the handle breaks off your mop bucket, don't toss it in the bin, because it can still help keep your house clean. Park that bucket in your mudroom and drop drippy or muddy boots into it as kids come in the door on a rainy or snowy day. The boots can dry out right there, without leaving the least bit of mess on your floor.

KEEP FIDO HYDRATED. You might not be happy with that old bucket anymore, but your dog will be delighted. In the summer, keep the bucket near a spigot and fill it frequently so your pets will always have a place to get a drink. Make sure the bucket is impeccably clean before giving it to your pet.

ONE DRIP AT A TIME. If you have plants or garden vegetables that would benefit from a slow watering, drill a few small holes in the bottom of a bucket that's lost its handle or has suffered a cracked rim. Place the bucket close to the base of the plant and fill it with water; the water will slowly drip out over the course of several hours and the plant will get a deep watering.

STORAGE

When the cleaning session's over, it's time to store everything neatly away. What's that? You're not sure how exactly you're going to fit everything you own into that small space? Don't worry; our experts have plenty of clever solutions.

GET YOUR FILL. If you start to think of your cleaning closet as the filling station for your arsenal of cleaning products, you'll run a much more efficient household. This is where you store all of your large economy-size refill containers of cleaning solutions. After you've finished your routine housecleaning and are returning your cleaning caddy to the storage closet, make it a habit to top off each of your squirt bottles—all-purpose cleanser, glass cleanser, disinfecting cleanser, and such. By using an easy-to-manage system such as this, you'll be more likely to continue buying the cost-saving refill bottles rather than the expensive smaller bottles—over time these savings will add up. And, of course, your squirt bottles will never come up short when you're knee-deep in a housecleaning project.

MAKE IT LAST

SORT THEM BY JOB. Have you ever had trouble finding a particular bottle of cleanser? Or have you discovered an old bottle once it's 5 years out of date? Arrange all of your cleaning products on a shelf according to function. For instance, you could group all of the dusting materials in one spot, floor-care products in another, and general cleaning fluids in another. Not only does this make your implements a breeze to find, but it also ensures that no bottle of cleanser will get forgotten in a dark corner—languishing until it's no good any more.

MAKE ONLY WHAT YOU NEED. Anyone with that Yankee penny-pinching sensibility likes to whip up a homemade cleanser now and then. When you do, keep this rule of thumb in mind: Try to make only the amount of cleanser you need for the current work at hand. There are a couple of reasons that this is a good idea: Homemade cleansers don't have stabilizing ingredients to preserve their cleaning power long-term, so your concoction may become useless sooner than you'd like. Also, if you have mixed up gallons of homemade cleanser, that's gallons of ingredients that are no longer available for other ingenious uses. If you do store your homemade cleanser, make sure it's well-labeled, and never use an old food container for this—there's just too much potential for accidental poisoning.

PASS IT ALONG

SAVE THOSE CABINETS. If you're remodeling the kitchen (or you know someone who is), those kitchen cabinets you're tearing out could have a new life in a less-visible spot in your home. They make glorious storage in the laundry room, for instance, or can serve as "cleaning central" in a utility room or basement. Kitchen cabinets are often replaced because the owner is tired of the look, not because they're in bad repair—so they'll probably need little or no fixing up when you reinstall them. Even if you're not remodeling, kitchen cabinets can often be picked up for little money at yard sales or second-hand stores.

MORE TIPS FOR THE LAUNDRY AND CLEANING CLOSET

Here's a roundup of the laundry room-related Pass It Along tips you'll find in the other chapters of *Don't Throw It Out!*

CHAPTER	TIP	PAGE
1	Reuse the Racks	7
1	New Life for Measuring Cups	23
1	Try These Tray Uses	25
2	Soften with Stray Socks	89
3	4 Super Ideas for Saved Socks	93
3	9 Something News from an Old Wedding Dress	97
6	Shower Curtain Cleaners	197
8	Slap Shot for Spiders	261
9	12 Ways to Reuse an Old Garden Hose	284

DOMESTIC CHALLENGE

There's nothing better than grandmother's tried and true cleaning solutions . . . most of the time! Try this quiz to see whether the old products and ways are still the best ways:

Questions

1. Kitchen curtains: old or new material?

   OLD: Cotton ruffles ironed with plenty of starch
   NEW: Panels or curtains made of patented Crypton material, which is integrally bacteria and odor-resistant

(continues)

2. Spots on stainless steel appliances: old or new cleanser?

   Old: vinegar or bleach diluted with water
   New: Soft liquid cleanser such as Soft Scrub (non-bleach) diluted with water

3. Plastic kiddie furniture: old or new cleanser?

   Old: a capful of Ivory dishwashing liquid dissolved in a gallon of water
   New: Scotch Brite scouring pads

4. Plastic rattles and small plastic toys: old or new washer?

   Old: hand wash in the sink with dishwashing liquid
   New: run through the dishwasher in a mesh bag or the silverware compartment

5. Athletic shoes: old or new odor prevention?

   Old: Upright metal shoe rack with plenty of air circulation in the closet
   New: Febreeze or similar odor eliminator on already musty shoes

6. Wood stove and fireplace doors: old or new cleaner?

   Old: straight razor and a mix of one gallon water per one cup vinegar
   New: commercial fireplace glass cleaner

7. Smoky laundry: old or new additive?

   Old: 1/4 cup baking soda per load
   New: Laundry stain remover such as Shout

8. Plastic shower curtains in the clothes washer: old or new cleanser?

   Old: 1/2 cup extra bleach added to the water along with twice the ordinary amount of detergent
   New: Spray with orange-based cleanser while it's still on the rod, then half the ordinary detergent in the washer

Answers

1. **New:** The starch won't keep out airborne particulates that

love to settle on kitchen textiles. The newer Crypton fabric sends particulates on their way so they'll settle on hard surfaces that are eaiser to wipe.

2. **NEW:** Stainless steel doesn't look porous, but it will absorb the vinegar or the bleach and get new marks, while soft rubbing with the Soft Scrub and a soft cloth can take care of most crusty bits.

3. **OLD:** Plastic scratches easily and the dishwashing liquid is usually sufficient for most marks on plastic.

4. **NEW:** The extra hot water and bleach in the dishwasher soap are better for disinfecting toys that will come in contact with little ones. If you've got a stubborn stain, try rubbing it with a bit of baking soda and a soft cloth before running the load.

5. **OLD:** The leading cause of smelly athletic shoes is bacteria breeding when the shoes are laying in a heap on the floor, covered with other clothes or inside a damp, warm gym bag. Odor eliminator is a fine temporary solution, but next time the shoes are completely clean and dry, try storing them where they'll have plenty of air circulating.

6. **OLD:** Either will do the job, but the vinegar's less expensive, easier to store safely and easier on the environment. Plus, you'll need to carefully scrape the tough gunk off with a razor even if you finish the job with the commercial cleaner instead of the vinegar mix.

7. **OLD:** The laundry stain remover is typically most effective on oil, grass, grape juice, coffee, baby formula, blood, and other protein-based stains while the baking soda will soften the water and break down the smoke so it rinses clear—plus it's hypoallergenic, ideal for use with clear and fragrance free detergents.

8. **NEW.** Bleach generally won't remove water marks, orange cleaner will. And you want less detergent, not more—and running the curtain with a couple of terry towels will help scrub any remaining gunk before you hang it back on the rod to dry.

PART

OUTSIDE THE HOUSE

8

OUTDOOR SPORTS
AND
HOBBIES

Outdoor sports are tough on gear. Sports equipment is designed to take plenty of abuse, but rain, snow, sun, mud, hard play, and plain old wear and tear take their toll. You'll get a lot more mileage out of gear if you know a few tricks, from the best way to wash a sleeping bag to experts' tips for getting more life out of racquet strings. In this chapter, you'll also find tips for buying used bikes and camp stoves, and you'll learn why duct tape isn't always everything it's cracked up to be—along with a few good alternatives.

The advice on the following pages also spells out ways to make repairs to outdoor equipment—at home and in the woods—after something goes wrong or just wears out. You'll learn how clever outdoors people make art from old bike parts and rugs from used climbing ropes, and how some folks use their old gear to help impoverished children live better lives. Now that's a good use of a worn-out pair of shoes.

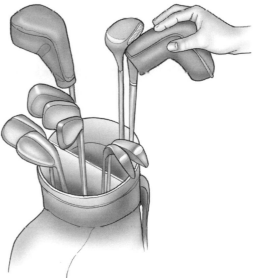

BASEBALL AND SOFTBALL

Who doesn't enjoy a good game of softball during a family reunion or company picnic. The following tips will keep gear in good repair whether you're a weekend player or the parent or grandparent of a Little Leaguer. We even have a tip for passing along an old bat.

FIX IT FAST

BREAK IN A GLOVE LIKE THE PROS. Breaking in a new baseball glove is a time-honored ritual, designed to make your glove behave like a vacuum cleaner for fly balls and grounders. You'll need a specially formulated glove conditioner, petroleum jelly, saddle soap—or even foam shaving cream. Here's how to do it.

1. Start by rubbing a thin coat of whatever you're using into the leather, starting in the palm and working outward, and coating both sides.
2. Once the glove is dry, head out for a good, long session of playing catch. This will start molding the glove around your fingers and hand.
3. Now reapply a light coat of the conditioner, put a ball in the pocket of the glove, and close up the whole package with a Rubber band or string.
4. Until the glove is fully broken in, always oil it after a game or practice and store it with a ball inside. Never soak a glove in water or dry it with an artificial heat source.

RESTORE LACES. The leather in a baseball glove may last for decades, but the lacing usually will wear thin or break much earlier. You can buy replacement lacing specifically designed for gloves or just use rawhide bootlaces. Here's how to upgrade the lacing.

1. Pull out the old laces, one set at a time.
2. Cut a 6-inch piece from a wire coat hanger with wire cutters.
3. Securely, but neatly, use some duct tape to fasten one end of the new lace to an end of the wire.
4. Use the wire to thread the lacing through the glove's holes, and

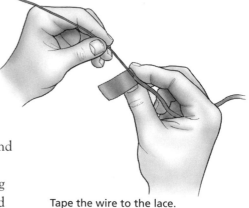

Tape the wire to the lace.

retie it in the same places the old lacing was tied with a simple overhand knot. Don't tie the knots too tightly, because after you use the glove a bit you'll have to retighten the lacing as it stretches.

5. Work some glove conditioner or petroleum jelly onto the new lacing, and you're ready to play.

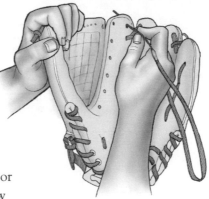

Thread the new lace into the glove.

GET EXTRA INNINGS FROM AN OLD BAT. A busted bat might seem like a useless—and even dangerous—piece of trash, exuding shards and splinters. But a length of smooth hardwood with a consistent taper isn't easy to make without an expensive mill. If you know an amateur woodworker, ask whether he would like to hang onto your old bat for a future project—a bung for a barrel, say, or the hull of a wooden model airplane.

PASS IT ALONG

Battered aluminum bats are easy to recycle because, well, they're made of aluminum. Just take them to your usual recycling drop-off, where they'll be processed, and may even end up becoming the raw material for new bats.

BICYCLING

It's one of the best forms of exercise, so it's no wonder that people everywhere ride their bikes for fun and for transportation. The expert tips we offer here will ensure that every riding experience is safe and that your bike remains in the best shape possible. Our simply ingenious advice about used biking gear is sure to give you a smile.

A CLEAN FRAME IS A HAPPY FRAME. The frame is the single most expensive part of your bike, and it pays to keep it clean. Wipe it off after every dirty ride with a clean rag or a sponge and soapy water. Wax the painted sections of the frame twice a year (at the beginning of riding season and mid-season) using auto wax or special bike wax. Inspect the frame regularly for nicks or scrapes, which can invite corrosion if not repaired. To fix scratches, cover them with durable touch-up paint available from car dealers, auto supply stores, and some bike shops.

MAKE IT LAST

CLEAN THE CHAIN. Reduce wear to your bike chain, derailleur, chain rings, and rear sprockets with a regular cleaning. For a quick cleanup, brush out the chain links with an old toothbrush and then reapply a lubricant such as Finish Line or Tri-Flow. Wipe off the excess lubricant with a rag, or it may attract dirt. Several times a year (more often if you frequently ride through mud or puddles), remove the chain and clean it with Pedro's Oranj Peelz Citrus Degreaser. Dry the chain with a clean rag, reinstall, and lubricate.

CHANGE THE CHAIN. To get the most life out of your bike's expensive chain ring and rear sprockets, replace the chain every couple of years (more often if you ride several times a week). As the bushings between the links wear, the chain gradually lengthens, and this causes uneven wear in your bike's drivetrain. The Park Tool Chain Checker (available at most bike shops) is an inexpensive device that determines precisely when a chain is ready to be replaced.

WATCH OUT FOR SNAKEBITES. If the pressure in your mountain bike tires is too low, your tire may get "snakebit" when you ride over a sharp bump. An underinflated tube can pinch against the rim of the tire, leaving side-by-side puncture marks. Keep the tire pressure within its recommended range and you'll be able to avoid having to make trailside repairs.

REMEDY A THORNY ISSUE. If you ride your bike in brushy country or an area with lots of broken glass, consider three options to avoid frequent flat tires.

1. **Try thorn-resistant inner tubes.** Available for both road bikes and mountain bikes, these tubes are a bit heavier and slightly more expensive than normal tubes, but they likely won't need to be patched or replaced as often.
2. **Give tough tire liners a try.** These strips of lightweight Kevlar or other tough material lie along the tire's inner wall and protect the tube inside.
3. **Get slimed.** This is a brand of puncture sealer that you put into your tube (or buy tubes prefilled with the stuff). When you get a puncture, the escaping air forces the so-called Slime into the hole and quickly seals it. It sounds like something from a straight-to-DVD horror movie, but cyclists swear it really works!

7 Uses for an Old Inner Tube

Don't chuck a bicycle inner tube just because it's no longer worth patching. These jumbo rubber bands may be useful around the house and garden in many ways.

1. **An extra hand.** You can use an inner tube as a flexible, wraparound clamp when you're repairing furniture or gluing other bulky items.
2. **Pad a rope.** Cover rope or wire with a section of the old tube before using it to brace a tree; the rubber sleeve will protect the trunk and branches.
3. **Hold on tight.** Make a simple set of slip-resistant grips for lawn and garden tools by cutting a length of tube and pulling it over the handle.
4. **Work out.** Wrap a section of the tubing around a doorknob or bedpost, and then pull on it with your hands or ankles to simulate the action of many weight machines at the gym.
5. **Bend and stretch.** Use a tube as an aid for stretching or yoga postures.
6. **Homemade hanger.** Hang a hose with a tube. Drive a nail into a stud in your garage or basement, slip one end of the tube over the nail, then pull the other end through a coil of hose, and hang that end over the nail, too.
7. **Dodge drafts.** Glue a few strips of old inner tube along a windowsill or doorjamb to block drafts.

RIDE WITH A WRECKED DERAILLEUR. Let's say you mush your front or rear derailleur against a rock and can't shift gears. Are you destined for a long walk home? Not necessarily. If you're carrying a chain tool and a wrench, you can make a field repair that will get you home, albeit with some hard pedaling.

First remove the derailleur from the bike. Now, using the chain tool, pop out enough links so the chain fits snugly on the middle chain ring and the third or fourth sprocket in the rear. Reinstall the chain and you'll be able to pedal home or to the shop using your new single-speed bike.

MAKING ART OUT OF CLUNKERS. You have an amazing photograph or a special biking memento; how do you frame the photo in a way that instantly says, "I love cycling!"? Here are two options.

1. **Turn to All Terrain Frames.** This company in Colorado recycles used tires by cleaning them up and fashioning them into picture and poster frames. It's your choice of knobby or smooth tires. For more information visit www.allterrainframes.com.

2. **Check out Resource Revival.** This Oregon-based business makes picture frames out of bike chains it buys in bulk from dozens of shops around the country, along with many other used bike parts (and now auto and computer parts). The company also sells bottle openers, CD racks, candleholders, clocks, and even beautifully crafted furniture made using cyclists' old junk. To learn more about Resource Revival's unique products visit www.resourcerevival.com.

SIMPLE SOLUTIONS

A Flat Coke for a Flat Tire

One time I was riding my mountain bike along a stream drainage, and I had a run-in with rock—I skimmed against a sharp rock and tore the sidewall of my tire. I could replace the tube inside easily, but if I tried to ride, the tube would just bubble out that slit in my tire. It was a long walk back, so I started looking for a solution. I found a plastic Coke bottle that was lying around as litter and, using a pocketknife, cut a piece of plastic to fit inside the tire. This formed a sleeve that kept the inner tube in place. It worked so well that I made it home and then rode a few more times before finally buying a new tire.

—Mike Lewis
Helotes, Texas

SPIN AN OVERHEAD TOOL RACK. How do you transform and old bike wheel into a hanging workshop rack? Use a pair of wire cutters, a little ingenuity, and follow these simple instructions.

1. Remove the tire and tube from the wheel, and then clean any stickers or gunk from the metal using rubbing alcohol or a spray-on lubricant such as WD-40 or Tri-Flow.

2. Using the wire cutters, snip off all of the spokes and remove the hub.

3. Attach four pieces of picture-frame wire, each about 2½ feet long, to the spoke holes at 90-degree intervals, so they come together in the middle.

4. Hang the contraption from your workshop ceiling with a hook screwed into a ceiling beam.

   Slip the ends of metal S-hooks through the spoke holes, and then you can hang tools, spare parts, and other workshop necessities from the end of the hooks. With some wheels, you may need to widen the spoke holes with a power drill and a bit slightly larger than the diameter of the hooks you'll be using.

> ## Duct Tape for the New Millennium
>
> For hard-to-fix busted gear, like a snapped ski pole or battered cage on a goalie's mask, nothing beats J-B Weld, a "liquid steel" and epoxy mix. Available at auto body stores, this compound is unaffected by cold or water, and it forms remarkably strong bonds between metal, glass, wood, and fiberglass. (It does not work on rubber, leather, or certain plastics.) Outdoors people have used it to repair climbing gear, ski equipment, fishing rods, and helmets. For best results, J-B Weld needs 4 hours to set and 24 hours to cure. For field repairs, the company also makes J-B Kwik, which sets in 4 minutes and cures in 4 to 6 hours.

BOATING

Whether you're into kayaking on a pond or enjoying a day of canoeing down a river, you'll find the following tips come in quite handy for keeping things afloat!

FLIP YOUR BOAT. Always store a small boat, canoe, or kayak upside-down to keep water out of the hull, especially if the craft is made of wood. Never leave a boat on the ground, or you'll invite rot and insect infestations; store it instead on blocks, sawhorses, or slings hanging from the rafters.

MAKE IT LAST

CORROSION-PROOF A BOAT. Electronic instruments on boats are particularly vulnerable to the corrosive forces of the elements. The solution is a coating and lubricant called Boeshield T-9, available at many marine supply stores. Designed by Boeing to protect aircraft components, the spray-on or liquid Boeshield lubricant creates a thin film that displaces moisture and seals metal parts, electrical connections, and electronic devices. (Boeshield also makes a lubricant for bicycles that protects components, trip computers, and lights from the elements.)

BOATS NEED SUNSCREEN, TOO. Lower-priced canoes and kayaks are often built of polyethylene. Although this material is strong and abrasion-resistant, it is highly vulnerable to ultraviolet (UV) radiation. Protecting the boat from the sun can extend its life span by 50 to 100 percent. Here's how to do that.

- **Stow it in the shade.** Always store your polyethylene craft out of the sun, with the deck side facing down.
- **Prevent warping.** When transporting one of these boats, make sure your roof rack supports the craft on its rails or beneath a bulkhead; positioning the boat with the unsupported deck over the rack may actually lead to the boat warping in the hot sun.
- **Use suntan lotion.** To protect the hull from UV rays while you're paddling or transporting the boat, spray on a coat of 303 Aerospace Protectant and rub it in with a clean cloth. You can find UV blockers for your boat at marine, auto supply, and hardware stores.

AVOID A BIG BANG. Inflatable rafts (or inner tubes) made of dark-colored rubber will heat rapidly in full sun, even if they're sitting in water, which means the air inside can expand dangerously. Splash cold water on the exposed surface periodically, and if you must leave a raft in the hot sun, let out some air first.

FIX IT FAST

GIVE YOUR CANOE A HEALTHY COAT. Fiberglass canoes and boats usually have a polyester finish called gelcoat. Here's how to restore a faded and scratched gelcoat hull.

1. Wet-sand the hull with 320-grit wet/dry paper using plenty of water for lubrication. Marine sandpaper is also available, but any brand of

---

BACK FROM THE BRINK
Beer Cans to the Rescue!

A good friend of mine was 18 and working with his father on their charter fishing boat out of Newburyport, Massachusetts. They were 25 miles offshore and had just finished up a day of fishing in rough weather when they blew the 3-inch-diameter hose that supplies seawater to cool the engine. They had no spare, and without it they were dead in the water. After a couple of hours of head-scratching, my friend's father had a brain-storm. Luckily, the party that had chartered their boat that day drank a lot of beer. Father and son spent the next few hours cutting apart the beer cans and making a metal hose out of the aluminum cylinders. They wrapped the whole mess in electrical tape, started the engine, and steamed home—a little late but very happy!

—Jim Ansara
Exeter, Massachusetts

wet/dry paper will work fine. Keep sanding with finer wet/dry paper, first 400-grit, and then 600.

2. Wipe off all the dust with a clean cloth, and then polish the hull with a rubbing compound such as 3M Super Duty Rubbing Compound and a chamois cloth.

3. Finally, wax the surface with a marine or auto wax, buff with a clean cloth, and spray on a coat of 303 Aerospace Protectant.

CROQUET

Experts in such matters think that the game was invented in Ireland during the early part of the 19th century. And even though it's not as popular as other backyard games, croquet is still enjoyed by many all around the country. We offer a tip about protecting your gear and another that will give you some options for recycling it.

WEATHERPROOF YOUR EQUIPMENT. Croquet sets naturally become caked with dirt and grass stains. Clean off the accumulated gunk with a dishwashing liquid and warm water, scrubbing with a soft-bristled brush. To restore the protective finish on older croquet mallets and stakes, clean thoroughly, allow them to dry, and brush a thin coat of spar varnish—a variety of marine varnish available at any marine supply store and some hardware stores—evenly on the wood.

RECYCLE OLD CROQUET GEAR. Even the most battered wooden croquet set can experience a second life in your lawn. Here are four ways to reuse them in your flower bed.

- **Make a hose guide.** Goal stakes can be driven into the ground next to fragile plantings to protect them from a hose as it's dragged from one position to another across the yard.
- **Claim it as a stake.** Mallet handles can be used the same way by unscrewing the handles from the heads (or sawing them off) and sharpening one end with a jackknife before driving them into the ground at key locations.
- **Special stakes.** To make fancier hose guides, using croquet balls, drive ½-inch wooden dowels into the ground. Now drill a ½-inch hole 2 inches deep in each croquet ball; you'll need a vise and a power drill or a drill press to do this safely and effectively. Put a few drops of yellow carpenter's glue inside the holes, slip the balls onto the dowels, and paint the dowels matching colors.

- **Support floppers.** Use the stakes or handles as plant supports for newly planted or floppy plants. If the stakes or handles have ridges, all the better to help hold the twine you'll use for tying up the plants.

FISHING

It's the most popular pastime in America, and with good reason. Fishing can be relaxing or exciting. You can participate from the quiet banks of a pond or the sea-splashed deck of a boat. Whatever your reason for fishing, you can make good use of the advice below.

MAKE IT LAST

PUT YOUR ROD ON A NO-SALT DIET. Just as salt rusts cars, it eventually also will lead to corrosion on the metal fittings of your fishing rod. To help give your rod a longer life, rinse it with fresh water, and then wipe it using a rag and some denatured alcohol. Use an old toothbrush and clean water to remove dirt and salt from around the line guides and reel seat. To protect the finish of your rod, complete your cleaning with Armor All wipes, available at auto supply or hardware stores.

DON'T BE A DRAG ON YOUR REEL. Before you put away your rod after a day of fishing, always back off the drag adjustment on the reel. Keeping the drag tight will lead to erratic performance in the drag system faster than a big bass can slice a line against a rock.

FIX IT FAST

STOCKINGS ARE A ROD'S BEST FRIEND. The line guides on your rod may develop little burrs or slivers that are practically invisible to the naked eye, but that may wear through a line under tension. To find burrs, pull a nylon stocking through the guides and look for snags, or swab the inside of each guide with a Q-tip and see whether it leaves behind any cotton threads. Gently use 320-grit wet/dry sandpaper to remove a small burr; replace seriously damaged line guides because they will corrode.

STEAM-CLEAN DAMAGED FLIES. Fishing flies may get crushed or deformed if you put them away wet or store them anywhere besides hard-sided boxes. To restore a misshapen fly, grab the hook with a pair of tweezers or pliers, and hold the fly over the steam from a boiling kettle. Often this will fluff the fly right back into shape. Air-dry the lure thoroughly before storing it.

BRIGHTEN AN OLD CORK GRIP. The cork grip on a fishing rod can start to look pretty dingy and stain covered after many days of fishing. To make it look like new, douse the cork in fresh water and sand it with fine, 220- or 320-grit, wet/dry sandpaper. Be careful not to sand the rod itself or any metal fittings. Clean the newly exposed surface with a household cleanser such as Soft Scrub with Bleach. Rinse and allow the cork to dry thoroughly before storing.

> ## The Downside of Duct Tape
>
> Ask outdoor experts how they fix their gear, and two words inevitably surface: duct tape. The stuff seems almost miraculously useful for mending busted ski poles, patching holes, and binding just about anything to anything else. But duct tape also leaves a nasty residue behind when it's peeled off, and those flecks and shards of old tape can make permanent repairs more difficult. Use the gray tape sparingly and only in emergencies. To remove duct tape residue, try cleaning with Duck Adhesive Remover, Goo Gone, WD-40, rubbing alcohol, or acetone. Always test these cleansers first in an inconspicuous area, especially on fabrics, as some products may alter colors.

ALCOHOL REVEALS HOLES IN WADERS. Breathable fabric fishing waders often suffer minor tears and punctures. If you know there's a leak but can't find the hole, try the following: Soak a rag in rubbing alcohol and dab around any areas where you suspect damage. Next, examine the fabric inside and out—pinholes usually show up as dark dots (we're not sure why, but they do). Small holes and tears can be fixed with adhesive patches, available at fishing retailers, or with a thin layer of Aquaseal, available online at www.aquaseal.com or from outdoor outfitters.

GOLF

People tend to be very passionate about golf. What is it about trying to put a tiny ball into a tiny hole that gets them so excited? Well, we can't answer that question, but we can tell you how to keep your gear in great shape and how to make use of that old golf set once it's outlived its usefulness.

GRAPHITE SHAFTS REQUIRE DRIVER ED. Modern drivers with graphite shafts offer superb performance, but the shafts need a bit more care than traditional metal shafts do. Here's how to make sure they last a lifetime.

MAKE IT LAST

- **Use club cozies.** Choose club-head covers that extend over the shafts to protect them from dings and dents.

- **Wash well.** Clean the shafts with mild soap and water, and always clean them immediately if they come in contact with fertilizers or other lawn chemicals.
- **Bath time.** Clean all clubfaces with warm, soapy water and an old, soft-bristled toothbrush. Compacted dirt can be brushed off the clubface or chipped out with the point of a tee.

FIX IT FAST **NEW LIFE FOR GRANDPA'S FAVORITE PUTTER.** Favorite old steel-shafted golf clubs can be easily restored. Many companies specialize in club refinishing; inquire at a local course for references. Or, do it yourself by very gently removing old crud, rust, and steel splinters from the shaft and head with a scouring pad or 320-grit or finer wet/dry sandpaper. Clean the surface with a metal polish designed for chrome or stainless steel. Be sure to dry the club thoroughly after each use to prevent future rust problems.

PASS IT ALONG **MAKE A CLEANING CADDY.** An old wheeled golf bag can be recycled as a cleaning caddy for garage or deck duty. A broom, mop, brush, and rake will stand inside; the pockets hold cleaning solutions, polishes, and hand brushes; and rags and dust cloths can be clipped to the outside with clothespins. Haul the golf bag around with one hand and a bucket of water in the other, and you'll save countless back-and-forth trips.

WALK THE GREENS. If you have an area of the lawn that's constantly compacted from foot traffic (you'll know compacted soil because it's the section that drains poorly), slip on a pair of golf shoes with spikes and walk back and forth over the area. The spikes create tiny holes that allow water to penetrate deeper into the soil.

HIKING AND CAMPING

These outdoors pursuits allow you to get back to basics, enjoy nature, and get some exercise. Check out the tips below for advice about everything from tents and sleeping bags to jackets and boots.

MAKE IT LAST **STORE LOFT LOOSELY.** For a warm night's sleep, your sleeping bag's insulation has to puff up and create pockets of warm air. Whether your sleeping bag is insulated with goose down or synthetic fibers, never store the bag crammed into its stuff sack, or you may permanently compress the insulation. When you get off the trail, fluff up your sleeping bags and leave them open and unstuffed (if you have room), or pack them loosely in a large mesh or cloth bag.

ADD A LINER. To extend the life of your sleeping bag, make a liner from a twin-sized sheet. Fold the sheet in half and sew it across the bottom and then half to three-quarters of the way up the side. The liner can be washed after every trip, reducing the number of times you need to wash your bag. Liners may also be warm enough by themselves in elder hostels or mountain huts.

A TENT YOU CAN PASS ON. Keeping a tent going for the long haul is mostly a matter of preventive maintenance and smart camping techniques. Here are some tips that will keep your tent snug and dry for many years.

- **Pitch on plastic.** Always pitch a tent on top of a groundsheet made of plastic, nylon, or even an old shower curtain. The groundsheet protects the tent floor from sharp rocks, sticks, and general wear and tear. Trim the groundsheet a couple of inches smaller than the tent floor, all the way around; a groundsheet that extends beyond the tent walls will just funnel rainwater under the tent floor.
- **Site it in the shade.** Protect your tent from ultraviolet (UV) radiation, which degrades the nylon walls. Never leave a tent standing for days on end unless it's absolutely necessary; if you must, then cover it with a cheap plastic tarp. If possible, pitch the tent in the shade. For additional UV protection, spray the exterior with 303 Aerospace Protectant or Nikwax UV Proof, and wipe it with a clean cloth.
- **Keep guy lines low.** Attach guy lines on the sides of the tent no more than halfway up the walls. Guy lines attached too high may allow the walls of the tent to collapse inward in high winds and break the poles.
- **Debug.** When you break camp, shake out the tent thoroughly to remove sand, stones, sticks, and dead bugs. If you must pack a wet tent, set it up and air-dry it thoroughly at the earliest opportunity. Never store a wet tent.
- **Clean it right.** Use a damp sponge and mild soap such as Ivory flakes dissolved in water to wipe off dirt and stains; rinse it with a garden hose. (Aim a

$mart Buys
OPT FOR ALUMINUM

Aluminum poles add significant cost to a new tent, but they're worth it. Aluminum tent poles last much, much longer than those made from fiberglass.

jet of water at the zippers from both sides to clean out grit.) Never wash or dry a tent in a machine, or you could damage it beyond repair.

REMOVE TEMPTATION FOR CRITTERS. Want your backpack to last forever? Never leave food inside it. The squirrels, marmots, ravens, and jays—to say nothing of bears—that live near popular trails and campsites quickly learn that packs equal snacks, and they'll chew right through the fabric to get at the food inside. When you reach a campsite, remove all the food from your pack and hang it out of reach of hungry animals. Between trips, scrub the pack inside and out with a sponge and liquid laundry detergent to clean out crumbs and wipe away tempting food odors.

CLEAN FILTER, CLEANER WATER. A portable water filter must be kept extremely clean, not only to ensure you're actually drinking clean water when you filter it, but also because dirty filters are much more laborious to operate and lead to their needing to be replaced before their time. Filters vary widely in their design and construction, but here's some advice that will help keep many filters sanitary and easy to use.

- **Give it a good cleaning.** If your filter uses a ceramic element, remove it regularly from its housing and scrub its surface with an old toothbrush. Rinse in clean water and replace it in the housing.
- **Unclog it.** If your filter allows it, backwashing is a good way to restore the flow to a clogged filter. Remove the intake hose from the filter and reattach it to the filter outlet, and then pump a backwash of water through the filter element.
- **Sterilize it.** At the beginning and end of the camping season, and after backwashing, sterilize the filter. Pump a solution, made of one capful of chlorine bleach in one quart of water, through the filter.

- **Air it out.** Store the filter in a breathable mesh bag, and keep it in a place that allows air to circulate.

DON'T START A WASTE DUMP. A water bottle or hydration pack that's stowed wet, especially with the dregs of a sugar-laden energy drink inside, is an invitation for microorganisms to set up house-keeping. To make sure your bottles keep delivering tasty, sanitary water, you have to clean them carefully.

Fill the hydration bladder or water bottle with warm water and add 1 teaspoon of chlorine bleach per liter of water. Leave this to soak overnight, and then rinse thoroughly. If your bottle stinks, try this formula: Mix 1/2 cup of baking soda in 1/2 cup of water. Fill the bottle with this mixture, and shake well. Hold the bottle or bladder over a sink, add 1/2 cup of lemon juice, aim the opening away from your face, and shake. The mixture will boil and bubble for about 10 minutes. Next, remove any air that you can, seal up the bladder, and put it aside for 20 minutes. Pour out the mixture and rinse in hot water.

THE RIGHT ZIPPER FOR THE RIGHT JOB.
Whether it's a rain jacket, pack, sleeping bag, or tent, zippers are the parts most prone to failure in outdoor gear. You'll curse the day you bought a tent with cheap zippers as dusk settles and the mosquitoes move in. To gain some peace of mind, choose out-door equipment with coil zippers rather than toothed zips. Coil zips have nylon loops sewn into the fabric tape on either side of the zipper opening. They're roughly twice as strong as toothed zippers, and they are usually self-healing: Just pulling the slider gently back and forth will often straighten bent coils. Toothed zips are common in parkas and other clothing, but always choose coils for packs, sleeping bags, and tents. In general, the bigger the zipper, the stronger and more durable it will be for a given use.

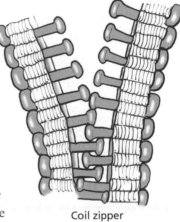

Coil zipper

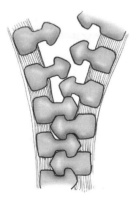

Tooth zipper

THE LOWDOWN ON DOWN. Washing down jackets and sleeping bags is essential to remove dirt and oils and restore the loft (puffiness) in the down. Never dry-clean a down product. For sleeping bags, the best bet is to wash and dry the bags at a commercial laundry with large machines; it's dangerous to use a home washer, with its relatively small agitator, or a home dryer, which will not allow the bag to tumble freely and could melt the fabric. Use a soap formulated for washing down or a mild, nondetergent soap such as Woolite or Ivory Flakes.

Close the zippers and pull the bag straight out of its stuff sack and into the washer, so it doesn't have time to puff up. If the bag has a waterproof-breathable shell, turn it inside out. Wash with warm water on the gentle setting, and run it through an extra spin cycle to remove excess water. Carefully gather up the wet bag and transfer it to the dryer on the medium heat setting. Add a couple of new tennis balls to break up the clumps in the down. When the clumps are gone, remove the bag and air-dry it overnight at home. Wash down parkas and other garments in a sink or tub at home, then dry them on the low, gentle setting in the dryer.

GET A GRIP ON LEAKS. Although most manufacturers of good tents tape the main seams in the fabric of the floor and fly to keep water from seeping through the needle holes, the seams still may need extra care to prevent leaks completely. Seal tents by drawing a bead of Seam Grip or Seam Sure along the inside of sewn seams, especially where the floor meets the wall of the tent and at vulnerable points such as air vents and corners. These sealants are available at most outdoor gear stores. Allow the coating to dry overnight before using the tent or putting it away for storage.

FIX IT FAST

GOT MILK? FIX A CHAIR. Those comfy fold-up camp chairs depend on metal stays that fit into fabric sleeves to give them structure. If the stays begin to poke through the fabric, you can still get more life out of the chair.

First, remove the stays. Now cut a plastic milk carton into little rectangles just big enough to fold over the ends of the metal stays. Fold one piece of plastic in half over each end, and use duct tape to fasten it in place. This padding will protect the sleeves from further damage.

KEEP DOWN IN ITS PLACE. A rip in a down parka or sleeping bag needs to be fixed right away, or down feathers will leak out and quickly fill the air inside your tent. Stock your repair kit with a bit of Kenyon K-Tape, an adhesive-backed nylon patch that comes in both rolls and squares. To mend the rip, simply clean and dry the fabric by the tear, round off the edges of the patch, and apply. Once you get back home, send the jacket or sleeping bag to a professional for a permanent sewn repair. Inquire at outdoor gear stores about sewers or mail-order outfits that specialize in outdoor equipment.

DRAW OUT A DRAWSTRING. Many parkas, ski pants, sleeping bags, and stuff sacks use drawstrings to cinch their openings. Sometimes those sneaky strings will slip inside eyelets or grommets and disappear into the hem of a garment or bag. To recover a drawstring, find the lost end and try working it back toward the eyelet with your fingers and thumbs. If this doesn't work (and it often doesn't), pull the cord all the way out. Now, attach a safety pin or paper clip to one end of the cord. (Make sure this is small enough to fit through the drawstring's eyelet.) Thread the pin through the eyelet, and use it to guide the cord around the hem with your fingers and thumbs. Once you've got both ends of the cord back in hand, knot them so they can't escape again.

DRAW A BEAD ON WATERPROOFING. Nearly all high-tech waterproof/breathable garments use a durable water-repellent (DWR) finish to help rain and melted snow bead up and roll off the fabric instead of penetrating. As this DWR treatment wears off, the garment may start to "wet out" as it absorbs moisture in damp weather, making it feel soaked and heavy even though it's not actually leaking. Here's how to make your garment shed water like it's new.

1. First, wash the item in cold water on the gentle cycle, using a mild soap such as Woolite.

2. Dry the garment in a machine on a low to medium setting; moderate heat will help restore the DWR treatment's

---

Zip It with Plastic

Plastic zip or cable ties, like the ones you use to secure fencing or bundle electrical cables, are superb all-around fix-it tools for sports equipment. Anytime you might be tempted to use wire or cord to repair an item or connect two or more, keep in mind that zip ties are quicker and usually just as secure, at least on a temporary basis. They're also inexpensive, super lightweight, and can be doubled up for more strength. Use them in a pinch to replace broken bootlaces or buckles, mend pack straps, reinforce the flotation on snowshoes, secure the bail on cross-country ski bindings, replace lost zipper pulls, or any of myriad other uses. Zip ties are widely available at home and garden stores and computer outlets—keep a handful in your workshop, boat, and backpack.

effectiveness. (However, always check the label in case a manufacturer has unusual washing or drying requirements.)

3. For a further boost to the DWR coating, iron the garment with a clean, warm iron set on low.

4. Finally, DWR treatments can be reapplied with spray-on or wash-in products, such as Nikwax or ReviveX. Follow the instructions carefully, and soon rain will be bouncing off your coat again.

LUBE A LANTERN. Many camp stoves and lanterns require pumping to pressurize the fuel before you can light up. Inside these pumps, there's usually a leather gasket that can dry out and shrink or bend, making the pump useless. If your stove or lantern doesn't seem to be pressurizing properly, or if the pump slides without any resistance, unscrew or pop off the pump cover, pull out the plunger, and check the gasket at the end. If it appears dry or misshapen, lubricate it with lightweight oil such as WD-40, cooking oil, or even lip balm; massage it in with your fingers to cover every surface. Replace the plunger and pump away!

$mart Buys
BUYING THE BEST CAMP STOVE

IF YOU . . .	BUY . . .	BECAUSE . . .
usually camp next to your car	a two-burner stove fueled by refillable propane canisters	although heavy, they're also clean burning, easy to operate, and efficient
backpack from spring through fall	a stove fueled by canisters of butane, isobutane, or a butane-propane mix; a stove that burns white gas; (Coleman fuel)	these are the most convenient options. These fuels are more economical, and don't create as much waste from spent fuel canisters
camp in winter	a hot-burning, white-gas stove	canister stoves don't operate well in the cold
travel overseas	a canister stove or a white-gas stove that can handle other fuels, such as kerosene or unleaded gasoline	a multi-fuel stove is the safest bet, since one of the fuels is likely to be available at your destination (but check before you leave); airlines will absolutely not allow you to bring stove fuel on board

PUT THE STICK BACK IN VELCRO. Sooner or later, the Velcro patches on your outdoor clothing and equipment always get tangled with dirt, fuzzy bits of fabric, and even twigs and burrs. The result? Those tiny hooks can't grab the little loops, and the Velcro stops sticking as well as it once did. The solution is simple: Comb out the hook side of the patches with a fine-toothed comb until the hook side is clean. Wash the loop side under a faucet, digging out the debris with an old toothbrush.

MEND MOSQUITO NETTING. BZZZZZZZZZ! If the whine of mosquitoes sounds a little too close for comfort when you're camping, you may have a hole in your tent's mosquito netting. Large holes or rips can be mended with a needle and thread; once you get home, send the tent to the manufacturer or a specialty repair shop for a permanent patch. If the hole is smaller than about an inch in diameter, you can make a permanent patch with a tube of Seam Grip (available at most outdoor gear shops), a piece of paper, and any kind of tape. Position the paper over the hole, tape it in place, turn the mosquito netting over, and cover the hole with a thick coat of Seam Grip, using another piece of paper to smooth out the layer of sealant. When the Seam Grip is dry, peel off the paper. A thin, flexible patch will remain. Don't try this in the field unless you can leave your tent standing around 48 hours; the Seam Grip must be completely dry before you pack up your tent.

UNSTICK A STUBBORN ZIP. The zipper is the weakest link in a tent or pack. Fortunately, stubborn zippers often can be fixed. Don't yank on it—you'll likely only worsen the underlying problem. Instead, try these zip tips next time you can't get in or out of your tent.
- **Brush it.** Scrub both sides of a balky zipper with a toothbrush dampened with water. Dishwashing liquid or hand soap can be used, too, but isn't absolutely necessary. Never oil or grease a zipper, because this only will attract more dirt and grit.
- **Salvage the slide.** If a zipper pops open in the middle of its track, a worn slider is often the culprit. Using a small pair of pliers, like those on some utility tools, you can often fix the slider. Open the zipper all the way, and then gently squeeze together one side of the slider opening; squeeze the other side the same amount, and try the zip again. Repeat this process until it closes properly, but be very careful not to overdo it.

• **Coil care.** Sometimes a coil (loop) in a zipper will be bent or crushed, putting it out of alignment with the others. Using a needle, straightened safety pin, paper clip, or the awl on your jackknife, reach under the offending coil and gently pull it back into proper position.

• **An interim solution.** If a tooth in a zipper breaks, the zip will have to be replaced, but you can still use the item until you get home by sewing the zipper shut just above the broken tooth; that way you can at least open and shut the zip partway.

• **Replace the pull.** Broken or lost zipper pulls can easily be replaced with cord, a plastic zip tie, a paper clip, or many other items.

PROVIDE SALVATION FOR A LOST SOLE. The soles of most hiking boots these days are glued, not sewn, to the uppers, and occasionally a sole will start to peel off and flap with every step. Here's how to repair it.

1. Thoroughly clean the exposed surfaces of both the sole and the upper; use rubbing alcohol and a stiff brush if available.

2. Apply a strong adhesive (Freesole is the most popular brand), and bind the sole and upper together using a C-clamp, tape, or a weight. (A full water bottle inside the boot works well for weighting heel repairs.)

3. Allow to dry overnight. To protect your boots, never leave them inside a hot car, which can weaken the glue bond.

KEEP SOCKS IN PAIRS. If your skiing, hiking, or hockey socks migrate to opposite sides of the house as soon as you get home, help is on the way. Sock-Locks, Sockpro, and other companies make small, plastic rings that keep socks together in the wash. As soon as you get home from soccer practice, a run, or a day hike, slip your dirty socks through one of these rings and toss the pair in the laundry hamper. You can wash and dry the socks while they're still linked together, and the pair will be ready when you need them.

DON'T AGONIZE OVER AN AGLET. Just about any Scrabble player knows that an aglet is the hard tip at the end of a shoelace that allows you to pass it through eyelets more easily. And any hiker knows what a pain it is to lace your boot if the shoelace breaks and one end no longer has a helpful aglet. The laces of most hiking boots (in fact, most any shoes) are made of a synthetic material such as nylon. Apply a lit match or lighter flame to the frayed end for just a second. Instead of burning, the nylon will melt and fuse together. Quickly dowse it with a little saliva or water. Let it cool a moment, but while the lace is still warm and pliable, pinch the loose ends together in a point. Voila! Instant aglet.

PAD JUST ABOUT ANYTHING. If your closed-cell foam sleeping pad is so tattered that your hips keep bumping the ground when you try to sleep, cut up the good parts of the pad for other uses. Try some of these ideas.

PASS IT ALONG

- A case for a camping lantern or camera
- A portable dog bed
- A seat for winter hiking lunch stops
- Insulation for a stove when you're cooking in the cold
- Insulation for a water bottle (secure it with duct tape)
- Knee pads for scrubbing camp dishes or gardening
- Padding for canoe or kayak seats
- Padding for roof racks

RUNNING

Doesn't matter if you're training for a fun run or a marathon, you'll get more use from those running shoes when you heed our expert tips.

MAXIMIZE YOUR MILES IN RUNNING SHOES. Running shoes should last 400 to 500 training miles—your mileage may vary, depending on whether you run on roads or trails (and how often you run in mud or snow). To get the maximum miles out of your shoes, treat them right.

MAKE IT LAST

- **Save them for running.** Not only will the shoes wear out more quickly, but their daily use reduces the effectiveness of the shock-absorbing padding. Ideally, you should own at least two pairs of running shoes and alternate their use to allow the padding to rebound and regain effectiveness between runs.

20 Hex Screws + 1 Pair Old Sneakers = 1 Pair Ice Walkers

Any comfortable old pair of rubber-soled sneakers or running shoes can be transformed into super-secure ice walkers for winter strolls or carrying in the groceries from an icy driveway. All you need is a drill or screwdriver and 12 to 16³⁄₈-inch #6 slotted hex screws (sheet-metal screws). Make sure to buy the ones with a sharp point and slotted head. Here's how it works.

1. Use an awl or ice pick to create 10 to 12 starter holes in a grid around the sole of each shoe.
2. Now install the screws in these holes, tightening until the bottoms of the screw heads are flush against the rubber.

You'll never feel the screw points, and the hex heads provide amazing traction on hard snow or ice.

- **Keep them clean.** Never wash shoes in a machine, or you may damage the glue and high-tech materials used to construct the shoes. Instead, remove the laces and insoles, and then scrub the shoes with warm, soapy water, using mild laundry soap like Woolite or liquid antibacterial hand soap. Rinse thoroughly and stuff the shoes with newspaper so they'll hold their shape as they dry. Never use a hair dryer or other artificial heat to dry the shoes.
- **Protect the seams.** If you frequently run off-road or along hillsides, the seams near the toes, especially along the outer edges, are vulnerable to wear. Protect them from abrasion by applying a bead of Seam Grip, available at most outdoor gear stores, along the outside of the seams. Allow it to dry thoroughly before using the shoes.

PASS IT ALONG

NEW HOMES FOR OLD SHOES. Once you're ready to retire a pair of running shoes, you can still make good use of them:

- **Paint in them.** Set them aside with your painting supplies and use them as who-cares-if-they-get-splattered painting shoes.
- **So others might run.** Donate clean, serviceable shoes to a charity, or ship them to Colorado-based One World Running (www.boulderrunning.com/oneworldrunning/), a group founded in 1986 by elite runners to collect running shoes, soccer shoes, and baseball equipment for needy athletes and children around the world.
- **Recycle them.** Many city recycling programs accept worn-out running shoes. The foam padding is ground up to make material for resurfacing tennis courts and playgrounds; the rubber soles eventually become weight-room flooring and running tracks. If no recycling is available locally, check out the Nike Reuse-A-Shoe program (www.nikereuseashoe.com).

RACQUETS AND BALLS

Finished with that old racquet and those old balls? Just take a look below for plenty of clever, crafty ideas.

SAVE YOUR STRINGS. The strings in tennis racquets need to be replaced frequently to maintain the racquet's performance. The rule of thumb is to replace strings as many times each year as the number of times you play each week; for example, if you play tennis twice a week, you should replace the strings at least twice a year. However, strings often need to be replaced because they break, usually as a result of wear and tear. To reduce such wear, many players (even some pros, who get strings for free) reinforce their racquets with simple elastics called Elastocross or String-a-Lings. These bands lock the strings in place so they can't rub.

MAKE IT LAST

SERVE UP A PICTURE FRAME. An old tennis or badminton racquet can be turned into an unusual picture frame—maybe to showcase that photo of you holding up your big tournament trophy! Here's how.

PASS IT ALONG

1. Using a sharp knife, cut and remove all of the strings.
2. Paint or lacquer a wooden frame and handle, or leave it in its natural condition.
3. Find or buy a piece of thin, colored cardboard large enough to cover the entire racquet head. Trace the shape of the head on the

---

6 Uses for an Old Tennis Ball

A tennis ball that's lost its bounce on the court may still have plenty of life at home. Try these tips to get an old ball back in the game.

1. **Slide silently.** Cut slits in the sides of balls and slip them onto the feet of chairs or other furniture that you want to slide easily and silently across a floor, such as a child's desk chair.
2. **Walk more easily.** Slip balls onto the feet of a walker, helping it slide easily without scratching floors. If you don't use a walker, consider donating them to your local nursing home.
3. **Hammer softly.** Pad a hammer head with a sliced tennis ball to quickly create a makeshift mallet.
4. **Tennis ball bumper.** Cut a small slit in a tennis ball, tie a paper clip to a length of string, poke the clip into the ball, and hang the strung-up ball inside your garage to mark the spot where you should stop your car.
5. **Roll away foot pain.** If you suffer from sore arches or plantar fasciitis, place an old tennis ball on the floor and roll your foot back and forth on it to soothe them.
6. **Go fetch.** Last but not least: Make your canine friend happy!

cardboard. Then cut out the oval shape and trim it so it fits behind the racquet head without peeking out from any of the edges.

4. With an X-Acto knife, cut a hole in the center of the cardboard to frame your picture—an oval frame matching the shape of the racquet head is best, but this is difficult to cut freehand.

5. Now attach the cardboard matte to the racquet frame using white Elmer's glue.

6. Tape the photo to the matte, facing through the frame.

7. Thread a small piece of picture wire through the top two string holes to create a loop, and use this to proudly hang up your new frame.

HOCKEY

Whether the gear belongs to you—or to a child or grandchild—it'll last a lot longer when you follow the tips below.

MAKE IT LAST

GET THE STINK OUT. There's no way around it: Hockey gear smells! To beat the stink, use Odor-Eaters, baking powder, or foot powder on gear, not just the skates, after every practice or game. Sprinkle the powder into the gloves, shoulder pads, shin guards, and skates, and it will inhibit bacteria that cause that funky smell.

Still Working After All These Years
KEEP ON ROLLING

I've been using the same pair of Rollerblades for 17 years now. I started to wear out the toes by dragging my feet, but then I found I could really beef up the plastic with layers of duct tape. I haven't put new laces in them for a decade. I bought high-quality hockey laces, and keep tying knots in them. I also cinch Velcro belts around my ankles to keep the boots tight. I spent a bunch of money on good bearings, and I haven't had to change them in a decade. (I do keep them clean and oiled.) I buy new wheels, but I rotate them regularly to get the maximum use out of them. Because the Rollerblades are plastic, they should actually last forever if you patch any holes, clean the bearings, and clean the insides and outsides of the boots regularly. Most important: You have to use them often so they don't get rusty!

—Lizzy Scully
Estes Park, Colorado

KEEP SKATE BLADES GLEAMING. To prevent rust on the blades of skates, always dry them thoroughly with a soft cloth after a session on the ice. Remove the insoles, and put away the skates with the toes pointing up to encourage the escape of trapped moisture. Never store the skates with their rubber or plastic blade guards in place, or you'll trap moisture against the blades. Store skates inside a terrycloth bag.

REGAIN YOUR SIGHT. A helmet visor is essential safety gear, but when the visor gets so scratched you can't see out of it, the game may become dangerous again. To fix minor scratches, smear non-gel toothpaste on the visor and buff it with a clean cloth. Rinse under a faucet. To keep your visor from fogging, rub dishwashing liquid onto the inside of the visor, allow it to dry, and then buff it with a clean, soft cloth.

 **FIX IT FAST**

SLAP SHOT FOR SPIDERS. Reuse an old hockey stick as an extension duster for out-of-reach nooks and crannies. Slide an old sock or nylon stocking over the blade of the stick, and use it to dust under and behind furniture or into overhead corners to clean out cobwebs.

PASS IT ALONG

THE PUCK STOPS HERE. Wondering what to do with old hockey pucks? If you know someone with a pool, a puck makes a great diving toy. No pool? Bring the puck indoors and use it as a paperweight.

One Man's Trash
A Bowl Gretsky Would Love

Given the right circumstances and a set of power tools, there's no telling what a creative person might do with someone else's trash—even old hockey sticks. Take Denis Roy, a woodworker in Winnipeg, Manitoba, Canada (naturally). Roy makes exquisite wooden bowls turned from hockey sticks that have been glued together.

Roy secures his supply of the raw materials from the manager of a local hockey arena. He's careful to use only all-wood sticks, because the fiberglass and graphite models are murder on his tool blades. Roy cuts down the old sticks into precisely measured shapes and then turns them on a lathe. Traditional wooden hockey sticks are made from mul-

tiple laminations of various woods. Designs on the bowls are achieved by using different brands of sticks and alternating their orientation in the rings that make up the bowls. Roy's bowls feature stripes and bull's eye patterns. Once the bowls are shaped, they are given 3 or 4 coats of salad bowl finish, making them wonderfully practical as well as pleasant to look at.

Roy sells his bowls online from his woodcraft Web site at www.ideasinwood.com. (Just click on bowls.) If you're feeling ambitious, he's also posted the plans for you to make one yourself. Oh, and Roy's advice for recyling old fiberglass or graphite sticks? Use them for tomato stakes in the garden.

RVING

Some many of us are hitting the open highways today that it seems like everyone is enjoying RVing. And why not? It allows you to always have the comforts of home close at hand. Our tips will help the novice and experienced RVer have more fun on the road.

TAKE A TEST DRIVE. New to RVing? Backing up seems to stymie lots of new RV drivers. So if you haven't been behind the wheel a lot, you can prevent costly fender benders by taking the RV to a big empty parking lot and practicing your backing-up technique, not just once, but on several different days before your first trip. Learning to stay within the lines of a parking space will take some of the stress out of backing up between two trees.

KNOW YOUR CLEARANCE. You're cruising along the highway when you see a "Low Clearance: 13′ 8″ sign. Will you make it? Why wonder? Before a trip, measure the height of your RV or motor home on a label, and place that label on your visor or dashboard. Then, get yourself a reliable, up-to-date map book such as the Rand McNally Motor Carriers' Road Atlas, which lists low-clearance overpasses and bridges. You'll never suffer that last-minute panic again.

MONITOR MOLD. Because they often spend extended periods sitting unused or traveling in warm and sometimes humid climates, RVs and campers are especially susceptible to mold and mildew. You can forestall this nuisance (and potential health hazard) by making a mold inspection part of your routine maintenance. Pay special attention to the caulking around the windows and doors, vents, shower, stove and refrigerator, and storage areas, and all hookups. Finding and attacking mold sooner, rather than later, can save you big money down the road on an expensive professional cleaning job.

THE FINE PRINT
Hold On to That Awning

Of course your RV or camper is insured; you couldn't drive it if it wasn't. But you may want to take a second look at the policy, because it may not cover your awnings, of all things. Damage to awnings that have not been stowed properly before traveling or prior to storms is among the most commonly reported accidents with RVs. And awnings can be quite pricey, with the largest costing more than $1,000. So do yourself a favor before you head out on your next adventure, secure your awnings and check your policy.

SET OUT A WELCOME MAT.
The inside of your camper or RV
starts out so nice and clean before a trip—but afterward, you've
tracked in all sorts of dirt from
the great outdoors. You can keep
your camper (nearly) pristine by
borrowing an idea from home:
a welcome mat. Visit any home
improvement store and purchase
a piece of indoor/outdoor carpet
and place it at the door of your
camper when you arrive at your
site. Shake it out before you leave,
and you'll have a lot less sweeping
up to do once you get home.

Drop Cloths for a Rainy Day

If you've spent any amount of time on the road in
your RV, you know that the days are not always sunny
and warm. But rainstorms, predicted or unexpected,
aren't just annoying. They can cause damage to an
RV or camper. If you get hit by a storm that damages
your vehicle's roof, you can make a quick repair—all
you need are some painter's plastic drop cloths and
duct tape (both of which you've packed plenty of,
right?). Wait until the rain has stopped—*never* get on
top of your RV during a storm—and then patch the
damage by covering it with the plastic. Secure it with
lots and lots of duct tape. The fix should hold until
you're able to make a more permanent repair.

MAKE A LAUNCH LIST. How many times have you driven off from
your campsite only to realize down the road that you left the television antenna up? To avoid this (and other) potential mishaps, take the
time to make a predeparture checklist. And to prevent your forgetting
about that checklist, write one item—take up chocks, lower antenna,
secure appliances, clean up site, and the like—on a brightly colored
clothespin with a permanent magic marker. As soon as you arrive at
your campsite, clip all the clothespins to the visors in the front seat.
At the end of your stay, take down the clothespins one a time, only
after tackling each job.

ELIMINATE ODORS. When an RV or camper sits unused during the
off-season, it can take on musty odors. To eliminate these unpleasant
smells, go to the kitchen and grab three or four disposable roasting
pans and a few small flat containers, and fill them with charcoal (not
the match-light variety). Set the containers around the interior of
your RV. Change the charcoal once a week or so if necessary, and the
odors will (almost) magically disappear.

FIX IT FAST

PUT MOLD ON HOLD. Once mold has shown up in your camper or
RV, there are several ways to get rid of it.
- **Fix it on the cheap.** Washing surfaces with a mixture of chlorine
  bleach and water (1 part bleach to 16 parts water, or 1 cup bleach

to 1 gallon of water) is the least expensive solution. Before using the mixture, be sure to try it on an inconspicuous area.

- **Try a brand name.** Several commercial products are designed specifically to target and remove mold. One popular brand is Tilex Mold & Mildew Remover.
- **Good for Mother Nature.** A more environmentally safe option is a product called MoldZyme. It's biodegradable and safe to use around your furry friends.

SO GLASSES STAY PUT. Tired of everything in your RV shifting with every turn? There's a simple step you can take before your next trip to make sure items stay where you put them. Line all of the shelves in the RV or camper with nonskid mats, which are available at home improvement and discount stores. The material usually comes in sheets that you cut to fit. This solution isn't just for kitchen items—use it anywhere you want items to stay put.

SKIING

Our experts put their heads together and came up with their best tips for those of us who ski the mountains or the trails.

MAKE IT LAST

KEEP YOUR SKIS IN TUNE. "Tuning" your skis' bottoms at least once a year will even out the bases, sharpen the edges, and remove rust, extending the life of your skis. Unless you're a well-equipped expert, a ski shop will do the best tune-ups with their precise machines. But you can save money and tune your skis more often at home with a few simple tools. Here are the basic steps.

1. Carefully scrape the bottom with a sharp, straight-sided metal scraper, moving from tips to tails with the scraper tilted toward the direction it's moving. Make sure the scraper's edge is completely square, and maintain even pressure across the base.

2. Then file the edges with a clean mill bastard file. Hold the file flat against the ski bottom, oriented at

---

FIX IT OR FORGET IT?
GET TO THE BOTTOM OF WORN-OUT SKIS

Waxless cross-country skis depend on plastic "scales" on their bottoms for traction in the snow. Eventually, these scales wear down and you may start slipping. You can apply ski wax over the worn-out scales, but then you'll get very poor glide out of your skis. There's no way to restore waxless skis to their original condition, but if you love the skis you can still salvage them. Take your old boards to a ski shop, and ask the professionals to grind off the remaining scales. You'll end up with a "new" pair of waxable skis.

a 45-degree angle to the length of the ski. File with long, even strokes, from tip to tail. Hold the file with your thumbs pressing gently in the middle of the ski's base to prevent the file from bending and rounding the edges. Your goal is a 90-degree corner on the edges.

More advanced tuning, such as beveling the edges to anything but a 90-degree angle, should be done by the pros at a ski shop.

LIGHT A CANDLE FOR SCRATCHES. Who hasn't been eager to start the ski season and skied right over a rock, leaving a long scratch in a ski bottom? Deep gashes that burrow into a ski (alpine or Nordic) or snowboard should be repaired professionally. But most nicks and scratches are easily repaired at home with a P-Tex candle, available at any ski or snowboarding shop.

FIX IT FAST

1. Use a sharp knife or scraper to trim away any shards of plastic at the edge of the cut.
2. Warm the ski or snowboard bottom with a hair dryer. In a well-ventilated room, carefully light the P-Tex candle using a match or a lighter (it will take a moment to get it going). Then hold the candle horizontally close to the ski and let molten plastic drip and flow into the wound. Be very careful not to let this plastic drop onto your arm, or a painful burn will result.
3. Completely fill the gouged-out ski bottom with plastic; too much is better than too little.
4. Douse the candle in water, allow the ski bottom and the P-Tex to cool completely, and then scrape it smooth with a sharp metal scraper.

Carefully light the P-Tex candle.

Make it smooth with a scraper.

PLAN AHEAD FOR SAFETY. A broken ski pole in the backcountry could mean an arduous trip back home, but not if you've planned ahead and carried a few simple items.

- **Spring for a spare.** Broken or lost baskets are one common pole problem. The solution is simple: Always carry a spare, available where you purchased your poles. Many baskets simply pop off and on. (Try bracing the basket between your boots and yanking on the pole.) Sometimes you may have to carefully slice off the busted basket with a sharp jackknife.

- **Splint it.** A bent or broken pole can be splinted for the ski out to civilization. To prepare for this emergency, wrap a few feet of duct tape around one of your poles, just below the grip. If a pole breaks, splint it with a tent stake, a green tree limb, or a piece of aluminum sliced from a soda can. Bind the duct tape tightly around the splint on both sides of the break. No duct tape? Adjustable nylon or leather straps from your pack or gaiters may also work.

PASS IT ALONG

SIT ON YOUR OLD SKIS. With a little ingenuity, old skis and snowboards can be turned into creative outdoor furniture. Vermont Ski Recyclers (www.skifurniture.com) and several other companies fashion skis and snowboards into chairs, bookshelves, glass-top tables, CD racks, benches, and other useful items. Or, how about a picket fence!

PERFORM A TOMATO STEM CHRISTIE. That busted ski pole may never see the slopes again, but just wait until summer! If you have a garden, an old ski pole makes a dandy tomato plant stake. Ski poles are designed to be tough and weatherproof. Plant it in the ground when your seedlings start to grow and even the largest beefsteaks won't droop when they're attached to this rugged trellis.

WALK OLD BOOTS TO THE GARDEN. A common problem many skiers face when they buy new skis is that the binding system that holds the boot to the ski doesn't match their old boots. While some backcountry ski boots are designed to be walked in, and so may have a second life as a backup hiking boot, most will probably never see a pair of woolly socks again. Instead, if

---

SIMPLE SOLUTIONS

All You'll Need is a Sled Dog

Those simple plastic sleds for kids make great wintertime totes. Once your kids or grandkids outgrow a sled, keep it in the garage to tow firewood, take out the trash, or bring in a heavy load of groceries.

you have a garden or patio, you can make use of the old footwear in an unconventional way. Just place an appropriately sized flowerpot inside. These flower-filled boots make an interesting arrangement in the garden or on the deck—and tell visitors that you have cold-weather outdoor hobbies, too.

SOCCER

When you're taking a break from watching the kids or grandkids' soccer matches, kick these ideas around!

THE GOAL? MULTIPLE SEASONS! Many folks think that expensive cleats will last about two seasons (spring and fall). But with a little preventive care, you can double or triple the life of soccer shoes. Clean the shoes thoroughly after each game or practice session. Knock off caked mud, and clean between the cleats with a stiff brush. Wipe the outside of the shoe with a rag and warm, soapy water to remove the remaining dirt and any chemicals used on the field. Stuff newspaper in the shoes to help them hold their shape as they dry, and never use an artificial heat source to dry them.

MAKE IT LAST

The life of leather shoes can be greatly extended by treating them regularly with Nikwax Liquid Conditioner (available wherever hiking boots are sold). If you find that the shoes wear out at a particular spot, take them to a cobbler who can sew on a leather reinforcement patch. Never walk across concrete or pavement in cleats; carry a pair of old running shoes or flip-flops in your training bag, and put these on after the game.

PASS IT ALONG

AN OLD BALL, DOG'S BEST FRIEND. If you have a dog (or know dogs that live in the neighborhood), deflate old soccer or footballs and give them to your furry friend as a chew toy that should last for weeks (Okay, days for some dogs). But check first with the dog's owner to make sure the dogs won't eat the torn pieces.

MORE TIPS FOR OUTDOOR SPORTS AND HOBBIES

Here's a roundup of the sport and hobby-related Pass It Along tips you'll find in the other chapters of *Don't Throw It Out!*

Domestic Challenge

In the world of expensive and sometimes infrequently used recreation equipment, which damaged goods warrant repairing, and which require the old heave-ho?

Questions

1. After spending a few too many days in the yard in the rain and sun, your bike helmet's strap is frayed and the buckle has come off. Has it taken its last ride in the park?

2. Who knows how it happened—a marshmallow roasting stick, the dog's toenails—but your nylon tent now sports a few punctures and burn spots. Assuming you can only use it if it's watertight, will you ever be able to pitch it again?

3. The badminton net is still operable, but one of the poles it's attached to is bent at the bottom. Can you make it better?

4. Now the birdie's little plastic tip is popping off at the critical moment of contact. Will it ever fly again?

5. Fess up. At least one of your croquet mallets is splintered from being used to pound stakes, and those scuffs and tooth marks on the balls come from unsupervised pets and improper storage. The wickets—if you have any left—are completely bent out of shape. So, is it time to find a new game for pleasant spring afternoons, or can you salvage this one?

6. You've discovered a treasured wooden tennis racquet and it's just got one broken string. Should you restring it and play on or is it played out?

Answers

1. For safety's sake, don't wear a damaged helmet to ride anymore—it will become a poorly fitting helmet, prone to slipping or covering the wrong parts of your skull, which can be just as dangerous as no helmet at all.

2. Sure, prepare to repair and enjoy dry camping once more. For any rips on the tent side, use adhesive-backed ripstop nylon repair tape, such as Kenyon brand, which comes in several colors. For the crucial tent fly and floor areas, make

it watertight again with Recoat, another Kenyon product that seals in place of polyurethane coating.

3. If the net's a nice one, salvage that pole in minutes with a splint approach. Use duct tape to attach an old broom or mop handle to the damaged section, leaving an extra 6 to 8 inches of the handle at the bottom. That way, you can slip it into a length of pipe or PVC in the ground to put the net in play once more.

4. Nope, even glue won't help a birdie with a loose tip since it must endure so much impact every time it meets the rac-quet—and it's most likely low-quality anyway. Pass the poor-performing birdies along to the cat as toys, slipping a little catnip between feathers and tip before gluing or taping it down. Then invest in some better models, they'll really enhance your game for just a few bucks.

5. Play on! Somewhat akin to billiards, you really only need a couple of mallets in good shape, since only one player hits at a time. As for the balls, you can buy many different qual-ity replacements for much less than a new set. And those bent wickets? Make replacements (you'll need nine total) from wire coat hangers cut with wire cutters and bent into a standard-size arch over a mailbox.

6. In most cases, while you can find someone to restring a wood racquet on any standard tennis website or even order the strings and do it yourself, a wooden racquet is no fun when you're playing someone with one of the more mod-ern graphite racquets—your racquet will bend and break if you string it tightly enough to return hard shots easily made by such racquets. If you have two, or a buddy who also has a wooden racquet, you can play the occasional wooden racquet game. Otherwise, see what your vintage piece will bring from the local antique shop or use it to decorate in the rec room.

9

LAWN AND GARDEN ACCESSORIES

Whether your yard is a lush carpet of grass, a vegetable patch spilling over with fresh produce, or a quiet corner of the deck, your outdoor spaces can be a retreat from the bustling stress of the world. To become that haven, your green space needs some work. That's where these tips come in. From keeping the mower working to creating a homemade planter that will last longer than your mortgage payments, these nifty pointers will help you extend the life of the tools and equipment that are essential to staying on top of your patch of earth.

Ponds? Paths? Feeders? Most any accessory that enhances your slice of the good life is addressed here, beginning with ways to "pick 'em and plant 'em" so they'll last a long time and advice about how to make quick fixes to your accessories when weather causes wear and tear.

No matter how careful you are, the sun will inevitably set on some garden equipment. When it does, there are loads of crafty ways to reuse your worn and outdated items.

BARBECUE GRILLS

Read on to smoke out ways to keep your outdoor cooking equipment right and ready, whether you'll use it again tomorrow or not until next year's annual event.

MAKE IT LAST

DON'T FEED THE SQUIRRELS. Of course the cooking surface on your grill will last longer if you wash it regularly, but did you know the all-important gas supply hose will thrive with a bit of the same treatment? Cats and dogs, squirrels, and other rodents are all drawn to the scent and flavor of grease, and if it spatters on the supply line, critters may not differentiate between gnawing on the oil and chewing up the hose. Next time you have the ammonia window cleanser out, wipe any stray grease from the gas supply hose using the cleanser and a paper towel or soft cloth, and that hose will live a long life.

DRESS THE GRILL WITH OIL. Sometimes it's what's on the outside that counts, like those little white spots, oxidation, and anything else the rain and wind feel like spattering to age a grill's exterior. Protect your grill from the elements by waiting until it cools, closing the lid, and then applying a light layer of vegetable oil with a paper towel to the body, paying particular attention to the top. Repeat the process every few weeks during the grilling season and again before you put the grill away for the winter.

FIX IT FAST

REPAINT WITHOUT PANTING. No matter how good the condition of its working parts, you won't really be happy with your barbecue or grill if it's dull and faded. Rejuvenate it, and maybe add a new color that complements your outdoor kitchen decor at the same time with a minimum of effort. First, clean off the dirt and oil. Then lightly abrade the entire exterior of the body with fine steel wool, wiping off any residue with a solution of half water and half vinegar and a soft, clean towel. Rinse the whole body with water, let it dry, and paint the prepared surface with high-temperature paint, which you should be able to find at any hardware or home improvement store.

PASS IT ALONG

GIVE THE GRILL ANOTHER LIFE. A gas grill is a complicated contraption, but simple charcoal grills with lids can lead a second life as patio planters after they're too worn to cook with anymore. Another neat advantage: If the grill has wheels, you can roll it around easily on a deck or patio to fulfill your plants' needs for sun or shade as the seasons change or the day wears on. Here's how to prepare the grill for its new role as the centerpiece of your backyard life.

1. Remove the hood and motor, if it has them.
2. Drill drainage holes in the bottom of the fire bowl and then remove rust or paint flakes with a wire brush.
3. To retard the formation of rust, consider painting both the inside and outside of the bowl before filling it with gravel (for drainage), potting soil, and then seeds or plants.

POTS AND PLANTERS

Simple plans help pots last many seasons in the sun, and then you can salvage worn ones with quick fixes. Or, give 'em a new job. Toad house, anyone?

THIS PLANTER WON'T CONK OUT. If you're a fan of container gardening but don't relish having to replace the containers every other year or so, consider a concrete alternative—it's virtually inde-structible, and ideal for anyone who doesn't need to move potted trees and plants or site them on a balcony or rooftop. Concrete planters are also the best choice for large plants or trees that need extra stability to support a large root system, and concrete has superior insulating properties to buffer plants and soil from temperature fluctuations. When your local garden center doesn't offer the tub or box you need or the price just isn't right, consider making your own durable con-crete box using ordinary cardboard boxes as the "mold." It makes a fun weekend project.

MAKE IT LAST

What you'll need:
- utility knife
- 2 cardboard boxes—1 should be the size you want the finished planter to be and the other should fit inside the first with about 2 inches of space all around
- about $1/3$ of a 60-pound bag of quick-setting concrete
- a piece of 2-inch mesh chicken wire the same dimensions as the larger box
- 3$3/4$-inch-diameter wooden dowels
- wheelbarrow or bucket in which to mix the concrete
- flat, stable surface to work on

To make the planter, follow these steps.

1. Use the utility knife to cut three 3/4-inch holes in the bottom of the smaller box, centering them along the width and in thirds along the length.

2. Following the package directions, whip up a batch of the concrete. Add water and then mix until it is about the consistency of peanut butter. The surface should be smooth and a groove cut into the concrete should hold its shape.

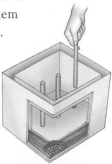

Step 5: Poke the dowels through the holes

3. Place the larger box on a flat dry surface. Spread a 1-inch layer of concrete onto the bottom of the box, smoothing it well with a trowel.

4. Cut a piece of chicken wire to cover the layer of concrete. Place it on top of the concrete, and then cover with another inch of concrete.

5. Center the smaller box inside the larger box on top of the concrete layer. To make drainage holes, poke the dowels through the holes and all the way to the bottom of the larger box, leaving them in place for the time being.

6. Cut the remaining wire mesh in pieces that will fit between the sides of the two boxes, minus an extra inch across the top. Stand the pieces on edge in the wet concrete on the bottom of the big box.

Step 7: Smooth the concrete to the height of the boxes.

7. Fill the spaces between the sides of the boxes with more concrete, completely covering the chicken wire and smoothing the concrete to the height of the boxes.

8. Let the cement rest for 1 hour, and then slip out the dowels. The concrete should hold its shape, forming drainage holes.

9. Allow the concrete to dry for 48 hours, and then remove the boxes to reveal the planter. If needed, use a drill with a masonry bit to ream out the drainage holes.

When you're finished, you'll have a durable, custom-made planter.

10. Let the planter cure in the shade for 3 weeks before planting.

Quick Fix for a Cracked Pot

If you've splurged on one of those fantastic, double-fired terra-cotta pots that's supposed to be impervious to freezing weather, it's frustrating to find a crack. Fortunately, you can fix the cracked pot quickly and easily, using nothing more than a drill that has a masonry bit and some copper wire. And do it soon, before that little fault line gets so wide you have to get rid of the pot. Here are the step-by-step instructions.

1. Use a small masonry bit to drill two ⅛-inch diameter holes about 2 inches apart on either side of the crack and 3 inches down from the rim. Drill more holes if the crack is long.

2. Cut a piece of .05-inch copper wire, available at craft and hardware stores, about four times the length of the diameter of the pot.

3. Poke the wire into one of the holes and then wrap the piece all the way around the pot until you reach the second hole.

4. Poke the other end of the wire through the second hole and then reach inside to join the two ends, winding them tightly together with pliers so they're supporting the cracked piece from inside the pot.

5. If the crack runs most of the height of the pot, drill and wire a second reinforcement an inch from the bottom of the pot.

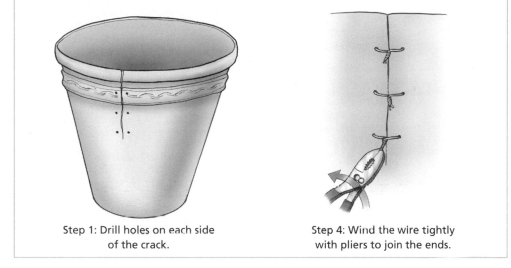

Step 1: Drill holes on each side of the crack.

Step 4: Wind the wire tightly with pliers to join the ends.

BABY, IT'S COLD OUTSIDE. Terra-cotta pots are very popular, and rightly so. They're beautiful and can work with almost any décor, indoors or out. But they're not indestructible. If you've decorated your deck or backyard with plants in terra-cotta pots, bring them indoors during the winter. The freezing temps can cause those pots to crack.

HANG IT UP. Hanging planters are great for getting your gorgeous greens off the ground and up to eye-level. But plants in these containers require different care than traditional planters to keep them happy and long lasting.

- **Choose birds of a feather.** If you plant more than one kind of plant in a hanging basket, make sure they all require the same growing conditions—all shade lovers or all plants that thrive in full sun.
- **Stagger bloom times.** If possible, try to choose plants that bloom at different times during the season or year so that the planter is always packed and flourishing.
- **Water early and often.** Hanging planters usually require more frequent watering to last longer. Make sure to check the soil often, especially during hot times.

FIX IT FAST

REEL IN BROKEN HANGERS.

If you accidentally break one or more of the sides (or the place where it clamps to the container) of a plastic hanger on a hanging basket, fear not: all is not lost. Here's how to fix it.

1. Cut off the broken plastic side support up to the top hook, using a utility knife or pruning scissors.
2. Heat a 12-penny nail in a 400°F oven for 10 minutes. Wearing oven mitts, carefully remove it.
3. Use the nail to poke a hole directly below the plastic lip of the pot on the broken side.

Step 1: Cut off the side support.

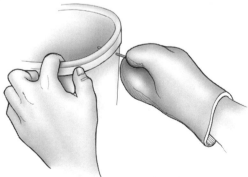

Step 3: Poke a hole in the pot with the blazing hot nail.

4. Thread the hole with invisible nylon fishing line, twice as long as the missing plastic support plus a couple of inches. Bring the two ends together and tie them in a double knot.

5. Slip the loop you've made over the plastic hook at the top and you're back in business. If the pots are supporting heavy plants, like full-grown ferns, double or even triple the number of fishing line loops per hole.

6. If you're interested in aesthetics as well as a quick fix, repeat this technique to replace the remaining two supports.

Once you're finished, the planter will be as good as new.

SHELVE UNUSABLE TERRA-COTTA POTS. A clay pot that's no longer watertight isn't a total wash. Consider turning it and a comparably sized pot into instant décor or storage. Wash and dry them, paint them with latex in the color of your choice, and use them to prop up a rectangular tempered piece of glass. *Voilà!* You have an instant shelf for paperbacks, collectibles, or, appropriately, small houseplants.

PASS IT ALONG

INSTALL A TOADY INSECT REPELLENT. That cracked terra-cotta pot could make a toad a fine home. Although it may seem silly to try to attract toads to your yard or garden, especially if you're squeamish, keep in mind that each one can consume an estimated 110 beetles, slugs, moths, sow bugs, armyworms, and other bugs every day. A remodeled clay pot offers the dark, cool housing they need to escape

4 Ways to Make a Window Box Work Longer

Whether you are purchasing or building a window box, you won't have to repair or replace it nearly as often if you follow these four guidelines.

1. **Keep out rust.** Use rust-proof brass screws, not nails in the construction.

2. **Paint lightly.** If you're painting wood, or purchasing painted wood, remember to choose light colors, which won't absorb heat. That's not only better for the plants,

but it also decreases the odds that the paint will blister or peel.

3. **Limit length.** Longer is not stronger. Make or choose a box in a length that's 36 inches or shorter—any longer and the sides will tend to bulge.

4. **Avoid costly collapses.** Make sure the window box brackets are anchored solidly to a structural part of the house, like a stud or the apron under the windowsill.

5 Ways to Help Planters and Plants Prosper

Increase the odds of healthy plants and long-lasting planters by following these five container gardening strategies.

1. **Give 'em shelter.** Just like any other garden plant, those in pots and planters need protection from the extreme sun and wind—and so do the containers. Make it a point to place them in spots where they will be sheltered by a building, fence, tree or bush, or plant shade. You can also create a windbreak nearby with an awning, arbor, or trellis.

2. **Be shy about commitment.** Play the waiting game to see how a few plants and different types of containers do on your patio, deck, or balcony before committing to others. Doing this will help you avoid making the same kinds of mistakes over and over again. Because some containers wick water away from the soil faster than other containers, you'll want to make sure your selections don't leave your plants high and dry after just a few hours and dictate that you have to water container plants twice a day. In addition, you'll also be much more likely to maintain containers when you have just a few at first. As you get a feel for the art of container gardening, gradually add new plants to your family.

3. **Don't pack 'em in.** Crowded plants, even plants in crowded containers, must compete with each other for sun and nutrients in the soil. In addition, when several containers are crowded together, it's hard to care for them all and keep the pots from drying out. Plus, crowded plants are more susceptible to insect attack and disease, and in shady, moist spots, the pots are more likely to mildew.

4. **Pamper plant roots.** If you're planting trees, shrubs, or perennials that will spend the winter outdoors and you live in a cold climate, choose containers that hold enough soil to keep plant roots from freezing. Mimic the same protection they'd get when planted in the earth by allowing at least 14 inches of soil below and beside the plant, and the plant should be able to ride out subzero temperatures.

5. **Groundwater lovers.** Hanging baskets are hard to get to for watering, and since heat rises, they're also the most likely to dry out first. Take it easy on yourself, and save wear and tear on the planters from all those watering sessions, by planting trailing succulents, like an Easter cactus (*Hatiora gaertneri*) or a burro's tail (*Sedum morganianum*), instead of water-loving annuals like impatiens.

the sun and their enemies while they're not acting as live insecticide. Here's how to enact the transformation (and don't forget to invite a young friend to enjoy the project with you).

1. Scout a sheltered spot in the vegetable or rose garden among the plants, where the pot will stay cool in the midday sun.

2. Wash the pot with mild dishwashing liquid, rinse thoroughly, and let it dry in the sun.

3. Draw a line on the pot that divides it into two sides (right and left). Paint the outside and bottom of one side with acrylic paints in earthy tones. If you feel especially creative, experiment with images of leaves, grasses, fossils, and bugs.

They Won't Fly But You Can Recycle Potted Plant Saucers

If the pot's long gone but the saucer still lives on, consider giving it a new life in the kitchen, home office, or out on the patio.

- **Set and spin.** If the saucer's diameter is more than 12 inches, wash it and use it to corral cans of food on a lazy Susan in the cupboard—the rim will prevent items from falling off when you revolve the base. Or corral small paint cans on the recycled lazy Susan in your workshop.
- **Spill-proof Spot's bowl.** If you've got a saucer that's still watertight, place it under the dog or cat's water bowl to catch overflow. Place another saucer under the dry food bowl to contain food that's been kicked up and out of the dish—presto, no more stepping on kitty's dry food pellets first thing in the morning.
- **Add a platform.** Use smaller saucers as trophy stands: Sand each saucer lightly if it's plastic, and paint it black or silver.
- **Light up the night.** Use small saucers to hold votive candles and larger saucers for bigger candles on a patio table.
- **Sort supplies.** Paint smaller saucers and use them to organize office supplies: paper clips, pushpins, erasers, loose change, and small Post-it pads.
- **Offer appetizers.** Serve chips in larger saucers for a festive and rustic décor. You may want to line the saucer with a fabric or paper napkin if it's been used before.

4. Dig a hole in the garden spot that's large enough to fit the pot laid on its side and deep enough to bury it halfway. Lay the pot horizontally and plant the unpainted half in the ground.
5. Place a few moist, dead leaves in the bottom of the house.
6. Check to see whether the debris has moved every couple days—that's a sure sign you have a toad tenant. If there's no action after a few weeks, try a new location.
7. When you can see that a toad has moved in, place a shallow saucer of water near the house—make sure to put it under some leaves or a bush for protection—so the toad can sit in the dish and absorb water through its skin.

PICK UP THE PIECES. Just because that terra-cotta pot is broken into bits doesn't mean it's time to take it to the trash. Here are three ways to recycle the shards.

- **Recycle it.** Place a shard over the drainage hole at the bottom of another pot. This will prevent soil from spilling out, while still allowing water to drain.
- **Make art.** Pass on the shards to a crafty friend (or use them yourself) for a mosaic project.
- **Try this sharp idea.** Use a large shard (or a whole pot) as a whetstone for your pruning knife or garden shears.

BIRDBATHS AND FOUNTAINS

Trickling water and a clean drink draw songbirds like nothing else and with these neat tricks your fountains and birdbaths will serve flocks of bathers for years.

MAKE IT LAST

SO DEPOSITS WON'T RETURN. Lime and mineral buildup can bring your flowing fountain to a permanent halt, but not if you practice a little preventive maintenance. Depending on how much debris falls into your fountain and how hard the water is in your area, clean your fountain pump from twice a week to once a month, any time you can see a bit of buildup. It doesn't require much muscle: Just mix 2 cups of white vinegar in 1 gallon of water and soak the fountain pump in the solution for 10 minutes. Then, while it's still submerged, rev up the fountain and let it pump the vinegar and water mixture for 30 minutes before replacing it in the birdbath. While the fountain's out, take the opportunity to scoop any twigs and leaves from the bowl, or clean algae from the sides if it's time.

PASS IT ALONG

GIVE IT A LOW-LEVEL JOB. A birdbath basin doesn't necessarily need its pedestal to function. Break (or unscrew) the bottom part, prop the top on a stump, the ground, or a couple of bricks for a low-down birdbath—just make sure there's nowhere nearby for a cat to hide— and count on other customers such as toads, raccoons, and neighborhood dogs.

BUTTERFLIES? THEIR NAME IS MUD. The birdbath may have outlived its usefulness, but you can still put the basin to work attracting butterflies to your garden. Males in particular like to hang out around mud puddles, where they ingest nutritious minerals and salt. To make your own permanent mud puddle, first choose

SIMPLE SOLUTIONS

A Birdbath Surface with Traction

It's hard to fix a birdbath that doesn't seem broken, but if it's too deep, steep, or slippery, birds aren't going to use it. Fortunately, there are easy ways to remedy the situation, whether you already own it or are in love with the look of an unsuitable model.

- **Add a platform.** For the birdbath that's so deep it retains more than 1 to 3 inches of water when it rains, add some flat rocks at the bottom for the birds to stand on.
- **Line it.** To alter the slippery surfaces that cause birds to dodge a birdbath, attach ordinary adhesive bathtub stickers to the bottom of the birdbath while it's still dry and clean, or try a couple lines of caulk sprinkled with sand.

a sunny spot in your yard or garden area, and place the birdbath basin in the ground so that it's flush with the ground around it. Fill it with sand or gravel and then water, and wait for the butterflies!

GARDEN HOSES

With these tips and minor mends, no more hose woes! And if the advice comes too late, use the useless hose to pad ice skates, tree trunks; heck, the list goes on and on!

STOW IT IN THE SHADE. Heat from the sun will make water inside the hose expand to stretch the fabric out of shape and encourage leaks and kinks. Store your hose in the shade if you can. Always release the pressure in a pressure nozzle when you're done for the day, so the hose won't contain as many droplets to expand if it does get overheated.

MAKE IT LAST

SHUT THAT SPUTTERING SPIGOT. When the connection between an outdoor spigot and a hose is always spraying or dripping, first try popping in a new washer—they tend to dry or deteriorate with time, and a replacement may be just the inexpensive fix that allows the hose to operate happily for a couple more seasons.

FIX IT FAST

If the washer doesn't work, you're still looking at only a few minutes' work to replace the coupling using a threaded brass repair coupler, sold to fit the male, female, or midpoint fitting. Cut out the offending hose section with a utility knife, slide the coupler over the cut end of the hose and down a few inches, and attach the rubber fitting to the outside of the cut end. Then slide the coupling back up the hose, so you can thread it onto the rubber fitting.

> ## FIX IT OR FORGET IT?
> ### IF IT'S NOT AT LEAST 4 PLY, LET IT GO BY
>
> Hoses are manufactured in layers, called plies, and the more plies a hose has, the stronger it is. You can buy a single-ply hose, or one with 6 layers, but unless your hose is at least 4-ply with brass end-fittings, don't fool with time-consuming repairs, because it's bound to develop new leaks and kinks after just a few more uses. Next time, consider investing in a more durable model, and also look for a protective sleeve at the female end to prevent kinks at the faucet.

LET LEAKS WATER LEEKS. When your garden hose keeps springing leaks, go with the flow—and let it leak water under the garden soil as a soaker hose. Use a craft or utility knife to cut half-inch slits every 3 inches along the length of the hose, leaving 3 or 4 feet uncut at the

PASS IT ALONG

12 Ways to Reuse an
Old Garden Hose

With this many ingenious ways to reuse pieces of a defunct garden hose, you may wish you had more of them! Use a razor blade, craft knife, or sharp hedge clippers to cut what you need, and electrical or duct tape to connect the ends, if necessary.

1. **Pot trivet.** Tape the ends of a piece of hose together to form a circle 8-inches in diameter. Place it beneath the saucer of a large houseplant to keep rings from forming or the floor getting scraped.

2. **Squeegee.** Cut a piece of garden hose long enough to cover the end of a leaf rake, slit it lengthwise, and slip it over the ends of the tines to make a large squeegee for big window-washing jobs.

3. **Padded hanger.** Slit two pieces of clean, dry garden hose lengthwise to slip over the diagonal pieces of a wire clothes hanger, and use it in place of a padded hanger to pamper delicate clothing. Or, slip a piece across the bottom rung of the wire hanger to hang dress pants without creasing. First, make sure the hose is scrupulously clean.

4. **Blade protector.** Protect ice skates with pieces of garden hose slit length-wise and slipped over the blades.

5. **Handle helper.** Cushion your hard-working hands using a piece of garden hose slipped over the cord or plastic handles of a heavy tote bag or a loaded ice chest—the handles won't cut into or chafe your skin no matter how long you're toting that heavy stuff around.

6. **Garden guides.** Instead of driving a nail or hook into a tree, attach bird houses and feeders by hanging them from a bough or tying them to the trunk with wire threaded through pieces of garden hose. The hose will keep the wire from scarring or accidentally girdling the tree. Don't forget to remove the whole contraption during the off-season and adjust the size for the next year.

7. **Family game.** A length of old garden hose makes a sturdy tug-of-war rope at a family picnic or a child's birthday party.

8. **Sanding helper.** To sand the rounded surfaces on a piece of furniture, cut a slit down the length of a 6-inch section of garden hose. Wrap a sheet of sandpaper around the hose and insert the ends into the slit. Secure the sandpaper with a narrow strip of duct tape, and sand away.

9. **Tree protector.** Use a piece of garden hose to tie a young tree to its stake. Thread wire or twine through the hose, wrap the hose around the tree, and then tie the wire or twine to the stake. The hose is strong, but won't damage the bark.

10. **Sheath.** To protect your fishing and camping knives, cut hose pieces as long as each knife blade. Slit each piece and slip it onto the blade.

11. **Pest repellent.** European earwigs feed at night on tender plants; to deter them, place sections of old garden hose on the ground near affected or vulnerable plants. Earwigs will collect in the hose. When morning comes, rinse the hose in a sink and wash the earwigs away.

12. **Garden guides, part II.** If you're planning a new planting bed, use an old hose to plan the space before you start digging, especially if you want a curved edge. Just lay the hose out in different shapes until you find the one you like best.

end where you'll attach it to the outdoor faucet. If you have one, attach the end cap so the water will spurt from the slits, not the other end of the hose. If not, plug the end under the soil with a cork or a piece of wooden dowel before burying the soaker hose in the garden.

LAWN MOWERS

Careful purchases and just a little pampering will keep your mower moving, and so will a measuring tape, flexible schedule, and an ability to watch grass grow. Honest!

RUN A CLEAN MACHINE. Your gas lawn mower will live a longer and more productive life if you take just one simple step: After each use, and after allowing the motor to completely cool, clean the underside with the hose and a strong stream of water. Built-up grass under the mower traps grass and grease residue and moisture; the former creates a dangerous fire hazard and the latter will eventually cause rust, if left unattended. And either of those two can send your mower to the dump a lot sooner than necessary. A quick hose-down is all you need to keep your mower mowing for a good long time.

MAKE IT LAST

SIMPLE SOLUTIONS

An Easy Way to Keep an Electric Mower Clean

For obvious reasons, you can't spray water on the underside of an electric mower to wash the grass off. For reasons just as evident, you can't leave the grass to mount up and eventually render the mower powerless. Hand brushing is tedious, though, so try this the next time the shroud is completely clean: Coat it with spray vegetable cooking oil and the grass will slide off without any effort from you. Repeat every other mowing or when necessary, depending on how much grass you cut each time.

KEEP THAT MOWER ROLLIN'. If you can't push the lawn mower around the yard easily, the sharp blades and tuned-up motor don't really matter. Here's a quick way to get those wheels rolling smoothly. Remove them with a ratchet and socket, smear automotive grease on the axle, and then replace them for another month or so of easy motion.

LAWN AND GRASS

Of course you take pride in your lawn—you put a lot of work into it. If you find that the grass in your yard isn't as green and healthy as you'd like it to be, just read on for tips that will make your lawn the envy of the neighborhood.

KNOW WHEN TO MOW. Doesn't it just figure that the way to have a long-lasting, lush lawn is to mow it more frequently? There's sound reasoning behind the advice, though: Cutting off too much height all

MAKE IT LAST

at once exposes the grass's tender lower stems to sunburn and takes off the green parts of the blade, which are the most productive parts of the stem. As a rule of thumb, cut the grass each time it adds another third to its height.

Following are some variety-specific recommendations for mowing. One note: Raise these height estimates by a half-inch when the weather is scorching hot.

GRASS VARIETY	MOW WHEN IT REACHES
Centipede and carpet grass	1 1/2 to 2 inches
Bermuda	1 to 1 1/2 inches
Kentucky bluegrass	At least 2 inches
Zoysia	3/4 to 1 1/2 inches
Tall fescue	3 inches

THE FINE PRINT

Great for the Environment, But Is It Good for You?

There's no doubt you should consider an electric mower if you're in the market for a new one that lasts a long time. Except for a battery replacement once every 5 to 7 years, these mowers require almost no maintenance. They don't even need oil changes, spark plugs, air filters, or tune-ups like gas mowers do, and electric mowers make the earth's energy last longer, too, using just a smidgen of electricity each year. The up-front costs are substantial, but tend to balance out over time with money saved on fuel and maintenance.

Still, savvy marketers might not make it clear that an electric mower will not be the best option for every homeowner. You have to decide whether these drawbacks offset the appeal of a low-maintenance mower with the potential to last indefinitely.

- **Not for the back 40.** Electric mowers with cords cost less, but you have to drag the cord around the yard—impossible unless you have a lawn that's smaller than a quarter of an acre—and still difficult if you must mow around lots of trees or shrubs.
- **Smaller is better.** Even a cordless electric mower's at a disadvantage on larger lawns—they're not self-propelled and are not designed for heavy or wet grass. A small person may not be able to handle the extra weight of the battery or the extra pushing.
- **Beware battery drain.** Depending on how powerful the mower's battery is or isn't, it may not last long enough to cut a larger lawn in one session.
- **Do you have the time?** Cordless mowers have batteries that may take 16 to 20 hours to fully recharge, with more powerful mowers' batteries taking the longest.
- **Keep it short.** If you want to cut easily with an electric mower, you'll need to cut when the grass is no more than an inch longer than you want it. If it gets longer than that, you're in for a lot of heavy pushing and the reel mower blades will tend to bind up.

Better Blades for Your Yard

Your yard isn't the perfect habitat for grass. It's dry, or shady, or you just don't have time to cut it frequently. The solution? There *is* a grass that will grow on your property—you just need to know which one to choose.

REQUIREMENT	CHOOSE THIS	NOT THIS
Shade-tolerant grass	Fescue	Kentucky bluegrass Ryegrass
Grass that will grow in dry conditions	Fescue	Kentucky bluegrass Ryegrass
Grass that will grow in high-traffic areas	Bluegrass Ryegrass	Fescue
Easy-to-establish grass	Perennial ryegrass	Kentucky bluegrass
Self-repairing grass	Kentucky bluegrass	Bunch grass
Fine-leaf texture grass	Fine fescue	Tall fescue
Grass that is tolerant to infrequent fertilizing	Fescues Carpet Centipede	Kentucky bluegrass Zoysia
Grass that is tolerant to less-frequent cutting	St. Augustine Tall fescue Kentucky bluegrass	Bermuda Zoysia

SERVE LONG DRINKS OF WATER. To help make grass roots grow deeper and the plants live longer, you need to water your lawn infrequently but deeply. Giving the lawn an inch of water once a week in sunny spots (and a little less in shadier areas) during dry spells should do the trick. Why should you avoid frequent light watering? Because roots go where the water is. And when you dampen just the surface of the soil, the blades can't take in the water and nutrients needed for growth and tenacity.

BANISH BARE SPOTS. Grass in winter is particularly vulnerable to heavy foot traffic, and the damage will keep it from popping back up and spreading come springtime. You can eliminate this problem by building a boardwalk. Set plywood or planks over 2-by-4 crosspieces in high foot traffic areas. After a couple of weeks, reposition the structure so the crosspieces won't damage the grass, either.

FIX IT FAST

One Man's Trash
Long Live the Lawn Rangers

It doesn't matter if the blades are too dull to cut grass or the motor sputters. As long as your push mower's wheels still work and you're within traveling distance of Arcola in Douglas County, Illinois, the weekend after Labor Day, you're welcome to drill with the Lawn Rangers. This self-described "precision lawn mower drill team" has performed annually since 1980 along the streets in the Arcola Broom Corn Festival Parade, marching in formation with brooms and lawn mowers while wearing cowboy hats.

As of the 2000 census, the city had a total population of 2,652, and a prominent community of Old Order Amish live in the countryside near Arcola. The parade honors Arcola's history as a center of broomcorn production in the late 19th century. The Lawn Rangers who participate hail from several states, but they all push mowers. Humor columnist Dave Barry marched with the Lawn Rangers in 1995; they also have an international following, with one Ranger from England and an associate chapter in Belgium.

FIX IT FAST

FIX THOSE BARE SPOTS. No need to reseed the whole lot just because one spot on the lawn has fallen victim to a bug or has been worn bare. Fix it quickly, first pulling out the dead grass, and then scraping the soil with a garden claw to loosen it. If you're growing a spreading variety of grass, such as Bermuda, zoysia, or buffalo grass, you can stop right there—it will fill in the spot itself in a week or so. But if you favor "clumping" grass, like fescue or rye, scatter a handful of its seeds on the spot, press them firmly into the soil, and keep the soil moist until they germinate, giving them 6 to 9 days to do so.

HAND TOOLS

You don't have to have a huge workshop to have lots of hand tools. Here are our expert ways to make yours last longer, how to make a quick repair, and how to make use of the ones that no longer work.

MAKE IT LAST

MATCH MAINTENANCE TO MATERIALS. Regular maintenance isn't particularly glamorous, but spend a few minutes doing it at the end of the season anyway if you want long service from rakes, hoes, shovels, and small hand tools. Thing is, you'll need two different—but simple—approaches for the wood and metal parts of each tool. To keep wood handles from deteriorating and also to make them smooth to the hand, rinse or brush the dirt from them, remove any splinters with fine sandpaper, and then wipe the handle with a heavy coat of

7 Savvy Moves
for Tool Shoppers

Ironic as it may seem, a lot of garden tools will last longer if you buy them used. Older shovels and hoes, for example, tend to be forged from a single piece of solid metal, which makes them stronger and the handle less likely to separate from the business end. Knowing the reputation of older tools, though, some unknowledgeable (or unscrupulous) people try to pawn off cheap, modern stuff in place of the older tools. Even if you know that a tool is more modern, like a weed whacker, it pays to keep your eyes open. Use these tactics when shopping flea markets or garage sales.

1. **ID the owner.** Ask who owned any hand tools previously. If a quick answer isn't forthcoming, walk away.

2. **Check the welds.** On tools like grass rakes and hoes, which have to withstand a lot of pressure, examine welded points and the spot where the metal attaches to the handle, looking for evidence of solid construction and aged, not new, metal.

3. **Rap and tap it.** Check out wood parts, looking for cracks, splintering, rotting, and loose connections to metal parts. Ask whether the salesperson minds if you rap the handle sharply on a table or chair—his or her answer may tell you whether it's poorly made or has dry rot.

4. **Skip the paint.** Be wary of painted handles—the color may be covering cheap or rotting wood.

5. **File it.** Test your metal when shopping for heavy-duty edge tools like spades. Bring a file and run it along the steel. If the file marks the metal without you exerting much pressure, it's probably too soft to give you long years of service, particularly if your soil is dense.

6. **Move it around.** If the tool has any mechanical parts, like an edger or long-handled bulb planter, make sure they move the way they're supposed to. Don't take anyone's word that all it needs is a bit of WD-40, unless they have some on hand and can demonstrate.

7. **Plug it in.** If you're shopping around for electric tools, bring an extension cord with you so you can test them on the spot.

boiled linseed oil. Use a wire whisk to remove the dirt from the metal portion of tools, sand with fine steel wool, give them a light coat of WD-40, and then poke them, metal-end down, into a bucket of dry sand to prevent rust between now and the spring thaw.

DIP YOUR TOOLS. Are you constantly leaving your hand tools in a forgotten patch to rust? If the top foe to your gardening tools' long lives is forgetfulness, fix the problem with a splash of color—and weatherproof your tool handles and improve their grips at the same time.

FIX IT FAST

Plasti Dip, a liquid synthetic rubber coating that dries solid, is the solution to the problem. You apply it by dipping a tool handle in and out of the mixture, and then letting it dry. Ever after, the tool will be easy to spot in the garden or lawn, which means you'll be less likely to forget it there. Not only that, but the tool will also have a more comfortable grip and resist water and frost damage.

MAKE A TEPEE FOR VINES. You can extend your garden space by growing veggie or flowering vines up poles. If you lean several poles together and tie the tops into a "tepee" for the vines to scale, you can also extend the season for cool weather crops like lettuce and cabbage by growing them below. A discarded rake is ideal for at least one of the tepee poles—it's about the right height and the tines provide a good starting place for young vines to twine. Here's how to assemble a multipole vine tepee.

1. Assemble five or six poles that are about 1 inch thick and about the same height of the discarded rake.

2. Use wire cutters or a utility knife to remove a few interior rake tines so that there's about a half-inch of space. Doing this will make room for the vines to scale.

3. Tie or wire the rake, tine-side down, and two of the poles together about 6 inches from the tops. Spread them out to form a cone shape, with each poles about 3 feet apart and resting on the soil.

4. Tie the end of a ball of twine to the rake handle where it joins with the tine section (around 20 inches up from the base). Then weave the twine around the other two poles at about the same height two or three times before cutting the end and tying it to the rake handle.

5. Prop the other poles in the spaces between the base poles, leaving one segment open if you plan to garden (or let kids play) inside the tepee. Tie or wire the ends of the secondary poles to the tops of the base poles.

6. To give the vines a place to climb between poles (and so they'll cover the sides completely), tie the end of the ball of twine to one of the outside poles about 12 inches from the top. Weave the twine under and over all the poles in a wide spiral to about 1 foot from the ground, leaving about 18 inches of

The finished tepee provides extra space in your garden for crops such as peas.

empty space between rows of twine. Cut and tie off the twine on one of the base poles.

7. To give vines that aren't growing near the rake tines a good place to start climbing, tie a piece of twine to a 3-inch stake and tap the stake into the ground near a pole. Run the twine diagonally to the pole, about 8 inches above the ground. Repeat for the other poles.

PONDS

Having a pond on your landscape can be a pricey proposition—here's how to make sure you get the very most for your money.

MAKE SURE THE WATER'S RIGHT. Ponds are lovely as both a landscape element and a songbird attraction, but don't expect one to last long in your yard unless you test the depth of the water table on your prospective site first. It's not that involved, but the information you'll glean is invaluable, because a high water table might bubble up and pop a synthetic liner right out of the ground. Dig a test hole as deep as you'd like the pond and keep an eye on it for a full 24 hours. Should the hole fill up with water when you haven't had rain during the test period, you can safely say the water table's high in that spot—and look elsewhere before creating any pond you plan to line with synthetic material.

MAKE IT LAST

Still Working After All These Years
POOLING POND LINER RESOURCE

The layer under a pond liner is all that keeps it from being punctured by rocks and roots, but digital designer Steven Lareau of Clinton, Tennessee, sees no reason to go to a lot of expense to add extra protection. Instead, he recommends staying in touch with your local pool supply house. "When I was putting in a pond on my new property, someone had mentioned using old carpet as the under layer for the liner, but I knew that would eventually deteriorate," he says. "Then I discovered the solar cover on the pool out back, all beat and dry-rotted. It's made of heavy-duty plastic and already has air bubbles to really cushion the liner. I jumped around on it barefoot and it held up, so I installed it bubble-side up, and so far, so good—I haven't had a bit of trouble with pond punctures for 6 or 7 years now."

You can still proceed even if you don't own a dilapidated pool cover. "Call your local pool supply store, and ask if it can have its customers save old covers when they buy a new one," says Lareau.

And he appeals to the same retailers for reusable sand for pond lining. "Your pool supply house is also a great source for old filter sand," says Lareau. Again, ask if customers will save their old sand for you when they buy new sand for their swimming pool filters. "It's kind of grungy, sometimes stinky, and may have a lot of small debris mixed in there, but hey—it's free!"

Mud-lined ponds don't present a problem in a high water table.

WAITING ROOM FOR WEBBED FEET. It's ducky to try to attract waterfowl to your pond, but make sure their sharp feet don't destroy the entire watery operation. Create a shore on the edges of the pond lining so ducks or geese have a launch pad for swimming, but make sure to build it from flat stones that will stay in place and protect the edges of the pond lining from being punctured.

WALKWAYS

Walk this way to read our clever advice about making your walkway last a lot longer. All you need is some sand and the will to weed.

FIX IT FAST

STRENGTHEN SAND FILLERS. In a flagstone or concrete paver walkway, sand provides drainage and helps hold the stepping stones

4 Ways to Protect Pavers

You probably aren't afraid of breaking your mother's back, but little cracks and improper installation can turn your concrete paver or flagstone path from a pretty passage to rubble. Take these precautions so you can walk safely and surely along your paths for a long time.

1. **Wait it out.** When you pour your own pavers from concrete, let them cure for a week after they dry before you move them to their outside spots—and before anyone steps on them!

2. **Add an inch.** Any large, flat piece of shale, sandstone, or granite will make a fine path placed right on sand or soil, but only if it's 1½ to 2 inches thick. Thinner flag-

stones are bound to settle unevenly and crack under pressure, unless they're primarily decorative or secured over a concrete path with mortar.

3. **Keep 'em grounded.** When you place flagstones in a path, never set them more than a half-inch higher than the ground, or someone may put too much weight on one of the edges and get enough leverage to break or crack the stone, especially if it happens all the time.

4. **Heave-ho to heaves.** To keep a flagstone walk from heaving in frost, dig a 2- to 3-inch hole beneath each stone and fill it in with coarse sand before placing the flagstone flush with the ground.

in place. But in some areas of the country, sand filler gets washed out in frequent or heavy rains. If that sounds familiar, give the sand some reinforcement: Mix 1 part Portland cement per 5 parts sand, and pat the mixture firmly between the pavers. Then spritz some water on top with the fine nozzle on the hose or a spray bottle to set the filler hard enough to resist washing away. Don't walk on the path for a day or so while you're waiting for it to set.

TAKE OUT WEEDS WHEN TEA'S ON. When just a few ambitious weeds, grass, and moss are growing out of cracks in your concrete, kill them without chemicals by pouring boiling water over them. Then let the sun finish the job before pulling them out or, in the case of moss, rinsing it off with the hose.

GARDEN GLOVES

Here's a handful of good ways to keep your garden gloves supple and strong, followed by more ideas for reusing worn gloves than you can count on 10 fingers!

LET LEATHER GLOVES GET YOUR GOAT. Any leather garden gloves will cost much more than their cotton, jersey, or rubber counterparts, but they'll also last a lot longer, with proper care. If your top priority with leather is comfort, choose goatskin or buckskin. They'll

MAKE IT LAST

SIMPLE SOLUTIONS

4 Airy Angles on Garden Glove Storage

Any type of garden glove will last longest (and smell and feel better) when you store it clean and dry in a well-ventilated spot or container. All of the following common household items can meet the criteria with a few easy alterations.

1. **Plastic or wicker baskets.** Just make sure to line the latter with something to absorb any dampness, like a section of newspaper covered with a paper towel.

2. **Ketchup anyone?** Slip each glove over one clean and empty slender-necked condi-

ment bottle, like the ones steak sauce or salad dressing come in. Fill the bottles with sand to weight them down and place them on a counter.

3. **It's a shoe-in.** Use wire shoe racks if you have several gardeners in the family—or several pairs of gloves.

4. **Have a six-pack.** Try using a six-pack of empty glass soda bottles, returned to their cardboard holder and weighted with sand or gravel. Leave the gloves on the bottles until the next time you need them.

last as long as the other leathers but they are soft and buttery and will mold themselves to your hands in time.

MAKE IT LAST

DON'T DUNK. Leather gloves stay supple and strong partly because of the oils infused in their surface—oil that comes out if you immerse the gloves in water for cleaning. Instead, use leather cleaner and a damp sponge when you can't get all the dirt off simply by brushing.

BREATHE EASY WITH COTTON GLOVES. Rubber gloves protect hands from most known garden foes—dirt, chemicals, water, and even thorns. But to keep the user comfortable and the gloves from getting sweaty and smelly (and that much closer to the trash heap), choose a pair with a cotton lining to breathe and wick away sweat in warm weather. You can hand wash the cotton-lined rubber gloves, too.

OVERCOAT WITH OVEN MITTS. Cotton or jersey gloves can be comfy for most gardening tasks, they're usually hand- or cold-water washable, and if you find a pair that fits the contours of your hand, you're set . . . until you need to pull up brambles or thorny weeds, or prune roses. No need to puncture your skin or set inexpensive gloves on the road to ruin on those rare occasions, though. Just take a quick kitchen detour to slide on some oven mitts, which will provide the extra padding and wrist cover you need. When you're done with the garden, run the mitts through the wash before using them to handle hot dishes again.

WHIP UP SOME CHICKEN SHOES. You can't use garden gloves any more when they get so many little rips and tears that your hands are no longer protected, so look down for a way to prolong their life . . . on a child's feet! Ten minutes or so is all you need to turn ordinary garden gloves and flips-flops or tennis shoes into poultry feet for a small-fry chicken costume.

PASS IT ALONG

What you'll need:
- discarded jersey, rubber, or cotton garden gloves
- cotton or rags to fill the fingers
- child-sized flip-flops or tennis shoes, depending on the weather
- around 18 inches of half-inch-wide elastic
- sewing machine or fabric glue
- measuring tape

1. Fill just the fingers of the gloves with cotton balls.
2. Place the gloves palm-side down and have the child who will wear the costume don the flip-flops or shoes. Then slip his right shoe into the right glove and left shoe into the left glove.
3. Taking one at a time, pull each glove toward the heel of the shoe until the fingers butt the end of the shoe.
4. With a permanent marker, make a mark on the cuff of one glove where it meets the right side of the child's foot. Make a corresponding mark on the left side. Repeat on the other gloved foot.
5. With a tape measure, measure the distance from the left mark, around the child's heel and back to the mark on the right side of the glove cuff. Cut a piece of elastic that long plus an inch.
6. To form a strap that will slip over the heel to help hold the "chicken foot" glove on the child's shoe (or heel if you're using flip flops), remove the gloves from the model's feet. Use a sewing machine or fabric glue to attach the ends of the elastic to the marks you've made, leaving a half inch at the end, and then tacking it down with thread or fabric glue.
7. Optional: If you can spare the shoes or flip-flops, use fabric glue to permanently attach the palms of the gloves to the bottoms of the

shoes. Complete the outfit with feather boas plus a baseball hat with construction paper beak and eyes attached with fabric glue.

BIRD FEEDERS AND SEED

Try these feeder designs tip, storage advice, and information about easy repairs to make feeders and food last longer and draw more birds. Oh, and mind what you put on the menu, too.

MAKE IT LAST

HOSE DOWN GRIMY FEEDERS. Keeping your bird feeder clean not only keeps the feeder from deteriorating, it protects the seed inside from going bad, and the avian diners from suffering—or even dying—from ingesting fouled bird seed or picking up infections at the feeder. With all these benefits, it's well worth the investment in a scrub brush hose attachment to make short work of washing the feeder. Available at most garden supply and home stores and sold over the Internet, the attachment fits an ordinary garden hose, extends your reach by at least a couple of feet, and spouts water while you scrub off grime and stuck-on seed.

4 Ways to Make Bird Feed Last Longer

Songbirds in the yard offer such pleasure that it's hard to think in terms of the money you must spend to attract them, but you can make your seed and feed last longer. Here's how.

1. **Butter up the grocer.** You can buy out-of-date peanut butter at a fraction of the cost and the birds won't mind at all—just make sure it's not rancid before you share it with your feathered friends. Look for jars with "Best Before" dates that are passed; resist any jars that have an "Expiration" date that has already passed. See whether you can strike a deal with the discount grocer in town to call you before tossing peanut butter, and ask for a deep discount anywhere else you see outdated jars on the shelves.

2. **Squirrel away safflower seed.** Most of the same birds that adore black sunflower seed will also come around for safflower seed, but the squirrels disdain it (in most areas, anyway).

3. **Fence in the fancy stuff.** Enclose a smaller feeder full of expensive sunflower seed inside a wire cage that only allows access to smaller songbirds. That way, larger pest birds won't come gobble up your stock in a matter of hours.

4. **Plan for no leftovers.** If you're constantly scraping out caked or spoiled seed that accumulates in your feeders, try monitoring precisely how much seed the birds consume in a day or so, and then filling up the feeders with just that much seed, particularly in wet weather. As you become more knowledgeable, extend the food to meet 2 or 3 days of feeding needs, but pull back any time you notice the birds are leaving leftovers to gather moisture and go bad.

7 Habits of Highly Effective Bird Feeders

When you want to decorate a patio or deck, you could buy a bird feeder made of flimsy or fragile materials. But to attract songbirds and keep them fed for the long haul, choose (or build) a feeder with these attributes.

1. **Poo poo plywood.** The best feeders are constructed of solid wood, not plywood, with nails and screws holding them together, not staples.

2. **Avoid seed traps.** Avoid dips and angles that will trap seeds or make the feeder hard to clean.

3. **Choose a big-mouth.** Look for a model with an easy-open lid large enough to pour seed without a funnel.

4. **Single-handed operating.** For convenience, you want an opening that can be filled with one hand and held open with the other.

5. **Big is better.** Get a feed that can hold at least a quart of birdseed, unless you plan to use it to hold "supplemental treats," and not the birds' core diet.

6. **Easy to clean.** Shop for a feeder that has smooth or flat sides that can be washed easily. A dirty feeder will actually repel, and not attract, the bird.

7. **Say no to mold.** Drainage in the bottom if it's a tray feeder, made from sturdy wire screen, will prevent mold.

WEED OUT WET SEED. The niger seed so beloved by finches and other tiny songbirds can be a health hazard if it absorbs moisture in the feeder and gets moldy—and it's also a shame to let the seed get wet, since it costs a premium. Borrow a tip from diners in the South to stave off the moisture in a bird-friendly fashion: Mix 1 part uncooked white rice per 4 parts niger thistle before filling the feeder. The rice harmlessly absorbs the moisture, protecting the seed.

MEND IT WITH L-SHAPED HINGES. Even the best-made bird feeder may start pulling apart at the corners over time, usually as the wood gets worn. Instead of tapping in a few more nails, which are likely to work loose, too, reinforce the area with L-shaped metal hinges attached with rust proof screws. They'll offer more reinforcement than screws alone and also have a better chance of staying put, since they attach to a fresh, unworn piece of the feeder.

FIX IT FAST

CUT SOME GLASS, FIX A FEEDER. When a piece of glass breaks in an otherwise sturdy hopper feeder, go to a business that cuts glass to size for a replacement. If the piece you're replacing needs to slide down a channel, make sure you know how thick it needs to be, or take a piece of the broken glass to the cutter for measurement.

Another option is to take the opportunity to make the hopper feeder look snazzier and deter those pesky squirrels, too, by replacing the glass piece with a piece of copper sheet. You can cut it yourself with heavy scissors or wire cutters, but make sure to wear gloves and protective eyewear while you work.

PASS IT ALONG

FEED THE NEEDS OF SHUT-INS WITH USED BIRD FEEDERS. Whether you've fallen out of the habit of feeding birds or have a few feeders that don't strike your fancy any more, think of shut-ins when you're considering passing along bird feeders. Local Veterans Hospital patients or residents of low-income senior citizen housing would surely enjoy a discarded feeder, particularly the kind that attaches right to a window. If you're not familiar with local organizations, ask at the library or check with United Way in your area. Or, check with Meals on Wheels to see whether any of their recipients might be interested, and make it a volunteer activity to fill and maintain the feeders at the home or hospital.

MORE TIPS FOR THE LAWN AND GARDEN

Here's a roundup of the lawn and garden Pass It Along tips you'll find in the other chapters of *Don't Throw It Out!*

CHAPTER	TIP	PAGE
1	Take the Spatula Outside	24
1	Old Utensils, New Uses	24
1	Try These Tray Uses	25
1	Save That Sieve	25
2	Satisfy Social Climbers	61
3	Spring into a Pea Prop	79
3	6 Ways to Draw a New Plan for Drawers	84
3	These Boots Are Made for Planting	93
4	Feather a Nest	112
5	Disks Redux	156
7	Let It Garden in Retirement	211
7	Bowl Them Over	212
7	Show That Basket the Door	212
7	Save the Stick	228
7	One Drip at a Time	229
8	Recycle Old Croquet Gear	245
8	Pad Just About Anything	257
8	Sit on Your Old Skis	266
8	Perform a Tomato Stem Christie	266
8	Walk Old Boots to the Garden	266
11	New Life for an Old Tire	350

DOMESTIC CHALLENGE

Gardeners are ingenious and frugal folks, but there are lots of ways to make things stand the test of time, especially if you have a few insider tips and tricks. For each garden item, try to guess which object or method will keep it in good working order.

Questions

1. For a two-stroke engine lawn mower, reach for this:

   A. Red spray paint
   B. The owner's manual
   C. A funnel
   D. All of the above

2. When you harvested sunflower heads for bird feed, store them in:

   A. Burlap bags and on a stepladder
   B. Discarded dry cleaner bags and the vegetable bin
   C. Copy paper boxes and mesh onion bags
   D. All of the above

3. To keep wood-handled small garden tools in working order, use:

   A. A terry cloth towel
   B. Sandpaper
   C. A discarded mailbox
   D. All of the above

4. Fallen leaves make a rich leaf mold soil amendment, and this handy item can help:

   A. A grass rake
   B. A handheld hole punch
   C. A 12' by 12' plastic tarp
   D. All of the above

5. Which of these will help container plants in container gardens survive a hot summer?

   A. A big pot and a small pot
   B. Heavy feedings once a month
   C. Rich, heavy soil
   D. All of the above

6. If your seedlings are just starting to emerge, use this to keep them safe from wind damage:

A. A 1′ by 8′ board
B. Several empty tuna cans
C. A layer of used newspapers
D. All of the above

7. For better rose blooms, try:

A. Clippers
B. A fixant such as alum powder
C. Cinnamon essential oil
D. All of the above

8. For the healthiest grass lawn in town, reach for:

A. A soaker hose
B. A day-by-day calendar with weekly mowing reminders
C. An easy-to-read ruler
D. All of the above

9. If you have a birdbath heater, you'll need:

A. An outdoor outlet protected by a ground fault circuit interrupter (GFCI)
B. Clean water in the bird bath
C. A model with auto shutoff
D. All of the above

10. To store a garden hose, recycle:

A. An empty Christmas popcorn tin with lid
B. A cut-down plastic garbage can with lid
C. A ping pong paddle and two golf balls
D. All of the above

Answers

1. **B.** The owner's manual will spell out the specific mix of fuel and oil your lightweight engine requires, which is crucial to keeping it running efficiently and prevent rapid deterioration (and smelly fumes!). While red spray paint may cover a few nicks and prevent rust, it really won't extend the life of

(*continues*)

your mower, nor will an easy-pour funnel for gasoline add any mileage to your tank.

2. **A.** Store sunflower heads in burlap bags and hang them from the rafters or the ceiling in the garage, where rodents can't reach them easily. Avoid storing any seed in cardboard or plastic, because moisture can cause mildew.

3. **D.** Use all three! The towel is great for wiping mud and moisture from the tools for rust-free storage, the sandpaper smoothes rough handles before they start splintering, and the mailbox on a post can store tools near your work site so they're free from rain or sunlight.

4. **B.** To keep leaves from blowing off and to form a rich leaf mold with minimum upkeep and water, rake them into heavy duty plastic garbage bags, water them down, tie the bags shut and punch several holes for ventilation. The leaves will stay moist as they break down and, in about four months, you'll have a bagful of rich leaf mold mulch to use as a soil amendment. You may even be able turn the bags inside out to wash and reuse next fall.

5. **A.** Nest a smaller pot inside a larger pot with peat moss in between to keep plant roots cool in hot sunny areas. The smaller pot of soil won't dry out as quickly because the larger pot will absorb most of the sun's heat. (And use a light soil mix in your pots, rather than heavy clay soil from your yard, so the plant can form plenty of feeder roots that will withstand high temps and frequent, light feedings.)

6. **A.** Use sticks or rocks to make a lean-to from the board that will shade seedlings from strong sun and harsh wind until they're a few inches tall.

7. **A.** A rosebush and clippers go hand-in-hand. While alum powder and essential oil are helpful for making rose-petal potpourri, you'll need clippers for the nicest possible blooms. To help a rose bush produce as many blooms as possible within a single season, make sure to clip the faded blossoms before the seed pods form, cutting the stem right above the set of five leaves below the bloom.

8. C. Time to measure! Every time your grass adds a third to its height, get out the mower, rather than mowing on a strict schedule. Keeping the lawn a little longer helps shade the roots and provides more drought protection. Avoid soaker hoses and sprinklers in most cases; they just don't water a large lawn efficiently.

9. D. A combo of all three! The GFCI is a necessity to cut off the flow of electricity to the heater in the event of a short, and an auto shutoff will protect the heater if the birdbath is accidentally knocked over or if the water evaporates. Be sure to provide fresh water as often as possible, too; running the heater in dirty water could ruin the heating element as well.

10. B. From trash to treasure, literally! Store the hose where it won't get run over with the car or lawnmower by coiling it in a plastic garbage can you've cut low enough to hold the coiled hose with a few inches to spare. Cut another hole in the side of the can so you can leave the hose connected to the bib faucet. You may even be able to keep the hose container free from debris by reusing the lid.

10
THE HOME WORKSHOP

The home workshop tends to reflect the various hobbies, projects, and interests of family members: In addition to the usual collection of hand tools and power tools, it might hold cans of paint that represent a history of room renovations, short lengths of dowel rod from a third-grade log cabin diorama, spare links from the chains on the backyard swing set, and so on.

In this chapter you'll find dozens of nifty ways to keep your tools in tip-top shape. We'll explain how buying yourself a new pair of shoes can extend the life of your tools and reveal how a trip to a restaurant may give you clues to an antique tool's provenance.

There's no right or wrong place for a home workshop, and no list of tools that everyone has to have. Your shop simply needs to be in the right spot for you and to contain the tools and materials you need to enjoy your hobbies and complete repair and renovation projects easily and successfully. Use the pages that follow to tweak, tune-up, or even clean out, your home workshop until it's just right for you.

HAND TOOLS

Whether you own an entire set of hand tools or just a screwdriver, wrench, and hammer, you'll find simply ingenious tips for all of them on the next few pages.

MAKE IT LAST

USE THE RIGHT TOOL FOR THE JOB. It might be handy to use your screwdriver as a chisel or a pry bar. But a few sessions of beating on the handle with a hammer will ding it up to the point that it's no longer comfortable to hold in your hand when you want to use it for its intended purpose. And a bent shaft will make it tricky to turn a screw. It's clever to make the most of the tools you own, but it can be destructive and dangerous to put tools to tasks they weren't meant to do.

KEEP A SET OF "UGLY" TOOLS. A set of tools that you don't mind abusing will help save your "good" tools for their intended purposes. Garage sales and flea markets are good places to shop for chisels you can use for pulling nails or screwdrivers that can double as paint stirrers—used tools will probably cost less and be of better quality than a new set of the lowest price tools you can find at a mass merchandiser.

BUY SHOES, PROTECT TOOLS. Simply keeping tools dry goes a long way toward giving them a long useful lifespan. Dampness spells destruction for metal parts, and rust has a way of cropping up on everything from nails and drill bits to carpenter's squares and saw blades.

- **Dry 'em out.** Recycle the small packets of silica gel that come inside shoe boxes, leather goods, electronics cartons, and vitamin bottles. Toss them into your toolbox and into the cases that hold your power tools. The desiccant material (silica) inside will help to absorb moisture before it attacks your tools. Replace packets as you acquire new ones, or "recharge" them once a year by heating them in your oven at 250°F for 30 minutes.
- **Lube 'em.** Lightly spray a rag with a lubricant, such as WD-40, and wipe metal tool parts after each use to clean them and help disperse moisture.
- **Keep 'em off the floor.** Store tools off the floor and away from pipes, plumbing, or other water sources.

STAY SHARP! Keeping your cutting tools sharp extends their useful life in your shop and makes them safer and easier to use when you need them. Dull cutting edges will crush rather than cut, and they're more likely to slip on the surface you're trying to cut. In the home workshop, keeping tools sharp is largely a matter of protecting their cutting surfaces from dings, nicks, and corrosion. Here's how to do that.

- **Use a cover-up.** Cover the cutting edges of hand saw blades to protect the teeth and to protect you from incidental contact with sharp edges. Cut a section of old garden hose to fit the length of your saw blade, slit it lengthwise, and slip it over the teeth. Make sure the hose is completely dry inside. Protect the narrow blade of a hacksaw or coping saw with the slender plastic spine that holds papers in a report cover.
- **Prevent rust.** Wipe saw blades and axe heads with a rag that's lightly spritzed with a lubricant, such as WD-40, to prevent rusting.

WARM UP BEFORE YOU WORK OUT. Cold temperatures can make metal tool parts brittle and prone to breaking. If you need to saw logs or split firewood or kindling outdoors in subfreezing weather, take a little time to warm up your saw blade, axe head, or hatchet before you put it to work. Don't worry—once that blade's in action, it'll stay warm, and so will you!

DON'T TOSS THOSE TOOLS. Most people aren't aware that the tray of a toolbox is the absolute worst place to store chisels and other cutting-edge equipment. Knocking around amid wrenches and screwdrivers can dull and ding sharp surfaces, so they won't be able to do their intended jobs when you need them most. New chisels may come with plastic caps to guard their edges; do your best to retain these for safe storage. Store chisels in a tool roll—a sturdy cloth or leather keeper with multiple pockets you tuck tools into—to keep them sharp, secure, and ready for action. You can shop for tool rolls at stores or Web sites that sell woodworking tools.

Make less elegant but functional chisel keepers out of empty toilet paper tubes by pinching one end closed and sealing it with a double layer of duct tape.

Shop Saftey Extends Your Life

Make sure your shop inventory includes basic equipment and devices to keep you safe while you work.

- **Dust masks and respirators.** Inexpensive paper masks provide protection from sawdust and other particles. When working around oil-based paints, finishes, epoxies, and solvents, use an organic vapor respirator mask approved by the National Institute for Occupational Safety and Health (NIOSH).
- **Safety goggles or glasses.** Find a pair that's comfortable enough that you'll wear them to protect your eyes whenever you're working with tools. Safety glasses should have guards on the sides to block flying particles; goggles offer better protection and may be worn over prescription eyeglasses.
- **Gloves.** Lightweight latex gloves make post-painting cleanup much easier and also protect your hands from harsh cleaning products. Choose heavy-duty butyl rubber for working with solvents, and sturdy canvas or leather gloves when you're handling rough wood or metal.
- **Floor mat.** Most workshop tasks keep you on your feet while you work. Do your feet and your legs and your back a favor and put a sturdy mat on the floor to reduce the pressure on your parts. A shop mat also helps protect dropped objects from breakage and protects you from the bouncing dropped objects might do on a harder surface.
- **Hearing protection.** Use earmuff-style hearing protectors or earplugs whenever you're using noisy power tools.
- **Smoke alarm.** Replace batteries at least once a year; twice a year is better. Let the beginning and end of daylight savings time remind you when it's time for fresh batteries—plan your semiannual battery change and smoke alarm test for the weekend each spring and fall when the time changes. Smoke alarm units wear out, too, and newer models may feature useful advances in technology. The Underwriters Laboratory recommends replacing smoke alarm units every 10 years.
- **Fire extinguisher.** For the same reasons you have a smoke alarm in your shop—flammable liquids, flammable sawdust, flammable wood scraps, oily rags, and other flammables—you should also have a fire extinguisher. Look for an Underwriters Laboratory or UL-approved extinguisher that's rated "ABC," which means it may be used on fires involving combustible materials, flammable liquids, and energized electrical equipment.
- **Carbon monoxide alarm.** If you have a wood- or coal-burning stove in your workshop, a carbon monoxide alarm is also a good idea. Improperly combusted fuels could cause a dangerous situation, and an alarm could save your life.

PICK UP A PRY BAR. Pulling nails with the claw end of your hammer's head can put a lot of twisting stress (torque) on the handle. If your weekend chores include a big renovation or demolition task that is likely to require pulling dozens or even hundreds of nails, save your hammer handle from forces that can crack or break it, and use a metal pry bar instead. A 12-inch pry bar with notched ends, one flat and one curved, makes nail removal quick and easy, and it saves your hammer for what it does best: putting nails in rather than taking them out. You can find pry bars at any well-stocked hardware or home improvement store.

HANDLE WITH CARE. Most tool handles are durable enough to stand up to years of service, provided you're using the tools for their intended purpose. (That is, not using screwdrivers as chisels or driving nails with the hammer's handle rather than its head.) Wooden tool handles need little more than an occasional cleaning with oil soap to give them a long life. Avoid treating them with polishes or finishes that might make them slippery or sticky when you use them.

MAINTAIN YOUR EDGE. A sharp axe is a safe axe: Cutting wood  or splitting kindling with a dull axe or hatchet is a tiring, frustrating, and dangerous process. A dull blade doesn't cut—it crushes. And it makes you tired as you pound away with it, taking more blows to do the job than you would with a sharp blade. Finally, the combination of fatigue and a dull axe puts you in danger of cutting yourself instead of the wood. And a dull axe never seems so sharp as when it meets with your foot or leg.

    If your workshop holds an axe or hatchet, it should also include a file and an axe stone for keeping the blade properly sharpened. Here's how to keep the edge on your axe.

1. Secure the axe in a vise or by pegging the handle against the side of a log with the blade pointing up.
2. Cut a piece of cardboard 3 to 4 inches square, and cut a slit in the center of it. Slide it over your file until it rests just above the handle. This will protect your fingers from the axe blade while you sharpen it.
3. Use the file or the rough side of a sharpening stone to remove visible burrs and nicks from the blade. File from the edge inward, using smooth, vertical, pushing strokes with a slight sideways motion along the blade. Do this on both sides of the blade.

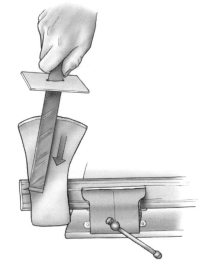

4. Use the smooth side of the sharpening stone in a circular motion to finish sharpening. Many axe stones work best when moistened with water or oil; follow the instructions for the particular stone in your tool kit.

5. Test the edge by dragging a piece of paper over it. A sharp blade will catch and cut the paper. Wipe the sharpened blade with a lightly oiled rag and store it in a sheath.

MAINTAIN YOUR EDGE, PART II. Put an edge on your hatchet before putting it away, and it will always be ready the next time you need it. Sharpening at the end of each job also ensures that the blade is clean, oiled, and dry when you store it, which guards it against the dulling effects of corrosion.

USE THE FORCE. Repairs and projects go much more quickly when the tools you need are close at hand. Outfit your workshop with heavy-duty magnetic strips on the wall next to your workbench or table, and you can count on finding the right tool within easy reach. Magnetic strips—a modern-day equivalent of Peg-Board and hooks—eliminate the problems of hooks that fall out when you take down a tool and peg holes that grow larger with use. The strips typically come in different magnetic strengths. You'll find heavy-duty strips for weighty tools such as hammers and large wrenches, and medium-duty and light-duty strips strong enough to secure screwdrivers, small pliers and vise grips, as well as nails and other fasteners. You can buy magnetic tool strips at home improvement stores and well-stocked hardware stores, as well as from online tool vendors.

WATCH FOR WIGGLES. A loose head on your hammer or axe demands immediate attention. Room to wiggle can quickly become room to slip off in mid-swing. Remove a loose head from the handle and remove the old wedge that fits in the slit at the top of the handle. Fit the tool head back onto the handle and drive a new wedge into the slit until there's no looseness left. Cut the wedge so it's flush with the top of the handle.

TUCK IN YOUR TOOLS FOR SPEEDY TAKEAWAY. When you need to take your tools to the job—rather than bringing the job to your shop—a tool roll makes a highly portable carrier that can help to ensure you have everything you need. Typically made of canvas or leather with multiple tool pockets, tool rolls come in different sizes for large and small tools. Some are designed specifically to hold all the pieces of a socket wrench set, for example.

A tool roll can save you from carrying a heavy toolbox that contains many unnecessary tools, and it keeps your tools from rattling around and banging against each other when you transport them. Cyclists find tool rolls handy for carrying the wrenches needed for quick roadside repairs, while serious climbers use them to secure and organize their rock-climbing equipment in their packs. Woodworkers prefer tool rolls for storing chisels and other sharp-edged tools to protect their cutting edges from dents and dings.

Look for tool rolls in stores and on Web sites that carry fine woodworking tools; you may also find them at motorcycle or bicycle shops or at camping outfitters.

FIND NEW HOMES FOR YOUR OLD TOOLS. A parent's move into  a smaller home may find you in possession of more tools than you'll ever use and more than your workshop can possibly hold. While there's not much of a market for broken, 20-year-old electric drills, old hand tools may be much sought after by collectors looking for antiques or antique-looking items. Sort through such "inheritances" and separate modern acquisitions from possible heirlooms, setting aside anything that improves on your own tool inventory or that has sentimental value in your family.

MAKE HISTORY. Contact your local historical society; such organizations may be very interested in acquiring old tools that are

> ## FIX IT OR FORGET IT?
> ### NO WISECRACKS
>
> Sad but true: A cracked axe or hammer handle is done for. If your wooden axe handle develops a crack in the middle of a job, it's time to stop using it. Tempting though it may be to try wrapping it with that all-purpose tool, duct tape, and carrying on, the risk of an airborne axe or hammerhead is not worth the gamble. And even if a crack seems insignificant, its presence indicates that the handle is failing and needs to be replaced before you use the tool again.

representative of the way things were done in the "olden days." Your great-grandfather's ice tongs, for example, might end up on display in a museum or living history exhibit, where you can take your own grandkids on a trip to the past. Look in the Yellow Pages of your phone book under "historical places" or in the white pages under the name of the county you live in.

DECK YOUR HALLS. Unique or particularly old tools might look great hanging on a wall or resting on a curio shelf in your home. Clean such objects carefully, keeping in mind that the patina of age may be a large part of their charm. Experts recommend using toothbrush-sized brass brushes, rags, and Murphy's oil soap to remove dirt gently from metal and wood surfaces.

GIVE TO A GOOD CAUSE. Universally practical tools, such as hammers, screwdrivers, and handsaws that are in good working condition, can find new life helping others through Habitat for Humanity, your local YM/YWCA, Scout troops, 4-H clubs, or other service organizations. Contact a local chapter to see whether tool donations are welcomed; be sure to get a receipt to keep with your tax records. You can use Habitat for Humanity's Web site (www.habitat.org) to search for a chapter in your area, or look in the white pages of your phone book. Look under "youth organizations" in the Yellow Pages to find Scout groups and boys' and girls' clubs; contact your county's Cooperative Extension office (listed in the blue pages of the phone book under "county government") to find 4-H clubs.

Solve a History Mystery . . .

. . . and enjoy a hot meal, too! Are you having a hard time figuring out what that odd tool from Grandpa's shed was used for? You might find its mate among the décor at a Cracker Barrel restaurant. With more than 475,000 artifacts on display in 41 states, Cracker Barrel considers each of its 535-plus locations a unique "museum of Americana." And each item on the walls has an inventory tag that allows the company to track down the answers to "what's that thing?" inquiries from its guests. Cracker Barrel also main-

tains a warehouse of artifacts in Lebanon, Tennessee, where items destined to become restaurant décor are cleaned, restored, and cataloged before being made available to the designers who carefully plan the displays for each new store.

If you're not planning a visit to a Cracker Barrel restaurant any time soon, you can view photos of some of its "old-time" tools and other treasures, along with explanations of how they were used, on the company's Web site at www.crackerbarrel.com.

SUPPORT THE ARTS. Seek out local artisans who might be looking for saw blades to paint or tools to turn into objets d'art. Inquire at community colleges, art schools, high school art departments, and artisans' guilds to find artists who work with "found" objects. Look up "art schools" in the Yellow Pages of your phone book, or check under the name of your county or region in the white pages to find area arts' organizations. You may also find such groups online by searching community Web sites or bulletin boards.

BE AN ANGEL. If your over-abundance of tools includes duplicates of basic implements you already own, make up your spares into "starter" tool kits for folks who are just setting up housekeeping. Agencies, such as homeless shelters (look under "housing" in the blue pages of the phone book) or the Red Cross (www.redcross.org), that assist people who are starting up—or starting over—may be able to direct your donation to someone who'll be glad to have it.

FIX IT OR FORGET IT?
GRANDPA'S HAMMER
(OR GEORGE WASHINGTON'S AX)

You can buy a replacement handle for your hammer, explains woodworker and high school technology education teacher Ken Burton of New Tripoli, Pennsylvania. But you can probably buy a new hammer for close to the price of a replacement handle—and save yourself the effort of fitting the new handle to the old head. Unless the hammer in question has sentimental value, it's probably easier to replace it with a new tool, Burton says, referring to an old joke about a family that claimed to have George Washington's ax: "It had been passed down through many generations and was the original ax, although they'd had to replace the head twice and the handle three times." Burton adds that he finds hammers with fiberglass handles put less stress on his elbow over the course of a day's work, noting that fiberglass handles rarely break, "unless you're doing something really bad!"

POWER TOOLS

Tools that run on electricity or battery power make work so much easier and more efficient. Here's how to keep each one you own working like a charm.

DON'T STARVE YOUR TOOLS. A voltage-hungry power tool at the end of a long and inadequate extension cord is a tool that's likely to perform poorly. It's also at risk of overheating and suffering permanent damage. The combination of distance (cord length) and resistance (insufficient carrying capacity in the cord) turns an adequate supply of power at the outlet into not-quite-enough juice at the other end. Match cord capacity to the needs of your tool, and

MAKE IT LAST

use the shortest cord possible to reach your work site. For example, a 4-amp drill that uses 120 volts needs at least a 14-gauge extension cord to deliver enough power over 100 feet; a 16-gauge cord will do for shorter distances. Look at the ampere rating of the tool you want to use and the voltage at which it's meant to operate. This information usually appears on a plate on the tool, as well as in the owner's manual.

GIVE RECHARGEABLES A LITTLE LOVE. All batteries wear out sooner or later. A few basic care practices will help extend the useful life of your rechargeable tool batteries.

- **Avoid extremes.** Chargers and battery packs perform best at normal room temperatures—above 50°F and below 100°F.
- **Don't overcharge.** Remove the battery from the charger when it is fully charged.
- **Discharge it.** Run the battery-powered device until the battery is completely drained, a process known as discharging, before storing batteries for extended periods (30 days or more).
- **Stow safely.** Store your discharged batteries in cool (below 80°F) conditions.
- **Let 'em cool down.** Allow batteries that are hot from use to cool for 30 minutes before attempting to recharge them.

SAVE THE PAPERWORK! Make it easy on yourself on the rare occasion when one of your power tools needs repair: Keep all basic documents such as receipts, warranties, and instruction booklets where they'll be easy to find.

Gone are the days when a broken tool could be repaired by its owner or by a handy neighbor. Like most other consumer electronics, modern power tools in need of repairs are destined to go to a manufacturer-approved repair center. If that happens, it's essential to have the paperwork.

Buy an expandable file folder, plastic for moisture resistance or cardstock if you're unwilling to spring for the plastic. When you buy a new tool or a replacement battery or any item that is going to spend the rest of its lifetime in your workshop, simply put the relevant documents in the folder for safekeeping. If you feel like getting fancy, use the dividers to separate materials for different tools. You can even use one section to store records that tell what color paint you used in the upstairs hall. How organized your folder needs to be depends upon how much paper you want to wade through if you have to find something. The point is, simply, to make sure you have the documents handy when you need them.

GIVE WORN-OUT RECHARGEABLES A SECOND CHANCE. When your rechargeable batteries finally bite the dust, you'll need to dispose of them in accordance with the laws governing hazardous waste disposal. Fortunately, getting rid of "dead" rechargeables is pretty straightforward, and it's good for the environment, too.

One Man's Trash
From Sawdust to Success

Bill Walsh, president of Walsh & Sons Trucking of Portland, Oregon, built his successful trucking business out of sawdust. As a college student tending bar in the late 1950s, Walsh learned that meat-packing companies would buy hardwood sawdust to use in the meat-smoking process. Meanwhile, the forest-products industry considered sawdust a waste by-product. Walsh saw an opportunity, and he went for it. Soon, he found himself hauling sawdust to meat processors throughout the Northwest. He nearly lost his product a few years later when paper mills began buying up the sawdust for paper manufacturing, but Walsh stuck with sawdust and began carrying it for the paper mills. Since 1961, his company has focused on hauling materials for the forest-products industry. Walsh & Sons Trucking now operates six facilities in the Northwest and has 270 trucks and 350 drivers, and Walsh and his five sons run the business that started with a pile of sawdust.

The Rechargeable Battery Recycling Corporation is a nonprofit, public service organization that promotes the recycling of portable rechargeable batteries and cellular phones. In 2005, the RBRC collected almost 5 million pounds of rechargeable batteries. The RBRC accepts the following battery types: nickel-cadmium (Ni-Cd), nickel-metal hydride (Ni-MH), lithium ion (Li-ion), and small sealed-lead acid (SSLA or Pb, up to 2 pounds). Cadmium, cobalt, iron, lead, and nickel are extracted from the recycled batteries and used to manufacture new batteries and stainless steel.

Many of the same retailers that sell rechargeable batteries and cell phones also serve as collection points for recycling. To find a collection site that's convenient for you, use the locator on the RBRC Web site at www.call2recycle.org or call the consumer help line at (800) 8-BATTERY or (877) 2-RECYCLE.

$mart Buys
GET MORE FOR YOUR MONEY

Top-quality power tools can command a pretty steep price, because they're built for precision and durability. If you need a reliable and long-lasting tool for regular use, it makes sense to shop for quality from the start. That doesn't have to mean spending a fortune if you're willing to consider a factory-reconditioned tool. Online retailers often sell remanufactured or reconditioned tools that offer performance (and warranties) that compare favorably with the same tools sold brand-new—the only difference is the price, which may be half to two-thirds that of a new tool.

Such tools may be a little banged up on the outside, but like-new where it counts, says Ken Burton, a high school technology education teacher from New Tripoli, Pennsylvania. They may also be unused returns that the manufacturer can no longer sell as new. Here are a few more ways to stretch your tool-buying budget.

• **Wrap up a (former) rental.** If you're in the market for a heavy-duty tool, check out the former rental tools at hardware and home improvement stores or rental centers. Retiring rentals may come with specialty attachments and often carry a very reasonable price tag. If you can make sure that the tool hasn't suffered ill use as a rental, you may get a great deal on a sturdy tool with many years of use left in it.

• **Watch out for "almost" brand-name tools.** Designer-brand knockoffs come in materials other than denim. Before you snap up an unbelievable deal on a big-ticket power tool, verify its credentials. What appears to be a steal from a well-known manufacturer may turn out to be a lesser-quality imitation with a name that differs by just a letter or two from that of the better-known brand.

• **Match spending to use.** For occasional jobs around the house, an inexpensive tool may be all you need. "You can buy a drill for $19 and, if you're only going to use it a couple of times a year, it'll probably last a long time," Burton says. "But if you use it every day, you're going to wear it out pretty quickly, at which point throwing it out is your only option. If you're buying a power tool for a specific project, it's worth it to spend a little more to get a tool that can withstand heavier use."

ELECTRICAL SUPPLIES

Back when Ben Franklin was conducting his experiments with electricity, he probably had no idea about the varied ways we'd discover to harness it. He would, however, appreciate the clever hints and tips we've come up with to keep all your electrical supplies happy and healthy.

CONSIDER AGE AND BEAUTY. When it comes to electrical equipment, older rarely means better. Innovations in materials and devices, updates to the National Electric Code, and increasingly complex electronics almost always make new equipment superior to, safer than, and more long-lasting than old materials that might be lingering in your workshop.

MAKE IT LAST

PRACTICE SMART CORD CARE AND USE. The thick layer of insulation that covers heavy-duty extension cords can make them seem invincible, but your cords still need care to keep them carrying power safely to where you need it.

- **Roll them.** Store extension cords on reels or other holders that let you wrap them up without causing sharp bends or kinks in the cord.
- **Lock it up.** Use a cord lock to secure the connection between your extension cord and a power tool if there's a risk that the cord will pull loose while you're working. An outdoor power tool, such as a leaf blower, may have a built-in cord lock, or you can buy these inexpensive plastic connectors at most hardware stores.
- **Protect during use.** Avoid accidentally shutting doors on cords or placing them where they'll be stepped on, driven over, or otherwise crushed.
- **Use on a temporary basis.** Household appliances such as air-conditioners should not get their considerable power needs through an extension cord.
- **Skip the "daisy chain."** It's tempting to connect two or

---

FIX IT OR FORGET IT?
CUT (OUT) THAT CORD

In addition to wear and tear from years of use and exposure, that old two-pronged extension cord that Grandma keeps with her Christmas lights was never intended to carry the amount of electricity required by modern appliances—or even by modern flashing, blinking, and moving Christmas decorations. No amount of electrical tape will make such a cord safe to use—and a heavily patched cord is a definite candidate for replacement. Do Grandma and everyone in the family a favor: Replace extension cords that are more than 5 years old, making sure to purchase new cords that have the carrying capacity for their intended places in your home's power chain.

When discarding old, damaged extension cords, the Electrical Safety Foundation International recommends cutting the cords so no one is tempted to remove them from your trash and reuse them.

more extension cords to get a power tool to where you want it, but increased distance equals increased fire risk, especially if one of the cords has a lower load-carrying capacity.

LIGHT UP YOUR LIFE—LONGER. By replacing regular on/off light switches with dimmers, you can easily double the life span of your light bulbs and reduce the electricity they use by anywhere from 10 to 60 percent. Installing a dimmer requires only a few basic tools and about 15 minutes of your time. Here are the step-by-step instructions.

1. Turn off the power at the breaker panel or fuse box.
2. Remove the faceplate and the switch-mounting screws.
3. Remove the switch, loosen the screws, and unhook the wires. Note that the ground wire will be green or bare copper.
4. Connect the dimmer wires to the corresponding wires in the outlet and then cap each connection with a wire nut (usually included with the dimmer).
5. Mount the dimmer and faceplate.
6. Turn on the circuit breaker or replace the fuse to restore power.

AVOID POWER STRUGGLES. Surge suppressors, also called surge protectors, work by absorbing spikes in the electricity flowing through the wires in your house, thereby protecting sensitive electronic equipment such as computers, televisions, and stereos from damage. Although surge suppressors may resemble multiple outlet power strips, they offer protection those devices don't.

When you're shopping for a surge protector that will last, make sure the label says, "UL Listed Transient Voltage Suppressor."

Surge protectors are rated by the amount of voltage they're able to suppress. Ratings range from 330 to 4000 volts; lower numbers indicate better surge protection.

A desirable feature in a reliable surge suppressor is an indicator light that indicates that the device is working. It's easy to forget about these useful tools, as they tend to be tucked behind the TV or under the desk. But surge protectors wear out and gradually lose their ability to absorb excess voltage coming through the line. Make a habit of checking the indicator lights on the surge suppressors in your home once a month; don't delay in replacing any that are no longer doing the job.

FIX IT OR FORGET IT?
FEEL THE HEAT

While it's not unusual for an extension cord to become warm after it has been in use for more than a few minutes, a cord that gets hot enough to soften its plastic outer coating needs to be replaced. Either it's inadequate for the power needs of the tool it is supplying or the wires inside of it have been damaged. Continuing to use the cord can create fire and shock hazards.

CORDS FOR THE COLD. Stiff, cold cords are at risk of developing cracks in their outer insulation, which increases your risk of getting shocked by dangerous electric currents. If your heavy-duty extension cord has to work in cold conditions, look for one that has some rubber in its insulating coating. The rubber will help keep the cord flexible even as temperatures fall toward 0°F and will save you from wrestling with a stiff, uncooperative cord.

CHECK FOR FAULTY GFCIS. Ground-fault circuit interrupters (GFCIs) are devices that detect when electricity seeks ground through an unintended pathway (a ground fault) and shut off (interrupt) the circuit when that happens. The National Electrical Code requires GFCI-protected outlets in kitchens, bathrooms, basements, garages, and outdoor areas in new constructions. GFCIs are a simple and effective way to prevent electrocution in places where water and electricity exist in close proximity. A GFCI can be damaged by power surges and lightning strikes and, although the outlet may appear okay and continue to work, the GFCI may have been destroyed. Underwriters Laboratory recommends testing GFCI outlets once a month and after strong thunderstorms.

To check your GFCI outlets—thereby ensuring that they last as long as possible—use a plug-in night-light with an on/off switch or a small lamp, then follow these steps.

1. Push the "reset" button on the GFCI to ensure normal operation.
2. Plug the night-light into the outlet and switch it on.
3. Push the "test" button on the GFCI. The light should go out.
4. Push the "reset" button again. The light should come back on.

If the light stays on when you push the "test" button, the GFCI is not working or is not wired correctly. Have an electrician test the outlet and rewire or replace the GFCI device.

FIX IT FAST

USE ELECTRICAL TAPE ONLY FOR TEMPORARY TOUCH-UPS. Because electricity is such a dangerous tool, it's better to err on the side of caution when making repairs to the devices through which it travels. Use a double layer of black vinyl electrical tape to wrap minor nicks and abrasions in electrical cords or to secure loose plug ends just long enough to get you through a task. If you're working outdoors where moisture may contact the damaged insulation, don't even reach for the tape—replace the cord right away. Even if the damage to the outer cord covering is minor, taping it may alter the cord's flexibility or create extra heat in that spot, both of which can damage the inner insulation and wires.

If your heavy-duty extension cord is damaged near an end, cut off the damaged area and put a new plug on your now-shorter cord. If damage is closer to the middle of the cord, cut out the damaged area and add new plugs to both pieces to create two shorter cords.

PLUMBING TOOLS AND SUPPLIES

Will you do anything to avoid calling a plumber? With the help of the tips below, you may be able to postpone that call—for good.

MAKE IT LAST

(HEAT-PROOF) GREASE IS THE WORD. Whether you're installing new washers in a bathroom sink or changing the showerhead, choose a plumbing-proper lubricant to smooth your way. Pass up the petroleum jelly—it will literally dissolve plumbing seals—and apply plumber's grease wherever a dab of lubrication is needed. Plumber's grease, also called heat-proof grease or key grease, is made to hold up under high temperatures (up to about 300°F), and it won't harm the parts inside your plumbing. You can buy plumber's grease at hardware and home improvement stores and plumbing supply outlets.

Shelf Life of the Stuff on Your Shelf

How long items such as paint and glue last depends a great deal upon how they're stored. Extreme temperatures—below freezing and above 80°F—shorten the shelf life of many products. If your workshop is in an unheated garage or shed, consider storing liquid and semiliquid materials in a place where conditions are more moderate.

MATERIAL	AVERAGE SHELF LIFE	NOTES
Caulk	1 year or more	Store tubes horizontally
Glue (wood or white)	1 year or more	
Lubricant sprays (WD-40, Liquid Wrench)	Indefinite	Follow label instructions when discarding aerosol cans
Mineral spirits, paint thinner, turpentine	Indefinite	Let paint particles settle out; pour off clear solvent back into storage container and reuse
Paint, latex	1 to several years	Ability to keep is highly dependent on storage conditions; older metal cans may rust inside and spoil paint
Paint, oil or alkyd	Several years	
Pipe joint compound	No more than 2 years	Discard if separated
Superglue (cyanoacrylate glue)	Up to 1 year	
Tape	Varies widely, depending on type	Store between pieces of waxed paper to keep dust and lint from sticking to sides

BEWARE TOO MANY GOOD TURNS. Teflon tape makes it extra easy to fasten threaded pipes into their fittings—so easy, in fact, that you can destroy a new fitting without even realizing it. To avoid this problem and make your fastenings last longer, you don't necessarily need to give up using Teflon tape. Instead, make it a point to work carefully when you are using it. As you thread new pipe into a fitting, you're basically inserting a wedge into the fitting, pressing outward against the weakest part of that particular shape. Teflon tape allows the threads to slide so smoothly that you may not feel the connection getting tighter, and before you realize it, you've destroyed the fitting. Take a slow-and-steady approach when working with this slippery substance, especially if it's your first experience. Err on the side of caution and under tighten until you get the feel of the tape and the right amount of turning, and test each joint for leaks before making the next connection.

FIX IT FAST

TAP THE ULTIMATE UNIVERSAL TOOL. Faucet specifications vary from one manufacturer to the next, and even among the models made by the same company. Faucets made in the last 10 to 15 years may have a cartridge insert, while older taps might have valve stems and replaceable valve seats. A typical home may have three or four different faucets from different manufacturers. Unless you're a plumber, it's unlikely that you'll have the tools necessary to make repairs on every one of the faucet sets in your home, and it really doesn't make sense to try.

When a plumbing problem arises, start with your computer. If you know the manufacturer of the faucet, go to its Web site. Most major brands offer specification sheets and exploded diagrams of their products that you can print out and take to the home improvement or plumbing supply store, so you can get exactly the right parts for the job and the proper tools, if necessary.

PAINT AND PAINTBRUSHES

We love paint! It just may be the best decorating tool out there. It's relatively inexpensive and it can change the whole look of a room or even the exterior of a home. Here's how to get the most out of each paint purchase.

MAKE IT LAST

PAINTS, PRESERVE US! Good paint-handling habits make a painting job go more smoothly and help ensure that any leftover paint remains in usable condition for as long as possible.

- **Keep it in a temperate climate.** Temperature lows and highs can cause the ingredients in paint to separate. Extended exposure to extremes can make the separation so severe that no amount of shaking and stirring will restore the paint's texture.
- **Don't paint from the can.** Pour paint into an open bucket or a roller pan and dip your brush or roller in that. The fewer items you stick into the paint can, the less likely the paint in the can will become contaminated (paint can spoil) or full of foreign matter that will make chunks and bumps on your painted surfaces.
- **Seal out air.** Keep paint cans closed as much as possible while you're working. At the end of the day, put a piece of plastic wrap over the

top of the can before securing the lid to help create an airtight seal.

- **Go "bottom's up."** When storing leftover paint, make sure the can lid is secure, then turn the can upside down to create an airtight seal and to avoid the formation of a "skin" of thickened paint on top.

- **Set some aside.** Keep some paint for touch-ups in a glass canning jar. You'll save yourself the trouble of opening and resealing the gallon paint can for a small amount of paint. You'll also extend the life of the paint that's stored in the can, by keeping it sealed.

WASH, WASH, WASH YOUR BRUSH. Extend the life of good-quality paint brushes, get a better coating of paint, and make cleanup easier by wetting your brush thoroughly before you start applying latex paint. Wet the bristles completely with water and shake out the excess, then clean your brush every half hour to an hour. Although this might seem excessive, it can save your brush by keeping paint from hardening in the bristles near the brush handle. If you wait until you're finished painting to clean the brush, you'll wind up pulling out a lot of the bristles along with the dried paint. Even if the brush survives such abuse, it won't apply paint as smoothly the next time you use it. If you've spent $25 for a brush and want to do a good job, it's worth the time to clean the brush more often than you think you need to.

WRAP IT UP BEFORE LUNCH. Taking a break from painting, in the middle of the job? Wrap your freshly cleaned brushes and rollers in plastic wrap or aluminum foil to keep them moist until you're ready to resume painting.

AGITATE FOR CLEAN PAINT ROLLERS. Wool rollers hold more paint and last longer than rollers with synthetic coverings. They also cost more, so it's worthwhile to clean them thoroughly after a latex painting session. Instead of messy scrubbing by hand, toss the rollers into your washing machine with some laundry detergent and run them through a normal wash cycle. The rollers will come out looking like new and ready to paint another day. Toss your painting clothes in the washer for the next load to clear away any remaining paint residue.

 **PURCHASE PAINT PRUDENTLY.** You're about to paint your living room, but you have no idea how much paint to purchase. You can quickly and easily solve that problem by going online. Many paint manufacturers' Web sites feature paint calculators to help you determine how much paint you need—you simply provide the dimensions of the space you plan to paint and the type of paint you'll use, and the program does the math for you.

STICK A FORK IN IT! That paintbrush you forgot to clean after the last paint job isn't necessarily destined for the trash. Even if the old paint is latex-based, you may need to start by soaking the brush in mineral spirits to loosen the residue. For brushes gummed up with other finishes, choose a solvent based on the recommendations on the finish label. Once the solvent starts to soften things up, don gloves and use your hands and an old fork (or a brush comb, available at most paint stores) to work it into the bristles.

Repeat this process as necessary until the brush is free of most of the gunk. Then soak it in a commercial brush cleanser or trisodium phosphate (sold at paint and hardware stores). Wrap the cleaned bristles in brown kraft paper to help restore their shape; store the brush flat or hanging from a hook.

 **PASS (UP) THE LEFTOVERS.** Whether it's latex or oil-based, the best way to get rid of extra paint of any kind is pretty straightforward—use it up. Give your room an extra coat. Paint your compost

bin, tomato cages, garden stakes, trellis, garden sheds, or other out-door items. Most household trash collection programs will accept dried latex paint and empty, dry metal paint cans with their lids removed. If you have a small amount of leftover latex paint, pour it over cat litter or sawdust in a paper bag and let it dry, then dispose of it with your regular trash pickup. Oil-based paint is considered house-hold hazardous waste and must be disposed of according to local, state, and federal regulations.

SHARE YOUR SPARE. Usable, leftover paint may find surfaces in need of a fresh coat elsewhere in your community. Recreation de-partments, churches, and service organizations that provide home maintenance to the elderly or disabled, theatre groups, and graffiti-abatement programs are all places that might welcome your extra paint. Ask your community's United Way office for help in identifying member agencies that could use your unwanted paint; you can find the United Way in the white pages of your phone book.

WORKSHOP MISCELLANY

These tips offer clever advice about all the doodads that seem to ac-cumulate in the workshop.

KEEP A LID ON IT. Fight the battle against dried-out glue and solidi-fied tubes of caulk with a handy latex device called Little Red Cap. The Little Red Cap is a flexible replacement cap that you can roll over the top of a bottle of glue or onto the cut tip of a caulk tube. The cap seals air out, helping to keep the contents from drying. You may appreciate these innovative doodads if you've ever sealed a tube of caulk with a nail only to have the nail rust and stain a large part of the caulk you squeeze out afterward. According to the product's Web site at www.littleredcap.com, these nifty items are sold in hardware stores in multiple-cap packages. A list of retailers that carry Little Red Caps appears on the Web site.

MAKE IT LAST

GET OUT OF A (SUPER) BIND. Ideally, you'll never make the mis-take of sticking your fingers together while working with one of the cyanoacrylate products more commonly known as superglue. But unfortunately, accidents do happen—and glue has a way of winding up on fingers and other surfaces where it's not wanted. If you do glue

FIX IT FAST

your fingers together, stay calm and don't attempt to pull your fingers apart—if you do this you'll remove skin as well as glue. Instead, slowly and gently rub bonded fingers together in warm, soapy water, working to gradually peel the bond apart. If you're after a speedier solution to this sticky situation, or need to remove glue from hard surfaces, apply an acetone-based nail polish remover to the glue. Wash up with soap and water when you're done.

7 Uses for Sawdust

Woodworkers sometimes joke that their hobby is turning wood into sawdust, but the truth behind the humor is that even a little bit of woodworking can leave you with a lot of sawdust. A well-equipped wood shop may include some type of sawdust collection system in association with its most-used sawdust-making tools. Whether you sweep the stuff up when the job's done or catch it while you work, the resulting pile of shavings need not wind up in the trash. As long as the sawdust you create comes from wood that has not been treated with chemical preservatives, give it new life in your garden, garage, or grill, among other places.

- **Mulch it.** Sawdust makes a good topping for garden pathways and will impede weed growth between vegetable rows.
- **Make speedy compost.** Mix 40 to 50 pounds of fresh horse manure with 10 pounds of sawdust; moisten, if necessary, to the dampness of a wrung-out sponge. Use a spading fork to turn the pile every 2 to 3 days. Within a few weeks, the compost should be ready to add to your garden. When it's finished, it will look and smell like rich, loose soil without obvious traces of its original ingredients.
- **Keep some in the kitchen.** If you have a below-the-sink bucket for holding compost-bound food scraps, top each meal's contributions with a handful of sawdust to soak up excess moisture and help control odors.
- **Spread it beneath the bunnies** (or hamsters, gerbils, guinea pigs, and other herbivores).

Spread a layer of sawdust under rabbit cages to catch droppings, creating compost on the spot. Put the resulting mixed manure and sawdust in your compost bin for final decomposition, or spread it over garden beds in the fall and dig it into the soil before you do your spring planting.

- **Soak up soggy spots.** Have a muddy place in the lawn along an over-traveled walkway? Use sawdust in place of a cloak to keep your sneakers out of the slop.
- **Take up smoking—meat, that is.** Sawdust and wood chips that are good for smoking include mesquite, hickory, alder, apple, cherry, maple, oak, and pecan. Do not use sawdust from resinous soft woods such as cedar, Douglas fir, pine, or spruce, or from any wood that has been chemically treated, painted, or finished. Soak the sawdust in water. Arrange charcoal briquettes in two piles on the charcoal grate in your grill and place a heavy-duty aluminum pan between them. Put 2 cups of water in the pan. Light the briquettes and let them burn for about a half hour. Then drain the sawdust and spread it over the hot coals. Replace the cooking grate and place meat over the drip pan; replenish the briquettes and sawdust every hour or so. Maintain a temperature of 225°F to 250°F for the duration of the smoking time.
- **Make it part of a paint job.** Put sawdust in a paper bag and pour leftover latex paint over it. Once dry, the paint/sawdust mixture can be put out for household trash collection.

KEEP TRACK OF TIME. "Did I buy this caulk last year or the year before?" Here's an easy way to have a ready answer to the "how old is it?" question. Hang a permanent marker in a handy spot in your workshop. Whenever you add a partial can of paint, a bottle of adhesive, a tube of caulk, or any other product to the shelves in your shop, write the date on the container. Don't rely on your memory to recall when you last painted the spare bedroom or when you replaced the faucet in the downstairs bath—the date on the tube will tell you exactly how old each item is. Easily visible dates simplify workshop cleanup, too—dispose of anything that's more than a couple of years old, unless you know for sure that it's still good. Plan your shop cleanup to coincide with your community's hazardous waste collection dates and dispose of chemicals safely and according to environmental regulations.

DISPOSE OF DUST CORRECTLY. Sawdust seems like a pretty harmless substance, one that can just go out with the trash—or into the compost bin, right? Not necessarily. Sawdust, shavings, and scraps from pressure-treated lumber are considered hazardous wastes and must be disposed of according to environmental regulations. Wear gloves and goggles and use a dust mask when working with treated wood; never burn scraps or sawdust from it. And when it's ready for the bin, contact your local sanitation department (you'll find the number in the blue pages of your local phone book).

PASS IT ALONG

MORE TIPS FOR THE HOME WORKSHOP
Here's a roundup of the workshop-related Pass It Along tips you'll find in the other chapters of *Don't Throw It Out!*

CHAPTER	TIP	PAGE
1	Transfer Trays	7
1	Old Utensils, New Uses	24
1	7 Uses for an Old Cutting Board	25
1	Organize Someone Else	32
1	Assign a Tube to Bag Duty	33
2	5 Ways to Say "Cheerio" to Chair Pads	61

(continues)

Keeping your hoard of equipment down to the well-honed necessities and the workshop clean and clutter-free isn't all about tidiness. It's also a surefire way to keep the tools you have in better shape, use up products before they expire to avoid messes and accidents that age the whole place. Ever tried to rescue your drill bits from a shellac spill? Find the quart of paint that matches the bathroom? Untangle six sets of cords for a simple welding job? Then you know what we mean.

While there are some tried-and-true methods for keeping your workshop shipshape and your stock to the most efficient minimum, there are just as many ideas that sound good but aren't worth a darn. Look over these 10 suggestions and pick out the seven genuine tips among the three bum steers:

Questions

1. Always send your significant other to the hardware store to buy supplies for projects—she might better resist buying extras or caving in to marketing ploys.

2. Sure, it destroys the surprise element, but write a specific wish list of tools and equipment, including size, model number, color, price, etc., you'd like to receive as gifts, and never make the same request of two different people.

3. Always clear and prepare the room you intend to paint or wallpaper before shopping for the supplies and you'll really cut down on the unused gallons and rolls hanging around.

4. Even though it's not cost effective, it's always a good idea to buy just a quart of paint in the color and brand you like so you can test it on the wall and avoid having several gallons of unsuitable paint lying around.

5. Sort spare nails, nuts and bolts and other small hardware by size into baby food jars mounted by the lid beneath a shelf for easy access and stockpile extra jars for future reference.

6. Whenever you can, shop for nails, screws, nuts and bolts somewhere that sells them by the pound so you can buy just what you need, or maybe a few extras.

(continues)

7. If you can't envision being able to use quality hand or power tools you've received as part of a legacy, keep one or two favorites and donate the rest to a Habitat for Humanity group or Boy Scout Group in honor of the person who willed you the tools—or sell them on eBay and donate the proceeds in their honor.

8. If you do a lot of woodworking, go ahead and buy (or build) an official workbench, but make each surface six inches shorter than the length you'd consider ideal to save on space.

9. Once a year, take everything off your workroom shelves and out of the cabinets if it can easily be moved by one person, move it out of the workroom, clean the shelves and then move back in only what you still need and will use within the next six months.

10. Strive to leave 20 percent of the space in your workroom empty after a clutter-clearing episode. You'll have room for new acquisitions if you really need them before the next purge.

Answers

Here are the three tips you shouldn't take:

1. While sending someone who won't succumb to impulse buys sounds reasonable, that person is even more likely to buy the wrong thing—or things—which will then either clutter up your workshop or require some speedy returns (and further exposure to impulse buys!). Instead, carry only limited cash or call ahead and have the order waiting for your arrival to limit temptation at the store.

5. How often do you use any but a few standard sizes of nails, screws, etc.? Do sort yours into baby food jars, but then sort them further into donations (or recycling material) and hardware to keep on hand because you'll use it within a couple of months. As for keeping extra empty jars at the ready, skip the precaution—it cuts clutter to reuse the few jars you have or come up with another container for donations.

8. It may be a good idea to commit some workroom space to a workbench if you'll use it for more than a couple projects each year. But don't make it too small or you won't be able to use it the way you need to and it will inevitably become another flat surface to hold unrelated junk. In fact, you may want to go a few inches larger than your largest anticipated project.

11

CARS, TRUCKS, AND OTHER VEHICLES

After your house, a car may be the largest financial commitment you make in your life. Protecting that investment used to be a lot easier: Back in the old days, a home mechanic could do all sorts of maintenance at home, and even take care of some simple fixes. But today, car maintenance and repair have become more complicated than ever because of computerized systems, compact engines, and new hybrid technology. In this chapter, you'll learn ways to help keep your automobile running for as long as possible, and we'll show you how proper upkeep is the key, not only to a car's long life, but to safety as well.

No car will last forever, but we'll help you get the most out of whatever you're driving. Keep the tires inflated, the oil and other fluids fresh, and the finish scratch and rust-free, and you're halfway there!

THE WHOLE VEHICLE

The tips on the following pages offer car repair and maintenance advice every car owner should heed. You'll learn how to save money by changing a fuse yourself (it's easy!) and tracking your gas mileage. And if you're thinking of donating an old car to charity—read on. It may not be the ideal write-off it once was.

MAKE IT LAST

MIND YOUR MANUALS. Read that owner's manual! Sure, it's a dry read, which is why you may be tempted to skip it. Don't. A car may be the most complicated piece of machinery you will ever own, and it's a good idea to discover what the manufacturer thinks you ought to know. You'll learn a lot, and mostly likely save yourself money on repairs and maintenance in the long run.

GO EASY ON THE CLUTCH. If your car has a manual transmission, remember that your foot belongs on the clutch pedal *only* when you're actually shifting gears. Resting your foot on the pedal, also known as riding the clutch, may cause the clutch to wear out prematurely. You may have heard this advice before, but it bears repeating—because most clutch problems are caused by riding the clutch! So, take care of the clutch, and it should last as long as the car.

One Man's Trash
A New A-Tire

In developing countries, sandals made from old tires are a common sight. Frustrated with shoes in general, Thomas J. Elpel decided to refine the tire sandal into a shoe that could withstand his hiking habit. Elpel, author of *The Field Guide to Primitive Living Skills*, was the kind of guy whose active lifestyle of hiking and camping could wear out six pairs of shoes in a single year. "It has always amazed me," he explains on his Web site: www.hollowtop.com/sandals.htm, "that tire companies can manufacture a tire and warranty the tread for some 50,000 miles, yet I can wear out the sole on any ordinary shoe in less than a year. Why can't we buy a shoe with a 50,000-mile warranty?" He refined his tire sandal design until it worked, and kept on working comfortably for miles. Elpel shares instructions on his Web site if you want to take some steps on recycled tires.

PROTECT THE TUMBLERS. Are your car keys on the same key chain as all of your other keys—and perhaps an extra heavy keychain doodad? If so, you may unknowingly be damaging your car's ignition. An overly laden keychain can wear out the tumblers inside the ignition and cause it to fail. The best bet is to keep your car keys on their own keychain.

BABY THE BATTERY. Most batteries today are billed as being maintenance-free. Even so, once a year it's a good idea to remove any accumulated corrosion from the battery connections. Clean metal connections are better conductors than dirty ones and will help prolong the life of the battery. (Here's a handy time-saver: Before you disconnect the battery, plug in a memory saver—available inexpensively at auto supply or electronic stores—to the cigarette lighter. This nifty device will save you from having to reset the clock and sound system in your car after you reconnect the battery). To clean battery connections properly, follow these simple steps.

1. Grab an old toothbrush, a little petroleum jelly, and some rubber gloves.
2. Mix 1 tablespoon of baking soda into 1 cup of water, and then don a pair of gloves.
3. This next step is *very* important: First disconnect the negative (grounded) terminal and then the positive terminal. If the ground is still connected while you unhook the positive terminal, you run the risk of creating a spark, or even causing the battery to explode.
4. Dip the toothbrush in the baking soda paste and scrub the clamps and terminals. If the battery terminals are really dirty, you may need to use a wire brush.
5. Wipe all surfaces until they are clean and dry, dab a small amount of petroleum jelly on each terminal to enhance conductivity, and then reconnect the terminals in reverse order (first positive, then negative). It's essential to reconnect the terminals in this order, or you could be in for a major shock!

KEEP YOUR EYE ON THE ROAD. The National Highway Traffic Safety Administration estimates that driver distractions cause 25 percent of accidents—that's 1.6 million accidents a year in the United States. Let's face it, if cell phones and latte sipping aren't enough, driving today offers plenty of other distractions. Here are some tips on how to stay safe on the road.

- **Stick with simple snacks.** If you must eat in the car, keep the food simple and neat, something you can hold with one hand—and nothing sticky or greasy.
- **Use care with GPS.** Some cars are equipped with GPS, or global positioning systems, that map your route as you drive. The computer speaks the directions, but the map on the little screen traces your every move. It's hard for the driver not to stare at this tiny television-like screen. Play it safe and let your passenger play navigator, or turn off the GPS feature.
- **Don't DJ and drive.** Automotive sound systems are another distraction, giving you the choice between AM and FM radio, CDs (often up to six of them), and sometimes even satellite radio with more than 100 channels each. Let your passenger play DJ, or find a station you like and leave the radio set there.
- **Focus on the road.** Of course, we all encounter loads of other fender-bender-causing sights during the morning commute: women applying their makeup in a rear view mirror, men wielding electric shavers, drivers reading the newspaper, and lots of people eating breakfast in the car. Remember to keep your eye on the road and your mind off all these distractions. And if you don't have a passenger, consider getting one—carpooling is good for the environment.

PROTECT YOUR CAR FROM THE ELEMENTS. Here are five ways to protect your car from rain, sleet, snow—and almost anything else Mother Nature might throw at it.

1. **Rid it of road salt.** You may not be able to stay home when it snows and the road is salted, but you can and should wash your car as soon as possible after the snow. If your garage is heated, be extra sure to rinse off road salt regularly; the heat in a garage can speed salt damage.
2. **Keep it covered.** Constant exposure to sunlight can cause your car's paint to fade and the upholstery and plastic dashboard to fade and crack. Consider a cloth covering or an inexpensive aluminum carport to keep the bright sun off your vehicle.
3. **Wash and wax.** At least once a month, wash with a soft cloth, being careful not to rub the dirt into the finish; it can leave scratches and dull the paint. A coat of wax will protect the finish from dirt, bugs, bird droppings, and road salt.
4. **Fix it quick.** Keep an eye out for dings and scratches in your car's paint and repair them quickly. The paint protects the metal underneath from rust.

Still Working After All These Years

ONE MAN, ONE CAR, MORE THAN 2 MILLION MILES

"Picking the Volvo was strictly an accident," says Irv Gordon, owner of the 1966 P1800S Volvo that holds the Guinness Book of World Records for highest mileage—as of this writing it has logged more than 2,450,000 miles. Two Chevys in a row had failed Irv, so he was ready to try something new. On June 23, 1966, he put down $4,150 for the cherry red Volvo and hasn't stopped driving it back and forth across the United States and Canada since. This car is so well traveled, that it's even visited five European countries.

His secret? Maintenance—and that doesn't mean waiting for problems to happen, it means preventing them before they happen. Says Gordon, "Oil changes are the easiest and most important service anyone can give a machine. Of course, checking the car over every time it goes on a lift is just as important and very easy to do. Brakes, tires, driveshaft, oil leaks, water leaks, and brake fluid are all things that should be looked at while the oil is running out of the car. One can save a fortune in repairs with a few cents in maintenance."

How much of that maintenance does Gordon do himself? Well, quite a bit. As he explains, "I do most of the work that does not require a lift, as I refuse to crawl under my car while in the driveway. I know about too many people who have been seriously hurt or killed when a car they were under fell on them. I do all the tune-ups, electrical service, cleaning and flushing the cooling and braking systems, and the oil changes, always using genuine Volvo parts. After owning the same car for 40 years, there is not much about it I do not know."

5. **Keep the inside clean.** Many of the same culprits that can cause damage to your car's exterior, such as dirt and water, are also a danger to the interior.

MPG: AN EARLY WARNING SYSTEM. Keeping a log of your gas  mileage does more than demonstrate whether your car's getting what the manufacturer promised. Knowing the usual numbers also allows you to recognize a potential problem: A decrease of 10 percent or more can mean something's wrong with your car. Here's how to accurately calculate your MPG.

1. Fill the gas tank and record the odometer reading or set the trip odometer to 0.

2. Next time you fill the tank, record the number of gallons of gas and again record the odometer reading.

3. Subtract the first mileage from the second, and then divide by the number of gallons of gas.

If you like, keep this up for a month or two and divide the total miles driven by the total number of gallons of gas. This will give you a better average of highway and city driving. With all of this information, you'll be able to spot-check your mileage after every fill-up or every few months. If you notice a dramatic difference in mileage, be sure to consult with a reputable service center or research possible causes online.

CHECK FUSES FIRST. Fuses protect a car's electrical equipment by acting as surge protectors and burning out before the equipment can get damaged. Next time your car's radio, clock, or headlights seem to go on the fritz, check the fuse box before heading to the mechanic. The owner's manual will tell you where to find the fuse box and which piece of electrical equipment each fuse protects.

Changing a fuse is as simple as changing a light bulb—maybe even simpler, because you don't have to stand on a chair—so you can do this repair yourself. Pull out the fuse, using your fingers or the plastic fuse puller in the fuse box, and examine it. You'll be able to tell if it's burned out, because the filament will be broken. Be sure to replace the fuse with one of the same size, and amperage. Fuses are cheap—about 25 cents each—so be sure to keep a few spare ones in your car. Beware of a fuse that blows repeatedly; this is a sign of a larger problem that will likely need to be addressed by a mechanic.

LET THERE BE LIGHT. Would you call an electrician into your house to change a light bulb? Probably not. Well, here's good news:

$mart Buys
FIND THE RIGHT MECHANIC

"Take it from me, a car mechanic can be your best friend or your worst enemy." These words of hard-earned wisdom come from Jamie Kitman, automotive journalist and old car collector. Modern cars, with their computerized systems, are complicated, and it's no longer easy to fix them yourself. Older cars may be easier to work on yourself, but the parts are getting harder to find. Either way, using a mechanic is your best bet.

The best way to find a mechanic is by word of mouth. Ask around, especially your friends who drive similar cars. A good mechanic is someone who cares about your car. As Kitman says, "What sets all better establishments apart is that they want to get it right. If for some reason they don't, they try again. Ideally you want someone who knows your specific make and model of car. If you're lucky, you'll find a service technician who wants to get a few moonlighting hours to fix your car."

If real-live word of mouth hasn't helped you find the right mechanic for your car, try the Internet. In addition to car club Web sites for every make and model and automotive bulletin boards on every topic you can think of, there's the Web site for the nationally syndicated (and hugely popular) radio show, "Car Talk." The Mechanics Files section at www.cartalk.com is a database of over 16,000 mechanics recommended by members of the Car Talk online community.

You don't need to call in your auto mechanic to change your headlights (or brake lights) either—unless you don't mind paying $25 for a $10 bulb. Here's how to proceed.

1. Check the owner's manual to find out the kind of replacement bulb you need. Bulbs are available at auto parts stores.
2. Switch off the headlights (if they're on) and open the hood.
3. Unplug the electrical connection and remove the bulb assembly. In some cars the bulb assembly turns to release, in others you need to unscrew a ring holding the bulb in place.
4. When inserting the new bulb, be careful not to touch the glass. Most newer model cars have halogen bulbs and the oil from your fingertips will cause a halogen bulb to burn out more quickly. (This is not the case, however, for xenon headlamps.)

RUN A CLEAN MACHINE. Out of your favorite car interior cleanser? Don't run to the store. Instead, head to the cleaning closet and grab some lemon oil wood polish. It's great for keeping your dashboard looking like new. And it smells nice too!

COLOR AWAY A SCRATCH. Temporarily repairing small scratches on your car's finish is child's play. If you don't have touch-up paint on hand, color in the scratches with a wax crayon, and buff the area with a soft cloth. This quick fix will keep rust away from the metal temporarily. As soon as you have a chance, permanently color in scratches with touch-up paint that matches your car's finish.

PUT AN END TO ICE. Waking up to your morning commute and facing a windshield coated in ice is a hassle. If you know an icy storm is approaching, there are two ways to prevent this buildup.

1. **Spritz it.** Mix one part water with three parts white vinegar and spray it on your windshield before the storm hits.
2. **Shield it.** Cover the windshield with rubber mats the night (or hours) before the storm. Either way, you should wake up to a clear windshield and a car that's ready to go.

BUMP OFF STICKERS. If you've decided that it's finally time to get rid of that Rolling Stones bumper sticker, but have had a hard time removing it, you've probably just been using the wrong method. There is in fact, an easy way to remove stubborn stickers. You'll need a bowl of vinegar and a rag. Soak the rag in the vinegar and sop the sticker.

Let it set for a few minutes and check to see whether the adhesive is dissolving. If it needs a little more help, soak it again. Then use a plastic knife (the kind you get with a take-out meal) to scrape it all off. Clean with an ammonia-based window cleaner, and buff to dry.

PASS IT ALONG

THINK TWICE ABOUT DONATING. For many years, donating a car was a great way to get a good tax deduction and help your favorite charity at the same time. However, recent tax law changes have made things more complicated. For instance, donating a car worth more than $500 no longer entitles you to deduct the fair market value. You can deduct only the actual amount the charity receives for selling your car—a number that is often much lower. Plus, you won't know what your deduction is until after the car is sold, and you need paperwork from the charity to prove it. And, in a few rare cases, titles have not been properly transferred, leaving the donor with liability issues if the car is involved in an accident.

If you decide that donating your vehicle is right for you, you must file Schedule A to qualify for the deduction, and the charity must be an officially registered not-for-profit organization. If you're not sure, you can call (877) 829-5500 to find out whether it is. All in all, it may be a better idea to sell the car yourself and then, if you like, donate the cash to the charity of your choice.

JUST FOR USED CARS

Just because a car isn't technically new doesn't mean it can't live a long and productive life. After all, it's new to you! Here's our best advice about buying and driving used cars.

RUST NEVER SLEEPS. When considering a used car, steer clear of rust and your "new" old car will last a good long time. Generally, mechanical repairs are easier and less expensive to make than rust repairs. Rust is expensive to eliminate, and left unchecked, can spread quickly. Road salt is a major cause of rust, so if you're looking for an older car, shop for cars that have spent their lives down south, in California, or anywhere they don't salt the roads in the winter. That said, remember that a car from a year-round beach town may be covered in ocean salt, which, if left on the car, can do the same damage to the finish. Even if you need to have the car shipped (after you've seen it and checked it out in person, of course) from a rust-free climate, the expense will likely be a fraction of what you would spend repairing a rusty car.

JOIN THE CLUB. If you have been longing to buy, for example, a 1963 powder blue MGB, but don't know which way to turn for advice, consider joining an MGB car club before you make your purchase. There's a club for every make of car, and usually even more than one for any particular model. The people in these car clubs have seen it all, made all the mistakes, and accrued a lot of knowledge along the way; and you can benefit from it. Ask questions and you will get answers on everything from selecting a good solid car to choosing a mechanic.

The Used Car to Avoid

Newer cars shouldn't rust because they've received factory-applied antirust prevention. That means if you see rust on a car made since the early 1990s, it will often indicate poorly repaired accident damage—the metal was not prepared properly, the way the factory did, and rust grabbed hold.

HAVE A BELT. If you're driving an old car with no seat belts (or one that has only lap belts), it's a good idea to install a set of three-point safety belts. Seat belts are relatively inexpensive to buy. The key is finding a mechanic who knows how to install them and feels comfortable doing so. (Fellow members of your car club can be helpful here.) You can't just bolt them to the floor or they will tear out; they must be properly moored. It's a bit of trouble, but it's worth it.

GAS AND OIL

Conserving gasoline and motor oil is a good idea for the planet and your wallet. Here are some simply ingenious ways to do just that.

MAKE GAS LAST. Here are nine ways to use less gas every day.

1. **Accelerate gently and slowly.** When you give the car a lot of gas, you're using a lot of gas.

2. **Carpool whenever possible.** And not just during your daily commute; organize shopping trips and other errands with friends and family. It requires a little organizing, but it's worth it.

3. **Combine multiple errands into one trip.** Shutting down and restarting the engine all day long wastes a lot of fuel.

4. **Don't bother warming up the car.** Modern engines don't need it and it only burns fuel.

5. **No idle engines.** Don't let the engine idle for more than a few minutes—turn off your car if you're going to be stopped for a while. Restarting the car burns less gas than allowing it to idle.

6. **Keep tires properly inflated.** Properly inflated tires encounter less roll resistance, thereby increasing fuel efficiency.

7. **Use air-conditioning only when necessary.** Turning on the AC activates a compressor that, in turn, causes the car to use more gas.

8. **Use cruise control.** Driving at a steady rate wins the race when you are talking gas mileage.

9. **Walk or ride a bicycle when possible.** It's good for your wallet and good for your body.

FIX IT OR FORGET IT?
TO SELL OR NOT TO SELL

Should you keep your car until it drops dead of extreme old age? Or sell as soon as the warranty is up?

My position is that for any American or European car, either sell it as soon as the warranty expires or buy an extended warranty (taking care to read the exclusions). If it's a Japanese car, I think bailing out at 99,000 miles, or sooner, is about right,.

Repairs at some shops are approaching $100 per hour for labor these days. And, the parts needed for repairs cost about three times as much as the labor. So essentially, just about any breakdown on a modern car out of warranty is a $400-plus situation, minimum. Break down two to three times a year, and this gets really expensive.

On top of that, the more complex and expensive your car, the more quickly it will depreciate as a rule, especially if it is out of warranty. Used car buyers are (rightly) shy of highly complex cars that have no warranty protection.

—Joe Troise
Edmunds.com host,
monthly contributor to *Road & Track Magazine*

UNLOAD THE JUNK. If you use your car's trunk or truck's bed as a rolling storage bin, you're wasting gas. That's because any additional weight in your vehicle reduces fuel efficiency. Keep your trunk or bed empty of all but the most vital items.

KEEP THE ROOF CLEAR. Next time you consider tying an item on your car's roof for transport, take a moment to consider whether it will fit inside the car. Carrying items on the roof increases drag on the vehicle, and that decreases fuel efficiency.

WALK TOWARD THE LIGHT (COLORS). When you're shopping around for a new car, choose a light color—white or silver, for instance. Light-colored cars absorb less heat (in the same way that a white T-shirt keeps you cooler than a dark-colored one). That means you'll need to use the air-conditioner less often, and less air-conditioning means less gas used.

CHILD CAR SEATS

If children ride in your car, you must have a car seat—in fact, it may be the most important piece of equipment you own. These tips will help you solve some of the most common issues you might encounter when fitting a seat.

BEWARE OF ILL-FITTING BELTS. Just using a child car seat is not  enough; it must be properly installed to keep your child or grandchild safe. The most common reason that car seats malfunction? Seat belts that are too loose. If you're having problems, use this checklist. The belt holding the baby should fit so that:
- You're able to insert only one or two fingers between the belt and your child or grandchild
- The lap belt lays across hips, not stomach
- The shoulder belt rests on her shoulder, not neck

The car seat itself, and this is the tricky part, should be attached so that it stays put and moves less than 1 inch when tugged firmly.

If you're having a hard time correctly fitting your car seat, there's a resource you can turn to: The National Highway Traffic Safety Administration runs a Web site at www.nhtsa.dot.gov. This site provides a list of locations that will make sure the child car seat you're using is fitted correctly. From the NHTSA home page, go to Child Safety Seat Information. The inspection service is free, but generally by appointment only. The Web site also rates the ease of use among different models of car seats.

Some other thoughts—try out a car seat before purchasing it, if possible, to make sure it works in your vehicle. *Never* buy a used car seat because you have no way of knowing whether it has been in an accident. (About the only place you can purchase used models is from garage sales; Goodwill and other charitable organizations will not accept donations of used car seats.)

Also, because car seats are difficult to install, keep a car seat in each vehicle your child will ride in, if at all possible.

PUT YOUR WEIGHT INTO IT. If you've ever installed a child's car seat, you'll know it's not as easy as it looks. The car seat needs to be firmly attached to the vehicle seat, and making those belts tight enough is difficult at best. If you're having trouble getting the car seat to sit tight, try kneeling on it or pressing hard on the seat with one knee; your weight will help you get the belt taut enough to stabilize the car seat. The car seat should not move if you try to wobble it. Seat belts on newer cars (after 1996) are supposed to lock to keep the belt

Still Working After All These Years
WELL, MAYBE

Burying your car in a concrete bunker is a really extreme way to make it last 50 years, but the people of Tulsa, Oklahoma, did just that in 1957. As part of Tulsa's Golden Jubilee Week, Tulsans buried a 1957 Plymouth Belvedere under the county courthouse lawn as part of a 50-year time capsule. The car will be dug up June 15, 2007; we'll be able to see then whether being buried alive has helped this notoriously rusty Plymouth last.

Citizens of 1957 entered a contest to win the car by guessing the 2007 population of Tulsa. The winner, or the heirs of the winner, will drive away in the old Plymouth (or more likely in the front seat of a tow truck) and its contents: a $100 trust fund that has been accruing interest since 1957 (estimated to be worth about $1,200), a case of Schlitz beer, and a glove box full of the contents of a real woman of 1957's purse—including bobby pins, lipstick, an unpaid parking ticket, and a bottle of tranquilizers. The good people of Tulsa—at least those who remember—are waiting and wondering how well the car survived. To find out more about the festivities, visit www.buriedcar.com.

from loosening once it has been adjusted. Some cars, though, will need a locking clip (see your owner's manual), a metal H-shaped device that is available wherever car seats are sold, to clamp the shoulder and lap belt portions of the seat belt together.

UPHOLSTERY AND CARPETING

Not only will taking care of your car's upholstery make for a nicer ride—it'll also help your car maintain its value. Read on for our expert ways to clean and protect upholstery along with some tips on how to choose the right seat covers.

KEEP IT CLEAN. Spill a little something on your car's upholstery? Not to worry. Just consult these simple ways to clean things up.

- **Lipstick won't stick.** To remove lipstick stains from fabric upholstery, dab a teeny bit of nongel toothpaste on the spot and rub gently with a damp cloth. Use another clean cloth, dampened with water, to wipe the spot clean.
- **Gets the squeak out, too.** The lubricant WD-40 is effective for removing all sorts of stains, including pen ink and crayon. Spray the area and work the lubricant in with a paper towel. Continue spraying and rubbing until the stain is gone. Next, use an old, clean toothbrush to rub a drop or two of dishwashing liquid into the area, and then dab off with a wet cloth.
- **And hold the onions.** Ketchup and mustard are two of the most common culprits of car stains. Luckily, the aptly named Kids 'N' Pets Stain & Odor Remover can remove both—along with other "mistakes" committed by those family members. It's available at home improvement stores and online through a variety of retailers.
- **Soap the seat.** Saddle soap is perfect for removing dirt and grime from leather car seats, but make sure to use a very small amount. Most people tend to go overboard on this mild cleanser. For best results, slightly dampen a sponge and dab a small amount of soap onto it. Work the sponge until it begins to lather, add a bit more water, then wipe the seats. Keep wiping them down until the leather is clean. Dry with a clean cloth.

BID ODORS ADIEU. Does the aroma of eau de dog linger on your car's upholstery or carpeting? Don't get rid of Fido. First, make sure the surface is dry, and then sprinkle on a generous amount of either

One Man's Trash
Hubcap Creatures

Most people would agree that old and battered hubcaps lying discarded along the side of the road are a sad sight. Not so for English sculptor Ptolemy Elrington who, for the past 6 years, has been picking up these bits of urban trash and fashioning them into shiny, intricate animal sculptures. He's created dogs, armadillos, and crocodiles from cut-up hubcaps, but his main fascination is fish.

A fervent recycler, Elrington hopes that his fish sculptures say something about our wasteful society. "Hubcaps, for instance," Elrington explains on his Web site, are "aesthetic in purpose but ultimately of very little use. They're automatically rubbish when on the side of the road, but with a little effort and imagination, I transform them into something which gives people a great deal more pleasure...Hopefully they will encourage people to reconsider before they discard something which apparently has no value."

Elrington's fish are intriguing because he makes no effort to hide the origin of his materials; the fish and other creatures look just like what they are—hubcaps and car parts cut up and welded back together. But, even so, magically they appear to be alive. You can see pictures of Elrington's hubcap creatures—and buy one for yourself—on his Web site at www.hubcapcreatures.com.

---

baking soda or a mixture of 1 part borax to 2 parts cornmeal. Let the mixture set for a couple of hours, and then vacuum it (and the odor) away. For stubborn odors, you may have to repeat the procedure.

COVER YOUR SEAT. If your car sees a lot of wear and tear, or has upholstery that has seen better days, a set of seat covers—not a new car—is the answer. Seat covers protect the car upholstery against sun damage and wear and tear, and will hide any old damage.

But don't just waltz into the auto supply store and buy any old seat cover. The best ones are custom made for your car model. Keep in mind that even if you supply the manufacturer with your car year and model, it's still a good idea to confirm seat styles (bench or bucket seats, headrests, and the like). Also, check your owner's manual to make sure that the seat covers won't interfere with your car's ability to deploy the side air bags.

PAW PRINTS ARE NOT PRETTY. Do you really need to spend a lot of money on a dog blanket for your car? No! Slip an old fitted sheet over the backseat and then tuck it in behind the seat. The benefits? Unlike a heavy blanket, the sheet washes easily. It also stays in place and covers the entire seat, which you certainly can't say about bath or beach towels.

TIRES

As the advertisement says, there's a lot riding on your tires, so it pays to purchase the right ones and maintain the ones you have. And when those tires are ready to bite the dust? No problem, because we have a clever ideas for using those old tires, too.

FULL OF AIR? Keep 'em that way! Not only do underinflated tires wear out more quickly than properly inflated ones, they can also cause a host of other problems: a car that handles poorly, has poor grip on the road, and uses more gas than necessary. (In 1995, the U.S. Department of Energy estimated that underinflated tires waste up to 4 million gallons of gas every single day in America.) Worst of all, tires that aren't fully inflated can fail and cause an accident. Follow these step-by-step instructions for making sure your tires are properly inflated.

MAKE IT LAST

1. Check pressure when the tires are cold and you haven't driven the car for at least 3 hours.
2. Use a tire gauge to check the pressure at home. This is known as the "cold" pressure.
3. If the car's been idle and you find that the tires are underinflated, drive to a gas station and check them again. This is the "hot" pressure. Unless you've driven only a minute or two, you should find that the tire pressure is higher.
4. Fill your tires with air until the gauge registers the correct number, plus the difference between the cold and hot tire temperatures. (For instance, if the cold tire pressure was 28psi and the hot was 32psi and your manufacturer's recommendation is 35psi, fill the tire so that the pressure registers at 39psi.)

THE FINE PRINT
Tire Recalls

Not all tire recalls get a lot of press, so it's possible that your tires could be recalled by the manufacturer without your ever knowing about it. To be safe, it's a good idea to register your new tire purchases with the manufacturer, so it knows where to find you in the event of a problem or recall. Since tires are not the kind of item one buys and takes home in the original wrapping, sometimes the buyer never even sees a registration form. Ask your tire retailer for the form, and the Department of Transportation identification numbers, which are used by the U.S. government to track tire production. Mail the completed form to the manufacturer. Some tire sellers will complete and file the form for consumers electronically, so find out when you make your purchase.

Experts recommend that you check the tire pressure at least once every month and before every long trip. Follow their advice and your tires will live a long life.

LET IT SNOW. If it snows in the winter where you live, snow tires are not just a good idea, but essential winter garb for your car—and to ensure your safety. With snow tires, your car will stop and go better on ice and snow and, let's face it, they'll pay for themselves if they help you avoid just one accident. In some places where it snows a lot, it's even against the law not to have snow tires, because cars without them delay traffic and cause accidents. And the best part? Using snow tires will actually make your summer tires last longer.

Snow tires of old were noisy and handled poorly when the snow was gone and the roads were just wet or dry and cold. Modern snow tires—marked with a mountain and/or snowflake symbol—are made of rubber compounds that can navigate all the possibilities, from snow to slush to a dry, cold road.

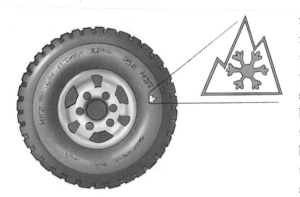

All-season tires aren't as effective as snow tires, because the rubber stiffens when the temperature drops, and stiff tires can't grip the road. People used to install snow tires only on the drive wheels, but with the new, improved snow tires, it's recommended that you buy a full set of four. Unfortunately, the extra grip factor of snow tires also causes the tires to wear out more quickly, so don't forget to switch back to your summer tires when the winter weather breaks. And remember, two sets of tires is not double the cost—your snow tires will allow your summer tires to last longer, and vice versa.

TAKE TURNS WITH YOUR TIRES. Your tires will wear more evenly and last longer if you have them rotated regularly—every 6,000 miles, or as recommended in the owner's manual. But take care; some cars have different-sized tires in the front and back, and swapping these would make for problems. Another tip: Never swap left to right with radial tires; this can result in tread separation and total tire failure.

You may know that there are a bunch of mysterious numbers and letters on the sides of tires, but you may not know what they mean. To choose the best tires for your car and your driving style, it's a good idea to do some research and understand all of the options before you start shopping around.

Here is a set of sample numbers that might appear on the side of a set of tires, and what they mean: P195/65R15 91V.

- The P stands for passenger (LT for light truck, T for temporary).
- 195 is the tire width, in millimeters.
- 65 is the aspect ratio, or the ratio of tire width to height. Tires with a low aspect ratio (from about 35 to 55) handle better than those with a high aspect ratio and are most appropriate for sports cars.
- R stands for radial construction, the most common designation today. The others are B (belted bias construction) and D (diagonal bias construction).
- 15 is the rim diameter, in inches.

- 91 is a load index, or the amount of weight a tire can carry. The number 91 stands for 1,356 pounds. Typically, the load index for cars and light trucks ranges from 70 to 110; the higher the number, the heavier the load a tire can handle.
- V is the tire's maximum speed designation (in this case up to 149 mph). Letters range from N (86 mph) to Z (149-plus mph).

Numbers for tread wear and letters for traction rating also appear on the sidewalls of tires. The base tread wear rating is 100, which means an estimated life of up to 30,000 miles. As the numbers increase, so does potential tread life. The highest number is 150. Of course, these numbers are only estimates, since the testing is done in ideal driving conditions.

Traction ratings—AA, A, B, and C—are based on the tire's ability to grip the road in wet conditions. Tires rated AA are best, C are worst. So if you live in a rainy climate, AA or A are the tires for you.

A PENNY FOR YOUR . . . TIRES? When is it time for new tires? **FIX IT FAST** Here's an easy way to answer that question. The tread depth on your tires needs to be more than 1/16 of an inch for the tire to grip the road safely. That's the exact distance between the tread's top edge and the top of Abraham Lincoln's head on a penny. Check your tread at least once a month by grasping Abe's body with your thumb and forefinger and then inserting the penny, Abe's head first, into the tread at its lowest point. If the tire treads cover any part of Abe's head, the tires have some life left. If the tread doesn't hit Honest Abe's head at all, it's time to buy new tires! Either way, safety dictates that you replace your tires every 5 years or when wear dictates, whichever comes first.

If you don't have a penny on hand, you can still check the tread. Tire tread patterns are designed with wear bars: small, raised parts of the tread pattern running across the groove of the tread pattern, marking minimum, allowable tread depth. When the tire tread grooves are even with the wear bars, you need new tires.

DON'T SPIN YOUR WHEELS. Stuck in snow? Spinning your wheels when you're stuck in mud, snow, or ice can be not only futile, but dangerous. In as little as 3 to 5 seconds, a rapidly spinning tire creates enough force to literally tear the tire apart, causing an explosion. When trying to free your car, never let your speed exceed 35 mph and don't allow anyone to stand near the spinning tire. Instead of spinning your wheels, gently rock your car back and forth by shifting the gear lever between reverse and second on manual transmissions, and between drive and reverse on automatics. If you still can't get the vehicle free, you'll have to call a tow truck. Check the owner's manual if your car is equipped with antilock brakes.

LET YOUR CAR DO THE WORK. The hardest part of changing a tire isn't getting 2,000 pounds of automobile up on that flimsy jack. That's nothing compared to loosening the wheel nuts. The trick is to loosen the nuts before operating the jack. It's easier to break the seal of dirt and rust and road salt when you loosen the nuts (but not remove them) with the full weight of the car on the ground. Elevated, the front wheels, in particular, are likely to spin when you try to turn the nut. If the nut is really and truly rusted stuck, try spraying with a penetrating lubricant (like WD-40), which you should keep in a car safety kit in the trunk. If you don't have a lubricant in the trunk, try any oily substance that you may have in the car with you—including lotion or even mayo from a sandwich.

PASS IT ALONG

NEW LIFE FOR AN OLD TIRE. Tire planters are retro-chic and easy to make. Here are the steps to follow to make your own planter.

Tire planters add a retro look to a yard, garden or deck.

What you'll need:
- chalk
- 1 tire
- sharp utility knife
- paints in the colors of your choice, if you want to decorate.

Step 1: Draw a scalloped line with chalk on the tire's sidewall.

1. Use the chalk to draw a scalloped or zigzag line around the sidewall on one side of a worn-out tire. Make a cardboard pattern if you want the pattern to be even.
2. Cut along that line with the knife.
3. When you've finished cutting, turn the tire inside out—this is the most difficult part and takes some muscle.
4. If you're feeling inspired, paint the outside of the tire planter and then place it in your garden. Fill the planter with dirt and plant some flowers. However, don't grow food crops in tire planters because chemicals from the rubber could leach into the soil.

Leave the tire's rim attached for a planter that sits off of the ground.

You can also make a tire planter out of a tire with the rim still attached. This kind of planter will sit higher off the ground and makes a country craft look a bit more formal. Tire planters are sturdy, can withstand any kind of weather, and are an American classic.

$mart Buys

NIX THE CAR ALARM

The first car theft in the United States occurred in 1896, not long after the first cars were introduced. Today in the United States, a car is stolen every 25 seconds, resulting in an annual loss of more than 1 million cars or $8.6 billion. You might think a car alarm would be the answer, but it's not.

According to the insurance industry—and those who are awakened regularly by alarms ringing throughout their neighborhoods—car alarms are useless. Most car thieves can dis-connect an alarm before anyone even thinks of calling the police. But the fact is, no one is calling the police anyway. Most times, car alarms are false alarms—the modern-day version of the boy who cried wolf.

If you want to keep your car safe, disconnect the alarm and install a brake lock, a vehicle tracking device that will lead the police to your stolen car, or a passive immobilizer or other kind of anti-carjacking device that will turn off your car in the event of a theft.

SWING OUT, SISTER. Think back to the lazy hazy days of your childhood summers, and one item probably features prominently in that daydream: a tire swing. Hanging a tire swing is easy, and it's a sure way to have the most popular backyard in the neighborhood—and to make good use of an old tire. Here's how to make your own.

What you'll need:

- 1 car or light truck tire (truck tires are more suitable for large teenagers or adults). Steel-belted tires are not suitable, as they can cause cuts and other injuries.
- power drill with a 1/2-inch bit
- 2-foot length of rubber tubing with a diameter large enough to fit over the rope. The tubing will protect the tree branch from abrasion over time.
- length of rot-proof rope that will reach from the branch to the ground, plus another 10 feet or so to accommodate the necessary knots and loops. Keep in mind that the rope must be strong enough to support the tire and the weight of the swinger. Ask the staff at your local hardware store for advice.
- 1 tree with a branch that is at 8 inches in diameter, at least 10 feet from the ground, and strong enough to hold the weight of a rope, the tire, and a child (or adult). Hardwood trees such as oak are stronger than evergreens.

1. Start by washing the tire thoroughly using hot soapy water. Then, wash it a second time with a mixture of 1 1/2 cups household bleach in 1 gallon hot water.
2. Drill holes around the tire to allow rain water to drain.

3. Tie one end of the rope around the tire using a sturdy knot such as a bowline or figure eight knot. If you're not a knot-tying expert, a good old square knot will do the trick, too.

4. Slip the rubber tubing over the other end of the rope and then loop the rope over the tree branch. Adjust the rubber tubing so that it covers the rope where it would rub the tree branch. Knot that end of the rope.

5. Make sure to inspect all parts of the swing—branch, rope, knots, and tire—periodically to make sure they're all secure.

ROAD TRIPS

Packing up your car for a family road trip can be a daunting; without the right planning, things can be a bit stressful. But our tips will make every journey a pleasure.

DEFOG THE WINDSHIELD. Foggy windshields are the bane of FIX IT FAST every driver's existance. Not only do they make keeping your eyes on the road difficult, but if there are kids in the car, they're certain to use their little fingers to make pictures in the condensation, which remain on the glass long after the fog has gone. The best way to cope is to prevent the foggy buildup altogether. Here are three easy tricks you can use to do just that.

- **Use soap.** Lightly dampen a paper towel, and then use it to rub a few drops of dishwashing liquid all over the glass. Buff dry with clean paper towels.
- **Or some vinegar and ammonia.** In a bucket, combine $1/2$ cup of vinegar or $1/2$ cup of household ammonia with 1 gallon of warm water. Wash the windows with the mixture, and then buff to dry with clean paper towels.
- **Add some alcohol.** Pour 2 cups of rubbing alcohol, $1/2$ cup of household ammonia, and a squirt of dishwashing liquid into a bucket of warm water. Wash the windows with the solution, and then buff to dry with clean paper towels.

ERASE THE FOG. If you're looking for an easy way to eliminate fog on your car's windshield, head on over to your local office supply store and purchase a chalkboard eraser—you can get one for around two bucks. Keep it in your glove box, and when the fog rolls in, you can just wipe it away.

WRAP IT UP. Maps, hotel reservations, and receipts pile up fast during a car trip. The good news is that you don't need to invest in a pricey visor organizer to keep it all contained. All you need to do is wrap a large rubber band or two around your car's sun visor and tuck those important papers under the rubber band.

BAN THE BUGS. Spend any time on the highway in the summer, and you'll find yourself peering through a windshield densely decorated with the remains of flying insects. All any crafty Yankee needs to get rid of them are a mesh onion bag and a dollop of dishwashing liquid. Squirt a small amount of dishwashing liquid onto your windshield, and then scrub with the mesh bag. The mesh won't harm the glass, and the dead bugs will come off easily. Finish up the job by wiping the window with a clean cloth.

BUGS BE GONE. It happens every spring and summer. After a long drive, your car's front grille is covered with a thick layer of dead bugs. Yuck. Who wants to spend time scraping that gunk off? Lucky for you, that's not necessary—if you have some laundry stain remover in the house. Spray the grille liberally with the cleaner, let it set for about 3 minutes, and then hose it off. Okay, you may have to scrub a *little*, but with a lot less elbow grease.

ORGANIZE THE TRUNK. Keeping a plastic laundry basket or two in your car's trunk can come in handy to prevent grocery bags from falling over on your way home from the store, to keep sports gear organized on your way to the park, or to stow wet towels on the way back from the beach. And because they're plastic, they're easy to clean.

BACKSEAT BACKPACKS. Kids plus cars usually equals clutter, which can be more than a benign nuisance. Loose Barbie dolls and portable MP3 players can become dangerous projectiles in the event of a sudden stop or an accident. The good news is that you don't need to buy a fancy backseat organizer for your kids' car toys and gadgets. An old backpack works just fine as a place to keep books, games, water bottles, and other necessities. Thread the straps of the backpack through the headrest of your car seat to hold the backpack in place.

WIPE AWAY THE DARKNESS. Are your headlights going dim? Can't see the road? Don't replace the headlights just yet. Keep a spray bottle filled with a vinegar–water mixture in your trunk along with some paper towels, and use that mixture to frequently clean the headlights (and wiper blades), especially in winter and early spring, when they are often splattered with snow melt.

A BRIGHTER LIGHT. Microscopic cracks in the headlight glass may be the reason your headlights seem dim. The teeny cracks may diffuse the light and affect your ability to see at night. Instead of investing again and again in new headlamps that you think are weak or dull, you may want to consider replacing the glass.

MORE TIPS FOR CARS, TRUCKS. AND OTHER AUTOMOBILES

Here's a roundup of the automobile-related Pass It Along tips you'll find in the other chapters of *Don't Throw It Out!*

CHAPTER	TIP	PAGE
1	Brew Up Clever Uses for Filters	16
1	7 Uses for an Old Cutting Board	25
1	Assign a Tube to Bag Duty	33
2	5 Ways to Say "Cheerio" to Chair Pads	61
3	Take Sheets to the Beach	88
6	Keep Vinyl in Your Vehicle	180
6	5 Uses for an Old Shower Curtain	180
7	Show That Basket the Door	212
7	Organize the Car	213
7	Vacuum Got a Flat?	222
8	6 Uses for an Old Tennis Ball	259

Domestic Challenge

Here's a true and false quiz that'll put your car knowledge to the test!

Question

1. You don't really need to monitor wear depth on your tires because most have a feature called wear bars that cause a "thumping" sound when the tires are ready to be replaced.

2. Experts recommend doing a visual check of your tires every time you get gas to make sure they don't need air.

3. The brakes on many cars, vans, and SUVs have a feature called "squeal pads" that emit a high-pitched sound when the break pads need to be replaced.

4. If you wash your car's wiper blades once a week with a little lighter fluid, they can last 2 years or more.

5. If you find that the locks are frozen in your car, just use the tried-and-true method of heating the key with a cigarette lighter.

Answers

1. **FALSE.** Most tires do have wear bars, but they do not start to thump until the tires are already dangerously worn. Use the penny test described above to check the wear on your tires.

2. **FALSE.** It can be difficult to determine whether tires are over- or underinflated just by looking at them. It's important to check tire pressure with a tire gauge at least once a month and definitely before a long trip.

3. **TRUE.** Once you can hear the squeal, you have about 1,000 miles to replace the break pads.

4. **FALSE.** Even good wiper blades will last no more than 18 months. And if you do clean them, it's important to not wash them with anything other than wiper fluid. Harsh cleaners can contain solvents that can cause the rubber on the blades to deteriorate more quickly.

5. **FALSE.** Inserting a red-hot key into a lock can cause expensive damage, especially on newer cars. Instead, use preventative measures. Squirt some graphite lock treatment or WD–40 lock treatment into the keyholes to keep them from freezing in the first place. Do not use too much, or you may clog the lock mechanism.

Resources

TOP 10 PASS IT ALONG PROJECTS

As we gathered the tips in *Don't Throw It Out*, we realized that we had compiled an especially impressive range of Pass It Along projects. So impressive, in fact, that we decided to make a list of our top ten favorites. But don't just keep these oh-so-clever ideas to yourself—pass them along to your friends and family!

1. MAKE A TEPEE FOR VINES, page 290
2. CLOSE THE BOOK ON SAFETY, page 122
3. NEW LIFE FOR AN OLD TIRE, page 350
4. THOSE BOOTS ARE MADE FOR PLANTING, page 93
5. SOCK AWAY A DOG BED, page 90
6. TRY A TIE SEAT, page 101
7. DISKS REDUX, page 156
8. SATISFY SOCIAL CLIMBERS, page 61
9. SERVE UP A PICTURE FRAME, page 259
10. KITTY IN THE CUPBOARD, page 83

HONORABLE MENTION:

- DO TRICKS WITH TOILET TUBES, page 183
- SAVE A TOOTHBRUSH, CELEBRATE A FRIEND, page 192
- MIRROR, MIRROR ON THE TABLE, page 67
- 5 OFF THE WALL USES FOR OLD FRAMES, page 69
- BABY, HANG THOSE QUILTS!, page 81

ARTS, CRAFTS, AND COLLECTIBLES

All Terrain Frames
www.allterrainframes.com
Picture and poster frames made from recycled tires.

American Institute of Conservators (AIC)
aic.stanford.edu/public/select.html
When looking for a professional to restore a collectible piece, this site can help you select a qualified conservator.

Aunt Philly's Toothbrush Rugs
www.auntphillys.com

Hubcap Creatures
www.hubcapcreatures.com
Intricate sculptures of fish, dogs, armadillos, and crocodiles made from recycled hubcaps.

Ideas in Wood
www.ideasinwood.com
Click "Bowls" to view wooden bowls made from hockey sticks.

The International Quilt Study Center
www.quiltstudy.org

Pick Up the Pieces
www.pickupthepieces.com
One of the country's oldest and largest art and collectibles restoration companies.

Resource Revival
www.resourcerevival.com
Picture frames made from recycled bike chains. Bottle openers, CD racks, candleholders, clocks, and furniture made using recycled bike, auto and computer parts.

Vinylux—Vintage Vinyl Design
www.vinylux.net
Bowls, clocks, coasters, sketchbooks, and note cards made from old 45s, LPs, and vintage album covers.

AUDIO AND VIDEO

PROTECT AND STORE VINYL

Archival Methods
www.archivalmethods.com

Metal Edge
www.metaledgeinc.com

University Products
www.universityproducts.com

TRADE AND SELL VIDEO GAMES

Swap-Bot
www.swap-bot.com

eBay's Half.com
www.half.com

DISPOSE OF OLD TVS IN AN ENVIRONMENTALLY FRIENDLY WAY

eBay's Rethink Initiative
http://rethink.ebay.com

EPA's Plug-in to eCycling
www.epa.gov/epaoswer/osw/conserve/plugin

Greener Choices
www.greenerchoices.org

Home Movie Depot
www.homemoviedepot.com
Transfer your super-8 or 8mm films to DVD.

AUTOMOBILES

Car Talk Radio Show
www.cartalk.com
The Mechanic Files is a database of over 16,000 mechanics recommended by members of the Car Talk online community.

Road Food
www.roadfood.com
Search for homemade ice cream, local diner, or rib shack while on the road.

BOOSTER SEATS

www.BoosterSeat.gov
Find out your state's requirements about booster seats.

The National Highway Traffic Safety Administration
www.nhtsa.dot.gov
Click "Child Safety Seat Information" for a list of locations that will make sure your child car seat is fitted correctly.

CELL PHONES

The Rechargeable Battery Recycling Corporation (RBRC)
www.rbrc.org
www.call2recycle.org
(800) 8-BATTERY or (877) 2-RECYCLE
Visit the RBRC for a list of retailers who will recycle or dispose of rechargeable batteries.

Wireless Recycling program
www.wirelessrecycling.com
Click on the big pink eraser or the home page to clear your phone's chip before donating it.

COMPUTERS, PRINTERS, AND ACCESSORIES

CLEAN OR ERASE A HARD DRIVE

http://safety.live.com
Click "Clean Up" on home page.

www.pcinspector.de
Select English from the pulldown menu on the home page.

www.heidi.ie
Download Eraser program from Heidi Computers.

www.jiiva.com
SuperScrubber program will erase any Mac hard drive.

ENVIRONMENTALLY SAFE DISPOSAL AND RECYCLING

www.earth911.org
Dispose of old computers and learn hot to refurbish newer machines.

www.emptysolution.com
Mail in empty printer cartridges using prepaid UPS labels for cash.

www.freerecycling.com
Company offers cash payments for empty laser or inkjet printer cartridges.

www.hp.com
Search for "product reuse and recycling."

INFORMATION GATHERING

http://gethuman.com/us
List of more than 500 companies, with each company's toll-free phone number and a shortcut to reach each company's live customer service department.

FIND A COMPANY OR SERVICE

1-800-555-1212
Use this number to find or U.S.-based company.

EDGAR (Electronic Data Gathering, Analysis, and Retrieval system)
www.sec.gov/edgar/searchedgar/companysearch.html
Use this Web site to locate the number of a public company

ORGANIZATIONS AND CHARITIES

Binky Patrol
www.binkypatrol.org
Donate quilts and blankets.

Boys and Girls Clubs of America
www.bgca.org

Goodwill Industries International
www.goodwill.org

Habitat for Humanity
www.habitat.org
Donate your universally practical tools, such as hammers, screwdrivers, wrenches, and handsaws.

Making Memories Foundation
www.makingmemories.org

The National Coalition Against Domestic Violence
www.ncadv.org
Used cell phones are redistributed to those in need.

Phones 4 Charity
www.phones4charity.org

Project Linus
ww.projectlinus.org
Donate quilts and blankets.

Red Cross
www.redcross.org

Salvation Army
www.salvationarmyusa.org

The Used Book Café, New York City
www.housingworks.org
Soho's Best-Kept Secret sells new, used, and rare books and donates all proceeds to HIV and AIDS services.

YMCA
www.ymca.net

OUTDOOR SPORTS AND HOBBIES

Aquaseal
www.aquaseal.com
Use Aquaseal to repair small holes and tears in breathable fabric fishing waders.

Nike Reuse-A-Shoe program
www.nikereuseashoe.com
Recycle your old running shoes.

One World Running
www.boulderrunning.com/oneworldrunning
Donate your clean, serviceable running shoes.

Primitive Living Skills
www.hollowtop.com/sandals.htm
Learn how to make sandals out of recycled tires from Thomas J. Elpel, author of The Field Guide to Primitive Living Skills.

REI
www.rei.com
Look under "Gear Care and Repair" in the "Expert Advice" section for a list of cobblers authorized to resole hiking boots with Vibram soles.

INDEX

Underscored page references indicate boxed text or tables and charts.
Boldface references indicate illustrations.

Plumbing tools and supplies, 320–22, <u>321</u>
    faucet specifications, 321
    pipe joint compound, <u>321</u>
    plumbing lubricants, 320
    Teflon tape
        using, 320–321
Polishes
    furniture, 48–49, <u>50</u>, 51–52, <u>225</u>
    metal, 223
    silicon-based, 51–52
    using, 48–49, <u>50</u>
Ponds, 291–292, <u>291</u>, <u>292</u>
    building edges of, 292
    liners for man-made, <u>291</u>, <u>292</u>
Pots. *See* Planters and pots
Pots and pans
    cleaning burned, 32–33
    cleaning mineral deposits from,
        33
    seasoning cast iron, 22
Power tools, 313–16, <u>313</u>, <u>315</u>, <u>316</u>
    batteries *vs.* corded, <u>314</u>
    extension cords for, 313–14
    paperwork on
        filing, 315
    purchasing, <u>316</u>
    rechargeable
        basic care of, 314
        recycling batteries of,
            315–16
Printers
    ink cartridges for
        disposing of, 152–53
        stocking up on, <u>153</u>
    selecting paper for, 149–50
    troubleshooting, 150–51
Project Linus, 115

Q

Quilting, <u>112</u>, 113–15, <u>113</u>
    dealing with extra fabric, 115
    International Quilt Study Center, <u>112</u>
    making templates, 113–14
    marking starting place, 114
    organizing fabric pieces, 113
    organizing fabrics, 113
Quilts, <u>112</u>, 113–15, <u>113</u>
    donating quilts, 115
    homemade rack for, 81
    Project Linus, 115
    removing blood stains from, 114
    storing, <u>112</u>

R

Racket sports
    rackets
        recycling as picture frames, 259–60, **260**
        reinforcing strings of, 259
    tennis balls
        uses for old, <u>259</u>
Rafts and inner tubes. *See also* Boats and other water
    craft
    sun and, 244
Raisins, rescuing over-dry, 39
Ranges, <u>6</u>, 7–9
    cleaning
        burners, <u>6</u>
        gas ovens, 8
        hoods, 8
    operating, <u>7</u>
    repairing
        burners, 7–8
        oven elements, 8–9
Razors
    electric, 190, 191
    extending life of blades, 190–91
Records
    caring for vinyl, 128
    recycling old, 131–32, <u>132</u>, **132**
Refrigerators, 4–7, <u>5</u>
    cleaning, 4, 5, 6
    operating, 4, 5, <u>5</u>
    reusing parts from old, 7
Rethink Initiative, 134
Rice steamers, protecting cabinets from, 27
Road trips
    defogging windshields, 353
    organizing paperwork from, 354
    planning, <u>352</u>
Rollerblading, maintaining rollerblades, <u>260</u>
Running, 257–58
    shoes for, 257–58
        recycling old, 258
RVing, 262–64, <u>262</u>, <u>263</u>
    awnings
        insurance for, <u>262</u>
    eliminating musty odors in, 262
    keeping clean, 262
    learning to drive, 262
    mold and mildew
        cleaning up, 262–63
        preventing, 262
    predeparture checklist, 262
    roofs
        emergency repairs to, <u>262</u>

S

Safety glasses and goggles, <u>308</u>
Salt
    keeping clump-free, 38–39
    removing excessive from soup, 39
Sauces, rescuing scorched, 39
Sawdust
    disposing of, 327
    uses for, <u>315</u>, <u>326</u>
Scanners, 149–150
    troubleshooting, 151
Scrapbooking, 115–118, **117**
    backing up work in scrapbooks, 116
    donating to historical societies, 118
    preserving old scrapbooks, 116
    tools for
        markers and pens, 115–16
        organizing, 117
        sharpening, 116–17
Shampoo, tips for using, <u>198</u>
Sheets
    converting flat to fitted, 86–86,
        86
    flannel, <u>82</u>
    purchasing, <u>87</u>
    recycling old, 87–88
    tie-dying faded, 85–86
Shoes
    athletic
        cleaning smelly, 90–91
        running, 257–58
    buying new, <u>94</u>
    canvas
        cleaning, 92
        keeping clean, 90
    donating dressy, 98
    for ice walking, <u>258</u>
    leather
        restoring dull, 92
    packing for traveling, <u>93</u>
    sandals
        from recycled tires, <u>334</u>
    shoelace tips (aglets)
        repairing frayed, 257
    slippers
        reusing old, stretched, 92–93
    trims for, <u>97</u>
Shower curtains, 179–80, <u>180</u>
    buying, 180
    making from recycled sheets, 87
    mending vinyl, 180
    preventing mildew on, 179

recycling vinyl, 180, <u>180</u>
    washing, 197
Shower doors
    recycling into mini-greenhouse, <u>179</u>
Showerheads
    fixing leaky, 177–78 <u>177</u>, **178**
Showers and bathtubs, 174–76, <u>174</u>
    caulking, 174–75
    preventing mildew in, 179
    setting water temperatures, 175
Shredders
    purchasing, <u>163</u>
    recycling waste paper from, 163
Silverware
    recycling old, 24
    washing fine, 20–21
Sinks
    acidic foods and, 26
    cleaning, 26
        metal, 29, <u>33</u>
        rust from, <u>33</u>
    polishing bathroom fixtures, <u>181</u>
    porcelain
        cleaning, 29, 30
        patching, 28
    protective pads and, 27
Skiing, 264–67, <u>264</u>, <u>265</u>
    ski equipment
        recycling old, 266–67
    ski poles
        emergency repairs to, 266
    skis
        fixing scratches on, 265, **265**
        "tuning" bottoms of, 264–65
        waxless cross-country, <u>264</u>
Sleds, plastic
    using for household chores, <u>266</u>
Sleeping bags
    cleaning down, 252
    liners for, 249
    recycling pads for, 257
    repairing down, 252–53
    storing, 248–49
Slow cookers, replacing ceramic pot,
    <u>21</u>
Smoke alarms, <u>308</u>
Soap
    liquid hand
        extending use of, 223
        preventing slimy, 201
Soccer, 267–268
    shoes
        expanding life span of, 267–68

Tools. *See* Hand tools, garden; Hand tools, home
    workshop; Power tools
Toothbrushes
    as cleaning tool, 192
    recycling, <u>191,</u> 192–93, **192, 193**
Towels
    caring for, 196–97
    recycling old, 197
Toys
    as craft material source, <u>120</u>
    doll beds
        from recycled furniture, <u>84</u>
    stuffed
        from recycled wedding dresses, <u>97</u>
    toilet paper tubes as, 184
Trucks and automobiles
    alarms, <u>351</u>
    antique
        installing seat belts in, 341
    batteries
        cleaning connections, 335
    car clubs, 341
    donating to charity, 340
    exterior
        cleaning grill, 354
        cleaning lights, 354–55
        cleaning windshield, 354
        protecting from the elements, 336–37
        removing bumper stickers from,
            339–40
        removing pine pitch from, <u>340</u>
        repairing scratches, 339
        rust and, 341
    fuses, 338
    gas mileage
        increasing, 342–43
        keeping log of, 337–38
    hubcaps
        recycling, <u>346</u>
    ignition system, 335
    interior
        caring for upholstery and carpeting, 337,
            345–46
        cleaning dashboard, 339
        defogging windshields, 353
        organizing, 354
    lights
        changing bulbs, 338–39
        cleaning, 354–55
        cleaning lenses, 354–55
    manuals, 334
    mechanics
        finding good ones, <u>338</u>
    rust and, 341

safety
    distractions and, 335–36
transmission
    manual, 334
used
    buying, 341
    rust and, 341, <u>341</u>
when to trade in, <u>342</u>
windshield
    defogging, 353
    preventing ice on, 339
Turpentine, shelf life of, <u>321</u>

U

Upholstered furniture
    cleaning, 62
        codes for, <u>65</u>
        vacuuming, 63, **63**
        with water-based cleansers, 65–66
    keeping pets off, <u>64</u>
    recycling old cushions, 66
    refurbishing
        oiling leather, 64
        repairing frayed piping, 64
        repairing linings, 64
    selecting durable fabric, 62
    sunlight and, 63

V

Vacuum cleaners, 219–22, <u>222</u>
    beater bars on, 220
    checking bag, 220
    cleaning brushes, 222
    handheld, 220
    powdered freshening products and, 220
    purchasing
        canister *vs.* upright, 219
    repairing snapped belts, 220–21, <u>222</u>
    technique for using, 222
    using old, 222
Vegetables
    artichokes
        keeping fresh, 35
    asparagus
        keeping fresh, 35
    mushrooms
        keeping fresh, 36
    onions
        storing in pantyhose, <u>92</u>
    saving cooking water from, 41
    tomatoes
        keeping fresh, 36

Vegetables *(cont.)*
    trimmings from
        using in soup, 36
Vegetable steamers, protecting cabinets from, 27
Velcro, detangling trash from, 255
VHS videotapes
    caring for, 130–31
    playing tips, 130–31
    storing, 130
    transferring to DVDs, 130

W

Walkers, tennis ball foot covers, <u>259</u>
Walkways, 292–93, <u>292</u>
    pavers
        installing, 292, <u>292</u>
    weeding, 293
Walls
    paint for in bathrooms, 188, 189
    stains on
        removing, 188–89
        sources of, 188, 189
    washing, 188–89
Washing machines
    detergent, 209
    drip pans and, 206
    filters
        cleaning, 210–11
    hoses to, 206–7
    mineral buildup
        avoiding, 208
        cleaning from interior, 208
    musty odors in, 211
    polishing, 208
    purchasing, <u>210</u>
    recycling tubs as planters, 211–12
    recycling window from old, 212
    ringer, <u>211</u>
    rust in, <u>213</u>
    ultra-dirty clothing and, 210
    vibration and, <u>212</u>
    wash cycles, 209
Water temperature, dishwashers and, 11
WD-40, <u>33</u>
    shelf life of, <u>321</u>
    as stain remover, 345
Wedding and formal attire, 96–98, <u>97, 98</u>
    bridesmaid dresses
        recycling as shoulder wrap, 97–98

donating used, 96, 98
recycling fabric from, <u>97</u>
storing, <u>98</u>
Whirlpools, cleaning jets, 176
Wine, freezing leftover, 41
Wood furniture, 47. *See also* Chairs;
    Tables
    bookcases
        replacing shelves, <u>51</u>
    buying
        determining quality of, <u>46</u>
        distinguishing between solid and
            imitations, <u>46</u>
        measuring house access points prior to,
            46
    caring for
        objects and substances to avoid placing on,
            <u>49, 55</u>
        removing stuck paper from, 51
    damaged
        disguising, 51, 52–53
        regluing, <u>52</u>
        repairing scratches and burns,
            51–52
        when to hire a professional refinisher,
            <u>53</u>
    dusting, 48–49, <u>48</u>
    humidity and, 47
    moving
        minimizing damage during, 46, <u>47</u>
    objects and substances to avoid placing on, <u>49,</u>
        <u>55</u>
    polishes, 48–49, <u>50</u>
        silicone-based, 51–52
        using, 48–49
    stenciling damaged, 49–50
    temperature extremes and,
        47–48
Working in comfort. *See* Ergonomics

Y

Yeast
    proofing, 39
    storing, 35

Z

Zippers, 251, **251**
    mending backpack, 255–56